Sexual Abuse in the Lives of Women Diagnosed with Serious Mental Illness

New Directions in Therapeutic Intervention

A series edited by *Marti T. Loring*, The Center for Mental Health and Human Development, and The Emotional Abuse Institute, Atlanta, Georgia

This book is part of a series. The publisher will accept continuation orders which may be cancelled at any time and which provide for automatic billing and shipping of each title in the series upon publication. Please write for details.

Sexual Abuse in the Lives of Women Diagnosed with Serious Mental Illness

Edited by

Maxine Harris
with **Christine L. Landis**

Community Connections
Washington, D.C.

 harwood academic publishers
Australia • Canada • China • France • Germany • India • Japan •
Luxembourg • Malaysia • The Netherlands • Russia • Singapore •
Switzerland • Thailand • United Kingdom

Amsteldijk 166
1st Floor
1079 LH Amsterdam
The Netherlands

British Library Cataloguing in Publication Data

Sexual abuse in the lives of women diagnosed with serious
    mental illness. — (New directions in therapeutic
    intervention ; v. 2)
    1. Mentally ill women   2. Sexual abuse victims
    I. Harris, Maxine   II. Landis, Christine L.
    362.2′082

ISBN 90-5702-504-3

Contents

III First Person Accounts

IV Policy and Research

V Special Issues

Introduction
to the Series

New Directions in Therapeutic Intervention is designed as a vehicle for the expression of innovative visions in the area of therapeutic intervention. Individual titles will examine the needs of special client populations and describe creative helping strategies within a theoretical context. The editor's hopes are twofold: That this series will serve as a collection of well-defined maps to guide caring professionals in their helping journey, and that it will provide new ideas and a sense of hope for intervention with individuals who, isolated and in emotional pain, reach out for connection with others in their human family.

Preface

The Key

Give me the key to your door
I want to come there some more
Open the door and I'll love you more
I'm a man, not a pin to tickle the lock
Let me back in. I will never hurt you again.

— Anonymous, early 1980s

This poem, discarded by a female client after a bibliotherapy session and retrieved by a curious case manager, illustrates some of the many problems we face in understanding and assessing the impact of sexual abuse trauma on the lives of women diagnosed with serious mental illness.

First, what meaning do we give to the above poem? Do we take it as evidence of a thought disorder? The author of this verse was a woman; yet, she wrote identifying herself as a man. Does this mean that she suffered from profound gender identity confusion? Was she delusional? Did she suffer from a multiple personality disorder and was this one of her alters speaking? We ask these questions because we already assume, based on the context in which this poem was written, that its author was accurately diagnosed as having a major mental illness.

Now imagine that the same poem was written by a woman seeking counseling at a rape crisis center. How do we then understand the verse? Is the author writing about her abuse experience from the more powerful perspective of the abuser? Is she struggling with her fears of being abused again? Is she offering a reasonable explanation for why she has locked herself away behind a wall of defenses?

Finally, assume that the poem was written by a college freshman as part of a writing assignment in an introductory poetry class. Would we ask any of the previous questions or would we now see the masculine voice as merely a literary technique? Would we be inclined to evaluate the poem as literature and not see it as a clue to the author's emotional and psychological status at all?

Once we have labeled a woman as suffering from a major mental illness, whether that label is an accurate assessment or not, we view her reports of sexual and physical abuse through the colored lens of her diagnosis. We do not need to concern ourselves with whether or not her memories are false or whether they have been suggested by an over-zealous therapist in order to discredit her report. The stigma of her diagnosis is often sufficient to call her account into question.

Given the complex interrelationship between sexual abuse and diagnosed mental illness, how do we begin to discuss the impact of sexual abuse trauma on the lives of women who receive treatment within the mental health system for a diagnosed illness? First, we must be clear about what we mean when we refer to sexual abuse. Sexual abuse is non-consensual or forced sexualized touching, fondling, or penetration committed by a perpetrator who is perceived as having greater physical or social power. The abuse may have occurred in the distant past when the victim was a child or it may be current and ongoing. The abuse may have been a single isolated event, such as a rape, or it may have been frequent and recurring. The relationship between the perpetrator and the victim may have been intimate and close, as when the abuse occurs within a family, or it may have been more distant or even anonymous. When women have spent much time within institutions, such as hospitals, foster care, or prisons, the abuse may have been committed by people designated as care givers.

Next, we must be clear about what we mean when we speak of a diagnosed mental illness. Some consumer advocates have argued that much of what gets labeled as symptoms is merely a response to trauma and fear of future abuse. For example, suspicious and guarded behavior may not be paranoia, but rather a legitimate response to repeated, unprovoked abuse. For some of these advocates, accurate assessment of a woman's abuse history may obviate the need for psychiatric diagnosis altogether. Others argue that at the very least, accurate assessment of traumatic events would allow us to revise a number of existing diagnoses, perhaps replacing some of the more severe labels with a diagnosis of post-traumatic stress disorder. In some cases, it might be reasonable to conclude that a woman suffered from both a major mental illness and the sequelae of sexual abuse trauma. When practitioners see these as discrete entities, they are far better able to design interventions to help women cope with and master disturbing symptoms.

While much has been written about the occurrence of sexual abuse in the general population, little has appeared in the professional or popular literature about the impact of such trauma on women diagnosed with serious mental illness. Perhaps the definitional complexity alluded to above has proven too daunting. Perhaps there is less interest in women who are personally, socially, and economically marginalized. Or perhaps the task of treating both men and women with serious mental illness is so demanding that practitioners are loathe to add one more problem to an already long list. In the present volume, the authors have attempted to address this gap in the literature by focusing specifically on sexual abuse trauma in the lives of women diagnosed with serious mental illness.

The volume is divided into five separate parts. Part I addresses issues of theory and assessment. The first chapter by Harris provides a conceptual and practical overview of how standard treatment interventions for persons diagnosed with serious mental illness would need to be adapted to accommodate the special needs of women who are also the survivors of sexual abuse. In the next chapter, Anderson and Chiocchio point out the complex interrelationships among homelessness, psychiatric symptoms, and substance addiction in the lives of many trauma survivors. Finally, the chapter by Spielvogel and Floyd provides a conceptual and practical guide for assessing trauma, both past and current, among women diagnosed with serious mental illness who present themselves to clinics, hospitals, or emergency rooms for treatment.

Part II focuses specifically on treatment issues. In their chapter on cognitive behavioral therapy, Mueser and Taylor present a clear and thorough discussion of one treatment approach and then apply that approach to a single case study. Stowe and Harris describe a social skills approach to trauma recovery designed specifically for women with serious mental illness. Wile focuses her attention on inpatient treatment of the survivor of childhood sexual abuse, domestic battery, or rape. She addresses issues of assessment as well as considering what treatment options are viable in an acute care setting.

Part III shifts the attention to the voices of women survivors of abuse. So often women's voices are silenced, either because they themselves fear reprisals or because others discredit their reports. In the personal accounts presented here, women tell their own stories about sexual and institutional abuse. The first chapter by Geller, Nicholson, and Traverso presents accounts of treatment from three separate historical eras: the mid-nineteenth century, the mid-twentieth century, and the 1970s. The chapter by Jennings poignantly recounts the mental health system's failure to recognize and treat her daughter's sexual and physical abuse trauma. Dende, Duca, Hobbs, and Landis serve as clinician/reporters, telling the stories of four inner city women who endured multiple abuses. Unzicker shares her experiences both as a patient and a healer as she tells the story of the safe haven she and her husband provided for many who were on the brink of despair.

Part IV reminds us that the personal must ultimately become political if it is to have widespread impact. These chapters address issues of policy and research. Reilly links policy initiatives to both research findings and current paradigms for understanding trauma. Rosenberg, Drake, and Mueser outline the conceptual and methodological problems faced by researchers studying trauma in the lives of women diagnosed with serious mental illness. They also speculate on the implications of the "false memory" debate for studies involving this population. Goodman et al. report, in detail, the results of one study investigating the incidence, severity, and impact of trauma in the lives of previously homeless, mentally ill women.

Part V deals with four special issues often not addressed in books on trauma and recovery. Blanchard and Jones focus attention on the needs of clinicians doing trauma work. Treating women with serious trauma histories can be vicariously traumatizing for clinicians working with them. Millet addresses the cultural awareness and sensitivity needed by clinicians working with African American women in particular and culturally diverse groups in general. Although many trauma survivors privately acknowledge that religion and spirituality have played a major role in their personal recoveries, few clinicians have addressed this issue. Fallot fills this gap in his chapter on spirituality in trauma recovery. Freeman and Fallot address the issue of trauma in the lives of men and offer an original conceptualization of developmental disruption resulting from trauma, one that has applicability to both men and women.

Although the present volume is an edited work and represents the thinking of nearly thirty contributors, almost half of the chapters were written by authors from Community Connections in Washington, D.C., so it may be useful to describe briefly the somewhat unique setting in which their work took place. Community Connections is a private non-profit mental health clinic serving women and men in the District of Columbia. The agency provides a range of services including case management, supported living, individual and group counseling, and vocational placement to clients with a history of mental illness, substance addiction, and homelessness. Eighty percent of the clients receiving services are African American and 60 percent are women. Since the early 1990s, all clinical work at Community Connections has been informed by the knowledge that many, if not most, of the clients have experienced severe and multiple traumas both in childhood and adulthood. This sensitivity to the impact of trauma on the lives of people diagnosed with serious mental illness has created an atmosphere in which clients have felt safe to share their stories of abuse and to begin the work of recovery.

Contributors

Catherine M. Anderson, M.Ed., Quality Assurance Coordinator, Community Connections, Inc., Washington, D.C.

Ellen Arledge Blanchard, M.S.W., Clinical Social Worker, Community Connections, Inc., Washington, D.C.

Katherine B. Chiocchio, M.Ed., Clinical Case Manager, Community Connections, Inc., Washington, D.C.

John D. Dende, M.A., Case Manager/Clinical Coordinator for Housing, Community Connections, Inc., Washington, D.C.

Robert E. Drake, M.D., Ph.D., Professor of Psychiatry, Dartmouth Medical School, Hanover, New Hampshire

Carolyn Duca, M.S.W., Clinical Coordinator for Housing, Community Connections, Inc., Washington, D.C.

Mary Ann Dutton, Ph.D., Research Professor, Department of Emergency Medicine, George Washington University, Washington, D.C.

Roger D. Fallot, Ph.D., Co-Director of Community Connections, Inc., Washington, D.C.

Alexia K. Floyd, Pre-Doctoral Psychology Intern, Department of Psychology, University of California, San Francisco

David W. Freeman, Psy.D., Clinical Supervisor, Community Connections, Inc., Washington, D.C.

Jeffrey L. Geller, M.D., M.P.H., Professor of Psychiatry, Director, Division of Public Sector Psychiatry, Department of Psychiatry, University of Massachusetts Medical School, Worcester

Lisa A. Goodman, Ph.D., Psychology Department, University of Maryland, College Park

Maxine Harris, Ph.D., Co-Founder and Co-Director of Community Connections, Inc., Washington, D.C.

Margaret Hobbs, M.S.W., Clinical Supervisor, Community Connections, Inc., Washington, D.C.

Ann Jennings, Ph.D., Psychologist, Maine Department of Mental Health, Mental Retardation and Substance Abuse Services, Augusta

Melanie Johnson, M.B.A., Psychology Department, University of Maryland, College Park

Mirta Jones, M.A., Clinical Case Manager, Community Connections, Inc., Washington, D.C.

Christine L. Landis, M.S.W., Clinical Social Worker, Community Connections, Inc., Washington, D.C.

Bronwen L. Millet, Ph.D., Research Department, Community Connections, Inc., Washington, D.C.

Kim T. Mueser, Ph.D., Departments of Psychiatry and Community and Family Medicine, Dartmouth Medical School, Hanover, New Hampshire

Joanne Nicholson, Ph.D., Assistant Professor of Psychiatry, Department of Psychiatry, University of Massachusetts Medical School, Worcester

Mary Anne Reilly, M.A., Associate Editor of *Moving Forward*, Arlington, Virginia

Stanley D. Rosenberg, Ph.D., Department of Psychiatry, Dartmouth Medical School, New Hampshire-Dartmouth Psychiatric Research Center, Hanover

Anna M. Spielvogel, M.D., Associate Clinical Professor of Psychiatry, Department of Psychiatry, San Francisco General Hospital, University of California, San Francisco

Heather Stowe, M.S.W., Clinical Social Worker, Community Connections, Inc., Washington, D.C.

Kathryn L. Taylor, Ph.D., Department of Psychiatry, Georgetown School of Medicine, Washington, D.C.

Amy Traverso, B.A., Research Assistant, Department of Psychiatry, University of Massachusetts Medical School, Worcester

Rae E. Unzicker, Activist and Consultant on Mental Health Policy, Sioux Falls, South Dakota

Joanne Wile, M.S.W., Associate Clinical Professor of Psychiatry, Department of Psychiatry, San Francisco General Hospital, University of California, San Francisco

Part I

Theory and Assessment

Chapter One

Modifications in Service Delivery

Maxine Harris

INVESTIGATIVE reporting within the popular press has brought to light the incidence of childhood sexual abuse trauma, domestic violence and sexual intimidation and harassment within the general population of women. More recently, scientific researchers have turned their attention to discovering the rates of sexual abuse trauma in the lives of women diagnosed with serious mental illness (Beck and van der Kolk, 1987; Craine *et al.*, 1988; Rose *et al.*, 1991). Before clinicians and program planners begin making alterations in treatment protocols to address sexual abuse trauma in the lives of women with severe mental illness, two definitional issues must be addressed. First, what do we mean by sexual abuse trauma? Second, how do we define the population of women diagnosed with severe mental illness?

Although distinctions can be made between sexual abuse trauma, which occurs in childhood (when cognitive and emotional schemas for understanding self and others are first forming) and abuse which occurs in adulthood as rape or domestic violence, many recent attempts to establish prevalence rates tend to aggregate sexual abuse which occurs in childhood with abuse which occurs later in adulthood (Jacobson, *et al.*, 1987). This tendency to combine the two types of abuse may stem from the fact that women sexually abused in childhood are more likely to be victimized as adults, resulting in

3

substantial overlap between the two groups (Muenzenmaier, *et al.*, 1993). The tendency to group childhood and adult survivors of sexual trauma may also stem from a recognition that similar treatments apply regardless of when the trauma occurred (Herman, 1993). For the purposes of this chapter, "sexual abuse trauma" will be used to refer to sexual assault experiences sustained during childhood and/or adulthood.

The designation "severe or chronic mental illness" also requires some clarification. It is generally accepted that such labeling does not refer exclusively to diagnosis, but rather that it takes into account both the duration of a person's psychiatric symptoms and the extent to which those symptoms impair level of functioning (Bachrach, 1988). It is unclear, however, what role, if any, a history of sexual abuse trauma might play in a woman's being labeled as "severely" or "chronically" mentally ill. One study of female psychiatric inpatients suggests that those with a history of abuse are more likely than a nonabused cohort to have severe, psychotic-like symptoms, to be diagnosed as having borderline personality disorder and to have suicidal symptoms (Bryer, *et al.*, 1987). It may well be, although it remains to be proven, that sexual abuse trauma is one route to patienthood for at least some women who come to be diagnosed as severely mentally ill.

Although it is true that more research needs to be done before we fully understand the role that sexual abuse trauma plays in the lives of women diagnosed with severe mental illness, those studies that have been done reveal prevalence rates from 34% in case management clients (Rose, *et al.*, 1991) to 51% in state hospital psychiatric patients (Craine, *et al.*, 1988). Clinicians and program planners need to begin modifying treatment interventions to accommodate the special needs and vulnerabilities of trauma survivors. Treatment services for clients diagnosed with severe mental illness generally include: case management, residential placement and supervision, inpatient hospitalization, medication management, network intervention and social skills training. Each of these treatment or service interventions must be grounded in an understanding of the trauma experience and adapted to accommodate the vulnerabilities of the trauma survivor. The purpose of this chapter is to suggest a series of clinical and programmatic modifications in customary and usual treatment for persons diagnosed with severe mental illness that might render those treatments more suitable to women who have experienced sexual abuse trauma.

Case management

Case management is a systems and a service intervention designed to coordinate, access and often provide the full range of care that a person with severe mental illness needs in order to live in the community. Regardless of their theoretical orientation, case managers often share a willingness to be flexible and to bend the rules of traditional treatment, a sense of informality and collegiality that extends both to co-workers and clients and a commitment to aggressive outreach (Harris and Bergman, 1993). Paradoxically, these very qualities, so important when engaging deinstitutionalized clients, may pose problems when working with trauma survivors. Trauma survivors are all too familiar with pseudo-intimate relationships in which traditional boundaries are violated and the will of the other is aggressively asserted "for their own good."

To avoid replicating the interpersonal dynamics of the abusive relationship, case managers must follow a set of guidelines that substitute structure and predictability for informality and flexibility:

1. Case managers should establish contracts with clients which spell out the obligations and responsibilities of both parties. The limits of the case management relationship should be articulated in these contracts; similarly, the terms under which the relationship will take place should be clarified.
2. Case managers should let clients know what they are going to do in advance of actually doing it. Even simple activities such as filling out a form should proceed with "Now we are going to fill out this form; I will ask you ten questions; the questions will all concern your medical history." By walking the client through an interaction before it occurs, the case manager makes the encounter predictable and safe.
3. While case managers might do well to ask permission before they intervene with any client, they must ask permission when

5

dealing with the survivors of sexual abuse trauma. Simple activities like making a home visit, riding in a car, or attending a recreational activity need to be agreed upon in advance and need to proceed with the stated consent of the client. Such agreements not only demonstrate respect for the client's wishes but also give the client control over the interaction.

4. Clients must have the right to say "no" to services. Case managers who are concerned with providing services to disenfranchised, "difficult" individuals sometimes forget that clients should always retain the right to reject services. When case managers foist services on unwilling clients, they risk creating an atmosphere in which a controlling adult asks a vulnerable child to do something that the child knows she does not want to do, in effect replicating the very dynamics of the trauma itself.

Because case management entails a relationship between two people in addition to being a service and treatment intervention (Harris and Bergman, 1987) case managers must be especially mindful of who they are when working with trauma survivors. One must be particularly cognizant of one's interpersonal style and how that style might be seen by a woman who has experienced abuse. Some variables that need to be considered are:

Degree of openness and friendliness. Because they have been abused in relationships that were supposed to be benign or positive, trauma survivors are naturally distrustful of new relationships. A case manager who is "too open" and "too friendly" may cause a client to ask somewhat suspiciously, "What does he/she want, anyway?"

Tendency toward being hierarchical and authoritarian. Since abusers use power to threaten and intimidate victims, clients are often wary of a case manager who is invested in being in charge. For some clients, any relationship in which a power imbalance exists may be reminiscent of the abuse relationship (Jacobson and Richardson, 1987).

Degree to which one appears self-effacing and fragile. Because trauma survivors have an ambivalent relationship to their own "victim"-selves, they are often disdainful or even rageful toward case managers who appear too vulnerable. The client needs to believe that the case manager is strong enough to handle the powerful emotions that might arise in working together.

Gender. Because most abuse is perpetrated by men toward women, the gender of the case manager is a significant issue (Jacobson, Herald, 1990). Male case managers tend to be feared as potential abusers. Clients may also try to seduce a male clinician, believing that all men are interested only in sex. Female case managers, on the other hand, may be seen as failed protectors and thereby become targets for rageful attacks. In general, it is wise to address issues of gender and the accompanying misperceptions early in the case management relationship. Also, case managers need to be aware of their own emotional reactions when working with trauma survivors. Both peer and individual supervision can be useful in helping case managers recognize and deal with their own feelings and responses.

Residential placement and supervision

At some point in their histories, most individuals who are severely and persistently mentally ill receive assistance in securing and maintaining housing. While housing options range from structured group homes to independent but supervised apartments, they almost always include some support and supervision on the part of residential counselors or clinical case managers (Bebout and Harris, 1991). Because of economic and programmatic realities, however, residents in supervised housing experience a *lack* of privacy, control and safety. Yet, privacy, control and safety are exactly what trauma survivors need if they are to succeed in residential placements. Moreover, concerns about privacy, control and safety apply equally to independent and group home placements. Regrettably, even on-site supervision does not eliminate the element of dangerousness from some group homes.

Privacy

In most group homes and supported apartments, residents must share not only living but also sleeping quarters. Boundaries are often blurred and a room that serves as a living or dining room by day may convert into a bedroom at night. Lack of secure, private sleeping space becomes especially problematic for a trauma survivor whose bedroom was violated by intruders in the past. It becomes difficult

7

for a clinician to help a client develop emotional and psychological boundaries when her most fundamental physical boundaries are not secured.

Control

In residential programs, rules about when and where people sleep are determined and imposed by residential staff. If an individual is residing in a group home, for example, there will be specific times for sleeping and individuals will be required to sleep in designated bedrooms on assigned beds. While this may seem like a relatively simple requirement, it can be problematic for the survivor of sexual abuse trauma who may have learned that the only safe time to sleep is during the day and that beds are unsafe places in which to sleep.

In most housing arrangements, residents do not have complete control over who is allowed to come into the home. While one may be able to control one's own visitors, in a shared apartment or a group home one may have no control over the visitors of one's roommates.

Safety

Because of the lack of affordable housing, most residential programs operate in marginal neighborhoods. It is difficult to feel safe where break-ins, rapes and murders are a daily occurrence.

To provide clients with much needed privacy, control and safety, residential planners must be mindful of the following guidelines:

1. Clients need private sleeping quarters. When economic realities prevent private bedrooms, room dividers and screens should be used to demarcate individual sleeping space. All residents should be helped to respect the privacy of roommates.
2. Residents should be allowed to maintain idiosyncratic sleeping patterns that feel safe to them. At the same time, they must be helped to respect group norms.
3. Rules about visitors and proper conduct within the home should be established to accommodate the needs of the most vulnerable house member. Whenever possible, needs for privacy should be considered and discussed when matching housemates.

4. Clients should be presented with a range of housing options and allowed to choose that which feels most safe.

5. Extra precautions such as door locks and window bars should be installed to help residents feel safe, even in those circumstances in which residential staff deem the precautions to be unnecessary.

6. Whenever possible, planners should establish creative public/private partnerships to develop or subsidize more safe, affordable housing.

Inpatient hospitalization

Most adults diagnosed with severe mental illness will experience at least one inpatient stay over the course of their psychiatric treatment. Hospitalization is often indicated for the survivors of sexual abuse trauma who are suicidal, homicidal, psychotic, drug-addicted, self-mutilating or otherwise decompensating (Courtois, 1988). However, because many women labeled as being chronically mentally ill have experienced sexual abuse or intimidation while being institutionalized, clinicians need to consider carefully how inpatient hospitalization will be used in the treatment of adult survivors of sexual abuse trauma who are diagnosed with severe mental illness (Geller and Harris, 1994).

Before assuming that the hospital is a safe place, the clinician must understand the role which hospitals have played in the lives of individual survivors. In some cases women were hospitalized and labeled as "crazy" when they first spoke of the abuse (Geller and Harris, 1994). The hospital, rather than being a place of treatment, was an instrument of control and punishment. Many women who were hospitalized for long stays at public hospitals were abused while hospitalized (Geller and Harris, 1994). The hospitalization thus became the site of more trauma.

When the need for inpatient, structured hospitalization does arise, clinicians need to carefully consider alternatives to traditional inpatient treatment as well as strategies for reframing inpatient treatment to render the hospitalization safe as well as therapeutic.

1. The alternative of using community-based and professionally staffed crisis beds should be considered. The need for a

structured and safe environment is real; however, individuals can receive support and safe haven in environments other than hospitals.

2. When a hospitalization becomes necessary, it should, if possible, be voluntary and under the control of the patient herself. It is often useful to establish contracts with chronically mentally ill survivors of sexual abuse trauma in which the client determines when and if a hospitalization will occur.

3. The rationale for an actual admission should be made explicit to the client as should the conditions for her release from the hospital. This explicit contracting makes the hospitalization a predictable experience rather than a frightening descent into a world over which the client has no control. Such contracting requires close coordination between the inpatient and outpatient treatment staffs.

4. Clinicians should also reframe the hospitalization as being different from previous hospitalizations. Rather than meaning that the client is out of control and crazy, this hospitalization means that the client is actually taking control of her life, asking for a safe space when she needs one and believing that she deserves to get the help that she requires.

Medication management

Most adults diagnosed with severe mental illness receive medications as part of their psychiatric treatment. Many receive several medications simultaneously. It is not uncommon to find a woman receiving anti-psychotic, antidepressant, anti-anxiety and possibly even anti-seizure medication all at the same time. Regrettably, clinicians often medicate any sign of powerful affect in a client who has been labeled as chronically mentally ill. Researchers have also found that there is a greater tendency to use psychotropic medications in adults who are survivors of abuse (Bryer, *et al.*, 1987).

Several factors may contribute to the manner and frequency with which psychotropic medications are prescribed. Some have suggested that the greater severity of symptoms has resulted in the increased use of medications (Bryer, *et al.*, 1987). It may also be possible that a lack of training and knowledge about sexual abuse trauma, coupled

10

with exposure to media portrayals of trauma survivors as being out of control, has served to frighten practitioners into believing that they must medicate the powerful feelings of anger, sadness and pain that accompany the exploration of a trauma history. Finally, medical practitioners historically have tended, in general, to "medicate away" the expression of powerful affect in female patients (Ehrenreich and English, 1978).

Regardless of the reasons clients receive psychotropic medications, practitioners must be aware that otherwise helpful medications can contribute to the affective numbing so characteristic of many adult survivors of sexual abuse trauma. The ready use of medications to subdue or control feelings may also contribute to the client's naive beliefs that her feelings are bad, dangerous and should not be felt.

In light of a diagnostic reformulation that takes into account a trauma history, the medications of women diagnosed with severe mental illness who are the survivors of sexual abuse trauma need to be reevaluated. For some of these women, medications that address symptoms of anxiety and depression may be used to replace antipsychotic medications. Furthermore, it may be possible to use medications episodically and for a shorter duration rather than on a long term basis. For other women, long term antipsychotic medications may continue to be therapeutic. These evaluations will need to be made on an individual basis. Recovery from sexual abuse trauma often entails that the survivor feel powerful emotions of anger, pain and sadness. Clients can, with the aid of clinical staff, experience their feelings and do so in ways that are safe and healthy. The relationship with a primary clinician or case manager creates a safe holding environment in which an adult survivor can begin to work through powerful feelings that have been locked away for a long time.

Both clinicians and clients must be trained to understand that starting to feel does not necessarily mean being overwhelmed by one's feelings. Clients can be taught to experience their feelings in small manageable doses and can be given permission to shut down when feelings seem too powerful to control. As one client so aptly put it, "I can nibble at feelings rather than swallow them whole."

Some of the expressive therapies used with non-chronically mentally ill women have applicability to this population with relatively little modification. Role plays, dance, movement and body work, anger and sadness rituals and writing and drawing exercises are all viable techniques for work with women who are diagnosed with severe mental illness. These techniques are especially effective when the individual is also engaged in a one-to-one relationship with a therapist or case manager in which the feelings can be worked through and further explored. By incorporating a variety of expressive therapies in treatment plans for clients who are trauma survivors, practitioners may find that they have to rely less on the use of psychotropic medications to control feelings and behaviors.

Network interventions

The social support systems of adults diagnosed with severe mental illness are frequently impoverished. Research reveals that these networks contain fewer members and have scarcer resources than the networks of healthier adults of the same age (Harris and Bergman, 1985). Moreover, the reciprocity between individuals in relationships is often distorted with one member of the dyad doing most of the giving and the other member doing most of the taking. Because social support networks enhance one's ability to cope with crises and to function in general, interventions often focus on rehabilitating impoverished and diminished support networks (Harris, *et al.*, 1986–87). These interventions seek to increase the size of the network or repair severed connections among network members. Clinicians often try to form an alliance with network members who can then assume some of the actual case management functions performed by mental health professionals.

Because trauma and abuse frequently occur in one's primary network, such interventions need to be modified when working with the survivors of sexual abuse trauma. First, clinicians must know the role that network members played in the abuse before routinely involving those network members in treatment. Clients should always have the option to refrain from contact with network members whom they deem to be dangerous and unsafe.

More difficult than honoring a client's request for no contact is the need to limit or modify contact when the network member is a past or current abuser and the client herself wants contact. Because their networks are so impoverished, these clients often desire to con-

12

tinue contact with network members that have been dangerous and abusive. In these cases, case managers need to find ways to permit contact to occur safely. Strategies similar to those used by child protective services with children whose abusive fathers have been removed from the home need to be adapted to working with adult survivors. It may be that contact should only occur, for example, when a disinterested and safe third person is also present.

Clinicians also need to be especially sensitive to the guilt and fear which a woman might feel if she is required to monitor and perhaps even report an abusive network member. Often abuse continues into the next generation and a survivor of sexual abuse trauma may be witness to current abuse that is being perpetrated on her nieces, daughters or granddaughters. Her own dilemma about whether or not to report a current abuser needs to be addressed within the clinical relationship. Issues of both loss and dangerousness must be considered.

Finally, case managers may need to focus on creating replacement networks for the survivors of sexual abuse trauma. New communities of women can join together to form replacement families (Bebout, 1993). Such efforts need to be encouraged and nurtured so that clients realize that distancing from an abusive network does not mean losing all social supports and human connections.

Social skills training

Training in social and interpersonal skills is often based on the assumption that adults with severe mental illness do not have the interpersonal and practical skills needed to succeed in normal community living. The content of many social skills courses, known as modules, includes such behaviors as proper grooming, the use of leisure time, budgeting and money management, conversation initiation and relationship building.

The first modification that clinicians must make in working with sexual abuse survivors in a social skills format is to understand the particular function that apparent skill deficits have served the abuse survivor. For example, many women consciously choose not to groom themselves because poor grooming protects them from further abuse and assault (Harris, 1991). Other women who have been given money and gifts in exchange for sexual favors have

13

difficulty managing money because, for them, taking money is shameful and reminiscent of acquiescing to sexual abuse. The difficulty these individuals have in managing their money is the result not of a skill deficit but rather it is the legacy of sexual abuse trauma.

In addition to understanding the meaning of particular skill deficits, clinicians need to modify social skills modules for abuse survivors by adding content areas that are particularly germane to the female survivor. Some areas that need to be added include: What are sexual and physical abuse? What links exist between abuse and psychiatric symptoms? Between abuse and homelessness? Between abuse and substance use or addiction? What does it mean to be a woman? What does it mean to be sexual? How does one become safe? How does one self-soothe? How does one parent? Modifications of social skills modules might therefore include:

Education about sexual and physical abuse

Many seriously mentally ill women lack even the most rudimentary information about sexual and physical abuse trauma. Consequently, education efforts must begin by defining sexual and physical abuse, sharing existing information on prevalence rates with survivors, discussing the long term effect of trauma and beginning to help women think about what rights they have in repairing the trauma that has occurred.

While this education can proceed in a didactic format, it is helpful to use current media portrayals to place sexual abuse trauma in a societal context. Clinicians need to remember that some of the information generally available in the culture via the news and television media may not be available to women with severe mental illness who continue to be more socially isolated than other women.

Education can also begin to give women a new set of cognitive labels that might be used to construct an alternative explanatory framework for understanding present difficulties. Current behavior may now make sense in light of a trauma history. For example, what has been labeled for years as paranoia may well be legitimate fear. Similarly, what has been called constricted affect and a lack of motivation may well be a self-protective device designed to limit the sphere of one's interaction and thus protect against the repetition of trauma.

Educational efforts must also focus on establishing the link between such extreme behaviors as homelessness and substance abuse and a history of sexual or physical abuse. "Running away" is often a first response to trauma; yet one can find many ways to run. A woman can run psychologically by consolidating powerful dissociative defenses; she can run biochemically by numbing herself with drugs and alcohol; she can run literally by taking to the streets. By understanding each of these as a response to intolerable circumstances, a woman can begin to take care of herself in less personally damaging ways.

Female identity

Many sexual abuse survivors do not have a clear understanding of what it means to be a woman. In fact, being a female has often been associated with being sexual and being victimized. Preliminary work at Community Connections with women trauma survivors who are also diagnosed with severe mental illness suggests that clients believe that to be female means to be a caretaker, a victim and an angry person. Discussions which clarify cultural, societal and racial stereotypes are especially useful in helping women to begin to understand how such images of womanhood influence their current behaviors. The goal of such discussions is to provide trauma survivors with a more realistic and positive sense of being a woman.

Sexuality

For most trauma survivors, sexuality is an area marked by confusion, shame and fear. First, survivors are often quite ignorant about sexual matters. Having been introduced to sex before they were able to fully understand what was happening, survivors who were abused as children retain many misconceptions about sexual behavior and feelings. Open and frank discussions about sexual practices, sexual pleasure, reciprocity and intimacy need to be conducted in a straightforward and nonthreatening manner.

Because of the forbidden and secret nature of sexual abuse, many survivors retain a sense of shame about their bodies, their sexual needs

15

and desires and their sexual activities. Clinicians need to employ cognitive interventions to help survivors distinguish between what was then and what is now, what are normal and acceptable feelings and what was and is under the survivor's control. Just talking openly about sexuality often lessens the shame that many women feel.

When sexual abuse was accompanied by physical abuse or the threat of physical abuse, women learned to be afraid of sex. The fear a woman feels about her sexuality needs to be addressed directly. Women need help in accurately assessing dangerousness, respecting their own perceptions and taking steps to make themselves safe.

Finally, decisions about sexuality need to address what it means to be seductive and flirtatious. Many women find themselves misreading the seductive behavior of others as well as being unclear about what non-verbal cues they themselves are giving. When sexuality has been confused, the whole idea of what it means to be seductive needs to be reexamined. Women need to be trained to attend to their own behavior as well as to learn what is normative behavior in a variety of different adult relationships.

Safety

Discussions of safety must address both physical and emotional safety and boundaries. Women need to be taught how to assess the actual dangers in their physical environment and how to take legitimate protective measures. For some women this means avoiding certain neighborhoods at night; for others it may mean taking a self defense course. All women must come to understand the limits on their abilities to avoid random physical violence. Establishing emotional boundaries is especially difficult for trauma survivors. Women need to learn what rights they have in relationships, how to say "no" in a clear and direct way and how to ask for what they need and want. For one whose most basic rights have been violated, it takes time and practice to begin to respect and to assert one's own needs and wishes in a relationship. A woman must be given support and encouragement that it is *always* right to take care of herself emotionally in a relationship.

In addition to addressing a woman's own safety, discussions must also focus on the safety of others when a woman has been a perpetrator as well as a victim. For many women, the most difficult abuses to discuss are those which they have inflicted on dependent children. Problem-solving must focus on strategies for keeping others safe as women learn to accept responsibility for their behaviors. Accepting legitimate responsibility must be distinguished, however, from gratuitous self-trashing and generalized self-blaming characteristic of many trauma survivors.

Self-soothing

Women with serious mental illness need to be instructed in ways in which they can soothe themselves when they feel anxious, depressed or frightened without using illegal substances, sexually acting out, or over-medicating themselves with prescription drugs. Techniques that help a woman to ground and center herself and to reestablish her own sense of who she is are especially important. It is also important for women to learn how to distract themselves from recurring intrusive thoughts and overwhelming feelings. Listening to music, meditating, watching television or exercising often help a woman gain control over her own internal state. Women need to learn how to "talk themselves down", how to convince themselves that they have a right to live and how to believe they can, in fact, get through the worst of times.

It is also important for women to know that certain standard defenses such as intellectual or compulsive activities are acceptable ways of modulating intense affect and anxiety. In the case of many, self-soothing begins by rereading notes or listening to tapes made by a therapist who instructs the woman in soothing "self talk" to help her to cope with a difficult situation. All of these techniques come to be under the survivors control and are understood as legitimate ways to manage one's anxiety and one's despair.

Regrettably, practitioners often believe that women diagnosed with serious mental illness do not have the same potential to soothe themselves that other men and women have and consequently soothing often comes only via medication or hospitalization. If these women are to live successfully and independently in community environments, they need to learn ways to soothe themselves in the face of anxiety and depression.

Parenting

Although most women with serious mental illness do not raise their children full-time, many are mothers and have serious questions about how to be a good parent. If one has been raised in an abusive home where parenting was either neglectful or hurtful, one does not have a model of how to be a nurturing and constructive parent. Many women express fears over becoming abusive themselves and need to understand how to monitor their own behavior with children.

Several other issues which apply to motherhood and are especially salient for adult survivors of trauma include: how to protect one's children without being over-protective; how to deal with one's envy over the safe childhood that one is providing for one's own children; and how to deal with the guilt one feels over not being able to raise one's children and guarantee their safety.

Implications for mental health services delivery

As clinicians and program planners begin to take into account the trauma histories of many women who have been diagnosed with severe mental illness, several modifications in service delivery must occur.

1. Assessment of current and childhood sexual abuse trauma must become part of the routine assessment of women diagnosed with serious mental illness (Muenzenmaier *et al.*, 1993). Moreover, in addition to being performed at the time of intake, assessments might need to be conducted at several different times in an ongoing clinical relationship since some clients only feel comfortable revealing a trauma history after they have come to trust a service provider.
2. Clinical staff accustomed to working with persons diagnosed with severe mental illness must be trained to work with trauma survivors.
3. Existing treatment interventions for persons with serious mental illness must be revamped so as not to inadvertently retraumatize women who have suffered sexual abuse. In general this

means paying special attention to physical, psychological and interpersonal boundaries.

4. Because trauma survivors often present with an array of symptoms (eating disorders, substance abuse histories and psychiatric problems) that might well be treated by separate service delivery systems, overall coordination of an individual's treatment by a consistent and informed case manager is important.

Conclusions

While it may seem daunting to add yet another area of concern to the treatment of seriously mentally ill women, program planners would be remiss not to recognize the extent to which many women diagnosed with serious mental illness have suffered from sexual abuse trauma. An accurate assessment of the extent of trauma will allow clinicians to devise treatments that are truly relevant to the experiences of their clients. Current treatment approaches are adaptable for work with trauma survivors if clinicians take the necessary steps to accommodate the treatment program to a history of trauma.

References

Bachrach, L.L. (1988) "Defining chronic mental illness: a concept paper", in *Hospital and Community Psychiatry*, 39, 383–388.

Bebout, R. and Harris, M. (1991) "In search of pumpkin shells: residential programming for the homeless mentally ill" In: Lamb, R. Bachrach, L.L. and Kass, F.L. (Eds.) *Treating the Homeless Mentally Ill.* Washington, D.C.: APA Press.

Bebout, R.R. (1993) "Contextual case management: restructuring the social support networks of seriously mentally ill adults" In: Harris, M. and Bergman, H.C. (Eds.): *Case Management for Mentally Ill Patients.* Langhorne, Pennsylvania: Harwood Academic Publishers, pp. 59–82.

Beck, J.C. and van der Kolk (1987) "Reports of childhood incest and current behavior of chronically hospitalized psychotic women", in *American Journal of Psychiatry*, 144, 1474–1476.

Bryer, J.B., Nelson, B.A., Miller, J.B. *et al.*, (1987) "Childhood sexual and physical abuse as factors in adult psychiatric illness", in *American Journal of Psychiatry*, 144, 1426–1430.

Courtois, C.A. (1988) *Healing the Incest Wound.* New York: W.W. Norton and Co.

Craine, L.S., Henson, C.E., Colliver, J.A., *et al.*, (1988) "Prevalence of a history of sexual abuse among female psychiatric patients in a state hospital system", in *Hospital and Community Psychiatry*, 39, 300–304.

Ehrenreich, B. and English, D. (1978) *For Her Own Good.* New York: Doubleday.

Geller J. and Harris, M. (1994) *Women of the Asylum.* New York: Anchor Books.

Harris, M. and Bergman, H.C. (1985) "Networking with young adult chronic patients", in *Psychosocial Rehabilitation Journal*, 8, 28–35.

Harris, M., Bergman, H.C. and Bachrach, L. (1986–87) "Individualized network planning for young adult chronic patients", in *Psychiatric Quarterly*, 58, 51–56.

Harris, M. and Bergman, H.C. (1987) "Case management with the chronically mentally ill: a clinical perspective" in *American Journal of Orthopsychiatry*, 57, 296–302.

Harris, M. (1991) *Sisters of the Shadow.* Norman, Oklahoma: Oklahoma University Press.

Harris, M. and Bergman, H.C. (Eds.), (1993) *Case Management for Mentally Ill Patients.* Langhorne, Pennsylvania: Harwood Academic Publishers.

Herman, J. (1993) *Trauma and Recovery.* New York: Basic Books.

Jacobson, A. and Richardson, B. (1987) "Assault experiences of 100 psychiatric inpatients: evidence of the need for routine inquiry", in *American Journal of Psychiatry*, 144, 908–913.

Jacobson, A. and Herald, C. (1990) "The relevance of childhood sexual abuse to adult psychiatric inpatient care", in *Hospital and Community Psychiatry*, 41, 154–158.

Muenzenmaier, K., Meyer, I., Struening, E., *et al.*, (1993) "Childhood abuse and neglect among women outpatients with chronic mental illness", in *Hospital and Community Psychiatry*, 44, 666–670.

Rose, S.M., Peabody, C.G. and Stratigeas, B. (1991) "Undetected abuse among intensive case management clients", in *Hospital and Community Psychiatry*, 42, 499–503.

Chapter Two

Homeless, Addictions and Mental Illness

Catherine M. Anderson and Katherine B. Chiocchio

A MONG the group of women who have experienced sexual or physical abuse at some time during their lives, there exists a subgroup of women who are episodically homeless, alcohol or drug addicted and diagnosed as having a serious mental illness. For this group of women, abuse is not a one time occurrence. These women experience repeated episodes of sexual and physical violence and are routinely confronted with events that fall "outside the range of usual human experience." (American Psychiatric Association, 1987)

The relationship between abuse on the one hand and homelessness, addiction and diagnosed mental illness on the other, is one of mutual causation. Women with a history of multiple abuse are more likely than other women to become homeless, substance dependent and diagnosed with a mental illness. Once women are homeless, substance dependent and psychiatrically symptomatic, they are at greater risk for being sexually and physically abused. Homelessness, substance abuse and having a diagnosed mental illness are thus both outcomes of a history of abuse and risk factors for future abuse.

These risk factors are not independent of each other. For example, a woman who is abusing cocaine and is homeless may be at great risk for suffering a major depression. Likewise, a woman who is hearing voices and drinking alcohol daily may be at risk for losing

21

her housing and becoming homeless. For the purpose of this chapter, however, we will focus on the separate and binary relationship between abuse and each of the three risk factors: homelessness, substance abuse and diagnosed mental illness. Only at the end, will we speculate on possible interrelationships.

It should also be noted that when a woman is episodically homeless, substance dependent and psychiatrically symptomatic, she is also likely to be poor and to be subjected to periods of prolonged and extreme stress. Both poverty and prolonged stress heighten a woman's vulnerability to future incidents of physical and sexual abuse.

Poverty and chronic stress

Poverty and constant and extreme stress may predispose a woman to physical and sexual abuse. Poor women experience more frequent, more threatening and more uncontrollable life events than do women in the general population. They are also exposed to more crime and violence (Belle, 1990). Conditions such as substandard housing, dangerous neighborhoods, oppressive responsibilities and financial insecurity are constant stressors that overwhelm an individual living in poverty (Belle, 1990). Exhaustion, lack of security and lack of social and psychological resources are associated with poverty and chronic stress and may impede a woman's recovery from trauma or expose her to further abuse.

Poor women often live in housing projects or disheveled urban apartment buildings. Poverty may result from a lack of social supports and may perpetuate a diminished social network. Poor women have more difficulty accessing existing resources due to lack of child care, transportation and information. Often a woman raising children on her own is overwhelmed by the lack of emotional and financial support and becomes too exhausted to focus on recovery from trauma or to protect herself from further abuse.

One needs only to watch the evening news to see that violent urban incidents have become daily occurrences in low income neighborhoods. These events produce an ongoing state of fear which creates a PTSD-like syndrome featuring prolonged hyperarousal (e.g. exaggerated startle response). Chronic fear is also likely to elicit feelings of hopelessness and despair which may lead to depression, self-hatred and violence (Garbarino, Kostelny and Dubrow, 1991).

Case:

Pat is a thirty-two year old single mother living in Washington, D.C. She is an abuse survivor diagnosed with schizoaffective disorder and alcohol and crack-cocaine dependence. Pat experiences symptoms of depression and psychosis and self-medicates with crack cocaine and prescription pain-killers and tranquilizers. The severity of Pat's illness became evident when her mother died four years ago and Pat became incapacitated by depression and psychosis. Pat has been in the application and appeal process for Supplemental Security Income (SSI) benefits since that time. Her first application was denied because of her substantial work history; her appeals were denied because she did not have sufficient assistance in providing documentation supportive of her disability diagnosis. Eventually, Pat stopped following through with the appeal process.

Because Pat has been unable to obtain disability income, she and her son depend on Aid to Families with Dependent Children (AFDC) funds to meet their basic needs. Pat was able to secure a highly sought after subsidized apartment. Unfortunately, the neighborhood was overwhelmed with drug dealers and street gangs. She expressed fear that her teen-aged son would be hurt or killed on the streets. As a result, she imposed strict curfews and other restrictions for her son which he perceived as punitive, confining and isolating. Her solution to entice him to stay home was to obtain a television set and a VCR.

Pat felt that having entertainment in the home was not a luxury but a necessity for her son's safety. Because of her financial situation, she was unable to actually purchase a television and was forced to rent one at an exceedingly high monthly rate. Consequently, Pat spent her monthly allotment by the third or fourth week and saw no alternative other than prostituting for funds to support herself and her son until the next AFDC payment.

Unfortunately, commercial sex recreates the dynamics of the abuse experience: the sense of having no choice or power, the physical danger, the secrecy and shame and the reality of being valued only for sex. Commercial sex also places a survivor at great risk for revictimization because women are often raped, severely beaten, or killed by their "tricks" or pimps.

Homelessness

Homelessness can take a number of forms and can be either episodic or chronic. Many homeless individuals reside in shelters, either temporarily or on a longer-term basis. Others literally live on the streets, sleeping in bus shelters, under bridges, on park benches, or over heating grates on city sidewalks. One subgroup of homeless adults does not consider themselves homeless despite being only marginally housed in friends' or relatives' homes. These persons often must move from friend to friend and are at risk for becoming homeless once they have exhausted their support networks (Bassuk, 1993).

Homelessness: as precipitated by abuse

Physical and sexual abuse are significant factors leading to homelessness. Young women often become homeless as a result of running away from an abusive home situation. Some families force children to leave after the children tell someone about being abused by a family member. A woman may choose to move to a shelter to escape an abusive relationship. Seventy percent of women living on the streets or in shelters report experiencing abuse in childhood (Goodman, 1991). From a study of 600 homeless men and 300 homeless women, more than half of the sample reported suffering a traumatic experience and most subjects stated that the traumatic event had occurred before they had become homeless. Rape was the most frequently reported trauma for the women. Most people interviewed for this study had experienced physical or sexual violence in childhood (North and Smith, 1992). Child and adult sexual and physical abuse may be the first experience in a process that culminates in homelessness for some individuals.

Case:
Melissa is a 28 year old woman diagnosed with schizoaffective disorder living in a supported housing program in Washington,

D.C. Melissa was molested by several of her mother's boyfriends and physically abused by her mother. At age thirteen, she was raped by her step-father and when she told her mother about the abuse she was not believed or protected. Melissa remained marginally housed or homeless for the next thirteen years. Melissa sought out older men to take care of her and protect her, many of whom physically and sexually abused her. She was pregnant six times and gave birth to three children. Melissa was hospitalized repeatedly for depression, suicidality and self-abuse and began using alcohol, marijuana, PCP and amphetamines. She was introduced to crack-cocaine by a drug dealer who threw her out of his apartment when she refused to prostitute for him. She reports that she has never prostituted for drugs or money; however, she has traded sex for security and shelter.

When Melissa presented for treatment, she was severely depressed and suicidal. She would disappear for days or weeks at a time and upon return she would report that she had been experiencing "blackouts." It is unclear whether these "blackouts" were dissociative or drug-induced or both. Every few months, Melissa experienced extreme agitation during which she would moan, cry, rock and attempt to harm herself by putting her arms through windows. These behaviors resulted in hospitalization.

Homelessness: as risk factor for abuse

Homelessness presents a constant threat to personal safety which places a woman at risk for trauma. Women living on the streets or in shelters are more likely to be beaten, raped, or exploited than women who are safely domiciled (Bassuk, 1993). Emergency shelters and other programs for homeless persons are often dangerous places as a result of overcrowding and poor supervision. Some women describe feeling intimidated by fellow residents shooting up drugs in the bathrooms or making sexual advances toward them after the lights are turned out. Sleeping in shelters or on the streets leaves a woman completely vulnerable and requires that she remain constantly on guard. In an interview study of women in a Manhattan shelter, D'Ercole and Struening (1990) found that respondents reported high rates of fear of physical harm. Individuals living on

25

the streets or in shelters experience more violence than those who are domiciled.

In a study of 99 women receiving case management services at a community mental health center in Washington, D.C., 30% of the respondents reported experiencing physical assault and 34% reported experiencing sexual assault during an episode of homelessness (Goodman, 1995). The pattern of victimization for these homeless women varies from the norm in that seventy-three percent reported being assaulted by a stranger. Of these assaults, 62% happened on the street, 31% occurred in a shelter and 23% took place in someone else's apartment (Goodman, 1995). These women are not in control of their surroundings or of what happens in their surroundings. Loss of control of circumstances places one at risk for trauma. These statistics highlight the fact that homelessness appears to increase a woman's likelihood for experiencing violence as a result of exposure to danger (Bassuk, 1993).

Substance abuse

Substance abuse is connected to trauma at several different levels. Children raised by substance abusing parents are at greater risk of experiencing sexual and physical abuse (Rose, Peabody and Stratigeas, 1991). Use of alcohol and other drugs by the abuse perpetrator can precipitate physical, sexual and emotional abuse. Children are often beaten severely when their primary caregivers are intoxicated. Women are frequently raped or beaten by partners who are inebriated. The victim can be forced to use substances in the process of being beaten or raped (Rose, Peabody and Stratigeas, 1991).

Substance abuse: as precipitated by abuse

Several studies link trauma with later substance abuse. From a sample of 100 male and female subjects receiving treatment for substance abuse, more than a third were diagnosed with some form of a dissociative disorder. Forty-three percent reported histories of childhood sexual or physical abuse which the authors suggest is a conservative estimate (Ross et al., 1992). They found that individuals with dissociative disorders seeking substance abuse treatment may have used

26

alcohol and other drugs to self-medicate the psychological symptoms from trauma. In an article describing the etiology of dual diagnosis, sexual abuse and physical abuse have been identified by Blankertz, Cnaan and Freedman (1993) as significant childhood risk factors for the development of addiction in adulthood.

The behaviors of commercial sex and substance use have been linked to early sexual abuse. Zierler, *et al.* (1991) note that survivors of sexual abuse use drugs and alcohol more heavily, as well as engage in sexual behaviors such as commercial sex, unprotected sex or sex with strangers, that place them at risk for disease or injury. Abuse survivors use alcohol and drugs to cope with both the emotional and physical pain associated with abuse, abuse memories and symptoms stemming from the abuse. Many women report that using crack-cocaine may help them to feel "more normal" or less dissociated in the short term. In actuality, cocaine worsens symptoms of hyperarousal, such as anxiety and paranoia. For women who have learned to use mind-altering drugs to cope with abuse pain, trauma histories can interfere with substance abuse treatment. Removal of substances as the primary coping mechanism without supplying an alternative may leave a woman vulnerable to traumatic memories. The probability of drug or alcohol relapse is high when the woman has no other means of coping with the emotional pain besides the use of substances.

Substance abuse: as risk factor for abuse

Violent crime is closely linked with illegal drug use. Drug-related murders are a daily occurrence in the inner city. Many women are physically or sexually abused in the process of obtaining and using drugs. Women using illegal substances live in danger of physical harm related to owing money, having dangerous networks, living in crack houses and exchanging sex for drugs. Drug dealers may beat or kill addicts who are unable to pay off their debts. The effect of mind-altering substances impairs judgment and reduces inhibitions which may eventually result in risk-taking behaviors.

Case:
Crystal is a thirty-eight year old African American woman dually diagnosed with chronic paranoid schizophrenia and

27

polysubstance dependence. Crystal experiences auditory hallucinations episodically commanding her to harm herself or others as well as severe paranoia, threatening visual hallucinations and fixed delusions about people intending to harm her physically or sexually. She began using heroin at age seventeen and used it for twelve years until forced to stop using while incarcerated for a shoplifting charge. Upon her release, she remained clean for a short time and then began using crack-cocaine. Crystal describes being routinely sexually and physically assaulted in the process of buying cocaine. In fact, she has been severely injured in the process of seeking drugs, to the point of requiring surgery. Because she is able to dissociate from these traumatic experiences, however, the high remains worth the risk.

During her most recent relapse, Crystal was intoxicated from alcohol and crack cocaine and was walking the streets in the middle of the night in a dangerous neighborhood looking for more crack. She reported encountering three young men and approaching them aggressively for crack. Eventually, the men beat her severely, broke her leg and stabbed her. Although Crystal did not cause the abuse to happen, her judgment had been impaired by the use of alcohol and crack and her inhibitions were lessened, causing her to persist in her attempts to purchase drugs from the three men who eventually abused her.

Substance abuse obscures the issue of victimization when it occurs in the process of using and seeking drugs. For example, rape is often not seen as abuse by the victim but simply as a part of life for a crack addicted woman. A woman who is heavily involved in drugs will think that the abusive experience is deserved or expected and, therefore, will not consider it abuse. Goodman (1995) notes "As one woman put it, 'I was asking for trouble when I went into the crack house. If I didn't want to get hit or fucked, I shouldn't have gone in there ... No, I can't call that forced.'"

All too frequently, an addicted woman's report of abuse is not taken seriously by helping professionals or she is blamed for the violence she has experienced. Because severe physical and sexual abuse occurs so commonly in the lives of substance abusing women, reports of violence are discounted or met with irritation. Clinicians sometimes forget that a woman can be simultaneously an addict and a victim. According to Cunningham, Sobell and Chow (1993) a diagnosis of addiction becomes a label that carries with it stigma and a loss of credibility.

Case:

Jackie is a thirty-five year old woman who lived most of her life with her grandmother in the family home in Washington, D.C. Jackie has been homeless or marginally housed in crack houses since the death of her grandmother. Jackie is heavily addicted to crack cocaine and will often exchange sex for drugs or money to buy drugs. She is well known in her neighbor-hood for behavior that demonstrates little regard for her physical integrity and, consequently, she is routinely humiliated and physically and sexually abused. Jackie reports being beaten, raped, gang-raped, threatened with a weapon or almost killed at least once a month. When she talks with her treatment providers about her abuse experiences, she is not seen as a true victim because she is living a dangerous lifestyle. Treatment providers often blame her for the abuse experiences because she puts herself at risk. Because she is seen as an addict, Jackie's abuse history is often ignored.

Mental illness: as precipitated by abuse

Abuse experiences precipitate entry into the mental health system in several ways. Physical and sexual abuse trauma create symptoms which can interfere with normal functioning and which worsen with time. Psychological treatment is often necessary to help the woman integrate her experience, heal damage done to the self and manage overwhelming symptoms. Trauma symptoms are often mistaken for symptoms of major mental illness and viewed as chronic; survivors are then tracked into long-term treatment.

The after effects of abuse, which include intense fear, anger, guilt and shame, a sense of worthlessness or contamination, chronic exhaustion and tension, exaggerated startle response and disrupted sleeping and eating patterns, require psychological and sometimes chemical treatments (Browne, 1993). Psychological survival may

29

require that the abuse survivor deny cognitive and emotional reality and distort her world view. These adaptations may result in psychiatric symptoms depending on the interaction between personal resources and the severity and context of the abuse. Rieker and Carmen (1986) describe the process by which a child abuse victim develops symptoms which precipitate entrance into the mental health system. The "victim-to-patient process" is an interaction between the abusive incident, the individual's psychological resources and the social context in which the abuse took place.

Women who have been physically and sexually abused as children are likely to experience severe deficits in coping, more severe symptoms of mental illness and an increase in self-destructive behaviors (Blankertz, Cnaan and Freedman, 1993; Carmen, Rieker and Mills, 1984). For women diagnosed with severe mental illness, coping capacity is further diminished; and therefore trauma appears to have a greater debilitating impact for this group.

Extreme abuse experiences are associated with severe psychiatric disorders. It has been established that women who have been hospitalized for symptoms of mental illness are likely to have been victims of childhood sexual abuse (Muenzenmair, et al., 1993; Carmen, Rieker and Mills, 1984; Fromuth and Burkhart, 1992). In a prevalence study of women diagnosed with serious mental illness, Muenzenmair et al. (1993) found higher rates of physical and sexual abuse histories, more frequent and ongoing abuse and more severe abuse within this population. Treatment for mental illness often ignores the possibility of traumatic etiology and focuses solely on medicating symptoms. Some symptoms of trauma, such as depression, anxiety and fearfulness, confusion, dissociation, nightmares and fantasies of doom and flashbacks and hallucinations, are often misdiagnosed and treated as symptoms of major mental illness. It is important to note that some women trauma survivors actually do have schizophrenia and that many PTSD symptoms respond well to medication. Central nervous system depressants mask these symptoms; therefore, dosage may need to be reduced so that a survivor may progress in her healing.

Psychiatric treatment is sometimes used to silence allegations of physical and sexual abuse. This silencing has been accomplished by the use of medications, restraints and seclusion and invasive surgical procedures. Sometimes the threat of these "treatments" is sufficient to restrict the survivor from speaking about the abuse (Jennings, 1994).

Case:

Elaine is a 70 year old single woman diagnosed with chronic schizophrenia. She reports that at an early age she was sexually abused by her father as well as by a neighbor. She graduated high school at the age of 18 and obtained a secretarial job with the federal government. She worked for nearly a year before her first hospitalization in 1944. Hospital records report that, Elaine exhibited hallucinations, delusions and crying spells. Following this initial hospitalization, Elaine remained institutionalized for nearly 47 years. Psychiatrists treated her symptoms aggressively with medication and electroconvulsive shock therapy. In 1950, Elaine's parents began demanding the psychiatrist to perform a lobotomy. When Elaine's treatment team did not support the procedure, her parents sought a psychiatrist who would perform the lobotomy. After two years of litigation, Elaine underwent a prefrontal lobe lobotomy. Elaine's current treatment team wonders if the lobotomy was sought as a means of silencing allegations of sexual abuse.

Mental illness: as a risk factor for abuse

Individuals diagnosed with mental illness have historically been abused in institutional settings. Great efforts have been made in the last 30 years to improve conditions in psychiatric hospitals as evidenced by court mandates requiring that psychiatric treatment be delivered in the least restrictive environment and the consumer advocacy movement. However, stigma still exists as an issue for both the diagnosed individual and for society; abuses still occur in the course of treatment and consumer rights are often violated. For example, in Montana damages were awarded to 371 individuals who were confined without justification in the late nineteen-eighties (Staff, 1992).

Abuse continues to be perpetrated within the mental health system to varying degrees. When symptoms are severe and a person requires involuntary admission, the police are often used to escort

her in handcuffs to the hospital. Seclusion, restraints and forced medication are misused on inpatient units as punishment for disruptive
but not necessarily dangerous behavior (Jennings, 1994). Treatment
providers at times sexually harass, seduce and rape consumers in their
care.

In fact, any treatment relationship has the potential for becoming
abusive because of the inherent difference in power possessed by
client and clinician. Moreover, individuals being treated for psychiatric symptoms may have problems defining boundaries. Nevertheless, it is always the responsibility of the treatment provider rather
than the consumer to create and protect boundaries in the treatment
relationship.

> Case:
>
> Elizabeth is a thirty-six year old woman diagnosed with
> major depression. When she was in her early twenties, her treat-
> ing psychiatrist initiated a sexual relationship with her during a
> hospitalization at a public institution. Upon learning that he was
> molesting several other female patients, Elizabeth complained
> about the psychiatrist to hospital staff. Elizabeth's persistent
> complaints resulted in her being transferred to another ward;
> however, the man continued to act as her treating psychiatrist.
> No disciplinary action was taken against him. Instead, Elizabeth
> was punished for "wrongly" accusing him.

Treatment providers, even when intending to act in the best interest of the individual, may actually be re-enacting a previous pattern
of abuse. Fromuth and Burkhart (1992), use Finkelhor's categories of
abuse consequences to demonstrate a parallel between abuse dynamics and inpatient psychiatric treatment. Stigmatization and powerlessness are central to the experiences of both trauma and psychiatric
hospitalization; betrayal and traumatic sexualization comprise
other dynamics of abuse that may be re-enacted in the process of
treatment.

In the mental health system, a consumer's complaints of abuse by a
treatment provider may be discounted because the system does not
see her as a credible witness. Abuse can be allowed to go unchecked
when reports of abuse are not believed because the reporting individual experiences disordered thinking. One woman reported to her

outpatient case manager that she had been sexually abused by a staff member during a recent hospitalization. Neither the case manager nor the psychiatrist believed the reports because of her history of delusional thinking. However, the report was later corroborated by a woman who did not have a thought disorder. The treatment provider may unwittingly reinforce one component of the abuse cycle when he or she does not validate stories of abuse.

Another way in which mental illness is a risk factor for abuse is the way in which many of its symptoms inherently interfere with an individual's ability to protect herself. Women responding to internal stimuli are often unable to fully attend to the world around them. Obviously, poor reality-testing and confusion leave a woman vulnerable to harm because they impair her ability to accurately assess a situation. In addition, women lacking a strong, integrated sense of self and demonstrating attendant compliant behavior may be more easily exploited. Moreover, individuals taking psychotropic medications which dull the senses and slow down responses may also be less alert to dangerous situations.

Case:

Ann is a forty-five year old divorced woman diagnosed with chronic schizophrenia. She experienced her initial psychotic break during her first year of medical school and was unable to complete school. Despite continued episodes of psychosis and hospitalizations, Ann eventually achieved a Master's degree in Library Science. However, due to debilitating psychotic symptoms she has never been able to work in her field. Ann's condition has deteriorated over the years. She experiences intense paranoia, unremitting auditory hallucinations of a persecutory nature, ideas of reference including a belief that the television and radio are talking about her, fixed delusions of sexual involvement with people in her social network as well as with celebrity figures and severely compromised boundaries and poor impulse control.

Ann's marriage ended following the onset of her mental illness. She describes feeling extremely lonely and undesirable and states that her self-worth depends on being involved with a man. Men exploit Ann's symptoms in order to sexually abuse

33

her and take financial advantage of her. Men appear at her door at all hours of the day or night whenever they want sex. Her self-esteem is so low that she pays them for their company. The man she considers her boyfriend will only allow her to give him oral sex. Therapists have been unsuccessful in helping Ann to set boundaries and protect herself from abuse.

Discussion

Homelessness, substance addiction and psychiatric symptoms are not usually mutually exclusive factors (Fischer and Breakey, 1991; Drake, Osher and Wallach, 1991; McCarty, Argeriou, Huebner and Lubran, 1991; Breakey *et al.*, 1989; Cuffel, Heithoff and Lawson, 1993; and Robertson, 1991). Many of the women presented in this chapter experienced childhood physical and sexual abuse and all have been diagnosed with a serious mental illness. The experience of abuse in childhood may have been the first step in a process that resulted in homelessness, substance abuse and/or entry into the mental health system.

For a trauma survivor, homelessness, substance abuse and psychiatric symptoms complicate the healing process because they have the potential to place a woman at risk for revictimization. In addition, women who are homeless, substance dependent or diagnosed with mental illness are likely to have fewer social and psychological resources for coping, further impeding the recovery process.

The interplay of all of these factors necessitates a multivariate treatment approach where these issues are addressed concurrently. Even though substance use is often the focus early in treatment, the impact of psychiatric symptoms, trauma after-effects and homelessness must be integrated into the treatment plan. In this discussion of trauma treatment and recovery, we have focused on the impact of the interface of homelessness, addictions and psychiatric symptoms on trauma recovery.

The treatment provider can easily become overwhelmed when beginning work with a woman presenting with the multiple, immediate issues of homelessness, substance abuse and psychiatric symptoms. In order to begin to stabilize the client, the clinician must form a relationship with her. The initial stage of a working relationship is usually based on meeting basic needs. For example, in the engagement phase of treatment of dually diagnosed homeless women, a first step could be to help the woman obtain a handicapped transportation pass so she can travel to secure other resources such as shelter and food. Basic human needs must be met before the more complicated issues of trauma and addictions can be addressed.

Containment and stabilization must be the primary focus in the early stages of treatment. The healing process begins with the formation of a working relationship; however, it can not move further until overt symptomatology and/or substance use are addressed. Hallucinations and delusions must be reduced and a beginning commitment to substance abuse treatment must be formed in order to secure safe housing for a homeless woman. A woman may remain homeless for an extended period of time during the containment and stabilization phase; clinicians must be aware that this process can take months. It is important to understand that essential work is being done even while the woman remains homeless.

Although stabilization must occur before intensive trauma work can begin, the relationship between trauma history and current functioning must be acknowledged and validated. Clinicians must understand and appreciate that what is stabilizing and containing for one woman in recovery may be destabilizing and fragmenting for another. For example, some women must become abstinent from alcohol and drugs in the beginning of trauma work and others may continue to use substances throughout the trauma work until they are feeling safer and have more coping resources and no longer need to self-medicate the pain, memories, flashbacks and nightmares with illegal substances.

Throughout recovery, an integrated treatment approach must be used to treat a consumer with multiple issues. The potential for relapse can occur at all stages of healing and can involve psychiatric symptoms, traumatic memories and homelessness as well as substance use. For women who are substance addicted, homeless and/or diagnosed with mental illness, the potential for relapse is greater because they are at risk for retraumatization. Because relapse precipitates crisis, crisis intervention is an ongoing need in trauma recovery. The clinician must remain flexible in his or her treatment planning in order to carry out the multivariate treatment approach.

References

American Psychiatric Association. (1987) *Diagnostic and statistical manual of mental disorders* (3rd ed., rev.). Washington, D.C.: Author.

Bassuck, E.L. (1993) "Social and economic hardships of homeless and other poor women", in *American Journal of Orthopsychiatry*, 63(3), 340–347.

Belle, D. (1990) "Poverty and women's mental health", in *American Psychologist*, 45, 385–389.

Blankertz, L.E., Cnaan, R.A. and Freedman, E. (1993) "Childhood risk factors in dually diagnosed homeless adults", in *Social Work*, 38(5), 587–595.

Breakey, W.R., Fischer, P.J., Kramer, M., Nestadt, G., Romanoski, A.J., Ross, A., Royall, R.M. and Stine, O.C. (1989) "Health and mental health problems of homeless men and women in Baltimore", in *Journal of American Medical Association*, 262(10), 1352–1357.

Browne, A. (1993) "Family violence and homelessness: The relevance of trauma histories in the lives of homeless women", in *American Journal of Orthopsychiatry*, 63(3), 370–383.

Carmen, E., Rieker, P. and Mills, T. (1984) "Victims of violence and psychiatric illness", in *American Journal of Psychiatry*, 141(3), 378–383.

Cuffel, B.J., Heithoff, K.A. and Lawson, W. (1993) "Correlates of patterns of substance abuse among patients with schizophrenia", in *Hospital and Community Psychiatry*, 44(3), 247–251.

Cunningham, J.A., Sobell, L.C. and Chow, V.M.C. (1993) "What's in a label? The effects of substance types and labels on treatment considerations and stigma", in *The Journal of Studies on Alcohol*, 54, 693–699.

D'Ercole, A. and Struening, E. (1990) "Victimization among homeless women: Implications for service delivery", in *Journal of Community Psychology*, 18, 141–152.

Drake, R.E., Osher, F. and Wallach, M.A. (1991) "Homelessness and dual diagnosis", in *American Psychologist*, 46, 1149–1158.

Fischer, P.J. and Breakey, W.R. (1991) "The epidemiology of alcohol, drug and mental disorders among homeless persons", in *American Psychologist*, 46(11), 1115–1128.

Fromuth, M.E. and Burkhart, B.R. (1992) "Recovery or recapitulation? An analysis of the impact of psychiatric hospitalization on the child sexual abuse survivor", in *Women and Therapy*, 12(3), 81–95.

Garbarino, J., Kostelny, K. and Dubrow, N. (1991) "What children can tell us about living in danger", in *American Psychologist*, 46, 376–383.

Goodman, L.A. (1991) "The prevalence of abuse among homeless and housed poor mothers: a comparison study", in American Journal of Orthopsychiatry, 6, 14, 489–500.

Goodman, L.A., Dutton, M.A. and Harris, M. (1995) "Episodically homeless women with serious mental illness: prevalence of physical and sexual assault", in American Journal of Orthopsychiatry, 65(4), 468–478.

Jennings, A. (1994) "On being invisible in the mental health system", in *Journal of Mental Health Administration*, 21(4).

Mayer, K. (1991) "Adult survivors of childhood sexual abuse and subsequent risk of HIV infection", in *American Journal of Public Health*, 81(5), 572–575.

McCarty, D., Argeriou, M., Huebner, R.B. and Lubran, B. (1991) "Alcoholism, drug abuse and the homeless", in *American Psychologist*, 46(11), 1139–1148.

Muenzenmaier, K., Meyer, I., Struening, E. and Ferber, J. (1993) "Childhood abuse and neglect among women outpatients with chronic mental illness", in *Hospital and Community Psychiatry*, 44(7), 666–670.

North, C.S. and Smith, E.M. (1992) "PTSD among homeless men and women", in *Hospital and Community Psychiatry*, 43(10), 1010–1016.

Rieker, P.P. and Carmen, E. (1986) "The victim-to-patient process: The disconformation and transformation of abuse", in *American Journal of Orthopsychiatry*, 56(3), 360–370.

Robertson, M.J. (1991) "Homeless women with children", in *American Psychologist*, 46(11), 1198–1204.

Rose, S.M., Peabody, C.G. and Stratigeas, B. (1991) "Undetected abuse among intensive case management clients", in *Hospital and Community Psychiatry*, 42(5), 499–503.

Ross, C.A., Kronson, J., Koensgen, S., Barkman, K., Clark, P. and Rockman, G. (1992) "Dissociation comorbidity in 100 chemically dependent patients", in *Hospital and Community Psychiatry*, 43(8), 840–842.

Staff. (1992) "Montana agrees to pay $3,500,000 damages for rights violations of state hospital patients", in *Hospital and Community Psychiatry*, 43(9), p. 947.

Zeirler, S., Feingold, L., Laufer, D., Velentgas, P., Kantrowitz-Gordon, I. and Mayer, K. (1991) "Adult survivors of childhood sexual abuse and subsequent risk of HIV infection", in *American Journal of Public Health*, 81(5), 572–575.

Chapter Three

Assessment of Trauma in Women Psychiatric Patients

Anna M. Spielvogel and Alexia K. Floyd

E XPOSURE to violence is increasingly commonplace for life in North America. While all sectors of the population are affected, disenfranchised vulnerable groups are disproportionately traumatized. This is particularly true of women of color, poor women, women with mental illness, women who abuse substances or women who engage in the sex trade. Violent acts against these women include homicide, assault, domestic partner abuse, childhood sexual and physical abuse, rape, sexual harassment and sexual boundary violations by health professionals. Exposure to one kind of abuse in childhood greatly increases the chance of other forms of abuse being present and repeated in adulthood (Chu and Dill, 1990; Rose, 1993; Carmen, *et al.,* 1984; Hamilton, 1989). Women and children experience violence predominantly from family members or close friends (Walker, 1994). Acknowledging and stopping the violence in this private sphere through increased awareness, community pressures and adequate resources for interventions have not been successful in most communities. Health care providers and therapists need to be fully educated as to the prevalence and sequelae of trauma in order to assure sensitive treatment. The important contribution of trauma to the development or manifestations of psychiatric symptomatology has been rediscovered over the last 20 years (Beitchman, *et al.*, 1992; Briere and Zaidi, 1989; Brown and Anderson, 1991; Bryer, *et al.*, 1987; Carmen, 1984; Craine, 1988; Herman, 1992 ii; Jacobsen and Richardson, 1987; Jennings, 1994; Malinosky and Hansen, 1991; Walker, 1994; Rose, 1993). Information regarding the particular impact of the nature, frequency, age of onset, duration and repetition of the trauma is still being elucidated. Repeated trauma with early onset can impair emotional, physical and cognitive development (Terr, 1991; Madonna, *et al.*, 1991). The long lasting effects of severe trauma characterized as post traumatic stress disorder (PTSD) alter the neurochemical balances and stress responses (van der Kolk, 1994; Vargas and Davidson, 1993; Southwick, *et al.*, 1993). PTSD can result in hyperarousal and sensitization to future stress or desensitization of the body's stress related neuromodulators accompanied by affective blunting and avoidance. Since trauma responses are varied and affect many areas of the mental status, they should be considered prior to arriving at other diagnoses. At the same time additional work needs to be done to delineate the interaction of trauma responses with other environmental, constitutional and genetic factors.

Considerable controversy persists about legitimate and reliable methods of assessing histories of childhood sexual trauma in adults and the appropriate treatments (Loftus, 1991, 1993; Herman 1992 ii; Walker, 1994). The questions about the appropriateness of assessing childhood trauma and the validity of reports are particularly problematic with severely and chronically mentally ill women. It might be argued that given the dwindling resources for mental health services routine assessment of trauma is impractical. Therefore care providers and institutions need to delineate what their rationale for assessment of trauma is and how to document the benefits of such an assessment. Several reasons for the assessment of trauma in a variety of settings can be cited:

1. Consequences of trauma obscure diagnosis and therefore lead to inaccurate assessment and treatment (van der Kolk, 1994; Herman, 1992 i).
2. Traumatized mentally ill women might present in the most acute ways and be at imminent risk for hurting themselves or prone to being victimized by others in the treatment setting unless the

assessment accurately reflects these risks (van der Kolk, *et al.*, 1991; Goodwin, *et al.*, 1990).

3. Traumatized patients are vulnerable to being revictimized by medical and psychiatric investigations that take control from them and render them powerless. Standard procedures in psychiatric emergency rooms can be traumatizing (Kurz, 1987; Jennings 1995). Therefore, knowledge of the trauma history can result in alterations in standard procedures to minimize negative effects.

4. Past trauma predisposes women to current violence and these acute dangers need to be accurately assessed and dealt with (Chu and Dill, 1990; Sandberg, *et al.*, 1994).

This chapter will describe the types of trauma to be assessed, the consequences and manifestations, the various settings where these assessments take place and recommendations for how to incorporate the data gathered into treatment decisions.

The DSM-IV (APA, 1994) defines trauma related to PTSD as directly experienced or witnessed events, including actual or threatened death or serious physical injury e.g., violent personal assaults, such as sexual assault or physical attack. For children, sexually traumatic events may include developmentally inappropriate sexual experiences without threatened or actual violence or injury. The likelihood of developing PTSD may increase as the intensity of and physical proximity to the stressor increase. The following associated constellations of symptoms may occur and are more commonly seen in association with an interpersonal stressor (e.g. childhood sexual or physical abuse, domestic battering, torture, etc.): impaired affect modulation; self-destructive and impulsive behavior; dissociative symptoms; somatic complaints; feelings of ineffectiveness, shame, despair or hopelessness; feeling permanently damaged; a loss of previously sustained beliefs; hostility; social withdrawal; feeling constantly threatened; impaired relationships with others; or a change in previous personality characteristics (DSM-IV, APA 1994).

Fullilove *et al.* (1993) reported structured interviews with 105 women attending substance abuse treatment programs in New York city and found that 104 of the women had at least one traumatic experience, suggesting the universality of trauma in urban socially disadvantaged clinical populations. The high percentage of women

41

(59%) reporting symptoms consistent with a lifetime diagnosis of PTSD was associated with exposure to violence, e.g., physical or sexual assaults as an adult or child and to the number of traumatic events. The authors suggested that nonviolent traumas e.g., serious accidents, death or injury of a loved one, loss of children to placement and homelessness, were equally frequent in women with or without PTSD. Human cruelty appeared particularly damaging to these women. Repeated trauma, rather than leading to habituation with a decrease in symptoms, seems to be associated with an increased risk of developing PTSD.

Women are at high risk for violence. Homicide is the leading cause of death in young African American females and fourth most common cause of death in white females (Stewart and Robertson, 1995). Prevalence data in nonclinical samples indicate that women have a 20–30% chance of experiencing sexual or physical assault over their lifetime.

Sexual contact between a child and a person at least five years older seems to occur in 20% of the population (Sandberg, *et al.*, 1994), predominately affecting females. Childhood sexual and physical abuse appears to be related to adult psychopathology. Increased rates of self injurious behavior, suicidality, dissociative disorders, PTSD, depression, borderline personality disorder (BPD), nonspecific Axis II disorders, substance abuse, somatization and repeated exposure to adult trauma are found in women attending crisis clinics who have childhood abuse histories (Forster and King, 1994; Roesler and Dafler, 1993; Malinosky-Rummel and Hanson, 1991; van der Kolk, *et al.*, 1991; Brown and Anderson, 1991; Lowenstein, 1990). The literature also documents higher rates of traumatic life events in patients with severe psychiatric disorders than in the general population (Carlin and Nicholas, 1992; Brown and Anderson, 1991; Briere and Zaidi, 1989; Bryer, *et al.*, 1987; Carmen, *et al.*, 1984; Herman, 1992 ii; Jacobson, 1989, 1990). Gallagher, *et al.* (1992) studied 22 female psychiatric inpatients and found that 73% of the subjects were victims of childhood sexual abuse and that 73% had experienced physical abuse. Using a standardized rating instrument regarding the nature and severity of the trauma resulted in reliable and specific reports of traumas.

The most popular way to assess abuse histories is through a clinical interview, with the interviewer directly asking about abuse history. Due to the fact that interviews can be highly variable, there have been studies to evaluate the efficacy of different measures in assessing the presence of trauma.

The Trauma Symptom Checklist (Briere and Runtz, 1989), the Childhood Trauma Questionnaire (Bernstein, et al., 1994) and the Retrospective Assessment of Traumatic Events instrument (RATE), which assess loss, physical, verbal and sexual abuse and severity of abuse (Gallagher, et al., 1992) are measures used to elicit histories of abuse. Tests to measure the presence of PTSD symptoms and disso- ciative disorders are also used to assess the sequelae of trauma since both disorders are strongly correlated with experiences of significant trauma (Spitzer, et al., 1990; Foa, et al., 1993; Robins, et al., 1981; Bernstein and Putnam, 1986; Forster and King, 1994). The relation- ship of PTSD and dissociative symptoms to other psychiatric diag- noses such as schizophrenia, affective illnesses, somatization, anxiety disorders, substance abuse and personality disorders is still being investigated (Davidson and Foa, 1991; Herman, 1992 i; Newman, et al., in press). There are several advantages to using a standardized interview format to assess the presence of violence and past experi- ences of abuse in most settings (see APPENDIX). Training clinicians to routinely ask specific, nonjudgmental questions about the pres- ence of violence or history of abuse (inquiring about specific events and experiences and avoiding terms like abuse, perpetrator and trauma) can increase the rate of detection and decrease the discom- fort of both clients and clinicians (Briere and Zaidi 1989). Chart reviews when structured interview protocols were not used indicate much lower rates of abuse. Women will rarely bring up the topic themselves, (Briere and Zaidi, 1989; Rose, et al., 1991; Sanders and Giolas, 1991; Brown and Anderson, 1991). Shame and confusion associated with past abuse can make patients unwilling or unable to initiate discussion about the abuse. Professionals not initiating discus- sion of the topic can confirm patients beliefs about the need to deny the experience (Bryer, et al., 1987). In addition, following a standard- ized protocol with all patients can protect clinicians from the accusa- tion that their inappropriate technique suggested an abuse history that is not factual (Loftus, 1991).

Even when rating scales are not directly applicable to the emer- gent or initial assessment of women because of the presence of confounding untreated psychiatric symptoms and time constraints, these standardized questions serve as a reminder to the clinician to obtain the information as soon as clinically appropriate.

The optimal approach of the clinician assessing a woman for trauma will vary with the woman's presenting complaints and motivation for addressing her trauma history, as well as with the treatment setting and the relationship between the clinician and the woman. The woman needs to feel as safe as possible, needs to be given control over the pace and format of the interview and needs to understand the reasons for eliciting a trauma history (Brown and Anderson, 1991; Forster and King, 1994). Women who experienced betrayal of trust by primary caretakers or intimates find it difficult to trust a clinician (Rose, 1986; Walker, 1994; Herman, 1992 ii). Understanding and responding appropriately to the women's overt and veiled questions regarding the care providers intentions, safety and ability to tolerate the trauma requires training and skill. Scrupulous honesty and integrity, clarity on the goal of the interview and the nature and duration of the relationship are important. In addition clinicians need to be aware of their own limitations and countertransference risks when eliciting trauma histories. Clinicians can err by avoiding the trauma because of their own discomfort or by becoming over-involved. Clinicians working with women with past or recent histories of abuse or rape must be vigilant in detecting the women's self-blame and counteract it (Walker, 1994; Rose, 1993). At the same time, especially in cases of domestic violence, they must be careful not to overly attack (verbally) the offender (Comas-Diaz and Green, 1994). Often the victims have close relationships with the offenders and may have mixed feelings toward them. In addition, women of color might be particularly reluctant to expose a member of their community and risk being held responsible for that person's abuse by the dominant society. In cases of domestic violence, verbally attacking the abusive partner when the woman remains in the relationship may increase her vulnerability to more severe abuse or danger in the future (Walker, 1994; Harway and Hansen, 1993).

Women who experience violence from a current partner, have been raped, or have been involved with gang violence, can present in a number of different treatment settings, e.g., the psychiatric emergency room, the rape treatment center, the medical emergency room, the obstetrician, family practitioner, at a substance abuse or mental health treatment center (Koss, *et al.*, 1991; Rose, 1993). Protocols for assessing the physical and psychological sequelae of violence and competent reporting to law enforcement agencies are essential for all these settings. Psychological sequelae of violence is self-destructive behavior, suicidality, PTSD and symptoms of dissociative disorders, somatization and depression (Goodman, *et al.*, 1993; Gelles and Straus, 1988; Stark and Flitcraft, 1988; Sonnenberg, 1988; Stewart and Robinson, 1995). A large number of abused women are encountered in substance abuse centers (Roesler and Dafler, 1993). Although it is not necessarily the main focus, assessment and treatment should address the sequelae of violence and abuse (Brown and Anderson, 1991; Roesler and Dafler, 1993).

Responding to the complex needs of women with trauma experiences is a daunting task. Treatment centers and clinicians can be assisted by guidelines of how to think through the priorities and address the obstacles.

1. In the initial evaluation clinicians need to address the woman's current exposure to violence and level of safety as first priority (Herman, 1992 ii; Harway and Hansen, 1993; Walker, 1994; Jacobson and Richardson, 1987).
2. The sensitive and effective assessment of violence and the management of risk to the women, requires awareness of the problems, training in eliciting the answers and comfort and ability to implement crisis interventions (Bryer, *et al.*, 1987; Harway and Hansen, 1993; Stewart and Robinson, 1995).
3. The woman's impulse control and tendency for self-injurious behavior needs to be immediately assessed and stabilized, given the association of self-destructive behavior with childhood abuse or neglect (van der Kolk, 1991) and exposure to domestic violence (Gelles and Strauss, 1988) and rape (Rose, 1986, 1993).
4. Physical injuries from the abuse need to be detected and comprehensive medical care and information provided (Rose, 1993; Stewart and Robinson, 1995).
5. Serious thought disorders, affective disturbances, or cognitive impairment as seen in acute psychosis or acute substance intoxication need to be stabilized first.

45

6. A semi-structured interview format asking for specific events or violent behaviors toward the woman is most effective in eliciting a complete trauma history. (See APPENDIX). Interviewers need to respect the pace of the individual and her preference for communication, verbal or written. They also need to be prepared to manage symptoms, such as hyperarousal, dissociation, hostility, or suicidal ideation by increasing the client's safety without rendering the woman powerless.

7. Whenever possible the woman's explicit permission should be sought for the interview and intervention. Confidentiality and its limits need to be explicitly negotiated. The woman's permission should be sought to share the trauma history with members of the treatment team and to record it in the chart while keeping it confidential from the woman's family or friends. Those pieces of information she explicitly authorizes for discussion may be shared.

8. Treatment centers need to be familiar with and address the stress of care providers working with trauma victims. Team approaches, access to consultation, supervision and therapy need to be in place to deal with staff's stress to safeguard the client's treatment.

9. Assessment and treatment centers should have procedures in place to investigate clients' allegations of sexual misconduct by clinicians. They should develop ongoing relationships with other agencies treating these women in order to implement a cohesive, sensitive treatment plan and avoid interagency conflict.

Some of these principles will be discussed in more detail in the next section of this chapter, especially as they pertain to clinical situations with seriously mentally ill women.

Assessement of immediate safety or risk

Intimate violence occurs between individuals in all racial, religious and economic groups and between those of every sexual orientation. It accounts for more injuries to women than rapes, muggings and car accidents combined (Straus and Gelles, 1989; Stark and Flitcraft, 1985). Domestic violence is defined in the California Penal Code as "abuse committed against an adult or fully emancipated minor who is a spouse, former spouse, cohabitant or person with whom the suspect has had a child, is having or has had a dating or engagement relationship (Penal Code 13700 (b)).

Pervasive domestic violence is often not revealed by the victim and, as studies show, is under-recognized by medical and psychiatric care providers (McLeer and Anwar, 1989). When information about domestic violence is sought, prevalence rates for women coming to medical emergency services range from 25–33 percent (Goodman, et al., 1993). In one psychiatric study, 26% of suicide attempts by women were found to be related to domestic violence (Stark and Flitcraft, 1985).

In spite of the increased awareness of the extent of violence against women and the risks posed to women's safety and life, adequate assessment of current risks are more the exception than the routine. Women should be asked about their current relationships and then in a matter of fact way if they have been physically or sexually hurt by their partner.

Intimate violence in lesbian relationships is particularly difficult to assess because of the lack of studies, lack of guidelines for assessment and treatment and stereotypes and discrimination facing lesbians as a group. However physical and sexual violence have been reported in 26 to 60 percent of women in a lesbian relationship (Lie and Gentlewarrior, 1991; Renzetti 1992). Important for the mental health care provider is the finding that lesbian victims did not perceive the services available for battered women (e.g., shelters, hotlines, police victim assistance programs etc.) as viable sources of help (Renzetti, 1992). Lesbians in that study also reported negative responses by shelter workers, physicians, police and attorneys. Clearly the mental health care worker assessing lesbians needs to be sensitive to the multiple discrimination and victimization these clients might experience.

Facilitation of acute and ongoing medical care for mentally ill women frequently falls to their mental health providers since women often have difficulties identifying the need for medical attention or encounter problems accessing sensitive care. Therefore, mental health professionals should be questioning women routinely about the presence of physical injuries, newly developed symptoms, their sexual practices and reproductive functioning. Symptoms of poor physical

47

health might be directly related to injuries sustained during a trau-matic event, or constitute a response to stress. Such symptoms might include headaches, insomnia, muscle aches, back pain, gastrointestinal disturbances, pelvic pain, fatigue (Stewart and Robinson, 1995; Goodman, Ross and Russo, 1993; Waigandt, *et al.*, 1990; Walker, *et al.*, 1988). A case manager working with a woman recently abused by a partner might find it easier to gain the partner's approval for intervention by offering to address the woman's need for physical care first (Rose, 1993). While being attended to for her physical injuries, the woman can receive information regarding shelters, legal recourse and can develop a safety plan.

Even when a woman reveals the presence of battering, therapists can underestimate the dangerousness of the situation and find them-selves at a loss for how to understand the situation and be unclear as to how to intervene (Harway and Hansen, 1993). If during an initial contact or assessment a client indicates that there might be violence, for instance "we fight at home," the specifics of the behaviors need to be explored. Appropriate questions might include, "Have you been hit, punched, shoved? Have any objects been used such as clubs, knives or other weapons? Have you been prevented from leaving home or has food or shelter been withheld? Have you been forced to have sex or engage in activities against your will, as a result of threats of injury?" The woman needs to be interviewed alone. Even then clinicians need to recognize that injuries are usually mini-mized and the behavior of the batterer is usually excused or rational-ized (Rose, 1993). If violence against the woman has become more severe and the episodes more frequent, or if the woman has threat-ened to leave, she is in imminent danger for escalating injuries or even death. Women need to be advised of the danger to their lives and encouraged to formulate a safety plan (Harway and Hansen, 1993; Hotaling and Sugerman, 1986). At a minimum, battered women should know the phone numbers of shelters for battered women and the police, know how to obtain an emergency restrain-ing order and identify when it would be safest to gather their chil-dren and necessary documents and leave. Unfortunately, many women feel they are unable to leave because they depend on the abuser for economic or emotional support and they realistically assess that the dangers that they face being on their own might be similar to those they face staying with the abusing partner. The role of mental health care providers is to assist the woman in formulating the best plan for her while being careful not to impose his or her own opinions, values or ideas on the woman.

Case one:

Ms. A, a 32 year old African American woman four months pregnant, presented to the emergency room with bruises over her left eye, her chest, arms and on her abdomen. When questioned about the injuries, she initially stated that she fell down stairs. She became increasingly hostile and irritable and refused to give further information. Hospital records revealed that she had a history of intravenous drug abuse and was HIV positive. She had been placed in foster care at age 12 because of five years of sexual and physical abuse by a stepfather and the substance abuse and mental illness of her mother. She was diagnosed with bipolar disorder and had received lithium carbonate in the past. She had two previous children removed from her custody at birth.

After attending to her injuries and assuring her by ultrasound examination that her fetus was doing well, the obstetricians suggested that she might like to talk to a psychiatrist working with pregnant women about all the stresses she was facing with her pregnancy. She was noted as looking depressed and had not gained weight appropriately. When questioned by the psychiatric consultant about what was of most concern to her, she revealed her fear that the child she was carrying would also be removed from her custody at birth. She described that she had been mostly drug free over the last six months, but that she recently relapsed after an argument with her boyfriend who questioned her ability to mother a child. She used cocaine and when her boyfriend discovered her relapse he assaulted her and threatened that he would abandon her and attempt to gain custody of the child. While angry at her boyfriend, she credited him with keeping her drug free and providing her with protection from assaults by other males. She described that this was the third time her boyfriend had hit her, that he had used his fist to punch her and stopped spontaneously after five minutes. She also explained that her boyfriend had a history of arrests which he and his community believed to be due to racial harassment. As a result, Ms. A considered it impossible to press charges against her boyfriend and risk losing his and the community's support. Her symptoms of depression were further explored and she admitted to crying spells, irritability and the wish to be dead.

A number of options were explored with Ms. A. The consultant expressed concern regarding the violence she was experiencing and explained the options of shelters or residential substance abuse programs for pregnant women. Psychiatric case management was recommended to assist her with all her life stressors since stabilization of her situation would improve the probability of keeping her child. Ms. A accepted the referral to a case manager, met the case manager prior to discharge but insisted on returning to her boyfriend to work things out. A safety plan was developed with her, rehearsing the steps she would take should she feel in danger in the future.

The case manager chose to meet with the woman and her boyfriend at their home and explained the health risks of HIV infection and the probability that the baby would be seronegative, especially if consistent medication was used. She complimented the couple on decreasing the substance abuse and attempted to enlist the boyfriend in supporting Ms. A's health care. She assisted Ms. A to obtain entitlements, so she could contribute financially to the couple's support. The case manager warned of the considerable stress health concerns and a pregnancy can place on a couple and insisted that the boyfriend commit to nonviolence. She also introduced Ms. A to a supportive substance abuse program for women with children and encouraged her to visit her local church and women friends regularly. She informed the boyfriend of the mandatory reporting law regarding violence and that she would be obligated to intervene and involve the police. The boyfriend accepted the interventions by the case manger and became invested in Ms. A's and the baby's health care.

This case highlights the dilemmas often faced by health care providers, in that one dangerous situation needs to be weighed against other risks. Ms. A's major concern was about her ability to mother and keep her baby, which is often the primary concern of women and can serve as motivation to accept abstinence from substances and to embark on treatment. Supporting this woman in her goals meant accepting that she was to continue to live with her boyfriend. Both for cultural reasons (suspiciousness of the law enforcement of the dominant culture) (Kanuha, 1994) and personal reasons, she wanted to be with the father of her baby to enhance her chance of finally having a family and was unwilling to leave or press charges against him. The case manager actively worked to explain and mediate the stressors the couple was facing and helped the woman to develop a supportive network to counteract the isolation which often is part of a violent relationship. The case manager made it clear to the boyfriend that there would be legal consequences for his continued violence. Usually legal consequences are necessary in order for the batterer to stop the assaults. Should Ms. A's boyfriend resort to violence again, she would be in a much stronger position to consider all her options.

Setting priorities with the acutely psychotic and impulsive client

When the histories of severely mentally ill women who have been hospitalized long term are examined, the women with sexual abuse histories have higher rates of seclusion and restraints, require more staff time and receive more neuroleptics (Beck and van der Kolk, 1987). The clinician assessing patients should be aware of how having a history of early sexual trauma may present itself and routinely ask about the range of traumas in women's lives. However, stabilization of acute psychotic disorders and providing safety for self-injurious or aggressive behavior must take priority. Yet survivors of abuse legitimately fear and feel retraumatized by the routine interventions in psychiatric or medical emergency rooms, such as the administration of medication against their will, being restrained on their backs, having to endure invasive questioning and physical exams (Jennings, 1995; Kitzinger, 1992).

Having past documentation regarding the presence of abuse and the woman's response to various interventions can guide the

clinician to help minimize retraumatization. Other helpful procedures involve having the survivor work with a staff member with
whom she is familiar or permitting a trusted friend or case manager
to stay with her. The clinician needs to recognize the survivor's fear
and explain in a calm voice what is happening and that she is safe.
Granting requests that make the woman more comfortable, such as
having the light on or off in the seclusion room or having female
staff assigned is important. In spite of sensitive treatment, survivors of
abuse can feel acutely panicked and reexperience their past trauma
in the present. Such a situation is illustrated in the following case.

Case two:
    Ms. B, a 47 year old woman of Italian descent, is brought by
the police to the psychiatric emergency room in an acutely
manic state. Her case manager had contacted the police. Ms. B
has a 20 year history of bipolar illness, recently presenting with
rapid cycling and a history of alcohol and cocaine abuse. At the
emergency room, she shouts that her father sexually abused her,
that she feels his fingers all over her body and that her husband
had recently raped and beaten her.
    She points to some fresh bruises on her arms. and insists on
pressing charges at that time. The next minute she is preoccupied with concerns that the Mafia is after her and hides under
the table from imaginary assailants. Her blood alcohol level is
high and she has a urine toxin screen positive for cocaine. She is
assigned a female staff person she knows from before and the
brief verbal and physical assessment focuses on ruling out acute
medical problems and delirium and establishing past medication
responses. She is placed in seclusion and restraints and treated
for her acute agitation and psychosis with benzodiazepins and
neurolepetics.
    When her husband requests to see her, he is told to allow
time for stabilization before that is possible. The husband reports
that Ms. B had stopped her medication three weeks earlier, has
been seeing her family of origin and has been using cocaine and
alcohol excessively. He denied that they had a fight or any violence occurred and accused her of routinely lying and lately of
staying out all night.

Ms. B's agitation and pressured speech improved with acute management over the next six hours. She then requested treatment with narcotics and large amounts of benzodiazepines, stating she had terrible withdrawal symptoms, which were not apparent by objective measures. After her release from restraints, she called 911 and requested the police come and get her because she was being forcibly raped at gunpoint by a staff person. The next day she asserted that she was raped by a male staff member while in seclusion and restraints. A rape treatment counselor was contacted and no evidence was found of recent penetration. However, the rape counselor found Ms. B's account of a sexual violation while in seclusion plausible. This occurred partly because Ms. B had recovered from her acute intoxication and mania and reported a reasonable story and partly because a rape counselor's training emphasizes belief in the client's story regardless of the circumstances. There also had been distrust between the rape treatment center and the psychiatric emergency services due to past allegation of patient mistreatment by psychiatric emergency staff. At this point the case manger was asked to provide more history and mediate between the two services. The case manager confirmed Ms. B had a history of childhood sexual and physical abuse, with a recent return of memories secondary to increased contact with her family. She reported that the patient had numerous dissociative episodes, flashbacks and somatic sensations probably linked to the trauma. Even when her affective illness was stabilized, she demonstrated features of borderline personality disorder. The case manager could not verify Ms. B's allegations of violence on the part of her husband but did note their relationship had become strained and that he had considered leaving. When the case manager spoke with Ms. B about all the events of the last month and her resulting anxiety and need for help, Ms. B admitted to feeling out of control and expressed doubt that her allegations against her husband and staff were accurate.

In Ms. B's case acute psychiatric symptoms and poor impulse control needed to be addressed first. Survivors of trauma are more likely to dissociate and can suffer from flashbacks or bodily memory

53

of the trauma (Sederer and Mayree, 1995; van der Kolk, 1994). In addition the presence of acute substance abuse can lead to dissociation and a distortion of perceptions (Roesler and Dafler, 1993). These factors need to be recognized without discounting the reports of childhood abuse. Hypnotic or trance states can easily occur because of clients' high hypnotizability even without any attempt on the part of the interviewer to induce such a state. With trauma victims in acute crisis, contact with reality can be enhanced by stabilizing their agitation and psychosis with medications, providing a here-and-now focus in the interactions and exposing them to familiar and safe people and environments.

Psychotropic medications are usually necessary to stabilize acute psychiatric crises even when a trauma history is also present. The choice of appropriate medication depends on the target symptoms and the woman's past history of medication response. Even though the woman in the example was apparently experiencing flashbacks and hyperarousal, both symptoms of PTSD, tricyclic antidepressants or serotonin uptake inhibitors (Southwick, 1993; Vargas and Davidson, 1993) were not appropriate because of the risk of worsening manic symptoms. Given the client's previous responsiveness to lithium and her symptoms of bipolar illness, the recommended medication treatment would target the manic symptoms. However, additional diagnoses of PTSD, multiple personality disorder or dissociative disorder need to be considered.

The case manager who had the longitudinal picture was crucial in this assessment. She also was extremely helpful in negotiating the differences between the two clinical services. Abuse of patients by caregivers has increasingly been the focus of media attention and professional literature. Survivors of trauma are particularly vulnerable to revictimization (Stewart and Robinson, 1995; Walker, 1994). Sederer (1995) recommends that treatment settings have a procedure for a swift and impartial investigation by a team appointed by the risk managers and actively work to reduce the patient's distress and that of the accused staff. In the case reported, the allegations were clearly false. The accusations changed with time, were easily explainable by the patient's mental state and inconsistent with the fact that the patient was assigned a female staff person at all times. However, in many cases the facts are not so clear-cut and certainly mistreatment of patients by staff has to be seriously considered. It should be noted that while having female staff does not rule out abuse, it does limit the likelihood of it happening.

Diagnostic puzzles

Clinicians doing assessment and treatment of survivors of childhood physical and sexual abuse also need to contend with the present political climate and media representation of these situations. While the public awareness of the frequency of violence against women has been raised by the media, focus on these topics has also created what some people call "a climate of victims and survivors." This climate complicates the accurate assessment of childhood abuse experiences in adults. In addition the memory of traumatic events can be impaired and therefore the "narrative truth" does not necessarily correspond to actual events (Ganaway, 1989). The probability for accurate assessments of a childhood history of trauma increases when clinicians avoid techniques that produce spontaneous or induced trance states and do not suggest the abuse to the patient.

Case three:

Ms. C was a 28 year old second generation Latina who presented to the Obstetrics clinic three months pregnant. She was described by the obstetrician as the "strangest person they ever encountered." While neatly groomed and superficially pleasant, she was noted to have a childlike demeanor, answering most questions including where she lived and who her family was with "I don't know," or contradictory information. She would at times be distracted, talk about other topics or stare off into space. The obstetrician was concerned that the woman was psychotic, developmentally delayed or suffering from dementia. Work up revealed a negative urine toxin screen and no physical abnormalities. The psychiatric consultant was also puzzled by the presentation, but noted intact cognitive functioning when neutral questions or problems were addressed. Ms. C denied psychotic symptoms but admitted to increasing symptoms of depression. Neuropsychological testing revealed the presence of a severe dissociative disorder, raising the possibility of multiple personality disorder (MPD) and major depression. Ms. C's intelligence was in the normal range. History obtained from collateral sources and the patient revealed that the patient's mother had a history of schizoaffective disorder with multiple hospitalizations while the patient was growing up. The patient described that she was like a wife to her father but would not provide clear or consistent answers to inquiries about childhood sexual contact with adults or physical abuse by her parents or exhusband. The patient had finished high school and two years of college, had been married for six years and given birth to a child three years prior. After the child was several months old, Ms. C changed, became withdrawn, uninterested in the child and started to talk strangely. The family, fearing she was developing symptoms of schizoaffective disorder like her mother, attempted to hospitalize her, but the patient disappeared and since then had lived a transient life style with only occasional contact with the family. The family stated that she lied to them about where she was staying and they had been unable to track her.

Ms. C was closely followed in the Obstetrics clinic and in psychotherapy. Her depression was treated with serotonin uptake inhibitors and therapy focused on improving her problem solving skills. A here-and-now focus was used to help her to develop a continuous sense of herself. She was motivated for treatment because she wanted to keep this baby. As delivery approached, she had a number of fugue states and her disorientation increased. She was psychiatrically hospitalized and delivered safely. She was referred to residential treatment with parenting classes and enrolled in an intensive infant parent program. The psychiatrist she was referred to after delivery questioned the diagnosis and insisted that she was schizophrenic. Considerable effort was required to assure appropriate treatment for Ms. C because her presentation was so puzzling.

Dissociative disorders are often difficult to diagnose and patients' behaviors often mimic other disorders. A patient with MPD, on the average, receives that diagnosis 6.8 years after entering mental health treatment and has an average of 3.6 other psychiatric diagnoses, (Puttman, 1986). The typical symptoms of dissociation, amnesia or denial of observed behavior are rarely reported to therapists initially. Patients often do present with depressions or rapid shifts in behaviors, often interpreted as an affective disorder. MPD patients often report somatic complaints such as migraine headaches, GI symptoms, unexplained pain, conversion symptoms and eating disorders. One third will describe auditory and visual hallucinations (Kluft and Fine, 1993). Often the voices are described as coming from the head, rather from an outside source. Patients with dissociative disorders usually do not respond to neuroleptic treatment and are in general frightened of the "control over them" when medication is offered. In the case presented above, major depression was diagnosed and Ms. C did partially respond to a course of serotonin uptake inhibitors.

In this particular case hypnosis was not used in the assessment or treatment. Instead each time she dissociated an attempt was made to help her connect to the painful feelings she avoided. For instance, one time when asked if she had seen the child protection worker about regaining custody of her three year old child, Ms. C suddenly smiled and focused on the tip of a pen and said, "This is an extraordinary pen. It has a golden tip." She was unable to explain her statement, but did acknowledge that it was stressful for her to talk about the Child Protection Services involvement with her older child. Therapy focused on helping her to develop concrete coping skills to prepare her for being a mother by improving her ability to trust and tolerate her own feelings and thoughts.

A third point raised by this case concerns the effect of dissociative disorders on pregnancy, child attachment and parental competency (van der Hart, *et al.*, 1991). Several studies report that while the majority of women survivors of abuse are competent parents, victims of physical or sexual abuse are more at risk for abusing their own children (Rose, 1993). Pregnancy and childbirth can trigger memories of abuse (Courtois and Riley, 1992; Rose, 1992). In one case treated by the authors (Spielvogel and Hohener, 1995), a woman who had been sexually abused by a cousin had a trigger of her memories when the cousin came into town two weeks before delivery of the woman's second child. She impulsively put her baby up for adoption after birth and denied awareness of her third pregnancy until the delivery. Bonnet (1993) reported that psychiatric interviews with women who anonymously relinquished their infants at birth revealed that a high percentage of these women had histories of childhood sexual abuse. In a number of cases of neonaticide, the mother was noted to be in a bewildered state, acting bizarrely and unable to remember the event. Other women with severe dissociative episodes experienced particular difficulties with their toddlers and in dissociative states either neglected the children or impulsively placed them out of the home (Spielvogel and Hohener, 1995). The impact of dissociative disorders on the pregnancy, the attachment to the infant and appropriate bonding is not fully understood. Risks resulting from the mothers' discontinuity of experience should be kept in mind when working with women having abuse histories and dissociative disorder.

Summary

Women with sequelae of abuse are encountered in a number of different treatment settings. Physical injuries, physiological stress responses and psychiatric manifestations need to be consistently assessed with detailed nonjudgmental questioning. Given the sensitive nature of the information and the possibility of retraumatization by intrusive and insensitive techniques, the interviewer needs to proceed carefully. The preference of the woman as to the gender of the interviewer and her wish of having trusted friends or family members to be present initially needs to be respected. The first issue to be addressed in any assessment is the women's current safety. The woman needs to be directly asked about the presence of an abusive relationship and a safety plan needs to be developed with her immediately. Her impulse control, tendency for self injury, suicidality or aggression towards others needs to be assessed and become a treatment priority. Trauma histories, the presence of complex PTSD or dissociative disorders can be assessed in mentally ill populations. Having this information on record is crucial in order to provide sensitive care for women in the psychiatric emergency department. Special care needs to be taken to avoid retraumatization by rendering women helpless and exposed. Boundaries, scrupulous honesty and confidentiality need to be observed when working with these women.

At times women will make accusations that care givers sexually violated them. Such accusations require swift and sensitive investigations by impartial professionals to decrease the distress of the patient and the accused care givers. Agencies routinely providing services to victims of abuse should have protocols in place to deal with these investigations.

Dissociative disorders are often misdiagnosed and patients inappropriately treated for years. Continuing education regarding the multiple manifestations of dissociative disorders, including MPD, is necessary for all care givers.

Appendix

Partners and Children: Do you have significant relationships? With whom? Have you been sexually active, with men, with women, with both? Do you know how to protect yourself from infection with HIV? How often have you been pregnant? How many children do you have? What are their ages and where are the children now? If children are grown, who raised them?

Physical abuse: As a child, were you hit with objects and/or punished in ways that resulted in bruises, burns, fractures or cuts? Was food or shelter withheld? Were you threatened with weapons or death? Did you witness anyone else threatened or hurt? Were you given medical care for injuries? Were you removed from your parent's care?

Sexual abuse: Did you have any sexual experiences as a little child? With whom? When? How long? Was there exposure, touching, oral/genital or genital contact? Were photographs taken? Were there threats of harm or violence? Were there any medical or social consequences or interventions?

If yes to sexual experiences, did you ever tell anyone? Was there ever a time you didn't remember these episodes? Do you have recurrent dreams or memories now?

Recent history: Are you safe in your current relationship? Have you been hit, punched or shoved? Have knives, clubs, ropes, guns or other weapons been used to punish or threaten you? How often, by whom? Did you seek any medical attention? Has food or shelter been withheld? Have you been prevented from entering or leaving your house? Have you been threatened with violence unless you agree to certain demands of your partner? Have you told anyone?

References

American Psychiatric Association. (1994) *Diagnostic and statistical manual of mental disorders.* Washington, D.C.: American Psychiatric Association.

Beck, J.C. and van der Kolk, B. (1987) "Report of childhood incest and current behavior of chronically hospitalized psychotic women", in *American Journal of Psychiatry,* 144(11), 1474–1476.

Beitchman, J.H., Zucker, K.J., Hood, J.E., DaCosta, G.A., Akman, D. and Cassava, E. (1992) "A review of the long term effects of child sexual abuse", in *Child Abuse and Neglect*, 16, 101–118.

Bernstein, D.P., Fink, L., Handelsman, L., Foote, J., Lovejoy, M., Wenzel, K., Sapareto, E. and Ruggiero, J. (1994) "Initial reliability and validity of a new restrospective measure of child abuse and neglect", in *American Journal of Psychiatry,* 151(8), 1132–1136.

Bernstein, E. and Putman, F. (1986) "Development reliability and validity of a dissociation scale", in *Journal of Nervous and Mental Disease*, 174, 724–735.

Beutler, L.E. and Hill, C.E. (1992) "Process and outcome research in the treatment of adult victims of childhood sexual abuse; methodological issues", in *Journal of Consulting Clinical Psychology,* 60, 204–212.

Bonnet, C. (1993) "Adoption at birth: Prevention against abandonment or neonaticide", in *Child Abuse and Neglect*, 17, 501–513.

Briere, J. and Runtz, M. (1989) "The trauma symptom checklist", in *Journal of Interpersonal Violence*, 4(2), 151–163.

Briere, J. and Zaidi, L.Y. (1989) "Sexual abuse histories and sequelae in female psychiatric emergency room patients", in *American Journal of Psychiatry,* 146(12), 1602–1606.

Brown, G.R. and Anderson, B. (1991) "Psychiatric morbidity in adult inpatients with childhood histories of sexual and physical abuse", in *American Journal of Psychiatry,* 148(1), 55–61.

Bryer, J.B., Nelson, B.A., Miller, J.B. and Krol, P.A. (1987) "Childhood sexual and physical abuse as factors in adult psychiatric illness", in *American Journal of Psychiatry,* 144(11), 1426–1430.

Carlin, A.S. and Ward, N.G. (1992) "Subtypes of psychiatric inpatient women who have been sexually abused", in *Journal of Nervous and Mental Disorders*, 180(6), 392–397.

Carmen, E.H., Reiker, P.P. and Mills, T. (1984) "Victims of violence and psychiatric illness", in *American Journal of Psychiatry,* 141(3), 378–383.

Chu, J.A. and Dill, D. (1990) "Dissociative symptoms in relation to childhood physical and sexual abuse", in *American Journal of Psychiatry*, 147, 887–892.

Comaz-Diaz, L. and Greene, B. (1994) *Women of Color: Integrating Ethnic and Gender Identities in Psychotherapy*, Guilford Press, New York.

Courtois, C. and Riley, C. (1992) "Pregnancy and childbirth as triggers for abuse memories: implications for care", in *Birth,* 19, 222–223.

Craine, L.S., Hensen, C.E. and Collier, J. *et al.* (1988) "Prevalence of history of sexual abuse among female psychiatric patients in a state hospital system", in *Hospital and Community Psychiatry,* 39, 300–304.

Davidson, J.R. and Foa, E.B. (1991) "Diagnostic Issues in Posttraumatic Stress Disorder: Consideration for the DSM-IV", in *Journal of Abnormal Psychology,* 100(3), 346–355.

Foa, E.B., Riggs, D.S., Dancu, C.V. and Rothbaum, B.O. (1993) "Reliability and validity of a brief instrument for assessing Post-traumatic Stress Disorder", in *Journal of Traumatic Stress,* 6, 459–474.

Forster, P. and King, J. (1994) "Traumatic stress reactions and the psychiatric emergency", in *Psychiatric Annals,* 24(11), 603–614.

Fullilove, M., Fullilove, R., Smith, M., Winkler, *et al.* (1993) "Violence, trauma and post traumatic stress disorder among women drug users", in *Journal of Traumatic Stress,* 6(4), 533–543.

Gallagher, R.E., Flye, B.L., Hurt, S.W., Stone, M.H. and Hull, J.W. (1992) "Retrospective assessment of traumatic experiences", in *Journal of Personality Disorders,* 6(2), 99–108.

Ganaway, G.K. (1989) "Historical versus narrative truth: Clarifying the role of exogenous trauma in the etiology of MPD and its variants", in *Dissociation,* 2(4), 205–220.

Gelles, R. and Straus, M. (1988) *Intimate Violence.* New York: Simon and Schuster.

Goodman, L.A., Ross, M.P. and Russo, N.F. (1993) "Violence against women: physical and mental health effects", in *Applied and Preventive Psychology,* 2, 79–83.

Goodwin, J.M., Cheeves, K. and Connell, V. (1990) "Borderline and other severe symptoms in adult survivors of incestuous abuse", in *Psychiatric Annals,* 20(1), 22–32.

Hamilton, J.A. (1989) "Emotional consequences of victimization and discrimination in 'special populations' of women", in *Psychiatric Clinics of North America,* 12(1), 35–51, 1989.

Harway, M. and Hansen, M. (Eds.) (1993) *Battering and family therapy, A feminist perspective.* Newbury Park, CA: Sage Publications.

Harway, M. and Hansen, M. "Therapist perceptions of family violence." (1993) In: M. Harway and M. Hansen (Eds.) *Battering and family therapy, A feminist perspective.* (pp. 42–53). Newbury Park, CA: Sage Publications.

Herman, J.L. (1992, i) "Complex PTSD: A syndrome in survivors of prolonged and repeated trauma", in *Journal of Traumatic Stress,* 5(3), 377–391.

Herman, J.L. (1992, ii) *Trauma and Recovery.* New York: Basic Books, Inc.

Hotaling, G.T. and Sugerman, D.B. (1986) "An analysis of risk markers in husband to wife violence: The current state of knowledge", in *Violence and Victims,* 1, 101–124.

Jacobson, A. (1989) "Physical and sexual assault histories among psychiatric outpatients", in *American Journal of Psychiatry,* 146, 755–758.

Jacobson, A. and Herald, C. (1990) "The relevance of childhood sexual abuse to adult psychiatric inpatient care", in *Hospital and Community Psychiatry,* 41(2), 155–158.

Jacobson, A. and Richardson, B. (1987) "Assault experience of 100 psychiatric inpatients: evidence of need for routine inquiry", in *American Journal of Psychiatry,* 144, 908–913.

Jennings, A. (1994) "On being invisible in the mental health system", in *Journal of Mental Health Administration,* 21(4), 374–387.

Kanuha, V. (1994) "Women of color in battering relationships", in *Women of Color,* Comas-Diaz and Greene B. (Eds.) Guilford press, New York, pp. 429–454.

Kitzinger, J. (1992) "Counteracting, not reenacting, the violation of women's bodies: The challenge for prenatal caregivers", in *Birth,* 19(4), 219–220.

Kluft, R.D. and Fine, C.G. (1993) *Clinical perspectives on multiple personality disorder.* American Psychiatric Press, Washington D.C.

Koss, M.P., Woodruff, W.J. and Koss, P.G. (1991) "Criminal victimization among primary care medical patients: Incidence, prevalence and physician usage", in *Behavioral Sciences and the Law,* 9, 85–96.

Kurz, D. (1987) "Emergency department response to battered women: Resistance to medicalization", in *Social Problems,* 34, 69–81.

Lie, G. and Gentlewarrior, S. (1991) "Intimate violence in lesbian relationships: Discussion of survey findings and practice implications", in *Journal of Social Services Research,* 15, 41–49.

Loftus, E. (1993) "The reality of repressed memorie", in *American Psychologist,* 48, 518–537.

Loftus, E. and Ketcham, K. (1991) *Witness for the defense. The accused, the eye witness and the expert who puts memory on trial.* New York, St. Martin's Press.

Lowenstein, R.J. (1990) "Somatoform disorders in victims of incest and child abuse." In: Kluft, R. (Ed.) *Incest Related Syndroms of Adult Psychopathology.* Washington D.C.: American Psychiatric Press Inc.

Madonna, P.G., Van Scoyk, S. and Jones, D. (1991) "Family interactions within incest and nonincest families", in *American Journal of Psychiatry,* 148, 46–49.

Malinosky-Rummell, R. and Hansen, D.J. (1991) "Long term consequences of childhood physical abuse", in *Psychological Bulletin*, 68–79.

Newman, E., Kaloupek, D.G. and Kaene, T.M. "Assessment of PTSD in Clinical and Research Settings", in (Eds.) MacFarlane, A.C., van der Kolk, B. and Weisaeth, L., *Comprehensive Text on Post Traumatic Stress*, Cambridge University Press (in press).

McLeer, S. and Anwar, R. (1989) "A study of battered women presenting in an emergency department", in *American Journal of Public Health*, 79(1), 65–66.

Puttman, F.W., Guroff, J.J., Silberman, E.K. *et al.* (1986) "The clinical phenomenology of multiple personality disorder: review of 100 recent cases", in *American Journal of Psychiatry*, 47, 285–293.

Renzetti, C. (1992) *Violent betrayal: Partner abuse in lesbian relationships.* Newbury Park, CA: Sage Publications.

Robins, L.N., Helzer, J.E., Croughan, J.L. and Ratliff, K.S. (1981) "National Institute of Mental Health diagnostic interview schedule: Its history, characteristics and validity", in *Archives of General Psychiatry*, 38, 381–389.

Roesler, T.A. and Dafler, C.E. (1993) "Chemical dissociation in adults sexually victimized as children: Alcohol and drug use in adult survivors", in *Journal of Substance Abuse Treatment*, 10, 537–543.

Rose, A. (1992) "Effects of childhood sexual abuse on childbirth: One woman's story", in *Birth,* 19, 214–218.

Rose, D. (1986) "Worse than death: Psychodynamics of rape victims and the need for psychotherapy", in *American Journal of Psychiatry*, 143(7), 817–824.

Rose, D. (1993) "Sexual Assault, Domestic Violence and Incest." In D. Stewart and N. Stotland (Eds.) *Psychological Aspects of Women's Health Care.* Washington D.C. American Psychiatric Press. pp. 447–483.

Rose, S., Peabody, C.G. and Stratigeas, B. (1991) "Undetected abuse among intensive case management clients", in *Hospital and Community Psychiatry,* 42(5), 499–503.

Sandberg, D., Lynn, S.J. and Green, J.P. (1994) "Sexual abuse and revictimization", in *Dissociation*, Lynn, S.J. and Rhue, J.W. (Eds.) Guilford Press, New York.

Sanders, B. and Giolas, M. (1991) "Dissociation and childhood trauma in psychologically disturbed adolescent", in *American Journal of Psychiatry,* 148, 50–54.

Sederer, L. and Mayree, L. (1995) "False allegations of sexual misconduct: Clinical and institutional considerations", in *Psychiatric Services*, 46, 160–63.

Sonnenberg, S.M. (1988) "Victims of violence and post-traumatic stress disorder", in *Psychiatric Clinics of North America*, 11, 581–590.

Southwick, S.M., Krystal, J.H., Morgan, C.A. *et al.* "Abnormal noradrenergic function in post-traumatic stress disorder", in *Archives of General Psychiatry*, 199, 50, 206–274.

Stark, E. and Flitcraft, A. (1988) "Violence among intimates: An epidemiological review." In: Van Hasselt, Morrison and Bellack (Eds), *Handbook of Family Violence*. New York: Plenum Press. pp. 293–317.

Stewart, D.E. and Robinson, G.E. (1995) "Violence against women in Review of Psychiatry" vol. 14, Oldham, J.M. and Riba, M.B. (Eds.) *American Psychiatric Press*, Washington D.C. pp. 261–282.

Spielvogel, A.M. and Hohener H.C. "Denial of pregnancy: a review", in *Birth*, in press.

Spitzer, R.L., Williams., J.B., Gibbon, M. and First, M.B. (1990) *Structured Clinical Interview for DSMIII-R-patient edition (SCID-P)*. Biometrics Research Department, New York State Psychiatric Institute, New York, New York.

Straus, M.A. and Gelles, R.J. (1989) "How violent are American families? Estimates from the National Family Violence Resurvey and other studies." In: M.A. Straus and R.J. Gelles (Eds.) *Physical Violence in American Families*, New Brunswick, NJ: Transaction. pp. 95–132.

Terr, L. (1991) "Childhood traumas: An outline and overview", in *American Journal of Psychiatry,* 148, 10–20.

van der Hart, O., Foure, H., van Cerve and Goodwin, J. (1991) "Unawareness and denial of pregnancy in patients with MPD", in *Dissociation*, 4, 65–73.

van der Kolk, B.A. (1994) "The body keeps the score: Memory and the evolving psychobiology of posttraumatic stress", in *Harvard Review of Psychiatry*, Jan/Feb 253–265.

van der Kolk, B.A., Perry, C. and Herman, J.L. (1991) "Childhood origins of self-destructive behavior", in *American Journal of Psychiatry*, 149(12), 1665–1671.

Vargas, M.A. and Davidson, J. (1993) "Post Traumatic Stress disorder", in *Psychiatric Clinics of North America,* 16(4), 737–748.

Waigandt, A. Wallace, D., Phelps, L. *et al.* (1990) "The impact of sexual assault on physical health status", in *Journal of Traumatic Stress*, 3, 93–102.

Walker, E., Kanton, W., Harrop-Griffiths, J., *et al.* (1988) "Relationship of chronic pelvic pain to psychiatric diagnosis and childhood sexual abuse", in *American Journal of Psychiatry*, 145, 75–80.

Walker, L.E. (1994) *Abused women and survivor therapy: A practical guide for the psychotherapist*. American Psychological Association, Washington, D.C.

Part II

Treatment

Chapter Four

A Cognitive-Behavioral Approach

Kim T. Mueser and Kathryn L. Taylor

OVER the past decade there has been a growing awareness of the high rate of sexual assault experienced by women throughout their lives. Although prevalence estimates vary greatly, most researchers agree that between one-quarter and one-third of all women are sexually abused as children or adolescents (Briere and Runtz, 1988; Finkelhor, Hotaling, Lewis and Smith, 1990). The prevalence of sexual assault continues to be high throughout adulthood, with most reports indicating that between one-fifth and one-quarter of all women are raped as adults (Kilpatrick, Edmunds and Seymour, 1992; Koss, 1993). Furthermore, even higher rates of childhood and adult sexual trauma are reported for women with severe psychiatric illnesses, with many estimates exceeding fifty percent (Goodman, Dutton and Harris, 1995; Hutchings and Dutton, 1993; Muenzenmaier, Mayer, Struening and Ferber, 1993).

Until recently, the lack of societal and professional recognition of the problem of trauma in the lives of women has obscured the pervasive effects of such abuse, often condemning women to a vicious cycle of abuse (Briere, 1992; Herman, 1992). The high prevalence of sexual trauma in the lives of women, coupled with increased understanding of the many sequelae of abuse (Rosenberg, Drake and

Mueser, in press), points to the need for effective interventions aimed at reducing distress and breaking the cycle of revictimization. This need is especially pressing for women with severe psychiatric disorders, who are most likely to be victims (Goodman, *et al.*, 1995) and who have the fewest economic and psychological resources for coping with such stressors.

In this chapter we present a cognitive-behavioral approach to treating the aftermath of sexual abuse in women. As a background to the method we provide an overview of one common syndrome resulting from sexual trauma, post-traumatic stress disorder. Next, we describe the principles of cognitive-behavioral treatment, followed by a detailed case presentation. We conclude with a discussion of the need for multi-faceted treatment approaches to address the diverse needs of sexually abused mentally ill women.

Post-traumatic stress disorder (PTSD)

PTSD is a psychiatric classification that encompasses a range of different symptoms that commonly occur following the experience of a traumatic event. Numerous clinical, historical and fictional accounts of PTSD-like reactions to trauma can be found in professional and literary writings (Grinker and Spiegel, 1945) dating far before modern diagnostic systems, such as the American Psychiatric Association's Diagnostic and Statistical Manual (DSM) series and the International Classification of Mental Disorders (ICM) series. Despite this, PTSD was not included as a separate nosological category in the U.S. until the appearance of DSM-III in 1980 (American Psychiatric Association, 1980). Because formal recognition of a psychiatric diagnostic entity is usually a prerequisite for obtaining clinical research funds, research on PTSD has lagged behind many other disorders, with the preponderance of knowledge accumulated over the past 15 years.

Symptoms of PTSD

The symptoms of PTSD identified by DSM-III have been modified only slightly in subsequent revisions, including the most recent version of DSM-IV (American Psychiatric Association, 1994). Of course, the diagnosis of PTSD requires an individual to be exposed to a traumatic event considered to be out of the realm of ordinary experience, involving some direct threat of death, severe bodily harm, or psychological injury, which the person at the time finds intensely distressing or fearful. Examples of common traumas include combat, torture, rape/sexual abuse, being the victim of another violent crime, accidents and natural disasters (e.g., earthquakes). In addition, the word "post" in PTSD refers to the requirement that symptoms of distress persist or develop over a period of time following exposure to the traumatic event (e.g., symptoms present one month or more after the trauma). The symptom clusters that comprise the PTSD diagnosis include: re-experiencing the trauma, heightened physiological arousal and avoidance of stimuli associated with trauma. According to DSM-IV criteria, at least one of each type of symptom must be present for a PTSD diagnosis.

Re-experiencing of the trauma is most frequently experienced in the form of flashbacks or intrusive images of the event, nightmares, or intense distress at exposure to cues that symbolize or resemble an aspect of the trauma (e.g., a woman who was raped in a dark alley experiences fear when walking past an alley at night). Symptoms of heightened *physiological arousal* include difficulty sleeping, irritability and anger outbursts, hypervigilance (e.g., constantly searching the environment for "threats" to one's control) and an exaggerated startle response (e.g., "jumping" in response to a sudden sound). *Avoidance of stimuli associated with the trauma* can include avoidance of thoughts, feelings, places, or persons. Other symptoms of avoidance include feelings of detachment or estrangement from others, restricted affect (e.g., emotional numbness) and a foreshortened sense of future. These additional symptoms are thought to reflect individuals' efforts to avoid traumatic memories by denying or submerging their feelings, their hopes for the future and affiliative needs.

Re-experiencing the trauma, heightened arousal and avoidance are the defining characteristics of PTSD, but many other symptoms typically co-occur with these symptoms. Traumatized persons frequently resort to alcohol and drug abuse in an effort to temporarily ward away unpleasant memories of their experiences (Keane and Wolfe, 1990) and they are at increased risk for suicide as an extreme effort to escape their past. Furthermore, hallucinations or delusions, usually but not always trauma-related, are sometimes part of the presenting clinical picture in the absence of schizophrenia or bipolar disorder (Mueser and Butler, 1987; Waldfogel and Mueser, 1988; Butler, Mueser, Sprock and Braff, in press). Finally, a host of interpersonal difficulties are often part of the natural sequelae of PTSD, due to the inability of many survivors to trust others (at times bordering on paranoia), their lack of skills in advocating for their own needs and pervasive feelings of guilt, worthlessness and despair.

PTSD in traumatized populations

A natural question that emerges when considering the diagnostic classification of PTSD is the prevalence of this disorder among persons exposed to traumatic life events. Although estimates of PTSD vary across studies, depending on the nature of the traumatic event and assessment methods, there is abundant evidence that PTSD is common in the population of traumatized persons. Estimates suggest that 40–50% of sexually abused children have PTSD (McLeer, Callaghan, Henry and Wallen, 1994; McLeer, Deblinger, Atkins, Foa and Raphe, 1988; McLeer, Deblinger, Henry and Orvaschel, 1992), while consistently greater than 65% of adults with a history of childhood sexual abuse met criteria for PTSD (Davidson and Smith, 1990; Donaldson and Gardner, 1985; Lindberg and Distad, 1985; O'Neill and Gupta, 1991). Similarly, 25–50% of women who are raped as adults develop a chronic PTSD syndrome (Resnick, Kilpatrick, Dansky, Saunders and Best, 1993; Rothbaum, Foa, Riggs, Murdock and Walsh, 1992) and about 25% of persons exposed to more general crimes or other civilian traumas have PTSD (Breslau, Davis, Andreski and Peterson, 1991; Resnick, et al., 1993).

Important determinants of the likelihood of developing PTSD include the severity of the trauma (e.g., violence, fear of death), whether injuries were sustained and multiple traumatization (Resnick and Kilpatrick, 1994). Indeed, when all three risk factors have been present, PTSD is present in the vast majority of cases (Kilpatrick, Saunders, Amick-McMullan, Best, Veronen and Resnick, 1989). Thus, while PTSD is not the only conceptualization for understanding the psychological sequelae of trauma, it is a common syndrome for abused persons and provides a useful heuristic for guiding treatment.

Treatment of PTSD symptoms

Treatment of PTSD can be divided into two broad goals. First, the fear network that leads directly to the PTSD symptoms of re-experiencing the trauma, avoidance and distress related to the trauma can be modified. Second, maladaptive behavior patterns that emerge secondary to PTSD symptoms can be corrected by teaching more adaptive interpersonal and coping skills.

According to Foa and Kozak (1986), two conditions are required in order to eliminate or reduce sensitivity and size of a fear network: (1) the fear network must be activated (i.e., brought into consciousness); and (2) information which is incompatible or inconsistent with the fear must be introduced (e.g., the person encounters a feared situation but nothing happens). In practice, almost all effective cognitive-behavioral treatments for PTSD have relied on the use of *exposure*-based approaches for decreasing the distress people experience when recalling traumatic events. These approaches involve helping the traumatized person expose herself to unpleasant memories of traumas, as well as to (safe) situations which have been previously avoided, in order to break the anxiety-avoidance cycle that amplifies PTSD symptoms. With increased imaginal and *in vivo* exposure, the person experiences a decrease in accompanying anxiety and avoidance.

Imaginal exposure to traumatic memories is usually performed in the context of individual therapy sessions. Following an assessment to identify the most crucial traumatic events, the person is encouraged to talk about one event at a time, repeatedly discussing that memory, including any accompanying thoughts, feelings, or sensory experiences and providing regular feedback to the therapist about the level of anxiety experienced. At first, the person feels high levels of anxiety when discussing a particular event, but the anxiety gradually decreases each time the event is recounted, until the person is able to describe the event with a minimum of distress. When the anxiety to one traumatic event habituates, another assessment is conducted to identify a second event for exposure. Simultaneous with imaginal exposure to traumatic memories, the person identifies feared situations which are typically avoided and begins the process of gradual re-exposure to those situations which are avoided but are safe.

71

Although most cognitive-behavioral treatment approaches for PTSD include exposure as a critical element, other strategies are often included as well. For example, teaching stress management techniques, cognitive restructuring (e.g., challenging beliefs, such as "no man can be trusted") and education (e.g., about normal physiological responses to fear) are commonly incorporated into treatment. However, the common element to different approaches is exposure to the feared memories of the traumatic events.

A growing body of research supports the efficacy of exposure-based approaches for treating persons with PTSD secondary to a range of different traumatic events. Single case study methodologies have demonstrated positive effects of exposure therapy, usually combined with other techniques, for PTSD following combat (Fairbank, Gross and Keane, 1983; Keane and Kaloupeck, 1982; Mueser, Yarnold and Foy, 1991), accidents (McCaffrey and Fairbank, 1985), crime victims (Vaughn and Tarrier, 1992), rape (Nishith, Hearst, Mueser and Foa, 1995; Waldfogel and Mueser, 1988), adult survivors of childhood sexual abuse (Elsenga and Emmelkamp, 1990; Rychtarik, Silverman, Van Landingham and Prue, 1984) and sexually abused children (Deblinger, McLeer and Henry, 1990). Furthermore, controlled or quasi-controlled research supports the beneficial effects of exposure-based treatment for PTSD due to both combat (Boudewyns and Hyer, 1990; Cooper and Clum, 1989; Keane, Fairbank, Caddell and Zimering, 1989) and rape (Foa, Freund, Hembree, Dancu, Franklin, Perry, Riggs and Moinar, 1994; Foa, Rothbaum, Riggs and Murdock, 1991; Resick and Schnicke, 1992).

Treating the other sequelae of trauma

While exposure techniques are at the heart of the treatment of PTSD symptoms, many different cognitive-behavioral strategies are used in the treatment of other trauma-related sequelae. When treating severely mentally ill women with a history of abuse, the importance of addressing a wide range of different cognitive, behavioral and emotional problems is of critical importance, because the origins of these impairments are so often unclear. For example, a woman may have poor interpersonal skills for managing conflict in close relationships. Such impairments may be due to avoidance of such relationships stemming from prior/current abuse, poor social skills due to another (non-PTSD) diagnosis, such as schizophrenia (Bellack, Morrison, Wixted and Mueser, 1990), or both. Similarly, persistent depression, substance abuse, or suicidality could be due to direct sequelae of PTSD, a primary major affective or substance use disorder, or both. In most cases of severely mentally ill persons, it is impossible to determine the etiology of the non-PTSD symptoms that so often dominate the clinical picture.

A wide range of different interventions are used to help individuals overcome the various sequelae of their traumatic experiences and other psychiatric disorders. Social skills training (Harris, in press; Liberman, DeRisi and Mueser, 1989) can be used to teach more effective interpersonal skills, such as basic conversational skills, assertiveness, conflict resolution, which may be impaired due to avoidance and/or cognitive deficits. Stress management techniques, such as relaxation and systematic desensitization, are often used to enable persons to cope with chronic, generalized states of anxiety often present in abused women (Wolff, 1977; Veronen and Kilpatrick, 1983). Cognitive therapy, including cognitive restructuring and challenging negative self-talk, can be useful in modifying negative thought patterns which contribute to depression and obsessional thinking styles in persons who have been abused (Forman, 1980; Frank and Stewart, 1983). Finally, psychoeducational and behavioral family therapy approaches (Glynn, et al., in press; Mueser and Glynn, 1995; Rabin and Nardi, 1991), in which families are educated about the symptoms and nature of psychiatric disorders (e.g., PTSD and major depression) and taught communication and problem solving skills, can improve the collective ability of the family to maintain a low stress environment and take steps towards individual and shared goals.

The needs of women with a serious mental illness and a history of abuse are wide-ranging and multi-faceted. Clearly no single technique or set of interventions can meet the individual needs of each woman, although treatment packages may be able to address many of the common needs of this population (Harris, in press). Thus, the individual tailoring of treatment to the personal needs of each woman, guided by repeated assessment, becomes an integral component of cognitive-behavioral intervention. To illustrate the dynamic interplay between presenting problems in mentally ill, abused women, the development of a cognitive-behavioral case formulation and treatment, we present a detailed case study. In this case, the assessment and treatment of PTSD is highlighted, as other issues could not be addressed without first reducing the severe symptoms of avoidance and re-experiencing the trauma. Following targeted treatment for PTSD, we describe cognitive-behavioral intervention aimed at addressing a range of long-term sequelae of trauma, such as problems with intimacy and vocational adjustment.

Case report

This case report outlines the extensive psychiatric history of a 32 year old woman (referred to here as "Sandra") with a history of sexual and physical abuse, who also experienced the untimely illness and death of her sister. Sandra's psychiatric history began at age 18. Over the subsequent 14 years, she has had 13 inpatient psychiatric hospitalizations, seven outpatient therapists and has attended three different day hospitals. Detailed information is presented on an exposure-based cognitive-behavioral treatment that took place when Sandra was 29–30 years old. The information presented was obtained from medical and psychiatric records, data collected by previous therapists, discussions with three of Sandra's former therapists and a recent interview with Sandra. Certain minor aspects of Sandra's history have been modified to protect her identity.

Medical history

At birth, Sandra suffered perinatal hypoxia and was subsequently diagnosed with a developmental disability. She was also diagnosed with congenital hypothyroidism and has been on hypothyroid medication (Synthroid) since approximately three months of age. In 1982, following multiple emergency room visits for abdominal pain, Sandra was diagnosed with a spastic colon. She underwent an appendectomy in 1986 and in 1990 an ovarian abscess was diagnosed. In 1990, Sandra also suffered a head injury and lost consciousness for approximately 24 hours. There was a question of seizure disorder following the head injury, but all EEG and CT scans were negative, resulting in a diagnosis of pseudo seizures and conversion reaction. However, approximately five years later she was prescribed Dilantin for control of seizures. In 1993, an ovarian cyst was removed. Sandra also has a history of renal calculi and multiple urinary tract infections. Finally, Sandra was diagnosed with multiple sclerosis (MS) in February, 1994. During the year following the diagnosis, she was hospitalized three times for diagnostic work-ups and worsening of MS symptoms. However, outside of these attacks, she has remained independent and is functioning well in terms of the MS.

Traumatic events

The traumatic events reported come under two general categories. First, Sandra's older sister died in 1980 from a brain tumor, when Sandra was 17 years old. Not only was this traumatic for Sandra, but also for the entire family, as the parents' marriage suffered following their daughter's death. Upon her sister's death, Sandra began having nightmares of her sister telling her that she should die and join her. Sandra found these dreams upsetting and also had some difficulty distinguishing between dream and reality. During her first psychiatric hospitalization in 1982, Sandra stated that she had seen her sister sitting in a chair and heard her telling her to kill herself and also stated that she heard her father's voice saying that he was going to kill her. She admitted to suicidal impulses and thoughts, which she related to her sister's death. These involved mainly a wish to be with her sister. In the majority of subsequent psychiatric hospitalizations, the presenting problem was a suicide attempt following command hallucinations of her sister telling her to kill herself. In addition, Sandra has reported that she assisted her sister in committing suicide, although her mother stated that her daughter died solely as a result of the tumor.

The second traumatic event is the extended sexual and physical abuse committed by her father. Sandra first reported the abuse during her fourth (1987) psychiatric admission and stated that it had occurred since nine years of age. Subsequent hospital discharge summaries indicate that the abuse began following her sister's death, when Sandra was 17. Presently, Sandra maintains that the abuse began when she was 10 years old and occurred intermittently until the age of 28. The sexual abuse included intercourse, being tied down during intercourse and being forced to perform oral sex. Physical abuse occurred primarily when Sandra refused to have sex with her father or attempted to move out of the home. The physical abuse included being dunked repeatedly in a bathtub of water, being slapped, hit with a belt and kept in the basement for several days at a time. According to Sandra, her sister and her cousin were also sexually abused by the father, who served three months in jail for abusing her cousin. Sandra states that she pressed charges against her father, but the charges were dismissed because of her psychiatric history. In addition, Sandra has reported sexual abuse by her brother and her uncle at different times during treatment, but it has not been clear whether these were delusional or actual occurrences.

Psychiatric history

Sandra has had an extensive history of inpatient psychiatric treatment, including a total of 13 hospitalizations. There are multiple similarities across the different hospitalizations, the most important of which include: 1) 9 of 13 admissions occurred near the anniversary of her sister's birthday or her sister's death; 2) 11 of 13 admissions followed a suicide attempt, which was most often by ingestion of pills and the remaining two admissions were for suicidal ideation with no attempt; 3) auditory and visual hallucinations of her sister telling her to kill herself were reported in 10 of 13 admissions; 4) an involuntary hospitalization was required in 10 of 13 admissions; 5) in 8 of 13 admissions an antipsychotic medication was prescribed; 6) the diagnosis at discharge was most often Borderline Personality Disorder (11 of 13), Brief Reactive Psychosis (5 of 13) and PTSD (4 of 13) and 7) PTSD was diagnosed for the first time during her tenth hospitalization.

Sandra has also received a variety of outpatient treatment services, including attendance at three different psychiatric day hospitals. She attended these programs sporadically at times and very regularly at other times, receiving treatment for a wide range of problems, including family conflict, nightmares, low self-esteem, suicidal thoughts and behaviors and hallucinations. She has received both group and individual therapy at these facilities over the years.

Substance abuse history

Sandra's records provide conflicting information about her history of alcohol abuse. The admissions prior to 1991 indicate either nothing about her alcohol use or state that tobacco was the only substance used. In 1991, Sandra reported that she drank five beers per day, since the age of 16. Currently, she reports that she does not drink at all because of the medications she is on for MS (Effexor). In addition, Sandra reported abusing laxatives and diet pills during 1992–1993 and again in 1995, due to suicidal ideation. Sandra has consistently denied illicit drug use. She smokes 10 cigarettes per day.

Family psychiatric history

Sandra's mother received one month of inpatient rehabilitation for alcohol dependence in 1991 and has been sober since this treatment. According to Sandra, her father was also a heavy drinker. Early in Sandra's records it is stated that her sister was hospitalized for "bizarre behavior" one month prior to her diagnosis of brain tumor, but no records were located. Sandra's mother denies any other family psychiatric history.

Social and developmental history

Sandra is the second of three children. She was close to her older sister (who died), but had also been jealous of her because of the extra attention her sister received from her father. Her younger brother is healthy, married and working full-time as a maintenance worker. She is friendly with her brother, though not close. She reports being close to her mother, but has not spoken with her father in at least two years (although she has seen him at family functions). She lived at home with both of her parents for the majority of her life prior to her marriage in 1994, with brief stints living with her brother, in transitional housing for psychiatric patients and once with a boyfriend for a week.

Sandra was born by emergency cesarean section 3 weeks prior to the due date, due to placenta previa. As mentioned, perinatal hypoxia resulted in a developmental disability. During her first three months she was cared for by two aunts because her mother was ill. Sandra's mother reports that Sandra was slow in developing: she sat up at 9 months, walked at two years, used single words at two years and spoke in phrases at three years. She began school at seven years of age, attending special classes in parochial school and when she was 16, was selected to attend a vocational training program. Sandra regularly attended Catholic church as a child.

When Sandra was 4 years old, her older sister was diagnosed with a brain tumor. Her sister was in remission and healthy until several months prior to her death. Upon her sister's death, Sandra dropped out of vocational school and her parents' marriage deteriorated. Sandra went to the medical emergency room 12 times during the two years following her sister's death, with complaints of abdominal pain, nausea and vomiting and ear and neck pain. A spastic colon was the ultimate diagnosis. Sandra's first psychiatric referral occurred during these ER visits.

In terms of vocational history, Sandra attended a cosmetology school for 4 months in 1986, worked for a few weeks at two different fast food restaurants and worked as an usher in a theater for a few months. From 1992 until the present writing in 1995 she has been intermittently working on her GED.

Sandra has been married for one year to a man three years her senior and of normal intelligence. They knew each other for approximately two years prior to the marriage and had dated off and on since meeting. Sandra's husband works as a waiter and is very invested in assisting her with her medical and psychiatric difficulties. Currently, much of the focus of outpatient treatment is on couples' related issues of communication and anger management, as they each have deficits in these areas. In addition, the couple reports that they have not engaged in sex since their marriage, as Sandra refuses due to her history of sexual abuse. She reports that in order to have sex, she must drink several beers beforehand and since she is unable to drink, she cannot have sex. Sandra reports feeling very guilty about this problem and attempts to avoid the issue by avoiding her husband. Sandra's husband finds this frustrating, but tries to be understanding. Sandra would like to work on this problem, but finds it an extremely difficult problem to approach in therapy.

Presenting complaints at initiation of cognitive-behavioral treatment

Sandra was first seen for cognitive-behavioral treatment during a hospitalization in February, 1992. This was an involuntary admission following a suicide attempt, which was reportedly due to command hallucinations of her deceased sister telling her to commit suicide. She was admitted the day following her sister's birthday, a historically difficult time for Sandra.

Following a clinical interview by the first author, it was hypothesized that Sandra's continuing symptoms were the result of chronic PTSD, due to either her sister's death, the sexual abuse, or both. Her PTSD symptoms included nightmares, intrusive thoughts and avoidance of reminders of the event. In addition, of course, were the auditory and visual hallucinations of the traumatic events.

Exposure treatment

Procedure. The approach to exposure therapy followed a similar format to that taken for victims of other traumas, such as combat and rape (Mueser *et al.*, 1991; Nishith *et al.*, 1995). After first discussing the rationale for and methods involved in exposure-based treatment, Sandra was taught how to rate her anxiety on a Subjective Units of Distress Scale (SUDS), ranging from 0 ("no anxiety") to 100 ("extreme anxiety"). Then, a comprehensive assessment of traumatic events was conducted by asking Sandra to briefly describe and imagine each event that she recalled, one at a time and to provide a SUDS rating for each. After reviewing the different traumatic events, a joint decision was made by Sandra and the therapist to focus the beginning of exposure-based treatment on two events that frequently recurred in the form of auditory and visual hallucinations, nightmares and intrusive thoughts. Scene one was an incident in which Sandra's father tried to drown her in a bathtub when she refused to submit to sexual abuse. Scene two involved her sister's reported suicide. During the assessment, Sandra gave SUDS ratings of 100 for both of these events.

The exposure treatment was conducted by having Sandra focus on one event at a time. The therapist instructed Sandra to describe the first event, talking about it and dwelling on any details related to the event that came into her mind while remaining focused on the incident. After describing the event, which usually required 2–5 minutes, Sandra provided a SUDS rating to summarize her overall distress while describing the incident. Then the therapist asked Sandra to describe the event again, as before and at the end to provide another SUDS rating. The therapist remained supportive and responsive to Sandra while asking a minimum of questions or probing for more details. The process of describing the traumatic event and giving SUDS ratings was repeated in the session until there was clear decrease in anxiety. At the end of each session (usually about an hour), strategies for dealing with anxiety between sessions were discussed and a homework assignment was given to confront situations which she was avoiding because of the disturbing memory. When clear decreases in anxiety across sessions were evident, the therapist gave Sandra an assignment to write down a description of the traumatic event which was then reviewed at the beginning of the next session. When the first event elicited minimal anxiety, exposure work began on the second event, with occasional re-visits to the first event to ensure that anxiety remained low.

During the first session, which included six exposures to the memory of the traumatic event, Sandra's SUDS ratings dropped to a 70 (from 100). Subsequently, over two more sessions her anxiety level dropped to a low of 20. These improvements in SUDS were associated with other general improvements in distress reported by Sandra and evident from her behavior in the session. On the fourth session, work began on the second traumatic event. During this session, her SUDS ratings dropped from 100 to 90 over the course of four exposures. Over six subsequent sessions, her SUDS ratings for the second event dropped to a low of 20, while additional exposure on first event dropped further to 10. Over the course of the 10 sessions, Sandra showed dramatic improvements in hallucinations, depression, suicidal ideation, as well as a range of other symptoms. She was discharged from the hospital and outpatient sessions were scheduled with the therapist.

Broad-spectrum cognitive-behavioral treatment

Following discharge from the hospital, Sandra was seen on an outpatient basis for an additional six sessions. Exposure to the above events was again conducted in three of these sessions and exposure to a third event (in which her father tied her down and raped her) was initiated. The cognitive-behavioral sessions conducted on an outpatient basis were not focused exclusively on exposure, but began to address a range of other needs.

Specifically, despite improvements in distress related to memories of traumatic events and avoidance of feared situations, Sandra, like many others with chronic PTSD, continued to experience difficulties with chronic anxiety, as well as managing interpersonal conflicts. To address these problems, Sandra was taught stress management strategies (e.g., relaxation, deep breathing) and social skills training was employed to enhance her ability to handle difficult interpersonal situations (e.g., assertiveness). Finally, problem-solving skills were taught to improve Sandra's ability to pursue personal goals, such as obtaining her GED and getting a job.

In September, 1992, Sandra was transferred to another therapist and since that time until the present writing (May, 1995) she has worked with two additional therapists as well, all at the same clinic (with supervision from the authors). Treatment continued along the same lines, gradually shifting the focus away from continued exposure therapy towards addressing new, emergent themes. For example, as Sandra has become more able to tolerate interpersonal intimacy, issues involving conflict resolution and sexual relations have become more critical. Similarly, strategies have been targeted to address Sandra's continued self-injurious behavior. In many instances, the core interventions of the cognitive-behavioral treatment have been consistent with the "dialectical behavior therapy" approach for borderline personality disorder espoused by Linehan (1993).

Measurement. Measures included the standardized self-report measures of the Beck Depression Inventory (BDI; Beck *et al.*, 1961, 1988) and the Symptom Checklist-90-R (SCL-90; Derogatis, 1977). The BDI is a 21-item measure of present mood state, with scores ranging from 0–63. A higher score indicates more severe depression. The SCL-90 is a 90-item measure of current psychiatric symptomatology, with subscales of obsessive-compulsive symptoms, anger-hostility, phobic anxiety, psychoticism, paranoid ideation, interpersonal sensitivity, depression, somatization and anxiety. These measures were given during the first year of cognitive-behavioral treatment when exposure sessions were being conducted.

Results. Figure 1 displays the results of the BDI and SCL-90 psychoticism subscale during the course of the exposure-based treatments. As can be seen in the Figure, BDI scores ranged between 33 and 50 prior to treatment and ranged between 13 and 35 during the initial phase of exposure treatment, with all but one score below 30. A rehospitalization was associated with a dramatic increase in BDI scores (45–49) and then further reduction in depression was noted once exposure sessions were reinstituted during the hospitalization, with scores ranging between seven and 12. The SCL-90 psychoticism scores reveal a very similar pattern and are representative of the other SCL-90 subscales. A BDI administered three years after the initiation of exposure therapy (March, 1995) indicated a moderate level of depression (BDI = 19), not especially high considering her recent diagnosis of MS.

Sandra's improved clinical status during cognitive-behavioral treatment has been accompanied by somewhat lower hospital utilization (see Figure 2). Sandra was admitted twice in 1992 following the initial exposure treatment and then hospitalized only once during the next 2.3 years. It is notable that this most recent admission followed an admission for a MS attack and was the first admission since the diagnosis of MS was made in February, 1994.

Summary and conclusions

Sandra is a 32 year old woman with a history of repeated physical and sexual abuse. She was committed by her father and experienced the untimely death of her sister when she was 17. She comes across as a childlike, engaging young woman, eager to please and not wanting to disappoint others. Her attentional and memory problems are marked and certainly have contributed to the "untruths" that have been noted over the years. Due to her desire to please, it seems that some of the untruths may simply be a result of her efforts to answer the questions that are asked of her and to not disappoint

BECK DEPRESSION INVENTORY AND SYMPTOM CHECKLIST - 90
PSYCHOTICISM

ASSESSMENT POINT	1	2	3	4	5	6	7	8	9	10	11	12	13	14	15	16	17	18	19	20	21
BECK DEP. INVENTORY	33	36	46	50	28	18	16	22	24	20	13	20	28	17	35	49	45	7	12	15	29
SYMPTOM CHECKLIST	25	37	40	44	38	25	20	23	29	17	14	24	26	17	28	30	46	16	19	17	18

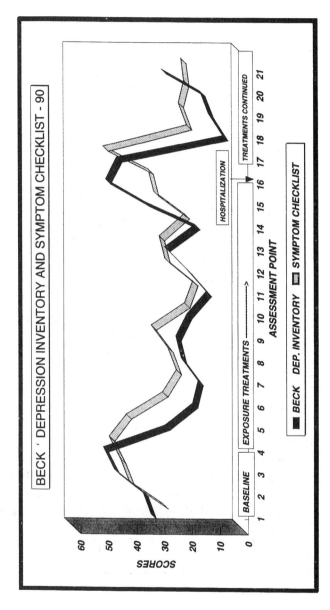

FIGURE 1

83

HOSPITALIZATION EXPERIENCE: A CASE STUDY-M.R.

YEAR	82	83	84	85	86	87	88	89	90	91	92	93	94	95
NUMBER OF HOSPITALIZATIONS	1	0	0	0	2	2	2	0	0	3	1	0	0	1
NO. OF DAYS HOSPITALIZED	43	0	0	0	17	21	33	0	0	23	17	42	0	38

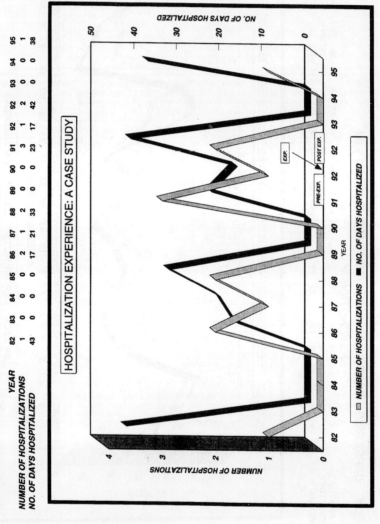

FIGURE 2

others by not knowing the answers. Sandra does not have the usual borderline quality of manipulating people in order to seek revenge, but rather to seek others' positive attention.

Sandra has had 13 inpatient psychiatric hospitalizations during as many years due to repeated suicide attempts which resulted from command hallucinations. She has received individual outpatient therapy from seven different therapists and attended three different day hospital programs over the past 15 years. The psychiatric diagnoses most frequently given to her have been PTSD, Borderline Personality Disorder and Brief Reactive Psychosis. Mental Retardation has also been noted (and documented in psychological testing).

Although Sandra reported the sexual abuse for the first time in 1987, the diagnosis of PTSD was not given to her until 1992. This delay in the recognition of symptoms may have been due to several factors. One factor may have been the relative unfamiliarity most practitioners had with the diagnosis in the mid-1980s and the tendency for psychiatric inpatient settings to fail to recognize PTSD even now (Cascardi *et al.*, in press). Second, her limited intelligence certainly resulted in practitioners calling her reports into question. Third, the behaviors consistent with Borderline Personality Disorder (e.g., suicidal "gestures," manipulations of staff) may have limited her credibility. Fourth, Sandra's symptoms were overwhelmingly described as "hallucinations," rather than the more usual PTSD symptom of "reexperiencing the trauma," in the form of intrusive thoughts and nightmares. Although hallucinations have been reported in persons with primary PTSD (Mueser and Butler, 1987; Butler *et al.*, in press), these symptoms are not formally recognized as part of the PTSD symptom cluster in the DSM series. Finally, Sandra was known to not tell the truth to staff on numerous occasions and it may have been thought that she was seeking attention by describing traumatic events that had not occurred.

In short, there were multiple contradictions in Sandra's history and symptoms with no certain way to verify her reports. Sandra's parents denied that the abuse had occurred, but of course they may have been motivated to protect the father. Or, Sandra's mother may have been unaware of the abuse, due to her alcohol history or to other reasons. Given the multiple PTSD symptoms demonstrated by Sandra, it was decided that even without verification of the abuse, it was worth believing her report and treating her for PTSD.

Thus, following 12 years of inpatient and outpatient treatment with multiple antipsychotic medications, milieu therapy, supportive therapy and imaginal exposure for the symptoms of PTSD due to sexual abuse was undertaken. Since this time, Sandra has remained in therapy on a consistent basis, has had a reduction in the number of hospitalizations, has married and is currently working on communication training and problem-solving techniques in treatment with her husband. These are skills that she has needed during her entire life, but that were not addressed prior to 1992, probably due to the overwhelming nature of her other symptoms. In addition, she has been consistently working on obtaining her GED certificate over the past two years. The recent diagnosis of MS is a severe stressor to Sandra, but she is managing it well with the assistance of her husband.

Sandra is a woman who is likely to remain in therapy for many years to come due to her multiple psychiatric and medical problems. Thus, goals for her treatment outcome will likely center around symptom management, reduction in psychiatric hospitalizations and skills development. From the self-report and hospital admission data presented, it appears that the imaginal exposure therapy, combined with other cognitive-behavioral treatment strategies, was beneficial to her overall well-being. Although Sandra describes the exposure as a very difficult treatment to undergo, she acknowledges that it has reduced her intrusive symptoms. Practitioners are encouraged to consider this mode of therapy with mentally ill women who have PTSD, even when the presentation is as difficult and complicated as the one presented.

References

American Psychiatric Association (1980) *Diagnostic and Statistical Manual of Mental Disorders, 3rd Edition, (DSM III)*, Washington, DC: APA.

American Psychiatric Association (1994) *Diagnostic and Statistical Manual of Mental Disorders, 4th Edition, (DSM-IV)*, Washington, DC: APA.

Beck, A.T., Steer, R.A. and Garbin, M.G. (1988) "Psychometric properties of the Beck Depression Inventory: Twenty-five years of evaluation", in *Clinical Psychology Review*, 8, 77–100.

Bellack, A.S., Morrison, R.L., Wixted, J.T. and Mueser, K.T. (1990) "An analysis of social competence in schizophrenia", in *British Journal of Psychiatry*, 156, 809–818.

Beck, A.T., Ward, C.H., Mendelsohn, M., Mock, J. and Erbaugh, J. (1961) "An inventory for measuring depression", in *Archives of General Psychiatry*, 4, 561–571.

Boudewyns, P.A. and Hyer, L. (1990) "Physiological response to combat memories and preliminary treatment outcome in Vietnam veteran PTSD patients treated with direct therapeutic exposure", in *Behavior Therapy*, 21, 63–87.

Breslau, N., Davis, G.C., Andreski, P. and Peterson, E. (1991) "Traumatic events and posttraumatic stress disorder in an urban population of young adults", in *Archives of General Psychiatry*, 48, 216–222.

Briere, J. (1992) "Methodological issues in the study of sexual abuse effect", in *Journal of Consulting and Clinical Psychology*, 60, 196–203.

Briere, J. and Runtz, M. (1988) "Symptomatology associated with childhood sexual victimization in a nonclinical adult sample", in *Child Abuse and Neglect*, 12, 51–59.

Butler, R.W., Mueser, K.T., Sprock, J. and Braff, D.L. (in press) "Positive symptoms of psychosis in posttraumatic stress disorder", in *Biological Psychiatry*.

Cascardi, M., Mueser, K.T., DeGirolomo, J. and Murrin, M. (in press) "Physical aggression against psychiatric inpatients by family members and partners: A descriptive study", in *Psychiatric Services*.

Cooper, N.A. and Clum, G.A. (1989) "Imaginal flooding as a supplementary treatment for PTSD in combat veterans: A controlled study", in *Behavior Therapy*, 20, 381–391.

Davidson, J. and Smith, R. (1990) "Traumatic experiences in psychiatric outpatients", in *Journal of Traumatic Stress*, 3, 459–475.

Deblinger, E., McLeer, S.V. and Henry, D. (1990) "Cognitive behavioral treatment for sexually abused children suffering from post-traumatic stress: Preliminary findings", in *Journal of American Academy of Child and Adolescent Psychiatry*, 29, 747–752.

Derogatis, L.R. (1977) *SCL-90: Administration, scoring and procedures manual, I. (for the revised) Version.* Towson, MD: Clinical Psychometrics Research.

Donaldson, M.A. and Gardner, R. (1985) "Diagnosis and treatment of traumatic stress among women after childhood incest." In C.R. Figley (Ed.), *Trauma and Its Wake* (pp. 356–377). New York: Brunner/Mazel.

Elsenga, S. and Emmelkamp, P.M.G. (1990) "Behavioral treatment of an incest-related trauma in an agoraphobic client", in *Journal of Anxiety Disorders*, 4, 151–162.

Fairbank, J.A., Gross, R.T. and Keane, T.M. (1983) "Treatment of posttraumatic stress disorder: Evaluating outcome with a behavioral code", in *Behavior Modification*, 7, 557–568.

Finkelhor, D., Hotaling, G., Lewis, I.A. and Smith, C. (1990) "Sexual abuse in a national survey of adult men and women: Prevalence, characteristics and risk factors", in *Child Abuse and Neglect*, 14, 19–28.

Foa, E.B., Freund, B.F., Hembree, E., Dancu, C.V., Franklin, M.E., Perry, K.J., Riggs, D.S. and Moinar, C. (1994) *Efficacy of short term behavioral treatments of PTSD in sexual and nonsexual assault victims*. Presented at the annual meeting of the Association for the Advancement of Behavior Therapy, November 1994, San Diego, CA.

Foa, E.B. and Kozak, M.J. (1986) "Emotional processing of fear: Exposure to corrective information", in *Psychological Bulletin*, 99, 20–35.

Foa, E.B., Rothbaum, B.O., Riggs, D. and Murdock, T. (1991) "Treatment of post-traumatic stress disorder in rape victims: A comparison between cognitive-behavioral procedures and counseling", in *Journal of Consulting and Clinical Psychology*, 59, 715–723.

Forman, B.D. (1980) "Cognitive modification of obsessive thinking in a rape victim: A preliminary study", in *Psychological Reports*, 47, 819–822.

Frank, E. and Stewart, B.D. (1983) "Treatment of depressed rape victims: An approach to stress-induced symptomatology." In Clayton, P.J. and Barrett, J.E. (Eds.) *Treatment of Depression: Old Controversies and New Approaches*. New York: Raven Press.

Glynn, S.M., Eth, S., Randolph, E.T., Foy, D.W., Leong, G.B., Paz, G.G., Salk, J.D., Firman, G. and Katzman, J.W. (in press) "Behavioral family therapy for Vietnam combat veterans with posttraumatic stress disorder", in *Journal of Psychotherapy Practice and Research*.

Goodman, L.A., Dutton, M.A. and Harris, M. (manuscript under review) "Physical and sexual assault prevalence among homeless women with serious mental illness."

Grinker, R. and Spiegel, J. (1945) *Men Under Stress*. Philadelphia: Blakiston.

Harris, M. (in press) "Treating sexual abuse trauma with dually diagnosed homeless women", in *Community Mental Health Journal*.

Herman, J.L. (1992) *Trauma and Recovery*. New York: Basic Books.

Hutchings, P.S. and Dutton, M.A. (1993) "Sexual assault history in a community mental health center clinical population", in *Community Mental Health Journal*, 29, 59–63.

Keane, T.M., Fairbank, J.A., Caddell, J.M. and Zimering, R.T. (1989) "Implosive (flooding) therapy reduces symptoms of PTSD in Vietnam combat veterans", in *Behavior Therapy*, 20, 245–260.

Keane, T.M. and Kaloupek, D.G. (1982) "Imaginal flooding in the treatment of a posttraumatic stress disorder", in *Journal of Consulting and Clinical Psychology*, 50, 138–140.

Keane, T.M. and Wolfe, J. (1990) "Comorbidity in post-traumatic stress disorder: An analysis of community and clinical studies", in *Journal of Applied Social Psychology*, 20, 1776–1788.

Kilpatrick, D.G., Edmunds, C.N. and Seymour, A.K. (1992) *Rape in America: A report to the nation*. Arlington, VA and Charleston, NC: National Victims Center.

Koss, M.P. (1993) "Detecting the scope of rape: A review of prevalence research methods", in *Journal of Interpersonal Violence*, 8, 198–222.

Liberman, R.P., DeRisi, W.J. and Mueser, K.T. (1989) *Social Skills Training for Psychiatric Patients*. Needham Heights, MA: Allyn and Bacon.

Lindberg, F.H. and Distad, M. (1985) "Post-traumatic stress disorders in women who experienced childhood incest", in *Child Abuse and Neglect*, 9, 329–334.

Linehan, M.M. (1993) *Cognitive-Behavioral Treatment of Borderline Personality Disorder*. New York: The Guilford Press.

McCaffrey, R.J. and Fairbank, J.A. (1985) "Behavioral assessment and treatment of accident-related post-traumatic stress disorder: Two case studies", in *Behavior Therapy*, 16, 406–416.

McLeer, S.V., Callaghan, M., Henry, D. and Wallen, J. (1994) "Psychiatric disorders in sexually abused children", in *Journal of the American Academy of Child and Adolescent Psychiatry*, 33(3), 313–319.

McLeer, S.V., Deblinger, E., Atkins, M.S., Foa, E.B. and Raphe, D.L. (1988) "Post-traumatic stress disorder in sexually abused children", in *Journal of the American Academy of Child and Adolescent Psychiatry*, 27(5), 650–654.

McLeer, S.V., Deblinger, E., Henry, D. and Orvaschel, H. (1992) "Sexually abused children at high risk for Posttraumatic Stress Disorder", in *Journal of the American Academy of Child and Adolescent Psychiatry*, 31(5), 875–879.

Muenzenmaier, K., Meyer, I., Struening, E. and Ferber, J. (1993) "Childhood abuse and neglect among women outpatients with chronic mental illness", in *Hospital and Community Psychiatry*, 44(7), 666–670.

Mueser, K.T. and Butler, R.W. (1987) "Auditory hallucinations in chronic combat-related posttraumatic stress disorder", in *American Journal of Psychiatry*, 144, 299–302.

Mueser, K.T. and Glynn, S.M. (1995) *Behavioral Family Therapy for Psychiatric Disorders*. Needham Heights, MA: Allyn and Bacon.

Mueser, K.T., Yarnold, P.Y. and Foy, D.W. (1991) "Statistical analysis for single-case designs: Evaluating outcome of imaginal exposure treatment of chronic PTSD", in *Behavior Modification*, 15, 134–155.

Nishith, P., Hearst, D.E., Mueser, K.T. and Foa, E.B. (1995) "PTSD and major depression: Methodological and treatment considerations in a single case design", in *Behavior Therapy*, 26, 319–335.

O'Neill, K. and Gupta, K. (1991) "Post-traumatic stress disorder in women who were victims of childhood sexual abuse", in *Irish Journal of Psychological Medicine*, 8, 124–127.

Rabin, C. and Nardi, C. (1991) "Treating post traumatic stress disorder couples: A psychoeducational program", in *Community Mental Health Journal*, 27(3), 209–224.

Resnick, H.S., Kilpatrick, D.G., Dansky, B.S., Saunders, B.E. and Best, C.L. (1993) "Prevalence of civilian trauma and post-traumatic stress disorder in a representative national sample of women", in *Journal of Consulting and Clinical Psychology*, 61, 984–991.

Resnick, L.M. and Kilpatrick, D.G. (1994) "Crime-related PTSD emphasis on adult general population samples", in *PTSD Research Quarterly*, 5(3), 1–3.

Resick, P.A. and Schnicke, M.K. (1992) "Cognitive processing therapy for sexual assault victims", in *Journal of Consulting and Clinical Psychology*, 60, 748–756.

Rosenberg, S.D., Drake, R.E. and Mueser, K.T. (in press) "New directions for treatment research on sequelae of sexual abuse", in *Community Mental Health Journal*.

Rothbaum, B.O., Foa, E.B., Riggs, D., Murdock, T. and Walsh, W. (1992) "A prospective examination of post-traumatic stress disorder in rape victims", in *Journal of Traumatic Stress*, 5, 455–475.

Rychtarik, R.G., Silverman, W.K., Van Landingham, W.P. and Prue, D.M. (1984) "Treatment of an incest victim with implosive therapy: A case study", in *Behavior Therapy*, 15, 410–420.

Vaughn, K. and Tarrier, N. (1992) "The use of image habituation training with post-traumatic stress disorders", in *British Journal of Psychiatry*, 161, 658–664.

Veronen, L.J. and Kilpatrick, D.G. (1983) "Stress management for rape victims." In D. Meichenbaum and M.E. Jarmeko (Eds.) *Stress Reduction and Prevention*. New York: Plenum Press.

Waldfogel, S. and Mueser, K.T. (1988) (Letter to the Editor) "Another case of chronic PTSD with auditory hallucinations", in *American Journal of Psychiatry*, 145, 13–14.

Wolff, R. (1977) "Systematic desensitization and negative practice to alter the after effects of a rape attempt", in *Journal of Behavior Therapy and Experimental Psychiatry*, 8, 423–425.

*The authors appreciate the comments of Melanie Bennett, Ph.D. and Michele Cascardi, Ph.D. on an earlier draft of this chapter.

Chapter Five

A Social Skills Approach to Trauma Recovery

Heather Stowe and Maxine Harris

G ROUP modalities, (psychotherapy, psycho-education and peer support groups) have been found to be highly effective with survivors of sexual abuse trauma (Browne, 1993; Courtois 1988). Clinicians frequently offer several caveats, however, as to whom among the cohort of trauma survivors will benefit from group interventions. Women with a history of psychosis, or those who exhibit weak ego strength, or those who have ongoing substance abuse addiction are generally considered unsuitable for group treatment. Yet public sector clinics serve increasing numbers of addicted and homeless women diagnosed with a severe and persistent mental illness who also present with a history of physical and sexual abuse. What treatment can clinicians offer this growing population of women?

Social skills training, a structured educational intervention, has long been used in the rehabilitation of persons diagnosed with chronic mental illness. Training modules focus on both practical, concrete skills such as money management and more general behaviors such as interpersonal communication. Clinicians need to be aware, however, that although social skill information is becoming more available, the population of disenfranchised women tends to be more isolated and consequently has less access to popular sources of information.

A social skills format has not yet been applied to recovery from trauma for women with serious mental illness. In an effort to address this gap, clinicians at Community Connections have designed a group treatment format to address issues of trauma and recovery for a population of women who have histories of homelessness, mental illness and substance addiction. This group treatment format involves a social skills component that is modified to include psychodynamic group techniques. It is important to understand the role that the apparent lack of social skills has served for women who have been sexually and physically traumatized. A lack of money management skills, for example, may be more related to the shame a woman feels at having exchanged sex for money in the past than to a cognitive inability to balance her budget.

Community Connections' trauma intervention is divided into two parts. The first part addresses general issues of victimization and powerlessness women experience on a societal level. During this first part of the intervention, women are also encouraged to look at issues of self-esteem and intimacy. The second part develops the themes of victimization and powerlessness from a general to a more personal level. The topics are designed to help women identify current life patterns or behaviors which are in fact sequelae of past abuses. Dysfunctional behaviors are accurately labeled and links are made between past and current actions. This linking of past trauma to current maladaptive behaviors helps participants to break the cycle of past trauma and avoid placing themselves in current situations in which they might become revictimized.

A significant part of the work of the groups is to provide concrete information and to help women accurately label feelings and behaviors. Many women lack the capacity to accurately label events which happened, or continue to happen, as being either traumatic or abusive. For example, being beaten with an extension cord might be understood as a sign of parental love – after all mom or dad would not do such a thing if they did not care and want to save a daughter from getting into trouble later in life. This mislabelling of events is carried into adult life when being harassed by men on the streets or beaten by a lover is framed as something one deserves or asks for rather than as an abusive act.

One especially damaging mislabelling occurs when some women see sexual abuse as an expression of affection. This then translates into an inability to link compulsive sexuality in adulthood with a search for comfort or affection. In adult life, many women are unable to frame the rapes and beatings they received in their search for drugs as abusive. After all, entering into a crack house is asking to get raped and beaten, is it not? It is this type of distorted belief system that is redressed in the second part of the trauma intervention.

Format

The intervention consists of a 24 topic social skills module based on issues of physical and sexual abuse. The weekly sessions combine psycho-educational techniques with more experiential interventions to address issues that seem particularly relevant to mentally ill women who are survivors of sexual, physical and emotional trauma. Each topic is designed to be covered over a period of two consecutive weeks. Leaders may choose how they divide the material, depending on the abilities and to some extent the preferences of the group members.

The time taken to fully discuss a topic is often a function of the particular topic and its relevance for the group members. Topics relating to current functioning and family or intimate relationships may take longer than two weeks. Many trauma survivors continue to struggle with how to manage past relationships and initiate new ones and therefore topics that stress interpersonal skills are particularly relevant and may take several weeks to exhaust.

Group leaders direct the session using a series of questions designed to facilitate conversation and to address the goals for a given topic. Leaders may use a flip chart or black board to record members' responses, but should avoid a format that becomes overly didactic or classroom-like. The flexible structure of a modified social skills approach allows members some emotional distance from and control over highly charged and sensitive material without it seeming too removed from the realities of their lives.

Membership

Leaders must pay attention to issues of psychosis, addiction and character style when considering group formation and membership.
Contrary to commonly held assumptions, women currently experiencing psychotic symptoms may attend the group. Generally, these
women either remain silent in the group or else become somewhat
more organized in response to a structured and relevant agenda.
Many women appreciate the chance to talk honestly about long
silenced abuse issues. Indeed, they may have become "crazy" as a
response to the trauma, labeled psychotic and delusional because
their stories were so horrible. Survivors are frequently misdiagnosed
in the mental health system and may often have a long list of diagnoses before the underlying history of sexual trauma is diagnosed
(Bryer, Nelson and Miller 1987). For some women the group provides the opportunity to be believed and validated for the first time.
As a result, members may actually experience a decrease in psychiatric symptomatology.

Similarly, a woman who is currently addicted to drugs or alcohol
may benefit from attending the group. However, she ought to be
meeting concurrently with her case manager and exploring the possible ways in which her addiction may be related to her trauma history.
For example, drugs or alcohol may have been part of a past abuse
experience insofar as either she or the abuser was drunk or high.
They may also be used to deaden her feelings about the abuse. It is
important to note that the life of an addict, including being on the
streets, can be viewed as a form of retraumatization in its own right.

A woman addicted to drugs may need periodic detoxification
while participating in the group. As the group develops cohesiveness,
members may grow increasingly disturbed by the self-destructive
aspects of another member's continuing addiction. Members may
choose to confront an addicted member as their initial compassion
grows into frustration with her behavior. When several women in
the group are in recovery, there may be an effort to turn the group
into an AA/NA meeting. In this instance, leaders must redirect the
focus to trauma issues. Another reason periodic detoxification may
be required is that women in trauma recovery may experience periodic relapses into substance use as they confront painful feelings and

memories of trauma. Such lapses do not necessarily mean that a woman needs to terminate her participation in the trauma group.

A woman may find it difficult to tell her story within a group format if her abuse history has left her with an extreme sensitivity to any criticism, an aggressive desire to monopolize the conversation, or hair-trigger and unfocused ragefulness. Groups of eight to ten women can, however, incorporate a maximum of one or two women with the above responses if leaders take the initiative to:

1. *Limit air time* – members with a tendency to monopolize the group are given two to three "open mike" periods, during which they can tell their stories. Once these periods are used, however, the members may only make relevant comments to other group members.

2. *Insure safety* – leaders must caution all women that they may express anger but that they may not frighten or bully other members of the group. Ridiculing or screaming at another group member should never be tolerated. One consequence of this behavior may be that the woman leaves the group temporarily to regain her composure.

3. *Reframe comments to acknowledge a woman's strength* – group members are often better able to hear limit setting or confrontational comments if their strengths and value are acknowledged first. For example, "You are such a compassionate woman, why do you think you are having trouble listening to Jane's story?" or "You obviously care about this group, why do you think you are having trouble coming on time?" Comments which first bolster self esteem are easier for a woman with a tenuous sense of self-worth to hear.

4. Group leaders or individual case managers should be prepared to provide one-on-one time for vulnerable members after the set group time ends. Limits should be set on the amount of time allowed.

Group attendance and participation

Leaders must be willing to grant some leniency with respect both to regular attendance and to punctuality, especially during the early

95

stages of group development. Highly anxious women may need to have some extra support and control over their attendance until they are certain that the group is a safe place. Further, people who are dependent on public transportation or on the schedules of others cannot realistically guarantee that they will be at their appointments on time.

Group leaders can improve attendance by as much as 50% by making weekly calls to all members just prior to the group to remind them of the meeting time. In this way women are made to feel that they are an important part of the group. The call demonstrates the care and concern of the leaders for the members and also allows the leaders time to check in with members, making sure that there are not problems a woman might be unable to talk about in the larger group forum. On a purely practical level, the call reminds people of the time and place of the meeting. However, if a woman requests that she not be called, this should be honored. Even after the group has been meeting for several months and a pattern of regular attendance has been established, members may still request that the weekly calls continue. The leader can structure the group to include a mechanism whereby the group members inquire after those who are absent at any given meeting. When participants assume responsibility for contacting absent members, cohesiveness and a sense of shared responsibility develop in the group. The leader may also suggest that group members contact one another before meetings so they can plan to arrive together or share transportation.

Group rules which discriminate against women who are unable to manage the time and attendance boundaries are often too inflexible for women diagnosed with a serious mental illness. At the same time, a given individual's need for flexibility must be balanced by the group's need to maintain its boundaries. A woman who has missed the beginning sessions, which are designed to socialize members to the group model and promote cohesiveness, is often unable to integrate into the group later. The leader may designate a specific date, perhaps three to four weeks after the group begins, when the early phase of group formation is considered complete, at which time women must commit to being part of the group and to regular and timely attendance. However, leaders should be aware that some women will continue to miss an occasional session.

Group leaders must remember that women who have received services for many years in the public mental health system have had varied experiences with group therapy. For some, groups have been intimidating and confrontational. Group members must be given the option to remain silent in the group or to leave the group if they feel overwhelmed or threatened by the content of the discussion. As group members feel increasingly comfortable with one another, active members may want to invite less vocal members to speak out. Having these choices and controls over one's participation often renders the group safe for a woman who has been diagnosed with a serious mental illness.

Confidentiality is an important part of what makes the groups safe for women. The group boundaries need to be established at the first group. Information shared within the group needs to stay within the group and anyone who feels unable to do so ought to be treated in individual therapy. Leaders need to make individual decisions about whether to include their own case management clients in their groups, but as a general rule it should be avoided when possible. Because case managers have some control over a client's access to resources, having one's case manager as a group leader may inhibit a woman's willingness to disclose what she might label as "damaging" information.

Content

Part I of the Skills Module consists of nine sessions and includes the following topics:

- Introduction to the Group
- What It Means to Be a Woman
- What Do You Know About Your Body?
- Physical Boundaries
- Emotional Boundaries: Setting Limits and Asking for What You Want
- Self Esteem
- Self Soothing: Developing Ways to Feel Better
- Female Sexuality/Masturbation
- Intimacy, Sex and Emotional Closeness

The first few sessions allow the group members to get to know each other. They also allow those who are not able to participate to physically withdraw from the group. Topics such as "What it means to be a woman," and "What do you know about your body?" emphasize those things which all women have in common. These topics provide a safe atmosphere in which group members can begin to feel comfortable exploring their beliefs about women in general and themselves in particular.

While the first section of the trauma recovery module is designed to introduce the women to the topic of trauma, it does so indirectly. The discussions do not require women to deal directly with their own trauma histories. This is the function of Part II of the intervention. All of the topics in Part I are linked to the topic of trauma in general. For example, when self-esteem is discussed, members are encouraged to speculate about how being abused may have affected their sense of self-worth.

The following is an example of the structure of one of the sessions in Part I. This session is called, "Developing Ways to Feel Better – Self Soothing." The goal in this session is to help the members to think about what they do when they feel bad. Many women might not be able to identify the strategies they use as "self soothing" but rather may see those behaviors as ways they have learned to make the pain go away.

Women who have been traumatized have a great need to self soothe and at the same time have few healthy soothing techniques at their disposal. Many trauma survivors have failed to learn how to label their feelings either accurately or specifically. Sometimes a woman feels dysphoric and labels her feeling as sadness when in fact it is anger or resentment. In other instances, women know they are feeling bad, but are not able to label the "bad" feelings any more specifically.

What do women do for themselves to gain comfort? Many trauma survivors who have been diagnosed as having a serious mental illness have had few available resources and certainly little instruction in positive ways of making themselves feel better. Often, they rely on a few "tried and true" methods – drugs (both street drugs and prescription medications), alcohol, binge eating, unsafe sexual encounters, compulsive activity or perhaps self-mutilating behaviors. Regrettably, many professionals within the mental health system have given these women the message, directly or otherwise, that they do not have the same ability as others to soothe themselves constructively. Women may need to be taught how to calm themselves and how to talk themselves down, ultimately finding non-destructive ways of overcoming their demons – whatever shape those demons may take.

The discussion questions during this session are designed to elicit the coping mechanisms that women have used in the past to deal with feeling out of control. Leaders encourage group members to consider what different coping strategies *cost*, i.e., "Some strategies are of the *feel good now, pay later variety*. What does it cost you to receive comfort? List your three most used comfort strategies in order of increasing cost." Hopefully, group members are able to see that some of their ways of dealing with stress and anxiety (such as drinking, drugs or self-mutilation) may offer temporary relief but cause more problems later on, the *soothe now, pay later* syndrome.

Many responses which women initially give fit well into the "fight or flight" response pattern described in the trauma literature as characteristic of those persons diagnosed with Post Traumatic Stress Disorder. Regrettably, many women who have been episodically homeless have all but exhausted the "flight" option. Further flight only tends to place them in even more dangerous situations. The same is usually true for the fight response. Unfortunately, many women who have spent years in public and private institutions have very dangerous or at least volatile networks, in which case to stand and fight may prove to be a very unwise, if not life-threatening decision.

The task of the group is to generate a list of healthy ways to take care of oneself. Initially this may require much input from the leaders. However, once led in this direction women soon begin to come up with ideas of their own. It may also be helpful to have pictures or magazines for the group to use in order to generate ideas. A healthy list might contain some of the following elements:

Auditory	Music
	Listening to the radio
	Talking on the phone

Visual	Looking at pictures of happy times
	Nature – tranquil scenes
	Going to the movies
Olfactory	Flowers
	Perfume
Gustatory	Favorite foods
	Good cup of coffee
Sensate	Exercise
	Massage
	Warm bath
	Wearing new clothes
	Soft touches – i.e., feathers
Self Esteem	Fixing yourself up and looking good
Relationships	Being with friends

The women are then instructed to make "comfort cards". These are folder sized pieces of poster board on which women can glue pictures, write words or draw things which might offer them comfort when they are alone and need support. They can then take these cards home with them and keep them in a prominent place. The cards serve as reminders of how to self soothe the next time a woman feels stressed or out of control.

When the first nine sessions have been completed, leaders conduct a review, check in with group members as to where they are in the process of personal healing and make sure that the group is ready to move on. This review allows the group to transition into Part II of the training in which members will begin to address their own trauma histories more directly.

Part II consists of the following 12 sessions:

- Gaining an Understanding of Trauma
- The Body Remembers What the Mind Forgets
- What is Sexual Abuse?
- What is Physical Abuse?
- Physical Safety
- What is Emotional Abuse?

- What is Institutional Abuse?
- Abuse and Psychiatric Symptoms
- Abuse and Substance Abuse
- Abuse and Homelessness
- Abuse and "Bad" Relationships
- Myths about Sexual Abuse

These sessions are more directly tied to an individual's own personal experience of trauma and its effect on current functioning. The work of this section is more intense and personal and consists much more of examining previous beliefs and ways of dealing with trauma. It also focuses on looking at what impact the past has on current functioning and on planning for how to minimize the negative impact as much as possible.

Judith Herman states in *Trauma and Recovery* (1994):

> Recovery unfolds in three stages. The central task of the first stage is the establishment of safety. The central task of the second stage is remembrance and mourning. The central task of the third stage is reconnection with ordinary life. (p. 155)

The framework of the social skills intervention bears a similar structure. Part I concentrates on 1) making the group a safe place, 2) providing some education about trauma and 3) giving women the opportunity to explore their perceptions about trauma and have validated or modified these perceptions as appropriate. Part II continues these goals, but also helps women to expand their behavioral repertoires in order to avoid repeating the same experiences time and time again. The emphasis now switches to making connections between the lack of power and control women feel and their continued experiences of abuse, whether in interpersonal relationships or in societally sanctioned "helping" relationships – i.e., by inpatient staff on a psychiatric unit.

The belief that each survivor needs to reconnect with ordinary life and find healthier ways of dealing with potentially traumatic situations is the focus of Part II of the intervention. Women need to learn or relearn that they ought to be able to trust their instincts in making good decisions. To do this, women need to be able to perform the accurate labeling mentioned earlier. An example of this process is found in the session entitled "Gaining an Understanding of Trauma." The goal is for each member to gain an understanding of what is meant by "trauma" and the role that trauma has played in her life.

The leaders begin the session with a general definition of trauma. Although it may be easy for women to come up with examples and definitions of physical and sexual trauma, it is usually much harder for them to recognize and define psychological or emotional abuse. In preparation for the group, leaders should have a definition of trauma on the board/flip chart that includes the following:

- intense fear
- helplessness
- loss of control
- threat of total destruction

Leaders can facilitate the discussion by asking members to generate a list of synonyms for trauma. Are there slang words women would use to identify their feelings? As with all sessions, it is important that the definitions used are those which have the most emotional reso-nance for the women in the group. Many women need to be given the technical words to describe the different feelings or feeling states often associated with trauma. By learning that there is a shared lan-guage to describe their feelings about what happened to them, women discover that others have felt this way and that their experi-ences and responses are not isolated and solely personal. Correct labeling ties their personal experience into universal experiences and makes those personal responses more legitimite.

The exercise for this session is to have women draw the feelings associated with trauma. Women are encouraged to use shapes and colors to draw what they feel. They need not draw a representational picture. This exercise is designed to elicit information from those women who are able to express themselves better in a less verbal way. For some, the unspeakable degradation perpetrated upon them can not be described in words. Women who were abused as children may know that something bad happened to them but may not have the vocabulary to express their feelings. Abuse became the secret that no one talked about. This session begins the process of developing a shared vocabulary for discussing and understanding the impact of trauma.

The other topics in Part II continue this discussion and allow women to explore specific ways in which trauma plays a part in addictions, in their involvement in the mental health system and in their current relationships. By looking into these connections, group members will begin to expand their understanding of how trauma has influenced their present life situations.

The final session of the social skills intervention is a healing ritual designed to close the group and allow women to reflect on what they have learned and what they would like to leave behind. Most importantly, the ritual celebrates what they will take with them. This is the "parting ritual," borrowed in part from Native American tradition, which gives the women something of the group to take away with them. The leaders collect artifacts – stones, carved animals, things from nature – anything which has traditionally symbolized healing and strength. A personal medicine bag is provided for each woman and she is invited to select things which she feels have totemic significance for her and which might help her continue in the healing process.

Each woman symbolically places whatever pain she is prepared to let go of on a communal rock which is then passed around the circle to other members. Once each woman has had a chance to give up her pain, the group rinses the rock with water in an act of cleansing and letting go. The group then shares a ritual meal of bread and juice.

What we have learned

Women in this population usually experience multiple traumas – physical and sexual abuse both in childhood and adulthood, homelessness, drug and alcohol addiction and institutional abuse from institutions such as child welfare agencies or public mental health systems (Goodman, Dutton and Harris, 1995). There is continued exposure to community violence, reinforced by dangerous social networks. They are resource poor and have inadequate social or economic reserves to escape the world of trauma and abuse in which they have been living since childhood.

Social skills models for chronically and persistently mentally ill women that focus on skills deficits are not always applicable to women who have severe trauma histories and who may have used those perceived deficits to protect themselves. This intervention clearly addresses three skill areas crucial to the treatment of chronically mentally ill women with trauma histories: intrapersonal, interpersonal and global (Harris and Fallot, 1995).

Intrapersonal skills

1. *Self Knowledge*: an understanding of biopsychosocial realities. These women range from knowing their bodies somewhat, to being totally disconnected from their physical selves. They have to be taught how to "read" their bodies in a realistic manner and to understand internal signals. There is a high incidence of somatization in this population; the ability to read the messages from their bodies might result in a sudden improvement in physical health.

They also need to be able to distinguish between what they think, what they feel and how they take action. Feelings need to be identified accurately. Often women begin the groups only able to identify a narrow range of feelings. For example, everything is either hurt or anger. As they develop a more sophisticated emotional vocabulary, their labeling becomes both more refined and more accurate.

Women are often unable to make distinctions between experiences of the past, present and future. Dissociation has served as useful protection in the past but accurate labeling of thought and affect will allow women to be able to enter future situations in a healthier manner. Women need to have their past experiences validated, but they also need to experience success in trusting their sense of themselves in the present and have confidence in their ability to go into future situations equipped with the skills and resources to handle potentially abusive situations.

2. *Self Soothing*: the ability to assuage feelings of distress, pain and hurt. Women with serious mental illness need to be instructed in ways in which they can soothe themselves when they feel anxious, depressed or frightened without using illegal substances, sexually acting out, or over medicating themselves with prescription drugs.

3. *Self Esteem*: the ability to generate and sustain positive images of the self. Many of these women are so confused because of prior abuse that they believe that to be a woman means to be a victim, to

be abused, or to be powerless. This intervention provides women with an alternate, more positive sense of what it can mean to be a woman in this world.

4. *Self Trusting*: the reliance on the validity of one's own feelings, thoughts and perceptions. These sessions allow women a safe place to explore their feelings and to develop the skills to know just what it is that they are feeling. It also allows them a forum in which to evaluate their own and others' behavior and to begin to form ideas as to the general reliability of their own and others' judgments and behaviors.

5. *Emotional Modulation*: the ability to control the expression of affective states. The stereotypical picture of the trauma survivor is usually one of extremes – hysterical and out of control or passive to the point of catatonia. Self-soothing techniques and appropriate labeling skills facilitate "evening out" some of the intense lability that may be a part of a trauma survivor's emotional make-up. Survivors discover that they can explore feelings without getting out of control and that they are able to deal with difficult situations without either exploding or becoming totally passive.

Interpersonal skills

1. *Self Expression*: the ability to express one's own feelings, thoughts, needs and wants. Trauma survivors have learned well to fulfill other people's needs at the expense of their own safety and well being. They need to be taught to take care of themselves and communicate those needs to others.

2. *Social Perception and Labeling*: the ability to accurately assess and respond to social situations. Many women need to learn, for example, that it is not safe to get into a car with someone you do not know, even if you do need to get to the store before it closes. Reciprocity in a relationship does not mean that just because someone buys you dinner you have to have sex in return. For many women knowledge of what is appropriate in social settings and what is potentially an abusive situation is deficient. Just as they have to develop the skills to read their own internal cues accurately, they need to be helped to transfer those perceptual skills to reading the interpersonal world accurately as well.

3. *Self Protection*: the ability to recognize, avoid and/or manage potentially harmful situations and relationships. Survivors are not accustomed to putting themselves first. They need to look at their past experiences, understand what it was that made those experiences abusive and develop skills that will help to protect themselves in the future.

4. *Self Assertion*: the ability to actively seek to meet one's own needs and wants in an appropriate manner. It is not enough to know one's own thoughts and needs. The next step is to develop the skills to articulate those needs and find ways of getting them met.

5. *Relational Mutuality*: the ability to listen to others as well as to express oneself, to engage in reciprocal meeting of interpersonal needs. Trauma survivors are often isolated and have had few, if any, successful experiences with mutuality in relationships. Respectful give- and-take between people, which is at the core of all healthy relationships, may be one of the most difficult areas for women with abuse histories. One must take the risk of trusting another individual even when past attempts have ended in betrayal and disappointment.

Global skills

1. *Identity Formation*: the ability to maintain a clear self-image, both when alone and in social situations, as well as the ability to define and maintain chosen social roles consistent with goals and values. This involves setting limits and boundaries and developing an internal point of reference (ego strength) which allows one to function effectively in different settings and roles. A woman is now no longer solely a trauma survivor; she is a sister, a trainee, a consumer of mental health services.

2. *Agency and Initiative Taking*: the ability to see oneself as a primary source of action and initiative in one's life. Abused women are those to whom things are done, upon whom abuse is perpetrated. Along with new skills comes the responsibility for one's own life. The intervention is designed to present positive images of women to encourage each woman to take responsibility for maximizing her own potential.

3. *Problem Solving*: the ability to combine cognitive, affective and social skills in resolving personal and interpersonal situations. Many of these women have been so diminished and demoralized by abuse that they lack the ability to make judgments about even the most obvious tasks. They need to integrate the skills they have developed in reading themselves and the world around them with solving the problems of everyday living.

This intervention is layered in such a way as to present these three domains of skill development in progressively more advanced styles, allowing women to practice ways of integrating new skills in more and more complex situations. Some skill deficits are addressed directly. In other cases, skills are enhanced indirectly as a result of group participation. For example, self-esteem is improved as women come to view themselves as resourceful problem-solvers. By providing women with information about abuse and dispelling myths, the intervention enables women to move beyond the limiting identity of their abusive experiences to a new and more positive definition of their place in the world.

For many women the group provides the opportunity to change something about themselves they thought was unchangeable. It allows them to normalize their experiences and begin to feel good about themselves. It gives them new skills which enable them to accurately label their experiences and safely express their feelings. Over the course of a year, they have experienced a safe place and they can take some of that safety out into the world with them. They have been able to practice asking for what they want or setting limits in a structured and protective environment. They have learned to value womanhood both in themselves and in others.

References

Browne, A.L. (1993) "Family Violence and Homelessness: the relevance of trauma histories in the lives of homeless women", in *American Journal of Orthopsychiatry*, 63, 3, pp. 370–384.

Breyer, J.B., Nelson, B.A. and Miller, J.B. *et al.* (1987) "Childhood sexual and physical abuse as factors in adult psychiatric illness", in *American Journal of Psychiatry*, 144, pp. 1426–1430.

Courtois, C.A. (1988) *Healing the Incest Wound*. New York: Norton.

Goodman, L.A., Dutton, M.A. and Harris, M. (1995) "Physical and Sexual Assault Prevalence Among Homeless Women with Serious Mental Illness", in *American Journal of Orthopsychiatry*.

Harris, M. and Fallot, R. (1995) "Trauma Recovery Skills: Development and Enhancement" (unpublished).

Herman, J. (1993) *Trauma and Recovery*, New York: Basic Books, p. 155.

Chapter Six

Inpatient Treatment of Psychiatric Women Patients with Trauma

Joanne Wile

Introduction

A sixty-eight year old single African American female screams from her room on a psychiatric inpatient unit, "Rape! Murder!" No one else is in the room and the physical and gynecological examinations on admission reveal no physical signs of battering or recent intercourse.

A twenty-one year old divorced Caucasian female in the room next door comes into the dining room to talk to the social worker about a new living situation. She wants to leave her home because she says she can no longer tolerate her father's sexual advances to her. The client conveyed this information in a disinterested, flat manner and then immediately changed the subject, talking about the paint color in the dining room.

A pregnant forty-two year old Latina widow is hospitalized for suicidal ideation. Three of her former husbands have been killed in gang-related battles. Six of her children are in foster care. She has recently used cocaine following an episode of battering by her current boyfriend. She has bruises on her face. She tells the psychiatrist that she hates herself and her unborn baby and wants to kill herself.

For the clinician treating clients admitted to the Women's Issues Consultation Team in the Department of Psychiatry at San Francisco General Hospital there is an almost constant bombardment of disturbing and stimulating behaviors and narratives, accompanied by an equally disturbing range of client feelings, from seeming disinterest to stark terror.

The Women's Issues Consultation Team was *not* initially established to study trauma. It was developed in 1984 to treat pregnant psychotic women. Various interventions were designed to ensure the safety of women and their babies during pregnancy, labor, delivery and the postpartum (Spielvogel and Wile, 1986 and 1994). Over the years, additional aspects of women's sexual and reproductive lives were included as treatment issues: birth control practices, abortion, child custody relinquishment, the development of sexual identity, problems related to sex trade work, sexually transmitted diseases including HIV, the passage through menopause, rape, domestic violence and childhood sexual abuse. We became increasingly aware of the connections between traumatic experiences and women's psychiatric presentations of depression, drug addictions, dissociative states, self-harm, eating disorders and anxiety disorders.

Women who come into inpatient settings may well be suffering from one of three sources of trauma: childhood sexual abuse, domestic violence, rape, or some combination of these experiences. When they are hospitalized, some women are victimized by inappropriate staff conduct. This widespread incidence of trauma requires careful assessment and well-designed inpatient treatment planning.

The study of the lives of women with major psychiatric disorders becomes the study of trauma

It has been observed that "sexual and physical abuse is so prevalent that it has been characterized as a normative aspect of female development" (Hamilton, 1989). Battering may occur in 25 to 50 percent of all women and rape (whether attempted or completed) may occur in 26 to 46 percent of women (Hamilton, 1989).

Too often, the high frequency of interpersonal violence which women are exposed to in the home and on the streets matches many or all of the descriptions of the stressors characterizing posttraumatic stress disorders. The symptoms these women experience include: chronic anxiety, psychic numbing, heightened physiological reactions, hypervigilance, dissociative responses, problems with intimate relationships, depression, substance abuse, sleep disturbances, fear, irritability, shame, low self-esteem, survivor guilt, helplessness and self-harm (Koss, Goodman, Browne, Fitzgerald, Keith and Russo, 1995; McNew and Abell, 1995).

Two studies of adult women hospitalized for treatment of severe and persistent mental illnesses found rates of retrospective reported abuse of 46 and 51% (Beck and van der Kolk, 1987; Craine, Henson, Colliver and MacLean, 1988). Because women who are admitted to an acute hospital setting may be in states of decompensation with impaired reality testing, the assessment of traumatic reports may be extremely difficult.

In gathering historical information clinicians need to guard against aggressive interviewing styles. Interviewers may adversely affect memory retrieval. Repeated questioning about particular childhood experiences or the immediate assumption of guilt toward accused adults may lead the client to assume the veracity of certain reports without sufficient exploration. The following guidelines have been developed to guard against these risks:

1. Maintain neutrality and guard against bias while facilitating the process of narrative reconstruction. Avoid the stance that it is desirable to 'produce' a trauma.
2. Avoid the use of hypnosis or pharmacological therapies to stimulate memory (e.g., sodium amytal).
3. Do not encourage bibliotherapy, self-help groups, or other forms of group therapy focused on abuse issues until there is reasonable certainty that sexual abuse actually occurred.
4. Allow clients to approach memories of abuse at their own pace, maintaining neutrality to avoid contamination by the therapist's suggestion about the existence of such memories or their content.
5. Focus on diminishing posttraumatic effects of abuse and enhancing current functioning rather than uncovering experiences of abuse. (Zweben, Clark and Smith, 1994)

An equally serious risk, of course, is the lack of detection of early experiences of physical and sexual abuse (Rose, Peabody and Stratigeas, 1991). Serious depressive episodes with suicidal ideation, impulsivity and dissociative states may be improperly treated and become even more persistent.

At San Francisco General Hospital, Brainin-Rodriguez has developed a protocol in which questions about childhood experiences of abuse are embedded in routine psychosocial and medical history gathering questions. After asking about the family constellation, she asks:

> "What was the home environment like?
> Who punished the kids and how were they punished?
> Were you ever punished in ways that resulted in bruises, burns, cuts or broken bones?
> If so, how long did it go on?
> Who else was involved?
> Did anyone else know?" (Brainin-Rodriguez, 1995)

Questions related to gynecology and obstetrics provide the framework for information on sexual experiences:

> "Any sexual experiences as a little child? Who? When? How long?
> Was there exposure, touching, oral/anal, or genital contact?
> Photographs taken?
> Threats of harm, weapons, or violence?
> Any medical or social consequences or interventions?
> If yes to the above questions, did you ever tell anyone?
> Was there ever a time you didn't remember these episodes?
> Do you have recurrent dreams or memories now?" (Brainin-Rodriguez, 1991)

The clinician should monitor the client's reactions to these questions, pacing the process, acknowledging that the discussion of certain experiences may be upsetting and allowing the client control in choosing when and how to reveal the information.

Obviously the clinician should not pursue discussion of these events in the acute hospitalization if the client becomes grossly psychotic, severely suicidal, assaultive or self-mutilating. The client needs sufficient ego strength and support to do exploratory work on traumatic events (Linehan, 1993).

However, linking certain disturbing behavior and perceptual distortions to childhood experiences of abuse and chaos may actually improve the client's sense of control and mastery in her adult life.

> Ms. L is a 24 year old European-American single woman, admitted to the inpatient unit for the third time in three months after a drug overdose of 35 tablets of phenobarbital, 20 milligrams of methadone, cocaine and intravenous amphetamine. She was 35 weeks pregnant, had been beaten by her boyfriend and kicked out of their apartment and had no place to stay.
>
> Following the protocol, a thorough history was taken. Ms. L reported that she knew nothing about her father. Her mother had used drugs, supported herself by sex trade work and was killed by a customer when Ms. L was three years old. She then lived in a series of foster homes. In her early teens she started supporting herself through prostitution, using a variety of drugs to dull her memories of sexual molestation in foster care and in her present sex trade work.
>
> On the unit Ms. L would become enraged, threatening staff and other clients at the slightest frustration. She required seclusion and restraint when she would slap and kick others. She was finally able to contract to take time in her room when she began to lose control. She complained about visual and auditory hallucinations. At night she would see dark figures around her bed who would try to grab her and call her derogatory names.
>
> Knowing the association of behavioral problems and sexual delusions in clients with childhood sexual trauma (Beck and van der Kolk, 1987), the staff helped the patient understand how her behavior was a desperate attempt to ward off the helplessness, intrusive memories and intense feelings associated with her past traumas. She spoke of feeling compelled to follow the path of her mother in a life of risk, suicide attempts, despair and substance abuse.

Some studies (Hughes, 1991; Kridler and Hassan, 1992) suggest that incest and other sexual traumas may be central precursors to women's drug abuse. Experts in the treatment of substance abuse disorders believe that if the psychological effects of incest are not addressed with recovering substance abusers the potential for relapse is increased (Janikowski and Glover, 1994). Many women report that street drugs are a means of blocking painful feelings and flashbacks of sexual abuse (Evans and Schaefer, 1987).

Fullilove, Lown and Fullilove (1992) describe how complex the interaction can be between childhood abuse, symptoms of posttraumatic stress disorder, substance abuse and retraumatization. In "crack" addictions the drug-induced euphoria effectively numbs the dysphoric feelings and memories associated with childhood traumas, but the craving for the drug leads both men and women to engage in high risk activities. For women the sex-for-drugs exchange system becomes a quick way to obtain crack or money, but it carries the risk of exposure to rape and other forms of violence, as well as expressions of disdain from others of being a "crack 'ho." Understanding the interaction of these forces may help women overcome the intense shame they feel for engaging in degrading acts in their effort to obtain drugs.

Not only substance abuse, but also other psychiatric symptom clusters can be treated more appropriately when the early abuse issues are identified. These clusters include: depression with atypical and dissociative features (Gelinas, 1983), somatization disorders (Briere and Runtz, 1988), dissociative disorders and self-harm through cutting and starvation (van der Kolk, 1989) and borderline personality disorders (Bryer, Nelson, Miller and Krol, 1987).

Some authors (Jennings, 1994; Rose, Peabody and Stratigeas, 1991), emphasize that the failure of clinicians to even ask about abuse experiences perpetuates an atmosphere of secrecy and nonresponsiveness which results in "institutional retraumatization" (Jennings, 1994). Others argue that asking about childhood victimization carries the risk of perpetuating false accusations against family members or other significant adults (Zweben, Clark and Smith, 1994). This is clearly a risk that needs to be considered.

As the woman tells her story, clinicians need to use a structured protocol, such as the one described earlier, which provides a consistent and neutral means of gathering childhood history. During the hospital stay, when the woman is in a place of safety and can receive treatment for her psychiatric condition, she and the staff can monitor the consistency of her reports of early and/or current abuse. When she is in a more stable condition, she can make the necessary decisions about how to pursue the issues she has raised.

When there appears to be risk of harm to the client or to another member of the household, the psychiatric social worker proposes a meeting in which the client's concerns are raised and family members have an opportunity to respond (J. Eastwood, personal communication, March 15, 1995). As Schatzow and Herman (1989) emphasize, "the session is being conducted at the initiative of the patient and for the benefit of her recovery. It is a family meeting, but not a family therapy session, as the family has not requested treatment" (p. 344).

> A twenty-three year old Chinese-American single female was admitted to the inpatient unit following a serious suicide attempt. A recent discussion with her sister, corroborating the father's sexual advances to both of them, led her to feel even more shame and hopelessness about herself and her family. She feared breaking the silence but felt terribly isolated with the secret of family incest. The staff talked with her about whether she wanted a meeting with her parents and sister to help her work on the effects of these experiences or whether she preferred to work on them in her individual psychotherapy. The client decided that the best choice for her was to have a meeting with herself and her mother.

In this situation the psychiatric social worker was respecting the client's sense of timing and disclosure. The object of the meeting was to support the client's wish to discuss issues that were bothering her. The clinician did not take a position with the mother of either supporting or denying the memories of the sexual advances.

The final reason for asking about childhood experiences of sexual and physical abuse is that epidemiological studies demonstrate that individuals who have experienced childhood abuse are at risk for repeated victimization in adulthood. Russell (1986) found that the risk of battering, sexual harassment and rape is nearly *doubled* for survivors of childhood abuse.

The adult female client treated in a public hospital is likely to experience trauma as a child and as an adult. Studies indicated that women living in poverty and women from ethnic minority groups are at particular risk for severe and life-threatening assaults (Belle, 1990; Merry, 1981; Steele, Mitchell, Graywolf, Bell, Chang and Schuller, 1982).

Domestic violence

When a woman is admitted to a psychiatric unit for treatment of symptoms of a major psychiatric illness, clinicians must keep in mind the possibility that she may be battered. Because of fear and shame, battered women may minimize the violence they experience. As Herman (1994) describes, the methods of psychological control used by the perpetrator "are designed to instill terror and helplessness and to destroy the victim's sense of self in relation to others" (p. 77). A physical examination performed in the medical emergency room may or may not have already revealed signs of physical violence. With the guarantee of confidentiality and privacy the inpatient staff should consider the possibility of domestic violence, as they assess the following factors:

> "She seems to be very isolated, with no access to money, to a car, or to other forms of transportation, to family or friends or to jobs or school;
> She experiences repeated injuries that are difficult to account for as accidental;
> She refers frequently to her partner's 'anger' or 'temper';
> She complains that her partner drinks excessively or changes personality when he (or she) drinks;
> She is afraid of being harmed;
> She frequently flees her home;
> She reports that her partner accuses her of sexual infidelity;
> She is reluctant to speak with you in the presence of the abuser;
> She alludes to her partner abusing the children or complains that he (or she) over disciplines them;
> Her partner has taken the children away from her;
> She is reluctant or terrified of speaking to those in authority because she fears reprisals by the abuser or because she wants to protect him (or her);

She has attempted suicide." (Jang, Lee, Madrigal, Morello-Frosch, Pendleton, 1991).

If there are initial indications of battering, the next assessment is the degree of violence. After commenting that most partners have disagreements, our clinicians ask, "What is it like when you and your partner have fights?" As the woman describes the fights, the clinician asks one or more of the following questions to clarify the degree of danger:

"Does your partner constantly criticize you, blame you for things that are not your fault or verbally degrade you?

Has he or she ever pushed, slapped, kicked, bitten, restrained, thrown objects at, spit at or used a weapon against you because he or she was angry or upset?

Does he or she prevent you from getting or maintaining a job, control your shared resources or restrict your access to money?

Has he or she ever threatened to harm you, your family, friends, children, pets or property? Has he or she threatened to blackmail or 'out' you if you leave?

Does he or she have a history of violence against former partners?" (Community United Against Violence, 1994)

Although the death of the battered woman or her partner is uncommon, the following indicate that the situation is becoming increasingly dangerous and should be documented in the medical record:

— An increase in the frequency or severity of the assaults
— Increasing or new threats of homicide or suicide by the partner
— Threats to the children
— Presence or availability of a firearm
— Failure of multiple support systems (McLeer, 1986)

It is important, of course, to convey to the woman that she is not alone in struggling with her situation and she is not to blame for what is happening. Her stay in the hospital may provide her with an opportunity to think through her situation, discuss the risk factors for her safety, review legal options and consider her needs for ongoing shelter and support.

Although the woman may have already been treated for a major psychiatric disorder on previous occasions, the clinician must be aware of the risk of suicidal and/or homicidal behavior and, in general, the possibility of a posttraumatic stress disorder. One of every ten battered women attempts suicide. Twenty-six percent of all female suicide attempts occur after physical abuse. For African American women the rate is fifty percent (Stark, Flitcraft, Zuckerman, Grey, Robison and Frazier, 1981).

During the inpatient hospitalization, staff may inadvertently contribute to "secondary victimization" (Brown, 1994). Because of complicated countertransference reactions involving denial, distancing and fears of helplessness, clinicians may find themselves blaming the woman for being depressed, indecisive, or failing to leave the abuser. They may attempt to direct her to leave the abusive partner prematurely, that is, when she does not have the psychological, social or financial resources to do so. This is dangerous. The woman may be at greater risk of harm if she decides to leave the abuser, so she must evaluate her internal and external resources very carefully. National crime statistics show that in almost seventy-five percent of spouse-on-spouse assaults, the victim was divorced or separated at the time of the incidents (U.S. Department of Justice, 1983). More than fifty percent of murders of women in the United States in 1990 were by husbands or boyfriends (Cooper, 1992).

A major countertransference effect which inpatient staff must constantly monitor is the activation of various prejudices and projections. Clinicians need to examine ideas and feelings about whom they consider to be "worthy" victims of domestic violence. Individual and institutional practices of prejudice against women of color, immigrants, lesbians, substance abusing women, poor women and prostitutes have often reinforced the helplessness, isolation and self-blame of these battered women. The life experiences of women in these groups may affect their behavior with hospital staff and their comfort in reporting episodes of abuse.

For lesbians and women of color there may be a fear that disclosing abuse will add to currently existing prejudices about the "deviant" behavior in these communities (Kanuha, 1994; Renzetti, 1992). They may feel protective of their partners because of the risk of abuse by the criminal justice system or the possibility of loss of child custody.

In many African American communities the history of police violence against male perpetrators may lead women to avoid contacting authorities (Richie and Kanuha, 1993). For Native American, African American (Takagi, 1991) and lesbian mothers (Renzetti, 1992) the reporting of their own victimization may lead to the loss of custody of their children. Staff in public social agencies are likely to conclude that they are inadequate mothers, rather than to institute measures which would provide support to them and their children.

There are certain class and racial definitions of femininity and respectability: white skin color, passivity, dependence, financial means and legalization of sexual behavior by a marriage license to a male partner. Women who do not meet these criteria are seen as "less feminine" and are dismissed.

In addition to these social and institutional barriers to receiving help, women may have cultural and religious values which contribute to their reluctance to confide in others about battering. Zambrano (1987) describes how certain gender expectations among Latino groups guide women's behavior: "the roles we are expected to fulfill very often limit what we can do in the world, confine our influence to the home and force us to make the needs of our partners and children our main concern" (p. 151). Ho (1990) and Lai (1986) describe a similar situation for some Asian women. The combination of religious beliefs, a tradition of family loyalty and the inculcation of a subservient female role to the males in the family may lead these women to stay in abusive relationships.

Women refugees and new immigrants may depend on their male partner because of limited language capability, lack of financial resources and separation from family and other traditional supports. They may fear that using health services could jeopardize their immigration status.

It is important for clinicians to evaluate which of the multiple traumas a woman faces is most intolerable to her. The clinician and client are evaluating harsh emotional and economic realities as they examine the woman's choices in situations of domestic violence. Harris and Bergman (1985) report that the social support systems of adults with severe and persistent mental illnesses are much more sparse than those in the general population of comparable ages. In this example the woman finds it more frightening to be totally without the support of her partner than to endure episodes of being hit by him:

Ms. R is a 20 year old single Latina with a long history of poly-drug abuse and depressive episodes. Her mother left her husband and children when the client was five years old. She was raised in a series of foster homes and reported episodes of sexual abuse which had been confirmed by other children in these homes. She made frequent attempts to run away and, when she met her current boyfriend at age 15, went to live with him. Beginning in adolescence, she helped to support both of them through sex trade work.

Ms. R and her case manager had been working to help her remain HIV negative and decrease her use of intravenous drugs. Ms. R made it clear that she did not want to leave her boyfriend, Mr. O, even though he would slap her periodically when he was intoxicated.

During one visit to the home, Ms. R presented with severe bruises on her face. She reported that she had been raped and beaten by a sex trade client who was high on drugs and who had refused to pay her. She feared that Mr. O would not believe her and would be enraged that she had failed to get money from the client. She had used their last supply of cocaine and now felt depressed and suicidal.

The case manager took Ms. R to the emergency room where she was given a physical examination and counseled about how to press legal charges against the rapist. She insisted on taking no action, continued to feel suicidal and feared that Mr. O would never take her back.

During the brief inpatient hospitalization, the case manager and inpatient staff reiterated that no one deserves to be raped or beaten. We expressed concern about her safety in doing prosti-tution and questioned Mr. O's concern for her well-being, given the risks on the streets. Ms. R remained adamant about staying with him and requested only that we help her explain what had happened.

In a meeting with Mr. O and Ms. R we helped her talk about the rape and emphasized how important his role would be in her recovery. Since his initial reaction was one of anger at the "john," we capitalized on this as an expression of his protectiveness toward her and that, unfortunately, rape is a serious risk in sex trade work (Hotaling, 1994). They talked about the need for her to have time off from the streets to recover emotionally and physically from the assault. The case manager helped the couple to develop a strategy to borrow money temporarily.

Experience has shown that we cannot attack the woman's partner when she feels dependent on him and chooses to remain with him. We can work with her to recognize signs of impending violence and to evaluate her choices should she decide to leave. If staff attack the abusive partner when the woman is choosing to remain in the relationship, they may actually increase her vulnerability to retaliatory measures (Walker, 1979).

Because of the peril to her life and the lives of her two sons, one woman eventually found both needed psychiatric treatment and safety in the hospital:

Ms. M, a 30 year old Pacific Islander woman who has two sons, ages four and seven, was residing with her husband in another state. She speaks limited English and relies on his income to support the family.

Following an episode in which her husband beat her and the sons with wooden slats, Ms. M took the children and boarded a bus headed for California where she had relatives. After only a few days the relatives demanded that she and the children leave. Knowing him, they feared the husband would come after her and harm them in the process. She left and came to a women's shelter. She soon showed signs of severe disorganization and depression. She reported seeing monstrous reptiles in the sky. She became too preoccupied and disorganized to cook or supervise her sons at the shelter. One day she attempted to walk into the ocean, saying that she no longer wanted to live.

The shelter staff brought her to the hospital and called Children's Protective Services to arrange temporary care for the sons. Through an interpreter the staff learned that she had been previously hospitalized for treatment of a bipolar affective disorder and had improved on a combination of lithium carbonate and mellaril. Although Ms. M initially reported visual hallucinations and a severe depression, she improved on the medication and was eventually discharged to a residential treatment program. In this program she was able to once again be reunited with her sons and work with the staff on establishing her family in a new city.

Without a residential treatment program for herself and her children the possibility of re-unification for the three of them would have been greatly diminished. Nicholson, Geller, Fisher and Dion, (1993) found that only a few states in the entire country offered such services to mentally ill mothers and their children.

Rape

Test and Berlin (1981) comment that "rape and other forms of sexual exploitation are particular problems for chronically mentally ill women, who are especially vulnerable to victimization" (p. 142). In a study of female inpatients with abortion and relinquishment of child custody experiences, the rates of reported rape were fifty-six percent for those who terminated pregnancies, sixty-six percent for those who relinquished custody and eighty-two percent for women who had both occurrences (Thomas, 1995). The reported rates for women in all these sub-groups are higher than the rates of reported rape given for the general population, from twenty-six to forty-six percent (Russell, 1984).

The most devastating experience for the clinicians on the Women's Issues Consultation Team was a rape which occurred while the woman was being treated on the psychiatric unit. This sexual assault revealed our inability to maintain a totally safe treatment environment:

Ms. A is a twenty-six year old single Spanish-speaking female from Central America who was brought to the hospital by her grandmother and sister. The family reported that she had not been eating or sleeping for the past two weeks. She would stare into space, not respond to direction and neglect her grooming.

Ms. A appeared to have developmental disabilities as well. She had delayed speech and, after two years of school in Central America, was told she could not continue and was kept at home.

Ms. A was abandoned by her mother at birth and had been raised by her grandmother and various aunts. She had come to this country for a brief visit. The symptoms had appeared prior to the visit, but worsened dramatically after they arrived in the city.

Without any confirming psychiatric data, Ms. A was given the tentative diagnosis of Psychosis, Not Otherwise Specified and started on 5 milligrams of haloperidol. In a week she had started eating again and was much more communicative. As the staff and family were planning her discharge from the hospital, the rape occurred.

On hourly rounds at 11 P.M. a nurse had found Ms. A in a male client's bathroom. She was sitting on the toilet seat and he was standing in front of her with his penis placed in her mouth. Staff immediately separated them, called administrative staff and hospital security. In an agitated state, crying, Ms. A related that she had come into his room to look at magazines with him and he had forced her into the bathroom and pushed her onto the toilet seat while he unzipped his pants and pressed his penis into her mouth.

The Rape Treatment Center was called and a Spanish-speaking counselor helped her talk to the police about the assault. The male client was taken to the Hall of Justice and booked on criminal charges. A gynecological examination was performed and evidence collected.

In the days that followed, Ms. A worked with her counselor from the Center about her feelings of anxiety and fear. The male client reported to the police that no one had ever "bothered him" about this behavior in a hospital before. In the community meetings that were held with staff and clients, we reiterated that there was a rule on the unit prohibiting sexual activities between clients because they often arrived to the hospital in very disorganized and vulnerable states and needed protection from unwanted and possibly unsafe sex during this recovery time.

In a series of meetings with the family, the social worker explained what had happened. After the initial shock and anger, the grandmother and sister reported that this was not the first time that a sexual assault had occurred. Ms. A's seemingly child-like trust, attractiveness, youth and eagerness for male attention made her vulnerable to unsafe situations in Central America as well. The family had been ashamed to bring this information to the staff previously, not wanting to reveal her loss of virginity (Ingoldsby, 1991).

In the week that followed, Ms. A saw the Rape Treatment Center counselor every day. She began participating in group activities almost immediately. The clients became more protective of her, joining her at meals and television-watching. Ms. A's appetite and sleep returned to her pre-rape status. Her family members made daily visits. Follow-up with the counselor was arranged and she was discharged to her family.

The medical record and incident reports were reviewed by the Patients' Rights representatives for the possibility of negligence. The findings were negative. The family also felt satisfied that the routine procedures to ensure client safety had been followed.

The staff continued to feel shaken by the rape. They questioned whether both men and women should be on the same acute psychiatric unit and whether they had missed any signs by the male client of previous predatory behaviors in his past history. Even though the legal findings had indicated the absence of negligence, the sense of having failed a young woman client who was also a visitor from a war-torn country lingered with the staff months after the incident.

Professional boundary violations

Women with histories of childhood physical and sexual abuse are vulnerable to inappropriate boundary violations by mental health clinicians. In our setting, the staff may hear allegations of misconduct by former and current psychotherapists or toward psychiatrists and hospital staff. All allegations are required by California law to be reported to Adult Protective Services for investigation. Such a report in the following situation was just one part of the clinician's interventions that to decrease the client's dangerousness to herself and others:

> Ms. R is a forty-one year old divorced African American female with a history of treatment for a bipolar affective disorder. She was admitted involuntarily following a period of cocaine abuse after a break-up with her boyfriend. Initially Ms. R was irritable, despairing and suicidal. She reported that she was hearing command hallucinations telling her to kill her boyfriend. She agreed to re-start her medication of lithium carbonate and fluoxetine.
>
> In exploring recent stressors, the client told the social worker that her boyfriend was a staff member in a local treatment program. He had become sexually involved with her when she was a client in the program and had helped her procure drugs. Even though she had just terminated the relationship, Ms. R was furious with him for crossing professional boundaries and becoming involved with her.
>
> Following consultation with Adult Protective Services and with the client's consent, the social worker contacted the administrator of the program. After hearing the allegations, the administrator discussed them with the accused staff person. He confessed that the allegations were true and offered to resign from his position.
>
> Upon hearing of the outcome of her complaint, Ms. R was satisfied and felt no need to pursue her charges in the legal system. She cried with relief and said that she had told two other service providers about the situation, but no one had done anything.
>
> Ms. R continued to feel less depressed and reported a cessation of the command hallucinations to kill the boyfriend. She no longer felt she had to "take the law into my own hands."

Possibly because of her substance abuse and severe mental illness Ms. R's complaints had been dismissed by others in the health care system. One direct consequence of having her allegations of professional misconduct taken seriously was the diminution of her suicidal and homicidal ideation.

Inpatient treatment approaches

Brainin-Rodriguez (1995) has observed that in the acute inpatient setting, clinicians who work with clients with trauma issues take on "multiple competing foci of treatment." The first goal must be stabilization of the woman's acute symptoms. The risks and benefits of receiving various medications are discussed with her. Staff explain that the goal is to reduce the client's distress so that she can address the psychological and situational issues that are troubling her.

Although the client may have a history of physical or sexual abuse, the current clinical presentation should be addressed first. In this example, psychological testing had confirmed that the primary diagnosis was Major Depression With Psychotic Features.

> Ms. T is a twenty-seven year old African American lesbian who was brought to the emergency service after cutting her wrists with a razor blade. In response to structured questions about her history, she reported that at age seven she had been sexually fondled by her father when her mother had been incapacitated by a physical illness. Ms. T is a high school graduate with a work history in the military service. Following a break-up with her partner of the last two years, she heard voices telling her to cut her wrists and stop taking food and fluids. During the brief hospitalization, she was able to mourn the loss of this relationship. She was treated with desipramine and haloperidol. The hallucinations ceased and, although sad about the loss of her partner, she was no longer suicidal.

When women present with uncomplicated symptoms of major affective, schizophrenic, or generalized anxiety disorders, medications addressing these symptoms should be initiated. When features of posttraumatic stress disorder, such as hyperarousal, avoidance, or intrusive symptoms, are also present, a range of medications may be considered, depending on the target symptoms (Southwick, Yehuda, Giller and Charney, 1994). Van der Kolk has found that fluoxetine is especially effective for treatment of the full range of symptoms in posttraumatic stress disorders (1994, p. 262).

Management of self-harming behaviors

Self-injury has been found to correlate with reported early sexual trauma (Calof, 1995; van der Kolk, 1989). Both the nature of the sexual abuse and age of the individual at the time affect the types of self-harming acts that are performed.

It is particularly difficult to identify and treat self-injurious behaviors. Often they are performed secretly. The individual may dissociate from both the experience of pain and the sense of meaning and motivation involved. The behaviors may also be mistakenly identified as suicide attempts. In fact, cutting, starving, burning and other harmful behaviors represent attempts to stay alive by expressing rage, punishing oneself, reducing tension, re-enacting traumas, or feeling real.

After assessing the specific meanings for the woman of her self-harming actions, various means of contracting for safety are established with her. Staff inform her that while they can monitor certain warning signs, she is ultimately the one who can keep herself safe.

Nursing staff developed the following plan with one client who made over fifty lacerations on her arms:

> Staff will ask, "Are you safe?"
>
> Client will respond clearly, with good eye contact and without delay, "I am safe. I will not harm myself in any way."
>
> If the client cannot carry out this interaction, she will be in constant eye contact with staff until she indicates she is safe, by completing the contracted interaction.
>
> If she cannot stay under staff's observation, she will agree to be placed in restraints until the contracted interaction can be completed.

The client had informed staff that either lack of eye contact or failure to give the full contracted statement meant that she was close to cutting herself.

Clients who perform self-mutilating actions inform staff that they are sometimes helped by being given substitute activities. One client used red marking pens to make bright red marks on her forearms when she felt like cutting herself. Another woman found that placing her hands in ice cold water provided the strong physical sensations she sought when self-cutting her thighs. Calof (1995) believes that these methods can be "alternative containers" for acts of tension regulation.

Many authors emphasize that it is not enough simply to extinguish these self-injurious behaviors. Although this goal is tempting for the relief of the staff, it does not provide the client with a means to cope with the intense feelings, states of unreality and flashbacks in new ways.

Susan Scheidt (personal communication, March 22, 1995), an attending psychologist on the inpatient unit, emphasizes two key aspects of treatment with clients who engage in self-harming behaviors: staff consistency and staff intervention when the client's behavior indicates that she is overwhelmed.

Ms. P is a twenty-three year old single European-American female hospitalized for self-cutting behavior and stopping her intake of food and fluids. Following seven days of starvation, the staff informed Ms. P that a nutritionist was being consulted. Ms. P, weighing 130 pounds, wished to lose another 15 pounds. Staff agreed that this was workable, but needed to be done safely. A daily calorie plan was instituted and she agreed that she would stay within sight 30 minutes after meals to avoid vomiting in her bathroom. For the first day the client was furious, refusing to participate. The staff held firmly to the need for a safe plan. The next day Ms. P began to adopt the new regimen.

As she became more comfortable, she was able to modify the plan to her wishes. She decided which foods and liquids she would choose to meet her caloric needs. Staff asked her to identify "loopholes" in the plan. She extended the time following meals to 45 minutes, stating that she was less likely to be able to vomit after that period.

In an attempt to discover the meaning of the starvation, she was asked to report the physical sensations she observed in her body. Ms. P initially insisted that starvation was a way that she felt "in control" of her life. Upon exploration, we learned that she actually experienced psychotic symptoms when starving herself and felt less in control. She experienced herself as more "in control" by having the choice of when to eat and when not to eat.

The clinicians made clear the danger to the client of her compulsive starving, tolerated her initial expression of rage and then adhered to the treatment plan. As she demonstrated the ability to regulate her intake of food and fluids, she was given more control of the treatment plan.

Group treatment modalities

Women's greater emphasis on affiliation and interdependence (Surrey, 1991) enables them to benefit from group modalities, even during hospital stays of only seven to ten days.

The clinicians on the Women's Issues Consultation Team have developed group modules addressing various aspects of women's psychiatric, medical, social and recreational needs.

The occupational therapist, Olivia Flores, has organized inpatient activities which create opportunities for clients to experience success, learn from one another, reinforce a sense of self and maintain a connection to core cultural roots (Dillard, Andonian, Flores, Lai, MacRae and Shakir, 1992). The first structured activity each day is a movement group in which clients use gross motor activities (exercises, dance, yoga, Tai Chi) to promote sensory integration, body awareness, stress reduction and energy arousal and release. The leader provides music, structures activities and monitors the performance of the clients.

Trauma for women often involves an assault on both the body and the spirit. The self-hatred and self-blame that are generated may take the form of self-mutilation, somatic preoccupations and a decrease in body awareness. Movement provides a safe means of recapturing body sensations which are under the woman's own control.

The weekly grooming group helps women learn grooming and personal hygiene skills, provides a forum for women to share thoughts and feelings about their appearance and leads to an increase in self esteem. Exchanges often lead to discussion of concerns about what looks attractive for each woman, racial differences in make-up and style, societal standards of attractiveness and group comments on the appearance and behavior of popular female performers.

The women's activity group uses art and media modalities to express themes in women's lives. Clay, art, readings from poetry, fiction, biographies and plays reflect issues such as family relationships, victimization, creativity, competition, body image and envy. Recently female clients from all the inpatient units participated in the Clothesline Project, a national effort in which abuse survivors, family members and friends decorated T-shirts. The images and graphic messages were designed to tell of women's survival of victimization by rape, domestic violence, incest, childhood sexual abuse and hate crimes against lesbians. At the end of the activity, clients and staff talked about their T-shirt productions and displayed their Clothesline in the activity room of the unit. The shirts, which went on display for the entire hospital and became part of the national display in Washington, D.C. for Women's History Month, were a tribute to women's survival.

Practical information about sexual issues is provided in a four-part group module for men and women. Based on the work of Steiner, Lussier, Maust, DiPalma and Allende (1994), the group combines didactic and discussion formats. Session one describes the sexually transmitted diseases of AIDS, hepatitis, herpes, gonorrhea and syphilis and outlines physical signs, transmission, prevention and treatment for each condition. Session two, about birth control methods, begins with a simple diagram of the male and female reproductive organs. The methods of condom with spermicide, diaphragm with spermicide, intrauterine device, sponge, oral contraceptive, contraceptive implant and surgical procedures of vasectomy and tubal ligation are described.

Session three is about intimacy and relationships. The group defines intimacy and then talks about types of intimate relationships: family, friends, lovers or spouses and pets. Members give examples of effective communication, verbal and nonverbal, from their lives. They discuss how past experiences of giving and receiving affection relate to current behavior. Participants are asked to describe the differences between productive and destructive relationships.

In session four, sexual myths are described and discussed. Using the Steiner model, group members are asked to decide whether the following five statements are true or false:

"You can't get pregnant the first time.
No means yes.

Alcohol or drugs make sex better.
There is no such thing as bad sex.
Talking about sex ruins the experience." (p. 381)

These questions help clients talk about consensual and nonconsensual sex, sex in exchange for drugs and sex with children.

Conclusion

The study of the lives of women with major psychiatric disorders becomes the study of trauma. Experiences of interpersonal violence, whether as children or as adults, in the home or on the streets, are almost normative aspects of women's lives.

Accordingly, inpatient treatment interventions must be designed to address the special requirements of trauma survivors. All aspects of the hospital program should reflect an awareness of trauma-related symptoms, the value of clear professional roles and boundaries, non-traumatizing decision-making processes and, most of all, the healing power of shared survivor narratives.

In the early phase of each woman's hospital stay, standard protocols are used for inquiry about child and adult experiences of physical and sexual trauma. This minimizes the dual risks of either lack of detection, on the one hand, or distorted memory retrieval, on the other.

Because of women's frequent experiences with abuse of power, clinicians need to be aware of how they use their authority and expertise so that the hospitalization is not re-traumatizing. In woman-centered treatment, decision-making should be as much of a collaborative process as possible. The reasons for the use of various medications are explained. The manner in which the woman has tried to cope with trauma is discussed with her so that she develops an appreciation of her own individual strengths and the vulnerabilities associated with her psychiatric symptoms. The goal of the staff's interactions is to constantly promote the woman's sense of mastery and control over her own life.

Just as few women can alone piece together the strands required for recovery from trauma, clinicians treating women with these issues need the help of the client and one another to create a holding environment for the recovery process. Individual and group consultation can enhance a clinician's knowledge of particular areas of trauma treatment, such as medication or comorbidity with substance abuse disorders. The consultation is also a core forum for discussion of countertransference reactions, such as self-righteousness, avoidance, rescue, hopelessness, rage and the myriad of other intense reactions that trauma work evokes. Weekly team meetings and case conferences are essential for establishing and coordinating a successful treatment plan with outpatient service providers. When the woman is involved in these meetings she is able to experience the hospital and community providers as a true therapeutic community for her.

Shinoda Bolen (1994) writes that for a healing community to work:

We need to see every woman in the circle as a sister who mirrors back to us reflection of ourselves. This means that whatever happened to her could have happened to us, that whatever she has felt or done is a possibility for us, that she is someone toward whom we feel neither superior nor inferior nor indifferent. (p. 221)

It is about bearing witness in the midst of the temptation to avert our eyes and not know the trauma that we see every day.

References

Beck, J.C. and van der Kolk, B. (1987) "Reports of childhood incest and current behavior of chronically hospitalized psychotic women", in *American Journal of Psychiatry*, 144, 1474–1476.

Belle, D. (1990) "Poverty and women's mental health", in *American psychologist*, 45, 385–389.

Bolen, J.S. (1994) *Crossing to Avalon*. San Francisco: Harper.

Brainin-Rodriguez, J. (1995) *Assessment of trauma in the female psychiatric inpatient: impact and treatment implications*. Manuscript submitted for publication.

Briere, J. and Runtz, M. (1988) "Post sexual abuse trauma", in *Journal of Interpersonal Violence*, 2, 367–379.

Brown, S. (1991) *Counseling Victims of Violence*. Alexandria, Virginia: American Counseling Association.

Bryer, J.B., Nelson, B.A. and Miller, J.B. (1987) "Childhood sexual and physical abuse as factors in adult psychiatric illness", in *American Journal of Psychiatry*, 144, 1426–1430.

Calof, D. (1994) *Chronic self-injury and self-mutilation in adult survivors of incest and childhood sexual abuse; etiology, assessment and intervention.* Manuscript submitted for publication.

Community United Against Violence. (1994). San Francisco.

Cooper, S. (1992, August 30) *San Francisco Examiner.*

Crane, L.S., Henson, C.E., Colliver, J.A. and MacLean, D.G. (1988) "Prevalence of a history of sexual abuse among female psychiatric patients in a state hospital system", in *Hospital and Community Psychiatry*, 39, 300–304.

Dillard, M., Andonian, L., Flores, O., Lai, L., MacRae, A. and Shakir, M. (1992) "Culturally competent occupational therapy in a diversely populated mental health setting", in *American Journal of Occupational Therapy*, 46, 721–725.

Evans, S. and Schaefer, S. (1987) "Incest and chemically dependent women: treatment implications", in *Journal of Chemical Dependency Treatment*, 1, 141–173.

Fullilove, M.T., Lown, E.A. and Fullilove, R.E. (1992) "Crack 'hos and skeezers: traumatic experiences of women crack users", in *The Journal of Sex Research*, 29, 275–287.

Gelinas, D.J. (1983) "The persisting negative effects of incest", in *Psychiatry*, 46, 312–332.

Hamilton, J.A. (1989) "Emotional consequences of victimization and discrimination in 'special populations' of women", in *Psychiatric Clinics of North America*, 12, 35–51.

Harris, M. and Bergman, H.C. (1985) "Networking with young adult chronic patients", in *Psychosocial Rehabilitation Journal*, 8, 28–35.

Herman, J. (1994) *Trauma and Recovery.* United States: Basic Books.

Ho, C.K. (1990) "An analysis of domestic violence in Asian American communities. A multi cultural approach to counseling." In L.S. Brown and M.P.P. Root (Eds.), *Diversity and Complexity in Feminist Therapy* (pp. 129–150). New York: Haworth Press.

Hotaling, N. (1994, May) "The lies about prostitution" (Letter to the editor). *San Francisco Examiner*, p. 15.

Hughes, T. (1991) "Research on chemical dependency among women: a women's health perspective", in *Family and Community Health*, 13, 35–39.

Ingoldsby, R. (1991) "The Latin American family: familism vs. machismo", in *Journal of Comparative Family Studies*, 22, 57–61.

Jang, D., Lee, D., Madrigal, T., Morello-Frosch, R. and Pendleton, G. (1991) "Domestic violence in immigrant and refugee communities: asserting the rights of battered women", in *Family Violence Prevention Fund*, 2, 1–12.

Janikowski, T.P. and Glover, N.M. (1994) "Incest and substance abuse: implications for treatment professionals", in *Journal of Substance Abuse Treatment*, 11, 177–183.

Jennings, A. (1994) "On being invisible in the mental health system", in *The Journal of Mental Health Administration*, 21, 374–387.

Kanuha, V. (1994) "Women of color in battering relationships." In L. Comas-Diaz and B. Greene (Eds.), *Women of Color* (pp. 428–454). New York: The Guilford Press.

Koss, M.P., Goodman, L.A., Browne, A., Fitzgerald, L.F., Keita, G.P. and Russo, N.F. (1995). *Male violence against Women at Home, at Work, and in the Community*. Washington, D.C. American Psychological Association.

Kridler, M. And Hassan, M. (1992) "Use of an interactional model with survivors of incest", in *Issues in Mental Health Nursing*, 12, 149–58.

Lai, T. (1986) "Asian women: resisting the violence." In M.C. Burns (Ed.), *The Speaking Profits Us: Violence in the Lives of Women of Color* (pp. 8–11). Seattle, WA: Center for the Prevention of Sexual and Domestic Violence.

Linehan, M. (1993) *Cognitive-Behavioral Treatment of Borderline Personality Disorder*. New York: The Guilford Press.

McLeer, S.V. (1987) "The role of the emergency physician in the prevention of domestic violence", in *Annals of Emergency Medicine*, 16, 107–113.

McNew, J.A. and Abell, N. (1995) "Posttraumatic stress symptomatology: similarities and differences between Vietnam veterans and adult survivors of childhood sexual abuse", in *Social Work*, 40, 115–126.

Merry, S. (1981) *Urban Danger*. Philadelphia: Temple University Press.

Nicholson, J., Geller, J., Fisher, W. and Dion, G. (1993) "State policies and programs that address the needs of mentally ill mothers in the public sector", in *Hospital and Community Psychiatry*, 44, 484–489.

Renzetti, C.M. (1992) *Violent Betrayal: Partner Abuse in Lesbian Relationships*, Newbury Park: Sage Publications.

Richie, B.E. and Kanuha, V. (1993) "Battered women of color in public health care systems: racism, sexism and violence." In B. Blair and S.E. Cayleff (Eds.), *Wings of Gauze: Women of Color and the Experience of Health and Illness* (pp. 288–299). Detroit: Wayne State University Press.

Rose, S.M., Peabody, C.G. and Stratigeas, B. (1991) "Undetected abuse among intensive case management clients", in *Hospital and Community Psychiatry*, 42, 409–503.

Russell, D.E. (1984) *Sexual Exploitation*. Beverly Hills: Sage Publications.

Russell, D.E. (1986) *The Secret Trauma*. New York: Basic Books.

Schatzow, E. and Herman, J.L. (1989) "Breaking secrecy: adult survivors disclose to their families", in *Psychiatric Clinics of North America*, 12, 337–349.

Southwick, S.M., Yehuda, R., Giller E.L. and Charney, D.S. (1994) "Use of tricyclics and monoamine oxidase inhibitors in the treatment of PTSD: a quantitative review." In M.M. Murburg (Ed.), *Catecholamine Function in Post-Traumatic Stress Disorder: Emerging Concepts* (pp. 293–305). Washington D.C.: American Psychiatric Press, Inc.

Spielvogel, A. and Wile, J. (1992) "Treatment and outcomes of psychotic patients during pregnancy and childbirth", in *Birth*, 19, 131–137.

Spielvogel, A. and Wile, J. (1986) "Treatment of the psychotic pregnant patient", in *Psychosomatics*, 27, 487–492.

Stark, E., Flitcraft, A., Zuckerman, D., Grey, A., Robison, J. and Frazier, W. (1981) "Wife abuse in the medical setting: an introduction for health personnel (Monograph No. 7)." Washington, D.C.: Office of Domestic Violence.

Steele, E., Mitchell, J., Graywolf, E., Belle, D., Chang, W. and Schuller, R.B. (1982) "The human cost of discrimination." In D. Belle (Ed.), *Lives in Stress: Women and Depression* (pp. 109–119). Beverly Hills, CA: Sage.

Steiner, J.L., Lussier, R.G., Maust, G.C., DiPalma, L.M. and Allende, M.J. (1994) "Psychoeducation about sexual issues in an acute treatment setting", in *Hospital and Community Psychiatry*, 45, 380–381.

Takagi, T. (1991) "Women of color and violence against women." In National Network of Women's Funds and Foundations/Corporate Philanthropy (C. Moliner, Ed.), *Violence Against Women Supplement* (pp. S1, S6). St. Paul, MN: National Network of Women's Fund and Foundations/Corporate Philanthropy.

Test, M. and Berlin, S. (1981) "Issues of special concern to chronically mentally ill women", in *Professional Psychology*, 12, 136–144.

Thomas, T.J. (1995) *A comparative analysis of women psychiatric inpatients who abort or relinquish custody and their responses to loss of child*. Unpublished manuscript.

U.S. Department of Justice. (1983). Washington D.C.: U.S. Government Printing Office.

van der Kolk, B.A. (1989) "Compulsion to repeat the trauma: reenactment, revictimization and masochism", in *Psychiatric Clinics of North America*, 12, 389–411.

van der Kolk, B.A. (1994) "The body keeps the score: memory and the evolving psychobiology of posttraumatic stress", in *Harvard Review of Psychiatry*, 1, 253–265.

Walker, L. (1979) *The Battered Woman*. New York: Harper and Row.

Zambrano, M.M. (1994) *!No Mas! Guia Para La Mujer Golpeada*. Seattle WA: Seal Press.

Zweben, J.E., Clark, H.W. and Smith, D.E. (1994) "Traumatic experiences and substance abuse: mapping the territory", in *Journal of Psychoactive Drugs*, 26, 327–344.

Part III

First Person Accounts

Chapter Seven

A Historical Perspective on Victimization

Jeffrey L. Geller, Joanne Nicholson and Amy Traverso

Introduction

It is not difficult to understand why, historically and currently, women are vulnerable to victimization by treaters. The argument of feminist authors is that women's voices have long been silenced by the "androcentric bias in psychiatry's ideology, epistemology and discourse" (Nugent, 1994, p. 113). Nugent suggested that the subjugation of women patients is allowed for by the interaction between deeply-held cultural stereotypes of women and the power and authority granted to treaters.

In taking a historical perspective, it is critical to consider the socio-political context of the events described – "symptoms" and "cures" – as that context relates to stereotypes of women at the time. Major themes that emerge in our analyses of women's illnesses and treatments and their consequent victimization over the past century, include the etiology of women's illnesses, the preferred treatment outcomes and the role played by treaters' perceptions of women.

The first recurrent theme is that women are construed as passive victims of their biology or their biological drives. The biological component is consistently alleged throughout discussions of the etiology of women's illnesses and attempted cures, whether surgical (in the late 1800's) or sexual (in the late 1900's). The stereotype of female passivity is reinforced by a woman's apparent "willingness to assume she is wrong, bad, neurotic ..." (Plasil, 1985, p. 71).

The second theme, an obvious corollary of the first, is that the treater or therapist, typically male, is placed in a superior position and imbued with trust and respect. The treater is empowered by the patient and family. His opinions regarding the course of treatment and goals are held in high esteem.

Coupled with and complicated by the first two themes, is the third which concern standards of care and the responsibility of treaters whose actions resulted in the victimization of women patients. It is now possible to view the physicians of the 1800's who performed surgeries that mutilated the reproductive organs of female patients with mental illness as operating with the best of intentions given the standards of practice at the time. It is not as easy to conclude that the contemporary treater who sexually abused the female patient in the course of her outpatient psychotherapy and perhaps in the name of helping her, was actually acting in the best interest of his patient given the current standards of practice.

These themes frame our analyses of patient and professional writings about trauma as the result of treatment and trauma as an artifact of treatment. We focus on three eras of psychiatric care: "biological" cures for women's woes in the mid- to late-nineteenth century; the experiences of women in public institutions in the 1930's to 1960's; and the sexual victimization of women by therapists reported from the late 1970's to the present.

Trauma as the result of treatment

Oophorectomy and other surgical procedures in the late nineteenth century

"My doctor tried all kinds of things, but still I was not better. It was then I began to suffer so from noises, even the slightest ... At last it was decided that I had some womb trouble and must be examined. I had some leucorrhoea and pain at my periods and walking hurt me and tired me so. I can't describe the shock I felt at having to be treated ...

besides, I had a feeling, which many women I know also have, that the womb is the weak point and is the cause of most of their nervous ills … I was ready to submit to anything and he "curetted" – that is the word – my womb. Instead of being better, I was a thousand-times worse. The shock and pain, or something, increased my nervous depression and I had, in addition, physical pain in back and head …" (Anonymous, 1896, p. 364)

Authors in the mid- to late-1800's embraced the notion that the majority of women's mental disturbances were caused by diseases of the female organs (Storer, 1870). As Dally (1991) pointed out, surgery became fashionable as a treatment, not only for ovaries that were believed to be diseased, but to address problem issues such as masturbation and "nymphomania," and other behaviors of women that were difficult for their husbands to control.

But according to Dally (1991), a highly controversial (and less common) procedure used during this time was the clitoridectomy, which was popularized by the London surgeon Isaac Baker Brown. While his fervent adherence to the operation ultimately led to his expulsion from the major medical societies in Britain, he was at the height of his popularity in 1864 when he established "The London Surgical Home for Diseases of Women." The clinic contained thirty-four beds at its peak and was "largely, though not exclusively" used for the clitoridectomy procedure (Dally, 1991). The "diseases" that Baker Brown alleged to "cure" included nymphomania, "peripheral excitement" (masturbation), epilepsy and "suicidal mania." In addition, five women whose "symptoms" included seeking a divorce were clitoridectomized; all returned to their husbands.

Baker Brown's work was first received by the British press with curiosity and some cautious optimism. There were devoted supporters who felt clitoridectomy was a safe and harmless removal of useless tissue. However, criticism quickly grew. Doctors in England and the United States called the operation "quackery". An article in the *Lancet* recommended that the medical establishment:

[protest] indignantly against the performance of a dreadful operation upon married women without the consent of their husbands and upon married and unmarried women without their own knowledge of the nature of the operation (Dally, 1991, p. 180).

By 1867, Dr. T.G. Thomas wrote in *A Practical Treatise on the Diseases of Women*:

> The excision of the normal organ for the cure of masturbation, nympho-mania, or general neurosis, which many years ago was introduced by Baker Brown of London, has long fallen into disuse (Dally, 1991 p.180).

This was not entirely true, as Baker Brown was performing the operation that very year, but it demonstrated both a shift in public opinion against clitoridectomy and an interest in covering up embarrassing mistakes of the recent past.

Storer, a prominent surgeon in the Boston medical community, labeled these cases of insanity as being of "reflex origin," and "not the result, primarily, of cerebral change" (p. 17). Storer summarized his opinions in a paper published in 1865, insisting that in women, "mental disease is often, perhaps generally, dependent upon functional or organic disturbance of the reproductive system"; that women's mental diseases are brought on or exacerbated by the menstrual cycle; and that successful treatment of mental disease in women "must be based upon" these conclusions (Storer, 1871, p. 30).

Goodell (1882) agreed with Storer's opinions, indicating that ovariotomy for insanity "is now one of the most successful of the major operations" (p. 294). Consistent with the attitudes of the day, Goodell indicated that the death of an insane woman is "always a relief to her dearest friends" (p. 285) and even if she recovered from her illness, the removal of her ovaries would prohibit her from transmitting her insanity to her offspring. It was Goodell's contention that it might be "sound policy and of commendable statesmanship to stamp out insanity by castrating all the insane men and spaying all the insane women" (p. 295).

Opinions such as Storer's and Goodell's ultimately met with some controversy, even though the mutilation of women's reproductive organs as treatment for mental illness became more common. Dialogue ensued in the medical journals, in both psychiatry and gynecology. Stone (1891) argued firmly for the role of the gynecologist in institutions for the insane, citing data that "insane persons who were quiet and gentle during the interval, fell into maniacal raving during the menstrual flow, not infrequently of an erotic character" (p. 870). It was the perspective of authors like Stone that insane women had as much right to relief from disease of the reproductive organs as sane women had.

In 1893, Thomas Morton indicated that "The increasing frequency of these experimental mutilations and their doubtful ultimate success, has caused conservative medical opinion to halt and to dispassionately discuss the whole subject ..." (p. 397). He reported that many "insane, epileptic and hystero-epileptic women" (p. 398) who were castrated were not cured and that insanity resulted from the operation. Morton, who was chairman of the Lunacy Committee of the State Board of Charities of Pennsylvania, was responding to the establishment of experimental surgical units in hospital settings. Colleagues of Dr. Morton's agreed that "Insanity is a disease of the brain, not of some organ remote from it" (Levick, 1893, p. 514).

As late as 1894, however, a case of successful recovery from "insanity due to the menstrual function" following oophorectomy was reported in the literature (Gorton, 1894). This was the case of a 16-year-old girl, who reportedly suffered mental instability during the time of her menstrual period. During her periods she exhibited many delusions of "an erotic character" (p. 236). The girl was operated on and had both ovaries and fallopian tubes removed. Following the operation she was reported to be mentally and physically well. Gorton maintained that oophorectomy was justifiable in circumstances in which women would otherwise become hopelessly demented.

The medical treatment of women's woes by professionals who assumed that the causes of women's difficulties were to be found in their organs and specifically their reproductive organs, did not always meet with success. The "nervous woman" in 1896 concluded:

> *"I am thirty, I have had thirteen doctors and my life has been a series of treatments. I do not complain of this. Most of my advisers have, I am sure, done their very best for me. But am I never to get well?"*
> (Anonymous, 1896, p. 367–368).

The rest cure of the late nineteenth century

> *"If a physician of high standing and one's own husband, assures friends and relatives that there is really nothing the matter with one but*

temporary nervous depression — a slight hysterical tendency — what is one to do? ... So I take phosphates or phospites — whichever it is and tonics and journeys and air and exercise and am absolutely forbidden to 'work' until I am well again ... He is very careful and loving and hardly lets me stir without special direction. I have a schedule prescription for each hour in the day; he takes all care from me and so I feel basely ungrateful not to value it more" (Gilman, 1892; reprinted, 1973, p. 10–12).

An alternative treatment to surgical intervention in the nineteenth century was the "rest cure," promulgated by S. Weir Mitchell (1878; 1885). Cases responding best to forced rest, excessive and controlled feeding, massage and electricity, according to Mitchell (1878), were those of "nervous women, who as a rule are thin and lack blood" (p. 9). Mitchell provided a description of one of these cases:

"A woman, most often between twenty and thirty, undergoes a season of trial or encounters some prolonged strain. She undertakes the hard task of nursing a relative and goes through this severe duty with the addition of emotional excitement, swayed by hopes and fears and forgetful of self and of what every one needs in the way of air and food and change when attempting this most trying task; or possibly it is mere physical strain, such as teaching. In another set of cases an illness is the cause and she never rallies entirely, or else some local uterine trouble starts the mischief and although this is cured the doctor wonders that his patient does not get fat and ruddy again" (Mitchell, 1878, p. 29).

According to Mitchell, uterine problems "soon appear" (p. 30). He recommended a thorough examination of each patient to correct all "womb troubles." These troubles were accompanied by the loss of self-control and moral degradation. Mitchell reassured the reader that he saw men who suffered from these symptoms.

Mitchell believed that an ensuing complication in the development of the symptoms of the dysfunctional female was the emergence of a sympathetic, devoted relative who ministers to the "caprices of hysterical sensitiveness" (Mitchell, 1878, p. 31). This companionship, Mitchell asserted, must be disrupted if a cure is to be achieved.

Mitchell's treatment regime included remaining in bed from six weeks to two months. The patient was not allowed to sit up, sew, write or read. After several weeks, activity was gradually reintroduced into the patient's life. Mitchell recommended massage and electricity as antidotes to the ill effects of rest on muscles (Mitchell, 1878).

As part of his treatment regime, Mitchell also advocated control of the woman's diet. "When a woman weighing one hundred pounds is lying in bed and does nothing, about three pints of skimmed milk daily will usually sustain her weight without other nourishment" (Mitchell, 1878, p. 74). Mitchell described the case of "a lady from New York" who lived for two years on two quarts of milk per day. "After a time I treated her as I would have done a child who had to be rapidly weaned and was thus successful by a series of changes in diet in enabling her to increase to a sufficient and comfortable extent the range of her dietary" (Mitchell, 1878, p. 75). After one week of treatment, one pound of beef was added to the daily diet, in the form of raw soup.

A further difficulty Mitchell aimed to treat was the consequent use of alcohol and drugs, i.e., chloral and morphia, by women prone to "the hysterical constitution" (Mitchell, 1878, p. 19). He reported great success in the case of "Miss L, age 26" who "went home changed no less morally than physically and resumed her place in the family circle and in social life, a healthy and well-cured woman" (Mitchell 1878, p. 96–97).

Mitchell's reported successes must be tempered by women's own reports of their conditions. Charlotte Perkins Gilman (Gilman, 1892; reprinted, 1973) described her deterioration during the time of her rest and confinement.

> "I lie down ever so much now. John says it is good for me and to sleep all I can.
>
> "Indeed he started the habit by making me lie down for an hour after each meal.
>
> "It is a very bad habit I am convinced, for you see I don't sleep."
> (Gilman, 1892; reprinted, 1973, p. 26)

Gilman attempted to cope with her boredom by studying the yellow wallpaper in her room; she slowly slipped into madness.

> "John is so pleased to see me improve! He laughed a little the other day and said I seemed to be flourishing in spite of my wall-paper.

145

"I turned it off with a laugh. I had no intention of telling him it was because of the wall-paper — he would make fun of me. He might even want to take me away ...

"Then I peeled off all the paper I could reach standing on the floor. It sticks horribly and the pattern just enjoys it! All those strangled heads and bulbous eyes and waddling fungus growths just shriek with derision!" (Gilman, 1892 reprinted, 1973, p. 34)

Trauma as an artifact of treatment

Women's experiences in public institutions in the 1930's to 1960's

"For eight years I was an inmate in a state asylum for the insane. During those years I passed through such unbearable terror that I deteriorated into a wild, frightened creature intent only on survival.

"And I survived.

"I was raped by orderlies, gnawed on by rats and poisoned by tainted food.

"And I survived.

"I was chained in padded cells, strapped into strait-jackets and half drowned in ice baths.

"And I survived" (Farmer, 1972, p. 1).

In 1948, the vast majority of the institutionalized patients in the U.S. were in state hospitals, according to Albert Deutsch, a professional writer, in the report of his survey of state mental hospitals (Deutsch, 1948). The American Psychiatric Association had minimum standards for mental hospitals at the time.

"It says there should be a least one psychiatrist for every 30 patients, in certain types of mental disease and at least one for every 200 in others. (In no mental hospital should there be less than one psychiatrist for every 150 patients.) There should be at least one graduate nurse for every 40 patients (for certain cases, one nurse is needed for every four patients). There should be at least one attendant for every eight patients. At least $5 a day should be expended for the care and treatment of each patient ...

146

"Not a single state mental hospital in the United States meets, or ever has met, even the minimum standards set by the APA in all major aspects of care and treatment!" (Deutsch, 1948, p. 39)

One of the challenges in the provision of hospital care for "mental defectives" in this era was that the average length of stay "had to be measured in years" (Deutsch, 1948, p. 35). Owen Copp, in 1921, indicated,

"the misconception, even among physicians, is prevalent, that mental patients, unrecovered after short, initial study and treatment, may properly be put aside for mere care in asylums during protracted illness without persistent and resourceful effort to alleviate and rehabilitate" (quoted in Solomon, 1958, p. 2).

Solomon (1958) indicated, 27 years later, that the field of psychiatry had failed to meet the challenge of caring for the chronically mentally ill.

"... one must face the fact that we are doing little by way of definite treatment of a large number of our chronic hospital population. It is not even the case that we are providing them with first class environmental care, much less loving and tender care" (Solomon, 1958, p. 8).

Less emphasis during these years was placed on causes of mental illness specific to women (Geller and Harris, 1994). Forms of "treatment" in the institutions included psychosurgery, i.e., prefrontal lobotomy; hydrotherapy, i.e., being placed in a tub of flowing lukewarm water to soothe the nerves or being shot with jets of water under high pressure; narcosis, i.e., prolonged sleeping; and shock treatments (Deutsch, 1948; Geller and Harris, 1994). Many states adopted sterilization policies to prevent the spread of mental illness (Geller and Harris, 1994).

Trauma resulted to patients during this era, not only as the consequence of inadequate treatment procedures and policies, but even more frequently and shockingly, as the consequence of the conditions in institutional settings. Deutsch described, for example, the conditions at the Philadelphia State Hospital for Mental Diseases, one of the six state institutions he visited in 1946 for his survey.

147

"I entered buildings swarming with naked humans herded like cattle and treated with less concern, pervaded by a fetid odor so heavy, so nauseating, that the stench seemed to have almost a physical existence of its own. I saw hundreds of patients living under leaking roofs, surrounded by moldy, decaying walls and sprawling on rotting floors for want of seats or benches.

"... I saw dirt and filth in many wards. Some of the buildings were modern; several wards were spotless, but these were the exceptions. The food was cold and unappetizing; dining rooms were filth-infested" (Deutsch, 1948, p. 42).

Ward attendants at the Philadelphia institution were in short supply – only one attendant covered 300 to 400 patients. Many of the attendants were vagrants recruited from courts and police stations. While many were loyal employees working in terrible conditions, many were drunks (Deutsch, 1948).

Women did not fare well in conditions like these, when receiving care or merely surviving in the wards.

"The physical was public and crudely done. Shy, confused women were stripped naked and laid out on worn-leather examination tables. With their heels forced into the iron stirrups, they spread their legs while an intern probed into them. The breasts were pinched, the stomach punched and blood taken for tests. Then each woman was rolled over and a thermometer was pushed into the rectum. When one is classed as insane, one cannot be trusted with an oral thermometer. Then the dreaded canvas straps appeared again and were buckled in place. Tied down and terrified, I felt the needle inch its way deep into the spine, strike home and suck out the fluid, throwing my body into a pool of swelling pain ...

"No semblance of dignity was left to us. We waited for our staff interviews defeated, sickened and for the most part, senseless" (Farmer, 1972, p. 95–96).

William Arnold (1978) documented the conditions Frances Farmer reported in her autobiography. He indicated that descriptions, like the one that follows, "hardly scratched the surface of what Frances actually experienced" during her institutional stays (Arnold, 1978, p. 140).

148

"... Orderlies raped at will. So did doctors. Many women were given medical care only when abortions were performed. Some of the orderlies pimped and set up prostitution rings within the institution, smuggling men into the outbuildings and supplying them with women. There must be a twisted perversion in having an insane woman and anything was permitted against them, for it is a common belief that 'crazy people' do not know what is happening to them" (Farmer, 1972, p. 118–119).

The conditions in city hospitals during this time were no better. Deutsch (1948) again described the nightmarish conditions in which Bellevue patients lived.

"You passed through the dimly lit, dingy, ill-ventilated ward swarming with sick humans, many strapped in camisoles or straitjackets, others rendered immovable in their beds by restraining sheets. Cots and beds jammed the narrow corridor where most of the patients spent 24 hours a day, awake and sleeping ...

"I passed by the hydrotherapy room on Ward N7 where, on a July night in 1945, a woman patient got off one of the cots in the jam-packed place converted into sleeping quarters, moved over to another patient's cot and strangled her with camisole laces" (Deutsch, 1948, p. 103–104).

Deutsch (1948) concluded that temporarily deranged patients, "might go through an emotional trauma as a result of their stay that could leave long-lasting scars on their memories" (p. 105).

By 1969, when Anne Barry, a journalist, contrived to have herself admitted to Bellevue, physical conditions had improved. However, what Barry reported is abuse of another sort. She wrote of the ways in which women were demeaned and belittled as part of the daily routine.

"In my baggy nightgown, my hair straggling down my back uncurled and unbrushed, no lipstick, I felt at a disadvantage with this neat young girl, but she owned me here, she was staff. And I had to call her Miss Garber, not Joan and she had to call me Miss Barry, as if we were equals and we were not" (Barry, 1971, p. 64).

"I gave up. 'May I have my nighttime medication then? I missed it somehow before bed.'

"Miss Foley flared. 'What do you mean, you missed it? You get right into bed this minute.' She followed me down the hall to my bed, scolding me all the way ...

"She looked sideways at me. 'You're a bad girl,' she said. 'It's your fault.' " (Barry, 1971, p. 153–154).

Outpatient psychotherapy and the sexual abuse of women patients

"As with everything Dr. X did and said in therapy, I accepted this action without rebellion; and as with other men in my life, I did not feel empowered to express my own desire. That desire, had I been able to verbalize it, doubtless would have been a plea for a sexual moratorium. But I could not even consider what I wanted, or needed, in relationships with men" (Bates and Brodsky, 1989, p. 31).

Gartrell and colleagues (1986) reported that 7.1% of the male and 3.1% of the female respondents in a national survey of psychiatrists acknowledged having had sexual relationships with patients. The vast majority of psychiatrists responding to Herman *et al.* (1987) survey indicated that sexual contact between therapist and patient is "always inappropriate" and "usually harmful" to the patient. Clearly women and particularly women with serious mental illness, are vulnerable for many reasons.

Psychotherapy is a process dependent upon a relationship; in fact, some would argue that the dynamic relationship between treater and patient is the process through which change is achieved. Central to that relationship are the patient's perceptions of the role of the therapist and expectations for the therapist's behavior. Because the therapist is assumed to be the expert, there is a basic power asymmetry to the therapist-patient relationship.

"It amazed me how much of Dr. Leonard's presence I could feel in the office, even in his absence. I felt the same sense of security as when he had been seated across from me behind the desk offering me understanding and guidance. I felt the same comfort as when he had consoled me and dried my tears. I felt the same awe of his wisdom glancing at his books as when he had given me advice. The associations held in that

150

room were powerful. I did not draw from its power, I surrendered to it and depended on it. I relaxed in the chair knowing that no harm could come to me there. " (Plasil, 1985, p. 54–55)

This power asymmetry is consistent with and reinforces many women's feelings of powerlessness in past relationships. According to Strean (1993), the victim of sexual abuse in the therapist-patient relationship often "appears similar to a battered child who has been emotionally abused and sexually exploited by a parental figure" (p. 155). The woman who was previously abused in the context of a relationship assumed to be supportive, i.e., the parent-child relationship, is re-victimized in a current relationship assumed to be one of support.

"A small voice inside her kept saying that she was not benefiting from his guidance, no matter how often he said she was getting better. She was astute enough to know the truth, but lacked the courage to act on it, as she had lacked courage so much of her life. She was still being the good little girl who did not make waves. And she could not believe that her psychiatrist could be in the wrong. When she suggested a woman therapist, he said that, considering her 'condition,' the worst thing she could do was to see a woman — that if he couldn't 'cure' her, nobody could" (Freeman and Roy, 1976, p. 64–65).

Abusive dynamics and events in the current treatment relationship may replicate those of an earlier, abusive relationship for the patient.

"I felt pushed and pulled in every direction, totally confused by what was happening. I just wanted him to hold me and stop being angry, but he kept yelling and I was so frightened I couldn't move away from the wall. I was a child again, cowering in fear of my mother's flailing arms" (Walker and Young, 1986, p. 122).

The blurring of boundaries between therapist and patient when sexual relations occur in the course of treatment contributes to the difficulties experienced by women with histories of trauma and with serious mental illness. Women patients have reported instances of therapists sharing personal and private feelings or experiences (Walker and Young, 1986), or situations in which therapists have

151

recruited them for other "jobs," i.e., typing letters in his office (Freeman and Roy, 1976). As roles blur, the transference issues abound (Trumpe, 1991).

It is not uncommon for therapists who become sexually involved with patients to consider their actions as helpful to the patient.

> *"Within six months of therapy, he had sexual relations with his patient on his office couch. In subsequent therapy sessions, the psychiatrist continued to have sexual intercourse with his patient. Although the doctor said that it was 'wrong,' he also told her that the sex would help in her therapy"* (Trumpe, 1991, p. 190).

> *" 'It would be good for you,' he said. 'If you can love me, you can love another man.' … He went on, 'It happens because of a process called 'transference.' If you love me, you can then transfer the feeling to other men who are more suitable' "* (Freeman and Roy, 1976, p. 55).

Treatment goals framed by therapists may reflect their perceptions of the "need" for sexual relations in the therapy.

> *"The stated goal of therapy became my evolution into a less depressed and more emotionally open, alive, reachable woman"* (Bates and Brodsky, 1989, p. 28).

> *"In the first session, he (the psychiatrist) pushed his legs and genitals against his patient, telling her this would be necessary to help her overcome severe sexual problems resulting from sexual abuse by her father"* (Trumpe, 1991, p. 77)

> *"The rationale usually given by the male psychiatrist or therapist is that if the female patient 'falls in love' with and/or sleeps with him, it will help her with her frigidity and/or will help her to become a 'normal,' genitally functioning, heterosexual woman …"* (Chesler, 1974, p. 77).

Trumpe (1991) concluded,

> *"It is interesting that physicians and therapists usually prescribe and administer this 'treatment' (sex) to women who are quite young and attractive and usually do not deem their more unattractive patients to be in need of this treatment"* (Trumpe, 1991, p. 83).

Herman *et al.* (1987) found that some offenders in their survey sample of psychiatrists felt there was an exaggerated concern for the welfare of patients. They reported the response from one offender who justified his sexual relationship with a patient as empowering, i.e., patients "should not be treated as children who need protection" (p. 167).

Therapists may justify the misuse of the treatment relationship by claiming that the relationship with the woman in therapy is different from, or has changed from the therapist–patient relationship.

> *"Dr. X responded: 'I can neither admit nor deny the above request for the following reason: She may have been charged for the session but was never charged for the time intercourse took place.'*
>
> *"... Dr. X insisted that the intercourse was separate from and in addition to, therapy. He asserted that a personal relationship existed between himself and each of us. Thus, he claimed, we were psychologically free of a patient identify and thereby able to consent to the intercourse"* (Bates and Brodsky, 1989, p. 53).

The mental status of the patient reporting sexual abuse may be called into question. In fact, the patient herself may have difficulty trusting her own impressions of what has transpired between herself and the therapist.

> *"And then, later in the day, I remembered what had happened and I thought: Was it real or was I dreaming that? I decided it had been real"* (Noel, 1984, p. 244).

The woman's lack of confidence or unwillingness to believe what has transpired may be "supported" by the therapist's offer of an alternative explanation.

> *"To give her every benefit of the doubt, Ms. Noel, having been relieved of a severe panic-depressive state, may have felt a surge of affection for her elderly, long-term therapist in the role of father-surrogate and, in a virtual fantasy, identified him with her own father, who she claimed had made what she interpreted as erotic advances during her childhood and adolescence."* (Masserman, 1994, p. 82).

Unfortunately, Herman *et al.* (1987) found, in surveying psychiatrists, that "Even those who believed that such contacts are usually harmful to patients and who regretted their own experiences had great difficulty recognizing that they had injured their patients"

(p. 167). The consequences of therapist–patient abuse can be disastrous. Victims of this abuse "suffer extreme psychological damage" (Trumpe, 1991, p. 65).

> *"But my insecurity continued to give way to shame and my inability to discern healthy relationships from unhealthy ones worsened. My judgment of what was destructive for me was terribly poor"* (Bates and Brodsky, 1989, p. 25).

Discussion

Psychiatry has all too often not been kind to the most vulnerable of women, i.e., those with histories of trauma and diagnosed with severe mental illness. The themes of biological drives and passivity; the role and power of the treater; and the perceived responsibility of the therapist, suggest points to highlight in these personal and professional accounts from three eras of treatment.

The tyranny of biology

Women's reproductive organs have been cast as the cause of their insanity in the nineteenth century and the means to curing their illnesses in the late twentieth century. With the advent of anesthesia and sterile surgical procedures, operating on women to cure them of their illnesses seemed the logical intervention to some treaters of the Victorian era. Essentially the argument was that while the brain was the seat of insanity it was not necessarily the seat of its cause. More often than not, insanity was due to a reflex causation from disordered functioning of another organ. Women were more vulnerable to this reflex then were men; and therefore, the organ of origin of the insanity must be those organs that differentiated women from men.

The idea that it was particularly women who were passive victims of the diseases of their organs was consistent with views about Victorian women. The treatment goals of eliminating the source of women's "malfunctioning" behavior and returning them to appropriate, moral family functioning obviously reflected the basic stereotype of women of the era.

Treaters of the late nineteenth century did not discuss the trauma directly inflicted upon women through the use of the surgical procedures. Young women, as in the example of the 16-year-old cited above, were sterilized before having the opportunity to marry and raise children. Older, married women were surgically treated or confined, which contributed to their insanity according to some knowledgeable women's accounts. It was not until late in the nineteenth century that these practices were called into question, as treaters began to examine outcome data on the surgical treatment of insanity and trauma induced by these interventions.

Women in institutions in the mid-twentieth century were the victims of conditions in treatment settings of the era. Attacks on women's reproductive organs, i.e., beatings and rape, were not imposed as a means of treatment *per se*, but were the correlates of conditions of overcrowding and poor staffing. Women languished in institutions for years. Those who were not insane when they entered the institutions were made insane during their lengthy stays. Frances Farmer, whose "outlandish" behavior prompted her mother to commit her, was severely abused in the institution, as were many other women who were employed in prostitution rings and raped by staff and visitors.

In the 1970's to 1990's, women were abused as an artifact of treatment. Again their "biology" played a significant role in the goals and means of intervention. Goals such as returning women to "full heterosexual functioning" following a history of sexual misuse dictated a sexual intervention as the treatment of choice. The definition of full heterosexual functioning was developed by the typically male treater who imposed his notion of appropriate sexual functioning and sometimes himself on the woman patient.

Father knows best

Treaters, typically male, in each of these eras are imbued with power, real and perceived, by women patients and their families. In the nineteenth century, husbands colluded with male physicians to seek the best outcomes for their wives, as defined from the male perspective. These outcomes maintained women in passive, dependent positions consistent with the stereotypes of appropriate functioning for women of the Victorian era. In spite of the fact that women expressed discomfort with these treatments, they often deferred to their husbands and treaters as persons of ultimate knowledge and wisdom.

In reviewing women's first-person accounts of life in institutions in the mid-twentieth century, it seems that only the male treaters felt they knew best. Certainly Frances Farmer was critical of the decisions and actions of her treaters and staff and may have, in fact, suffered more because of her voiced criticisms.

In the detailed accounts of women victims of sexual abuse by out-patient psychotherapists more of the subtle but significant aspects of the asymmetrical power relationship between therapist and patient are evident. Women who were victims of previous abuse and/or suffered a severe mental illness were most vulnerable to therapist abuse. The abuse of these women often left greater scars, as the treatment relationship replicated the pain of the past. Women questioned their own judgment rather than that of the therapist, as the therapist-patient dyad replicated the father-daughter relationship and abuse was repeated.

She made me do it

The responsibility of the treater for perpetrating abuse or allowing abuse to be perpetrated is a complex issue. The physicians of the 1800's, who employed surgical and rest cures to treat women's illnesses, may bear less blame than the treaters of the 1990's, who actively sexually exploited their women patients, albeit in the name of "helping" them. Even though the goal of nineteenth century treaters was to "control" women's thinking, moods and sexuality, their interventions reflected acceptable practices of the time.

The notion that women's impaired functioning, sexually and otherwise, demands intervention was twisted in this century into a rationale to rape and engage women in sexual activity contraindicated by their illnesses and past histories of maltreatment. The issue of whether hospitalized women diagnosed with mental illnesses were capable of providing true informed consent to participate in sexual activities was obviously not considered by institution staff in the mid-twentieth century and all too often ignored by psychotherapists in the late-twentieth century.

Contemporary therapists have justified their misuse of women patients by invoking the empowerment rationale, i.e., patients should not be treated like babies who can not make up their own minds, or by suggesting that sexual interaction was an integral part of treatment. Women with mental illness, who were sexually mistreated in past relationships, have described their own judgment in relationship situations as impaired. These women required therapists who were extremely sensitive to issues of responsibility and true empowerment and capable of maintaining appropriate boundaries with their patients.

Conclusions

Throughout the nineteenth century, the best minds in American psychiatry and neurology repeatedly pointed out the inherent weakness of women.

> Isaac Ray: *"With women it is but a step from extreme nervous susceptibility to downright hysteria and from that to overt insanity. In the sexual evolution, in pregnancy, in the parturient period, in lactation, strange thoughts, extraordinary feelings, unreasonable appetites, criminal impulses, may haunt a mind at other times innocent and pure"* (Ray, 1866, p. 267).

> S. Weir Mitchell: *"At seventeen I presume that healthy girls are as well able to study, with proper precautions, as men; but before this time overuse, or even a very steady use, of the brain is in many dangerous to health and to every probability of future womanly usefulness"* (Mitchell, 1899, p. 35–36).

While perhaps well-meaning and probably in tune with the thinking of the era, such proclamations laid the groundwork for therapeutic interventions that were at their best demeaning, at their worst abusive. This mode of treating women did not disappear throughout most of the twentieth century.

Women patients, even women patients of the more illustrious of the nineteenth century alienists, tried to refute their treaters' pronouncements. They proclaimed their strengths and decried their treatments. Their voices went unheeded. They were, of course, not only women, but also insane women.

This theme is not simply a phenomenon of a century gone by. The issue remains alive today. Hearken to the voice of a contemporary woman.

157

"You file a sexual assault grievance against a MHP [mental health professional]. The investigation is as painful as the episode and you are depressed for days. But the examining board finds in his favour. You get the transcripts of the testimony. It's said that you have a personality disorder (news to you). It's said that you put people in no-win situations. Only he wins the suit and you've been losing all your life. It's his word against yours and you have a psychiatric label. He's the respected professional. You're only a CMI [chronically mentally ill].

"What have you learned as a CMI? Abuse. Physical, emotional, spiritual, sexual and financial. Vulnerability. Lack of credibility. Reduced to a three-letter acronym. Denied your own inner convictions. Frustrated. Stigmatized. Always wrong. Put in double binds.

"Until today. Today you speak out. Today you reclaim yourself. Today you begin to heal, to heal others. Today life begins anew ..." (Blaska, 1992, p. 285).

References

Anonymous. (1896) Confessions of a nervous woman. *Post Graduate Monthly. Journal of Medicine and Surgery*, 11, 364–368.

Arnold, W. (1978) *Frances Farmer: Shadowland*. New York: Berkley Publishing Corporation.

Barry, A. (1971) *Bellevue is a state of mind*. New York: Berkley Publishing Corporation.

Bates, C.M. and Brodsky, A.M. (1989) *Sex in the therapy hour*. New York: The Guilford Press.

Blaska, B. (1992) "What it feels like to be treated like a CMI – and 'prevail'-ing over it." *Changes: An International Journal of Psychology and Psychotherapy*, 10, 282–286.

Chesler, P. (1974) "Rape and psychotherapy." In N. Connell and C. Wilson (Eds.), *Rape: The sourcebook for women*. New York: New American Library.

Covan, F.L. and Kahn, C. (1994) *Crazy all the time: Life, lessons and insanity on the psych ward of Bellevue Hospital*. New York: Simon and Shuster.

Dally, A. (1991) *Women under the knife: A history of surgery*. New York: Routledge.

Deutsch, A. (1948) *The shame of the states*. New York: Harcourt, Brace and Company.

Farmer, F. (1972) *Will there really be a morning?* New York: Dell Publishing Co., Inc.

Freeman, L. and Roy, J. (1976) *Betrayal*. New York: Stein and Day.

Gartrell, N., Herman, J., Olarte, S., Feldstein M. and Localio, R. (1986) "Psychiatrist-patient contact: Results of a national survey." I: Prevalence. *American Journal of Psychiatry*, 143, 1126–1131.

Geller, J.L. and Harris, M. (1994) *Women of the asylum*. New York: Doubleday.

Gilman, C.P. (1892) "The yellow wallpaper." *New England Magazine*, 5, 647–656. Reprinted in 1973, New York: Feminist Press.

Goodell, W. (1882) "Clinical notes on the extirpation of the ovaries for insanity." *American Journal of Insanity*, 38, 294–302.

Gorton, E. (1894) "A case of insanity due to the menstrual function – oophorectomy – recovery." *Medical Record*, 46, 235–236.

Herman, J.L., Gartrell, N., Olarte, S., Feldstein, J. and Localio, R. (1987) "Psychiatrist-patient sexual contact: Results of a national survey." II: Psychiatrists' attitudes. *American Journal of Psychiatry*, 144, 164–169.

Levick, J.J. (1893) Correspondence to Dr. Morton. *American Journal of Insanity*, 49, 514.

Masserman, J. (1994) *Sexual accusations and social turmoil*. Oakland, California: Regent Press.

Mitchell, S.W. (1878) *Fat and blood and how to make them*. Philadelphia: J.B. Lippincott and Co.

Mitchell, S.W. (1885) *Lectures on diseases of the nervous system, especially in women*. Philadelphia: Lea Brothers and Co.

Mitchell, S.W. (1899) *Wear and tear or hints for the overworked*. Philadelphia: J.B. Lippincott.

Morton, T.G. (1893) "Removal of the ovaries as a cure for insanity." *American Journal of Insanity*, 49, 397–401.

Noel, B. and K. Watterson. (1992) *You must be dreaming*. New York: Poseidon Press.

Nugent, C.D. (1994) "Blaming the victims: Silencing women sexually exploited by psychotherapists." *The Journal of Mind and Behavior*, 15, 113–138.

Plasil, E. (1985) *Therapist*. New York: St. Martin's.

Ray, I. (1866) "The insanity of women produced by desertion or seduction." *American Journal of Insanity*, 23, 263–274.

Solomon, H.C. (1958) "The American Psychiatric Association in relation to American psychiatry." *The American Journal of Psychiatry*, 115, 1–9.

Stone, I.S. (1891) "Can the gynecologist aid the alienist in institutions for the insane?" *Journal of the American Medical Association*, 16, 870–872.

Storer, H.R. (1870) "Notes on the relations of the female sexual organs to mental disease." *Gynaecological Society of Boston*, 2, 290–304.

159

Storer, H.R. (1871) *Causation, course and treatment of reflex insanity in women.* Boston: Lee and Shepard, Publishers.

Strean, H.S. (1993) *Therapists who have sex with their patients: Treatment and recovery.* New York: Brunner/Mazel, Inc.

Trumpe, P. (1991) *Doctors who rape.* Wakefield, New Hampshire: Longwood Academic Press.

Walker, E. and Young, P.D. (1986) *A killing cure.* New York: Henry Holt and Company.

Chapter Eight

On Being Invisible in the Mental Health System

Ann Jennings

"... You're constantly being bumped against by those of poor vision. Or again, you often doubt if you really exist. You wonder whether you aren't simply a phantom in other people's minds. Say, a figure in a nightmare which the sleeper tries with all his strength to destroy. It's when you feel like this that, out of resentment, you begin to bump people back. And let me confess, you feel that way most of the time. You ache with the need to convince yourself that you do exist in the real world, that you're a part of all the sound and anguish and you strike out with your fists, you curse and you swear to make them recognize you. And, alas, it's seldom successful." (Invisible Man," by Ralph Ellison, 1947)

This chapter tells the story of my daughter Anna's sexual abuse as a child and subsequent experiences as a chronically mentally ill client in the mental health system. Information from 17 years of mental health records and anecdotal accounts are used to illustrate the effects of the abuse, her attempts to reach out for help and the system's failure to respond. There is evidence that a significant subset of psychiatric patients were severely sexually traumatized in childhood. Yet standard interview schedules consistently neglect to ask questions about such abuse, appropriate treatment is seldom available and clients are often retraumatized by current practices. Psychiatry's historic resistance to addressing abuse as etiology is being challenged today by economic, political and professional forces. The basic assumption that mental illness is biological or genetic in origin and is therefore treatable primarily by symptom control or management is being brought into question. The following "case study" of my daughter Anna demonstrates the need for inclusion in the field of an additional view of the etiology of mental illness. Forces supporting the emergence of a new trauma paradigm are highlighted.

Anna's story

From the age 13 to her recent death at the age of 32, Anna was viewed and treated by the mental health system as "severely and chronically mentally ill." Communication about who she was, how she was perceived and treated and how she responded, took place through her mental health records. A review of 17 years of these records reveal her described in terms of diagnoses, medications, "symptoms," behaviors and treatment approaches. Unresponsive to treatments proffered her, she was consistently termed "noncompliant" or "treatment resistant." Initially recorded childhood history was dropped from her later records. Her own insights into her condition were not noted.

When she was 25, Anna was reevaluated after a suicide attempt. For a brief period, she was rediagnosed as suffering from acute depression and a form of post-traumatic stress disorder. This was the only time in her mental health career that Anna agreed with her diagnosis. She understood herself – not as a person with a "brain disease," but as a person who was profoundly hurt and traumatized by the "awful things" that had happened to her.

What happened to Anna?

Anna was born in 1960, the third of five children, a beautiful healthy baby with a wonderful disposition. At the age of about two and a half, she began to scream and cry inconsolably. At four, we took her to a child psychiatrist who found nothing wrong with her. When we placed her in nursery school, her problems seemed to lessen.

162

That Anna was being sexually abused and traumatized at the time is clear now, verified in later years by her own revelations and by the memories of others. Her memories of abuse by a male babysitter were vivid, detailed and consistent in each telling over the years. They were further verified by persons close to the perpetrator and his family, one of whom witnessed the perpetrator years later in the act of abusing another child.

Anna described the experience of being forcibly restrained and sexually violated at the age of about three and a half: "He tied me up, put my hands over my head, blindfolded me with my little T-shirt, pulled my T-shirt over my head with nothing on below, opened my legs and was examining and putting things in me and all that ... Ugh. It hurt me. I would cry and he wouldn't stop. To do that when I was a little kid was like ... uh, I don't know. It made me feel pretty bad. I remember after he did that I was walking toward the door out of the room and I was feeling like I was bad. And why not Sarah and Mary (her older and younger sisters) and why just me? And I had this feeling in me that I was bad you know ... a bad seed ... and that I was the only one in the world ..."

Evidence that Anna was betrayed and sexually violated at an even earlier age by another perpetrator, a relative, came to light eventually through the revelations of a housekeeper whom Anna had confided in at the time. She had told this woman that a man "played with her where he wasn't supposed to," and the man "hurted her." This abuse was kept secret for nearly 30 years.

Anna remembers trying to tell us, as a little child, what was happening, but there was no one to hear or respond. When she told me a man "fooled" with her, I assumed she meant a young neighborhood boy and cautioned his parents. When we took her to a physician, she experienced the physical examination as yet another violation. "I remember the doctor you took me to when I told you. He did things to me that were disgusting (pointing to her genital area)."

The trauma Anna experienced was then compounded by the silence surrounding it. She tried to communicate with her rage, her screams and her terror. She became the "difficult to handle" child. Her screaming and crying were frequently punished by spankings and confinement to her room. No one then could see or hear her truth; sexual abuse did not "exist" in our minds. When later, as a young girl, she withdrew within herself, somehow "different," and "apart" from her peers, we attributed it to her artistic talent or independent personality. We did not see or attend to the terror, dissociation, loneliness and isolation expressed in her drawing, nor did we heed the hints of trouble expressed by her behaviors. Two grade school psychologists were alone among the professionals we encountered in sensing the turbulence underneath her silence. One reported, "Anna is confused about her sexual identity. You must help her." The other wrote, "It would seem that Anna has suppressed or repressed traumatic incidents."

Chaos and parental conflict existed in Anna's family from the age of 11 to 13. Though her four brothers and sisters survived the multiple geographic moves, alternative lifestyles, disintegration of their parent's marriage and episodic violence and alcoholism, Anna did not. She "broke" at the age of 13. A psychiatrist prescribed Haldol to "help her to sleep." She suffered a seizure in reaction, requiring emergency hospitalization. Thus, was she introduced to the mental health system.

Annas invisibility in the mental health system

Anna was a client of the mental health system for 19 years, until age 32. For nearly 12 of those years, she was institutionalized in psychiatric hospitals. When in the community, she rotated in and out of acute psychiatric wards, psychiatric emergency rooms, crisis residential programs and locked mental facilities. Principal diagnoses found in her charts included: Borderline Personality with Paranoid and Schizotypal Features, Paranoia, Undersocialized Conduct Disorder Aggressive type and various types of Schizophrenia including Paranoid, Undifferentiated, Hebephrenic and Residual. Paranoid Schizophrenia was her most prominent diagnosis. Chronic with acute exacerbation, subchronic and chronic courses of Schizophrenia were identified. Symptoms of Anorexia, Bulimia and Obsessive Compulsive Personality were also recorded. Treatments included family therapy, vitamin and nutritional therapy, Insulin and Electroconvulsive "therapy," psychotherapy, behavioral therapy, art, music and dance therapies, psycho-social rehabilitation, intensive case management, group therapy and every conceivable psycho-pharmaceutical treatment including Clozaril. Ninety-five percent of the treatment approach to her was the use of psychotropic drugs. Though early on there were references to dissociation and though Anna articulated details of childhood and adult sexual assault experiences, her mental health records contain no information about or attempts to elicit the existence of a history of such trauma.

Anna was 22 when she learned, through conversation with other patients who had also been sexually assaulted as children, that she wasn't "the only one in the world." It was then that she was first able to describe to me the details of her abuse. This time, with awareness gained over the years, I was able to hear her.

Events finally became understandable. Sexual torture and betrayal explained her constant screaming as a toddler, her improvement in nursery school and the reemergence of her disturbance at puberty. It explained the tears in her paintings, the content of her "delusions," her image of herself as shameful, her self-destructiveness, her involvement in prostitution and sadistic relationships, her perception of the world as deliberately hurtful, her isolation and her profound lack of trust. I thought with relief and with hope, that now we knew why treatment had not helped. Here at last was a way to understand and help her heal.

The reaction of the mental health system was to ignore this information. When I or Anna would attempt to raise the subject, a look would come into the professionals' eyes, as if shades were being drawn. If notes were being taken, the pencil would stop moving. We were pushing on a dead button. This remained the case until she took her life, 10 years and 15 mental hospitals later.

There was one exception. When Anna was 25 years old, the chief psychologist on a back ward of a state hospital listened to her after a suicide attempt and took what she told him seriously. He initiated a new treatment approach which addressed her experiences of sexual abuse. Antidepressant medication was prescribed, but neuroleptic drugs were viewed as suppressing the thought processes and emotions she needed to feel fully in order to begin healing. Rather than relying on drugs as a solution to escalating stress, Anna was helped through these crises and taught how to deal with them. Art "therapy" was de-emphasized and art lessons were begun, building her artistic talent and increasing her self esteem. Discussions began about what she needed in order to leave the hospital and live in the community.

This situation was not to last. The state hospital was closed because of rampant and intractable abuse. Anna's treatment team disbanded. She returned to the system of public mental institutions and community mental health agencies, a world where she was – once again – invisible and undefended. In and out of the "protected environments" of mental health institutions, she repeatedly experienced coerced or manipulated sex, verbal and physical abuse and rape. When she "broke," she became like a three or four year old consumed by rage and terror in the face of sexual invasion. The thoughts, voices and nightmares that tormented her were sexual and torturing in nature. Violent itches, twitching, stabbing pains, ice cold spots and innumerable other somatic symptoms invaded her slight body.

Over her remaining years, in community agencies, acute psychiatric hospitalizations, medical and psychiatric emergency rooms and the back wards of state mental institutions, she experienced night terrors and insomnia; fears of being taken over by outside forces and of "becoming someone else"; voices telling her she was evil, commanding her to be raped and punished; and eating disorders, dysmenorrhea and amenorrhea. She painted self-portraits covered with tears, bodies in bondage without hands or arms and images of multiple persons and sexual acts. She was plagued by intrusive thoughts of abusing her own child, of being tortured, of being "seen" naked by everybody and of people "getting off sexually" on her torment.

She would often "flashback" into experiencing her childhood trauma, screaming in terror and pleading for help. On one such occasion I went with her to a psychiatric emergency service. Calmed enough to answer questions, she stated her diagnosed to be "Post Traumatic Stress Disorder." The psychiatrist seemed to be recording this information on the form, when my daughter went over and looked at what she had written, turned to me and said, "Mom, she wrote down 'schizophrenic'.

She disclosed in words and behavior fragmented details of the "awful things" that had happened to her. Once while in restraints she screamed over and over again, I'm just a sex object, I'm nothing but

166

a sex object." She told her therapist of the "voices" inside her saying, "I'm a very young person," "I want you to help me," and "the baby is crying." Once she called her therapist late at night, pleading for her to come to the hospital because "the baby wants to talk to you." Permission was denied by the psychiatrist in charge.

Believing herself to be "bad," "disgusting" and "worthless," as child sexual abuse victims often do, she hurt, mutilated and repeatedly revictimized herself. She put cigarettes out on her arms, legs and genital area, bashed her head with her fists and against walls, cut deep scars in herself with torn-up cans, stick hangers, pencils and other sharp objects up her vagina, swallowed tacks and pushed pills into her ears, attempted to pull her eyes out, forced herself to vomit, dug her feces out so as to keep food out of her body, stabbed herself in the stomach with a sharp knife and paid men to rape her.

Again and again, as victims of sexual assault often do, Anna sought relief through suicide. She tried to kill herself many times – slashing her wrists, attempting to drown herself, taking drug overdoses, poisoning herself by spraying paint and rubbing dirt into self-inflicted wounds, slitting her throat with a too dull razor and hanging herself from the pipes of a state hospital. She dared men to kill her – on one occasion by throwing her off a bridge and on another by stepping on her back to break it. Many times she would have succeeded had it not been for outside interventions or her own fears of dying or eternal damnation.

Many of the mental health professionals she encountered were highly skilled in their disciplines. Many genuinely cared for Anna. Some grew to love her. But in spite of their caring, her experience with the mental health system was a continuing reenactment of her original trauma. Her perception of herself as "bad," "defective," a "bad seed" or an evil influence on the world, was reinforced by a focus on her pathologies, a view of her as having a diseased brain, heavy reliance on psychotropic drugs and forced control and the silence surrounding her disclosures of abuse.

In the months prior to her death, Anna and I began to reconstruct her story. She completed more than two hundred pages of detailed memories of her childhood from birth to age 15. In her own words, including her writings and artwork and the memories of her brothers, sisters and others who had been close to her, she spoke her truth. "Mom," she said, "I'm gonna try not to live in these places, because I want to get my life – find some friends – get out some day. Maybe this book will help. Maybe someone will come along and understand me. And they won't just say 'drugs, drugs, drugs!' " She gave her doctor a draft of her book. It was never read.

Just four days after her thirty-second birthday, after another haunted sleepless night, she hung herself, by her T-shirt, in the early morning bleakness of her room in a California State Mental Hospital. She was found by a team of three night staff who were on their way in to give her another shot of medication.

The wall of silence and invisibility

The tragedy of Anna's life is daily replicated in the lives of many individuals viewed as "chronically and severely mentally ill." Unrecognized and untreated for their childhood trauma, they repeatedly cycle through the system's most expensive psychiatric emergency, acute inpatient and long term institutional services. Their disclosures of sexual abuse are discredited or ignored. As happened during their early childhood, they learn within the mental health system to keep silent.

Clinicians who acknowledge the prevalence of traumatic abuse and recognize its etiological and therapeutic significance, are deeply frustrated at being denied the tools and support necessary to respond adequately. Sometimes, as Anna's psychologist did, these clinicians leave the mental health system entirely, deciding they can no longer practice with integrity within it.

A seemingly impenetrable wall of silence isolates the reality and impact of childhood sexual abuse from the consciousness of the public mental health system. No place exists within the system's formal information management structures to receive this data from clients. We do not elicit the information, nor do we record it. Yet to respond therapeutically without such knowledge is analogous to "treating a Vietnam veteran without knowing about Vietnam or what happened there" (Gise and Paddison, 1988). Why, with childhood sexual abuse an open issue for discussion and treatment elsewhere, is it not addressed in the public mental health system.

A paradigmatic explanation: the inability to see

"... I am invisible, understand, simply because people refuse to see me. Like the bodiless heads you see sometimes in circus sideshows, it is as though I have been surrounded by mirrors of hard, distorting glass. When they approach me, they see only my surrounding, themselves, or figments of their imagination – indeed, everything and anything except me ... That invisibility to which I refer occurs because of a peculiar disposition of the eyes of those with whom I come in contact. A matter of the construction of their inner eyes, those eyes with which they look through their physical eyes upon reality ..." ("Invisible Man," by Ralph Ellison, 1947) (Author's underlines)

Although rehabilitative, psycho-therapeutic and self-help approaches operate within the system, the dominant paradigm within which these approaches operate is clearly that of biological psychiatry.

Thomas Kuhn (1972), in his analysis of the history and development of the natural sciences, brought the concept of "paradigm" into popular usage. He defined "paradigms" as the conceptual networks through which scientists view the world." Data that agrees with the scientists' conceptual network is seen with clarity and understanding. But unexpected "anomalous" data which does not match the scientific paradigm is frequently "unseen," ignored or distorted to fit existing theories.

In the field of mental health, a biologically based understanding of the nature of "mental illness" has for years been the dominant paradigm. It has determined the appropriate research questions and methodologies, the theories taught in universities and applied in the field, the interventions, treatment approaches and programs used and the outcomes seen to indicate success.

Paradigmatically understood, the mental health system was constructed to view Anna and her "illness" solely through the conceptual lens of biological psychiatry. The source of her pain, early childhood sexual abuse trauma, was an anomaly – a contradiction to the paradigm and as such could not be seen through this lens. Her experience did not match the professional view of mental illness. It did not fit within the system's prevailing theoretical constructs. There was not adequate language available within the professions to articulate or label it. There were not reimbursement mechanisms to cover its "treatment." It was not addressed in curricula for professional training and education, nor was there support for research on the phenomena. There were no tools – treatment, rehabilitation or self-help interventions, for responding to it. And there was no political support within the field or from advocacy groups for its inclusion. Screened through the single lens of the biological paradigm, Anna's experience could not be assimilated. It had to be "unseen," rejected or distorted to fit within the parameters of the accepted conceptual framework.

As a result of this paradigmatic "blindness," conventionally accepted psychiatric practices and institutional environments repeatedly retraumatized Anna, reenacting and exacerbating the pain and sequel of her childhood experience. The following table illustrates that retraumatization.

Institutional retraumatization

Early Childhood Trauma Experience	Common Mental Health Institutional Practices
Unseen/Unheard	
Anna's child psychiatrist did not inquire into or see signs of sexual trauma. Anna misdiagnosed.	Adult psychiatry does not inquire into, see signs of or understand sexual trauma. Anna misdiagnosed.
Anna's attempts to tell parents, others adults, met with denial and silencing.	Reports of past and present abuse ignored, disbelieved, discredited. Interpreted as delusional. Silenced.
Only two grade school psychologists saw trauma. Their insight ignored by parents.	Only two psychologists saw trauma as etiology. Their insight ignored by psychiatric system.
Secrecy: those who knew of abuse did not tell. Priority was to protect self, family relationships, reputations.	Institutional secretiveness replicates family's. Priority is to protect institution, jobs, reputations. Patient abuse not reported up line. Public scrutiny not allowed.

Perpetrator retaliation if abuse revealed.	Patient or staff reporting of abuse is retaliated against.
Abuse occurred at pre-verbal age. No one saw the sexual trauma expressed in her childhood behavior and artwork.	No one saw the sexual trauma expression in her adult "symptoms" or artwork, with the exception of one art therapist.

Trapped

Unable to escape perpetrators' abuse. Dependent as child on family, caregivers.	Unable to escape institutional abuse. Locked up in co-ed wards, defenseless against male staff and patient perpetrators. Kept dependent: denied education or skill development.

Sexually Violated

Abuser stripped Anna, pulled T-shirt over her head.	Stripped of clothing when secluded or restrained, often by or in presence of male attendants.
Stripped by abuser to "with nothing on below."	To inject with medication, patients' pants pulled down exposing buttocks and thighs, often by male attendants.
"Tied up," held down, arms and hands bound.	"Take down," "restraint"; arms and legs shackled to bed.
Abuser "blindfolded me with my little T-shirt."	Cloth would be thrown over Anna's face if she spit or screamed while strapped down in restraints.
Abuser "opened my legs."	Forced 4-point restraints in spread eagle position.

171

Abuser "was examining and putting things in me."	Medication injected into her body against her will.
Boundaries violated. Exposed. No privacy	No privacy from patients or staff. Co-ed wards. Staff free to walk in room anytime. No boundaries.

Isolated

Taken by abuser to places hidden from others.	Forced, often by male attendants, into seclusion room.
Isolated in her experience: "why just me?	Separated from community in locked facilities.
"I thought I was the only one in the world."	No recognition or validation of patients' sexual abuse experiences.

Blamed and Shamed

I had "this feeling that I was bad … a bad seed."	Patients stigmatized as deficient; mentally ill, worthless. Abusive institutional practices and ugly environments convey low regard for patients, tear down self-worth.
She became the "difficult to handle" child.	She became a "noncompliant," "treatment resistant" difficult to handle patient.
She was blamed, spanked, confined to her room for her anger, screams and cries.	Her rage, terror, screams and cries were often punished by meds, restraint, loss of "privileges" and seclusion.

Controlled

Perpetrator had absolute power/control over Anna.	Institutional staff had absolute power/control over Anna.
Pleas to stop violation were ignored. "It hurt me. I would cry and he wouldn't stop."	Pleas and cries to stop abusive treatment, restraint, seclusion, over medication, etc., commonly ignored.

Expressions of intense feelings, especially anger directed at parents, were often suppressed.

Intense feelings, especially anger at those with more power (all staff) suppressed by medication, isolation, restraint.

Unprotected

Anna was defenseless against perpetrator abuse. Her attempts to tell went unheard. There was no safe place for her even in her own home or room.

Mental patients defenseless against staff abuse. Reports disbelieved. No safeguards effectively protect patients. Personnel policies prevent dismissal of abusive staff.

Threatened

As child, constant threat of being sexually violated.

As mental patient, constant threat of being stripped, thrown into seclusion, restrained, over medicated. Sexual violation common.

Discredited

As a child, Anna's reports of sexual assault were unheard, minimized or silenced.

As a mental patient, Anna's reports of sexual assault were not believed. Reports of child sexual abuse were ignored.

Crazy-Making

Appropriate anger at sexual abuse, seen as something wrong with Anna. Abuse continued-unseen.

Appropriate anger at abusive institutional practices, judged pathological. Met with continuation of practices.

Anna's fear from threat of being abused was not understood. Abuse continued-unseen.

Fear of abusive and threatening institutional behavior is labeled "paranoia" by the institution producing it.

Sexual abuse unseen or silenced. Message: "you did not experience what you experienced."

Psychiatric denial of sexual abuse. Message to patient: "you did not experience what you experienced."

Betrayed

Anna violated by trusted caretakers and relatives.	Anna retraumatized by helping professionals/psychiatry.
Disciplinary interventions were "for her own good."	Interventions presented as "for the good of the patient."
Family relationships fragmented by separation, divorce. Anna had no one to trust and depend on.	Relationships of trust are arbitrarily disrupted based on needs of system. No continuity of care or caregiver.

The effect of this institutional retraumatization was to continually leave Anna "in a condition that fulfilled the prophecy of her pathology" (Stefan, 1993). This was especially true in the use of psychotropic medication. Survivors of trauma tell us the capacity to think and to feel fully is essential for recovery. Psychotropic drugs continually robbed Anna of these capacities. Several years ago, she had been through a crisis period without medication. For days following, she asked for me to hold her. She talked softly about her feelings, crying gently, showing trust through touching and hugs. One day after her newly prescribed meds were beginning to "take effect," she said to me with a flatter voice and her eyes again haunted. "Mom, the feeling of love is going away." As her feelings of rage, grief and terror were suppressed, so were her feelings of love, laughter, caring and intimacy, isolating her again from herself and from others and preventing the possibility of healing.

Medication can be helpful if used cautiously, with the full understanding and consent of the patient. But without particular knowledge of the kinds of medications which can alleviate symptoms and facilitate recovery from trauma, medications can cause incalculable damage. For Anna, the system's reliance on psycho-pharmaceutical treatment was a metaphor for her original trauma. As sexual assault had violated physical and psychological boundaries of self, forced neuroleptic drugs also intruded past boundaries, invading, altering and disabling her mind, body and emotions. She once said to me, "I don't have a safe place inside myself."

The emerging paradigm- or- nescience: the decision not to know

Although the established paradigm may help to alleviate the suffering of those whose mental illness is strictly genetic or biological in nature, it failed Anna and it continues to fail a significant group whose histories contain sexual and/or physical trauma. Rising cognizance of this failure is one of several factors currently impacting on the mental health field, indicating the need for a new paradigm, based on trauma, to emerge. Resistance to such a paradigm has been extraordinary. Why, despite evidence that a significant number of psychiatric patients were sexually abused in childhood, is this information still "taboo" in the public mental health field?

The following statement was made several years ago, to a consumer, by the chair of a major city's public mental health advisory board: "You know why there are 'chicken hawks' (pedophiles) don't you? It's because there are so many chickens running around." The consumer, a young man labeled manic depressive, had just spoken before the board, disclosing how he had been raped by his father at the age of three and by his stepfather at the age of thirteen. He expressed concern that the issue of childhood sexual assault was not being addressed anywhere by the system. He spoke of how it was a significant factor in his own illness and that of many other clients in the system. He though that, surely, his concerns would be shared by other advocates. He was mistaken. Board members responded by attacking his judgment, discrediting his concerns, or ignoring him altogether. He was met with averted eyes, disavowal and ridicule, then was blamed for his own victimization. He never broached the subject publicly again.

Although today his disclosure would more than likely not be responded to with such open hostility, this incident demonstrates the aversion which often meets any discussion of childhood sexual abuse when related to mental illness. Resistance to a sexual abuse trauma paradigm has existed in the field for over 130 years, during which time the etiological role of childhood sexual violation in mental illness has been alternately discovered then denied. In 1860, the prevalence and import of child sexual abuse was exposed by

Amboise Tardieu (Masson, 1984), in 1896 by Sigmund Freud (Freud, 1896), in 1932 by Sandor Ferenczi (Ferenczi, 1932), in 1962 (Kempe, Silverman and Steele, 1962) and 1984 (Kempe R and Kempe C, 1984) by C. Henry Kempe. Each exposure was met by the scientific community with distaste, rejections or discreditation. Each revelation was countered with arguments which in essence blamed the victims and protected the perpetrators. Freud, faced with his colleagues' ridicule of and hostility to his discoveries, sacrificed his major insight into the etiology of mental illness and replaced his theory of trauma by the view that his patients had "fantasized" their early memories of rape and seduction (Masson, 1984). Today, 100 years later, in spite of countless instances of documented abuse, this tradition of denial and victim-blame continues to thrive.

Paradigm shifts, though they mark the way to progress and opportunity, are always initially resisted. They cause change, disrupt the status quo, create tension and uncertainty and involve more work. Yet psychiatry and the mental health field's persistent reluctance to consider a sexual abuse trauma paradigm for understanding the experience of so many of its clients, is indeed extraordinary, a form of "madness" in inactivity. Psychiatrist Roland Summit refers to this denial as "nescience" or "deliberate, beatific ignorance." He proposes that "in our historic failure to grasp the importance of sexual abuse and our reluctance to embrace it now, we might acknowledge that we are not naively innocent. We seem to be willfully ignorant, "nescient." He adds, "Perhaps it is worth considering at this point that the complementary derivatives of the same root are 'conscience, conscientious, conscious, consciousness, science and omniscience' " (Summit, 1989).

The decision not to know extends beyond the mental health field and into the broader culture. People labeled "crazy" are thought of as aberrant – different from the rest of us – made deficient by some biological accident for which no one is responsible. The pervasiveness of the sexual abuse of children, the fact that it can result in such devastation to the human psyche and our complicity in the damage as witnesses or perpetrators, may be a reality too painful to contemplate and too dangerous to expose. "We are all players in a strange charade in which everyone assumes the role of the untouched," says psychiatrist Roland Summit. "Perpetrators circulate in unknown numbers, making policy and influencing opinion while a horde of survivors shrinks from one another as if each were the enemy. Some of those who assume they are untouched by sexual abuse are aggressively indifferent to the problem, protective of adults and judgmental of victims in order to distance themselves from their own hurt child imprisoned within. In the absence of someone to call roll and in the preservation of agonizing shame, each survivor exists as an alien hiding among an army of peers. If we could find the courage to face our superstitions head on, we would see that the apparitions veiled in the fog aren't really monsters at all. They are our children. They are us." (Summit, 1989).

Today's nescience in the public mental health field is also reflective of some current economic and political forces that pull toward short term, primarily pharmaceutical, solutions to manage spiraling costs in the mental health care industry and psychiatry's and the family movement's impetus to gain insurance parity for "mental illness" with other medical illnesses. Both these forces depend on adherence to the established bio-medical paradigm and its view of "mental illness" as biologically determined.

At this point in history however, multiple and divergent forces are confronting nescience with truth. Although these forces will continue to meet resistance, they appear to be forming a powerful movement which will help to protect children from adult violation and will promote acceptance of a trauma-based paradigm recognizing the pain of individuals like my daughter and offering them "the radical prospect of recovery." (Summit, 1989).

Acceptance of a new trauma paradigm: implications for the field

> "... I learned the virtues of memory as redemptive ... Only by remembering our pain, sadness, agony and the responses that we have invented, can we save ourselves and our children ... What more could you do for your patients, but help them regain their memory?" (Elie Wiesel, Childhood Trauma Symposium, Albert Einstein Center, Philadelphia, PA, October 7, 1988)

The continual re-emergence of a paradigm that acknowledges the significance of sexual abuse trauma in the lives of persons considered to be mentally ill – in spite of the extraordinary resistance with which it is, again and again, met – is indicative of its power and truthfulness. Mental health professionals, administrators and policy makers are in a unique position today to prevent the re-creation of tragedies such as my daughter Anna's. The tools and resources they need to do so can be found in the following forces supporting the emergence of the new trauma paradigm.

★ Among the most significant forces for change are the victims themselves. For the first time in history, survivors of sexual trauma are speaking out – revealing their experiences of having been sexually violated as children, lobbying politically for services and legislative action, challenging societal denial and nescience and keeping the reality of the sexual assault of children in the arena of public awareness.

★ Political support for a new trauma paradigm is growing as governmentally sanctioned committees are formed and local, state and federal governing bodies pass legislation requiring mental health systems to address issues of physical and sexual abuse trauma in their clients.

★ New therapeutic approaches to sexual and other trauma in people who are called seriously mentally ill, are being used and developed outside of and on the fringes of the public mental health system. Examples can be found in the dissociative disorder units of private psychiatric hospitals; in the work of art therapists using imagery and play therapy with traumatized children; in the treatment of severely traumatized war veterans; in the specialized victims and offenders services now serving severely mentally ill individuals; in incest survivor self-help groups; in rape treatment centers; increasingly in the field of child psychiatry; and in the work of private therapists.

★ Respected national and international professional associations focused on research and treatment of severely traumatized children and adults have formed over the last decade and networks of professionals, advocates and ex-patient survivors increasingly proliferate.

★ Women's rights and mental health litigators are being asked to recognize the connection between sexual violence, "craziness," and the treatment of women in psychiatric institutions. These connections are seen to have consequences for rights to treatment, rights to refuse treatment and forced medication and seclusion and restraint cases.

178

★ A powerful force for paradigmatic change at this time in history is the advent of health care reform, introducing managed care, captitation and the need for public mental health organizations to compete in providing quality services to consumers/survivors in a cost-effective way. Incorrect diagnoses and treatment exacerbate the condition of traumatized patients, making them dependent on the system's most restrictive and expensive services. An analysis of 17 years of Anna's records shows that she was hospitalized a total of 4,124 days. The total cost for this hospitalization, figured at $640 a day, was $2,639,360.00. This figure does not include residential treatment, case management, legal, medical and other costs estimated to be over $1,000,000, for a total cost of almost $4,000,000.00. With studies showing prevalence rates as high as 81% of hospitalized patients to have histories of sexual and/or physical trauma (Jacobson and Richardson, 1987), the fiscal implications to exploring a trauma paradigm are obvious.

★ Finally, a shift is occurring in the scientific field. The number of studies, instruments, articles, books and professional journals based on a trauma paradigm is multiplying, making visible the most hidden and most damaged victims of childhood sexual assault and heightening awareness of such anomalies to the psychiatric paradigm. Research findings showing inextricable connections between trauma, physiology and the brain are now pointing the way to new relationships between these areas of data under a trauma paradigm (van der Kolk, 1994). Research is revealing significantly higher prevalence rates of childhood sexual abuse among female psychiatric outpatients and inpatients (as high as 50 to 70%) (Briere and Runtz, 1991) than is found in the general population. Many of these clients require emergency, acute inpatient care and long term hospitalization services. The growing pool of data indicates that when trauma is recognized and responded to in specific therapeutic interaction, possibilities of recovery exist even for those survivors of sexual abuse who are viewed as schizophrenic, depressive, or borderline.

This is what I knew — that recovery was possible. It is what I hoped for my daughter and what she hoped for herself. It is what

---

★This article was previously published in *Journal of Mental Health Administration*, 1994, 21(4)

must be made possible for others like Anna, still hidden on the back wards of state mental institutions, in psychiatric emergency rooms and locked wards, in prisons, in seedy rooming houses, dangerous shelters and on even more dangerous city streets, dismissed as "crazy," with stories of abuse no one asks about, listens to, or believes.

References

Briere, J. and Runtz, M. (1991) "The long-term effects of sexual abuse: a review and synthesis", in *New Directions for Mental Health Services*, 51, 3–13.

Ferenczi, S. (1932) "Confusion of tongues between adults and the child: the language of tenderness and the language of [sexual] passion", [Masson, J.M., Loring, M., Trans.] In: Masson, J.M. (1984). *The assault on truth: Freuds suppression of the seduction theory*. New York: Farror, Straus and Girous, pp. 283-295, Appendix C.

Freud, S. (1896) "The aetiology of hysteria", [Translation by James Stachey] In: Masson, J.M. (1984). *The assault on truth: Freuds suppression of the seduction theory*. New York: Farror, Straus and Girous, pp. 252–282, Appendix B.

Gise, L.H. and Paddison, P. (1988) "Rape, sexual abuse and its victims" in *Psychiatric Clinics of North America*, 11, 629–648.

Jacobson, A. and Richardson, B. (1987) "Assault experiences of 100 psychiatric inpatients: evidence of the need for routine inquiry", in *American Journal of Psychiatry*, 144, 908–913.

Kempe, C.H., Silverman, F.N., Steele, B.F., *et al.* (1962) "The battered-child syndrome", in *Journal of the American Medical Association*, 181, 17–24.

Kuhn, T.S. (1972) *The structure of scientific revolutions*. Chicago: University of Chicago Press.

Masson, J.M. (1984) *The assault on truth: Freuds suppression of the seduction theory*. New York: Farror, Straus and Girous.

Stefan, S. (1993) *The protection racket: violence against women: psychiatric labeling and law*. Unpublished Manuscript, University of Miami.

Summit, R. (1989) "The centrality of victimization: regaining the focal point of recovery for survivors of child sexual abuse", in *Psychiatric Clinics of North America*, 12, 413–450.

van der Kolk, B.A. (1994) *The body keeps the score: memory and the evolving psychobiology of post traumatic stress*. Harvard Review of Psychiatry, 1, 253–265.

Chapter Nine

As Told To …

John D. Dende, Carolyn Duca, Margaret Hobbs and Christine L. Landis

T HE trauma stories that female survivors of abuse tell have a significant therapeutic role. The recounting of their trauma stories serves to acknowledge and verify women's experience. In writing the painful accounts, or telling them to a "safe" listener, a survivor may gain a sense of relief and control just by having her story expressed and believed. While some female survivors recount their stories for personal healing and recovery, others express a desire to pass on their stories as a way of sparing others from a similar fate. The timing of the disclosure, however, needs to be a woman's own. Pressure to recount past abuses may only serve to increase defenses and symptomatology. The role of the "witness" is to hear and support. To be believed is the single most important gift that can be given to any survivor of abuse.

The stories told in this chapter are of pain, grief, anger, numbness and near despair. They are stories of physical, sexual and psychological abuse. The women who chose to tell their histories are true survivors – survivors who continue to deal with past abuses on a regular basis, yet women who are reflective about their experiences and determined to move on. The abuse is woven into the fabric of their lives, a significant and influential part of who they are. It is their own strength and determination which have helped them to endure and given them a vision for a life free from victimization.

Each woman's story in this chapter is individual and unique. There are, however, similar elements that run through them: loss of innocence, threats of violence against them if the abuse is reported, the pain in telling others who do not believe and/or do nothing to stop the abuse, the self-destructiveness that results and the difficulty, in some cases, of establishing healthy, non-abusive relationships. Listen now, as they recount their experiences.

Sharon's story

As told to John D. Dende, M.A.

I'm a 36 year old gay African American female who has been sexually traumatized – raped – by my stepfather for seven years starting when I was eleven. Because of this trauma, I have felt like an outsider all my life.

My father died when I was one year old. For a long time I believed he would come back. It's sad living your life believing a dead person is going to save you.

On my eighth birthday my stepfather married my mother. Before my stepfather moved into our life, I went everywhere with my mother and was always around women.

My mother had a job that took her throughout the country. That left me and my stepfather alone a lot. He insisted I call him "mister." He drank quite a bit and became so nasty that his own two sons stopped coming around.

When I'd wrestle in the basement with my stepfather's sons, he would get angry. He would snatch me up and throw me and tell his sons "I better not see you like that again." We were confused; it wasn't anything sexual, just two little kids wrestling. The problem was that someone else was touching me and that was enough to trigger him. Once he almost killed his best friend for trying to touch me.

By the time I was eleven, when I started to develop as a young female, my stepfather began raping me. He started out showing me pornographic films. I really didn't want to see these films but I was forced to watch them. I was forced at gunpoint to watch these films. He fondled me, penetrated me and threatened me. I can remember the bleeding and the pain that I felt and I was real hurt. He said if I told my mother, he would kill me. I was scared more than anything else that I might cause him to shoot me. I never doubted that he would shoot me.

He justified his rapes by saying "I'm going to make it so you don't like women anymore. You're not supposed to like women." He knew I had infatuations for other girls. I was homosexual, something I knew from the second grade on, well before the rapes.

Sometimes I would go to my friend's house and wait until he went to work and my mother came home. But all throughout my adolescence he continued to have sex with me. I really don't remember exactly what he did. I just remember the sex, the forced sex. He would leave money on my dresser and tell my mother he gave me some money for doing something good in school.

I became disruptive in school hoping someone would ask me what was wrong. My mother took me to a psychiatrist, but the psychiatrist didn't understand because I couldn't talk to him. I was scared for my life. If I tell this doctor and he tells my mother, my mother might get hurt.

One teacher did spend extra time with me outside of class. She felt something was wrong, but I was too afraid. I never told her, but I told her it's at home; the problem is at home; I don't want to go home. I became attached to her. When she became pregnant, I got angry with her because this baby was going to take my place. People I get close to have either died or left my life somehow, but I do have a handful of friends today.

I have always used writing and painting as a way of unburdening myself. When the abuse started, I remember going to the office with my mother. She used to give me a desk by myself and I would draw pictures and write poetry. People in the office were impressed. They hung the pictures up. They took me to lunch. But no one figured out what I was trying to say.

I used to write weird stories in my diary and leave them in my drawer so my mother would find little hints of what I was trying to tell her. I would write that I'm not a virgin anymore, that someone is taking my body. My mother just thought I was having some sort of experience with a boy or girl in school. The other girls in my neighborhood were into dolls and such and I never was. I was one of the boys. I figured if I acted like them, they wouldn't think of me in a sexual way.

183

The neighborhood boys used to like that I could play rough stuff with them. What I was really doing was retaliating for the abuse that was happening at home and they never knew this.

I used to go to my (maternal) grandmothers' a lot just to get away from my stepfather; I would pack my bag and walk ten miles. My uncle was there; he was my age and I played football with him and watched him fight. I felt safe with him, but I wouldn't go up into his room when the other boys were there because I thought they would have sex with me. My grandmother drank a lot and I could do anything I wanted.

I have been able to talk about my homosexuality with my grandmother and she accepts me. She doesn't try to change me or tell me something is wrong with me because of the way I feel. My mother to this day has not accepted it.

I never had an opportunity to grow on my own. I would fight my stepfather and it still wouldn't do me any good. I was just a kid against this big man and thrown into a position which seemed hopeless. I wanted to die.

I felt like I really didn't exist. I felt like I was a "walking anything." I was dirty. I was bad. I remember fearing that the other kids would find out about me and spread it around. I had to miss my graduation from high school because I was out for some type of surgery. I don't even remember what part of my body the surgery was on. They mailed me my diploma.

I was dealing with a very sick individual and to me he's still sick because he has never owned up to the fact that this is something that he did. I know he's never going to do that, though, because he just feels he didn't do anything wrong. I guess he would lose out for real if he admitted it to my mother. I believe in my heart that my mother does know and does believe me. But she was sexually abused herself and hasn't really dealt with it.

I could never trust a man again, because of what had happened to me and I really didn't trust women either. I stayed away from everybody.

I was always afraid of being killed by him. One Saturday my stepfather's best friend and his wife and my mother were all in the basement, with their drinks and all, watching pornographic films. When they went downstairs, I had gotten into the tub to take a bath. When I came out, I had my robe on but I didn't have anything underneath my robe. My usual custom was to lie there in my room and thaw out before I put on lotion and underclothes.

So I was just laying on my bed. I thought it was my mother entering my room, but it was my stepfather's friend and I screamed and my stepfather came upstairs and beat him up. This man never touched me, but, he never had a chance to touch me because I screamed. Before he could get down the hallway, my stepfather was already there, in the room.

After my stepfather beat him up, my stepfather went and got the gun. He made his friend lay in the yard and he was getting ready to shoot him in the yard. He shot but he missed. If the man hadn't moved, my stepfather would have shot him. But by this time my mother told him please don't shoot him, don't shoot him – just let him go. "He's messing with my property." I felt like I was his property. I didn't feel human. I felt like a piece of property. If there was some way I could have gotten myself out of this I would have, but it never happened. I kind of thought, well, if he does this to his friend what would he do to me.

I asked my mother if I could go to my grandmother's for a few days. From what had happened she thought I was scared of that man, but she didn't know about her own husband.

I think I was about 15 or 16 when I had my first drink. Drink knocked me out and I didn't have to think about the pain anymore. If the memories started creeping into my mind, I got shaky and took a little drink here and there, but not every day. It was nasty, but it knocked me out and by the time I woke up my mother would be home. Or if she wouldn't be home I'd make sure to get out of the house because sometimes he would attack me after he came out of the shower. He would have sex with me, then he would go to work. I would make sure I was somewhere where he couldn't see me to tell me to come back to the house.

I chose to go away to college to get away from him and survive. I had a choice, a scholarship from three different schools. My mother wanted me to go to school around here. I chose a private girls' school far away in the South because I felt it would be safe there: among all women I would be okay. It was 99 percent white.

College was the one place that I did learn how to have some feelings for people and that it would be okay. I loved one woman there so much that I tried to break up any contact she had with men because I wanted her all to myself. She was my first love.

It became a little hard for both of us because she felt I wanted sex. When she approached me with it, I told her I loved her too much to do that to our relationship.

What I knew of relationships was that somebody just takes you whenever they want. I never had the opportunity early on to just grow on my own.

It's just recently I'm able to talk to somebody about having a relationship. I've lost a lot of "would-be" relationships because I couldn't respond to what some people would call natural feelings, spontaneous feelings. I would freeze up. And I would get angry. For a long time I wouldn't let anyone touch me or kiss me, even my family.

As I've been recollecting incidents of my life, I remember something really bad happened to me in college which I've never told anyone.

A friend of mine let me use her car to pick up some marijuana. On my way back the car stopped and at the time I didn't know much about cars.

This guy pulled up behind and he asked me what was the problem and said maybe you need a jump. So he went in his trunk and got a shotgun out and said you're going with me. I told him to kill me first and then do whatever he wanted to me. I said I could not live through this.

He took me to his apartment; it was all men in every chair, everywhere a man was sitting there. I was like, "Oh my goodness." I was like eighteen years old and all these men, they just wanted to "do" me. I thought I'd come to college for freedom and to escape all this. I was really scared; I guess he saw how really scared I was ... he apologized, then he took me back to my car. I was already a ball of nerves when I went to college. After this, I couldn't go to class and sit there because my nerves wouldn't let me. I had memories of what had happened to me.

My school advisor was a psychologist; I majored in psychology and I would ask to change classes, to get into classes where I might be able to concentrate better. I really was shit when I went to school.

I was put in a speech class. I told parts of my own story, but they just didn't know that it was my story.

One night I started hearing things and seeing things and thought people were chasing me. I was put in a hospital, put on tranquilizers that made me kind of half in and half out, so I had to take a tape recorder to class. I was doing other peoples' homework for them so they could graduate. I went to a therapist twice a week but I never told him about the abuse or the shotgun incident.

The woman I was in love with in college locked me out of the dorm room after an argument one night. She had some guys in the room. Later that night, I locked her in a closet and told her to do what I said or I would cut her up. I caught myself and said what am I doing? I love her. I tried to do everything in my power to show her I wouldn't hurt her. She helped me the most because she always stood by me. If I didn't have her I probably would never have gone back to classes.

I dropped out of college, but I didn't want to go back to my mother's. I joined the military and went to Panama. I thought of the military as a way out where I might actually get some of the tension away from me. I could be an aggressive soldier. Coming home or visiting relatives I could wear my uniform and look proud, feel proud.

My drill sergeant would stand right in front of me and call me all kinds of names and do things to intimidate me. I was so mad inside, but it didn't even phase me and she left me alone. She was the enemy like my stepfather was the enemy. I would look her dead in the eyes and I could see she couldn't take it. Sometimes people would catch me being in a trance, just staring. They thought I was different and strange.

There weren't many women in the military at that time. It was two years of loneliness. I was a damn good soldier. I was tough, real hard. If I had to do it over again, I would have gone to a therapist before going to the military and dealt with the things I hadn't dealt with growing up. I would have been able to function better as a soldier.

I really snapped when I went into the army. I lost it completely. I don't know what triggered it or anything. A lot of it is gone. All I remember is they put me in the hospital and I stayed there a long time.

187

I have blocked out so much, but a portion of me still knows I did this, I lived through this for all those years. I remember wondering whether it will stick to me so bad that I'll end up in institutions for the rest of my life. I guess if I didn't have certain nurses at the VA I probably would have stayed withdrawn and it would have hurt me mentally and physically for the rest of my life.

I returned to D.C. and stayed with my grandmother and grandfather. Some guys from the service came by and introduced me to crack cocaine and PCP. I had real bad flashbacks of seeing my stepfather having sex with me and I would fight the very guys who were drinking and smoking with me. I was going to be tough and show these people, these men especially, that I was not afraid of anything. I would hit them and that would start a fight.

I've fought many men, many men. I was asking for the fights. It was my way of releasing tension from being abused. I wanted to show a man that I could hurt him. I've fought many men and fortunately I've survived.

I can become dangerous. I've been in situations where I become very dangerous. I'm always the one they take away. They take me away every time. Fighting is one behavior I've learned to control over the years. Part of me still wants to fight and always will. Today I just walk away or ignore it. I write a lot in my journal. It helps me manage the rage I feel.

The first time I was put in a psychiatric hospital in D.C. was when I took a security guard's gun from him when he snatched me up by the collar. My first reaction was to take his gun. But I gave the gun to the store manager and walked on out and forgot all about it.

Forty-five minutes later the police came to get me and I didn't like the way they were handling me and I didn't know why they were coming to get me. I fought six police officers and fought them real good. I called my grandfather and he came and got me before they could put me in a room and give me Thorazine. I've been put in the hospital a lot of times for fighting.

When my grandmother died, my mother's mother, the one I always ran to, I started hearing the voices of my uncles and my cousins and my grandmother. After she died, I was 29 then, my grandfather wanted to have sex; he said it's just you and me now. I told him he was crazy and to get out of my face.

I never liked my grandfather from the start, but my mother always told me that no matter what he's still my grandfather; she would tell me I had to take care of him. And this was the man who had abused her.

Three years ago he came up to the room and tried to have sex with me. I screamed, I hollered for help because there were other people in the house, but no one did anything. I really felt betrayed by my uncle because he heard it and didn't do anything. At this time my uncle, the one I felt safe with when I was a kid, had – and still has – a bad cocaine habit and is living off my grandfather.

I had the same hatred for my grandfather that I had for my step-father. When I see my grandfather now, I really don't have any feel-ings, it's just total numbness toward him … like he's dead physically and I could look right through him and he's really not there. I just go there to protect my 13 year old cousin who lives with him. Nothing will happen to that girl as long as I'm alive.

I've called Child Protective Services. I let the whole family know I've been raped by my stepfather and grandfather and told them that if anything ever happens to me or my cousin, somebody is going to jail. You can throw me out of the family, whatever you want to do, but let it be known that I'm here. I'm not going to do like I did when I was a young girl and just clam up and go on with this thing for another twenty years. He is going to jail. My feelings have to be expressed and somebody is going to listen. It hasn't gone well with a lot of people, but they know where I stand today.

I am committed to helping my cousin grow and move on. She will not be touched until she wants to be touched by someone who's not in her family. If her mother and father want to get high all the time and leave her out, I'll take care of her the best I know how. I'll protect my cousin so that she doesn't become an abused young girl. I have survived and I will teach her how to survive.

Cheryl's story

As told to Carolyn Duca, M.S.W.
The first person narrative of trauma that follows is derived from a series of interviews with a woman whom the writer will refer to as Cheryl. Cheryl's account is a story both of incest and of abandonment. Cheryl's experiences of

being sexually abused by her father as a small child led inexorably to a pro-found and global sense of being left and alone. Despite the original link to sexual trauma, abandonment occupies a separate and distinct space in Cheryl's consciousness. Abandonment has taken on a life of its own and has become a source of trauma in its own right.

My dad was a music teacher. He played piano in bars and would get drunk all the time. When he would come home he would either yell and scream or would pick on my mom. I don't remember if he beat her. The first thing I remember him doing to me was knocking me out of my high chair after I wouldn't eat a plate of peas. I was around three years old. There were other abuses, but that was the first one that clearly sticks in my mind … also that I would always hide when my dad came around.

I guess he abused my mom too. I was four and a half years old when she first left him and we went to live with my grandparents. But then my mom decided she was going to try to get back with my dad, when I was maybe six years old. We went to where he lived. One day she left me with him while she went to get milkshakes down the street at a little store. While she was there he – you know – incest and all that.

I remember that I had been playing with clay when my father told me to come into the bedroom. Every time I think of it I see the multicolored clay. Then he asked me to suck on his you-know-what. It went further from there. It got worse. He actually entered me and all that stuff. I don't remember a lot of it but I do remember scream-ing and telling him "No!" and "This doesn't seem right" and "I don't think I'm supposed to do this with my father." He assured me that it was okay and normal and what was expected. So I did what he said. I was afraid so I just wanted to get it over with, whatever he wanted. I wanted my mother to come back from the store, you know. I felt I had to do it his way or I would be the biggest creep on earth or I would feel guilty if I didn't do it. I already felt guilty if I *did* do it, but he was bigger than me. And he had hit me before. I can't remember everything but I do remember this incident. I know there were more, especially when he was drunk.

My mother came in on it. She caught him. I remember them fighting – they screamed and yelled. I went back into another room. Then I guess she called the police. So, we ended up in night court. I remember sitting and playing with something on the judge's bench or desk. I don't know why he never went to jail. He was a veteran and he always ended up in the VA hospital.

This wasn't the first time either. It had happened before, but my mother didn't believe me. I had told a lady at our church that my father had done something. This lady confronted my mother. But then my mother left me there alone with him anyway. I guess she didn't feel or think anything of it. I resent her for that now. But, in my heart, I wanted it to work between my parents so I tried not to be afraid and I tried to act like it didn't happen.

After that my mom never went back with my dad. We went back to live with my grandparents. But my father used to like to watch me at school and I used to get scared. Then, he started molesting other children. There used to be things in the paper about my father. I had to live through this with the kids in the class and everything. I was afraid of my dad and the kids teased me. They would call me names. Even though what the kids called me was stupid, I took it to heart.

We felt deserted because my father didn't pay child support and there wasn't a lot of money. My mother worked in a factory. She wasn't very well educated. I think she's autistic and others in my family say that she's autistic. She didn't have the ability to love me then so I felt deserted by her. I did have my grandparents and if it wasn't for them I think I would have died. But they didn't really want me either and I knew that, so I always felt like I was on tiptoes. In addition, I didn't understand why my father deserted me. I recall this stuff that happened but as a kid you don't realize how terrible it is and why your mother won't let you see your father. I always felt abandoned and I still sometimes do. I do a lot.

When I was a teenager, I didn't want my mother to tell me I was just like my father so it was important to me to be the best that I could be. So I joined the Seventh Day Adventist Church. They were as strict as they could be – they don't smoke and they don't drink. All my efforts were geared toward entering their Academy. I was so glad to get away from my home because of all this stuff. At age 14 I went to the Junior Academy and when I was 16, I went to the Boarding Academy and stayed overnight. I tried to do everything right. I was what you would call a hyper-vigilant person because

191

I didn't want my mom to say I was just like my father. I look like my dad. My dad has blonde hair and blue eyes. My mom has black hair and brown eyes.

So, I always felt deserted, like I was no good and like my mother was waiting for something awful to happen, so I had to keep going and going and going. I got through high school, then college. After I was married, when I was 23 years old, I started having problems.

At first the problems were chemical. Premenstrual syndrome (PMS) was part of it but they hardly knew anything about PMS back then. So even though I'm Bipolar, the PMS made it worse. I was finally diagnosed with PMS about seven years after I had been treated for all kinds of other things and the medicines weren't working. At times I wouldn't take the medicines because they would make me sick. They put me on drugs that I was allergic to like Lithium. It made me have diarrhea and some of the meds made me hallucinate. This affected my marriage really badly because I had been a strong and regular and stable person until then. Then I became inconsistent. Several times I was suicidal. I scared myself. But we got through it for 11 years. I was married for 11 years. Finally, because I thought I was a nut, a *real* nut that wasn't going to get cured, I kicked my husband out of the house. I just told him to leave and told him it was his fault. After I divorced my husband, they tried me on a MAO inhibitor. That made me hallucinate and it made me feel higher than God. One February weekend, when I was out of it, I married this foreign guy. At the time he was like my Persian fantasy. The relationship lasted only two weeks. I think that had to do with the drugs. I can't believe that I married this guy. I'm still married to him and I know I need to get this fixed but I'm afraid to do so because he's an illegal alien. So I just don't do anything about it.

I always ended up having to talk with therapists because my mom is not able to deal with emotions at all. She's very hard. She's always saying "Don't blame it on me." I bring her a problem and she says that it's not her fault and she doesn't want to hear it. For three years I didn't talk to her at all, I just said goodbye to her because she was being ridiculous. I got tired of all the bad feelings she gave to me or put on me. She would visit me and always tell me what she didn't want, but never what she wanted.

I've had a lot of different therapists. The reason I started in therapy was because I wasn't able to take things to my mom and talk to her about them without her getting defensive and saying that I should have a therapist to talk to. I'm sorry I always have to have therapists and that therapists always leave. I have this really hard problem because it always feels like they die. Like to me, they really do die. I had the same therapist for 10 years. We were friends before she was my therapist. I had a really hard time because I was into music and I expected her to be my manager. I had these expectations that she didn't have so I feel like I wasted 10 years. I hate dealing with therapists. I wish I didn't have to, I wish they didn't leave and I wish that once they left I wasn't totally nothing.

Every time a therapist leaves it just feels like another abandonment, so I relive all of my losses. I relive them all and feel all of the old pain. I ended up in the hospital three times – before it was all over – when my first therapist left. I was somewhat autistic before I had her as a therapist and she helped me to be able to be touched. My husband and I didn't have any children and we were married for 11 years. What happened to me as a child affected my sex life. I was always finding a reason not to be in the same room or in bed with my husband. Unfortunately he had a problem too, so it wasn't hard for him not to be in the same room as me. We were more like brother and sister. Later, after my husband and I were divorced, I experimented with sadomasochistic sex (S&M) because I had these feelings that I was no good. Part of me always thinks I need to be beaten and I went through a period of time where I beat myself. My mom was a beater. Back then I thought that all parents beat their kids so I never thought my mother was abusive. Anyway, I wasn't altogether sure what S&M was but reading it was the only thing that would turn me on. I finally grew out of it and realized that I only enjoyed reading it, not being a part of it. I also did all of the experimenting I did because I was a virgin before I was married. One of my friends asked me how I could be a virgin if my dad did what he did to me. Well, I said I was a virgin as far as my choice.

Even though my dad had done what he did, I still wanted to love my dad. I was a lot like my dad. I always used music to be close to him. Before I got married, I went to see him – he was in a VA hospital – and I took my husband-to-be to meet him. I wanted him to know I was getting married and I wanted him to come to my wedding.

I was afraid to have sex and afraid to have kids because of what had happened with my dad. I wrote a letter to him to ask him what I should do about my fears. He wrote me several times and said that if I came up to visit him, he and I could get a motel room and do all kind of things. I never did go to see him alone as an adult except once. I remember his being in my car with me and looking at me with sexy eyes and acting weird. So I just told him point blank, "Don't fuck with me. If you mess with me, your ass is going to jail." I wasn't taking any chances. But I pissed him off.

One of the worst examples of my father not being there for me happened on my wedding day. It might not be a big deal, but it was to me at the time. I had wanted my dad to come to my wedding but my mom and my family didn't want him there. If I invited him no one was going to come. So I didn't invite him. My grandfather gave me away. But my grandfather was deaf so when the minister asked, "Who gives this woman to this man?" he didn't hear it. Nothing. Total silence. The minister just moved on. All of a sudden I was so angry at my father. I started shaking violently thinking about his not being there and what he had done to me. I was angry because he couldn't be there.

I sometimes resent my therapy because I'd rather have a family who I could just talk things over with. I've had to spend thousands and thousands of dollars for hospitals. I managed to go all the way to age 20 without being hospitalized. Then I was hospitalized because I was exhausted. They said I was trying to do too much. So at first they didn't think I was mentally ill. When I was 23, my real hospitalizations started. I was having bipolar symptoms then. I was just high, high, high and I couldn't sleep. I went 10 days without sleeping and developed pneumonia. Other times I would get in my car and drive. Once I drove all the way from D.C. to Florida to pick up a container of orange juice and then drove back. Another time I drove to Dallas to get rid of my manic energy. Within two days of getting there I had gotten myself my own place and had even gotten a job. Then after the mania passed I said to myself, "What the hell am I doing here?" A friend flew down and helped me to drive back.

Sometimes in the hospital I used to get hurt by some of the patients when they weren't medicated right. One time a girl pulled out a fist full of my hair. I would get scared in the hospital, so much so that I did stuff to get kicked out. Once when I was in the hospital working on some of this stuff about my dad and the sexual abuse there were several multiple personalities on the unit. I had never seen people with multiple personalities before. I don't believe I have that problem. So I went into the nurses' station and pushed everything off the desk. They said I was throwing things, but I just pushed the stuff off. They put me in a body bag. I told them I didn't want to be on that unit any more because the patients scared me and they moved me to a different unit with manic depressives. At another hospital, they were supposed to take us out to smoke right after breakfast. Well, right after breakfast turned out to be right after lunch. I got impatient and I kicked the door by the nurses' station and they all jumped on me and knocked me down. I chipped my tooth and they put me in restraints. I wasn't in them for very long when they found out my frustration was just over a cigarette break.

I always feel abandonment and I have trouble dealing with rejection. If I think that someone is rejecting me – even if it may not be the case – I can't deal with it. There are two things that set me off – if someone makes me feel stupid and if I feel rejected. I become visibly upset and want the other person to go away. Usually I'm the one who will leave. If I couldn't leave the situation, I don't know what I would do. I've never had to actually stay in that spot.

On the other hand, I'm really insecure with any change. For example, I do well in jobs until they change me or promote me. If I have to move my office or my desk from where I've gotten used to it, it's like I'm in a totally new place and I can't function. Suddenly it's like I've never had any smarts about anything. I don't understand it but that's how it is. I find it embarrassing and, more than that, frustrating not to be able to function from place to place. So, I would often leave jobs because of my illness. I didn't want people to see me not functioning; I wanted them to remember me the way I had been, so I would just leave. Or, if I had an anxiety attack at work I'd leave and end up at the hospital. Sometimes they put you in some intensive care unit where you couldn't call and say "Hey, I'm sick and can't come to work." If my employers could have given me time and space, say a couple of weeks, then I'd probably be ok but they hardly ever had that much time for me.

I naturally feel that the best thing I can do for people is just stay out of their way. That is how I feel that I can make my best contribution. That's pitiful. I worked long and hard and went through a lot to get through school and to get my teaching certificate because I had wanted teaching to be my contribution. But inside I'm really afraid to teach, to do the thing I love best, because lately there have been so many issues about child molesting. I'm afraid that I'll be accused of being a child molester. I feel that when I'm brave enough to teach and to present myself to the world despite having gone through all this crap then I'll have healed.

Constance's story

As told to Margaret Hobbs, M.S.W.

Constance was born several months prematurely to an addicted mother, Betty. She spent the first months of her life in an incubator, abandoned by her mother. Betty made one attempt to care for Constance when she was six months old. However, Betty soon returned Constance to the hospital. Constance was one year old when she left the Washington, D.C. hospital to live with Betty once again. By this time, Betty was a single mother with another infant. Constance knows that when she was two or three she was sent to a children's receiving home, but she is uncertain about what caused her second institutionalization. She has been told that she stabbed her younger sister, but she does not remember having a knife or her sister's being stabbed. Constance stayed there until she was five years old.

When she was five, Constance was placed in foster care with a family named Jackson. She remembers this as the best time in her life. The Jacksons were an older couple with successful grown children. Constance describes her life with the foster parents she believed were her real parents: "We went to church and Bible studies. We'd eat at a certain time. We'd go to bed at a certain time. We had family meals. We'd sit down and watch T.V. and talk and laugh. We had a family day when the whole family would go out on trips, for outings and stuff like that." School attendance was perfect; "mom" made sure home work was done. Constance saw herself as thriving. Constance

196

thinks that she lived with the Jacksons until she was about nine years old. She remembers clearly what happened next. One day while riding her bike in her neighborhood, she noticed two strangers, a man and a "white lady in a tan car with a government sticker." Constance thought they were the police. In reality they were a child welfare worker and Constance's father. Constance was upset and confused; she thought that the Jacksons were her parents. Mr. Jackson told her that she was their adopted daughter and that she must go with her real father. Constance got her things and left with her real father. She never saw the Jacksons again.

Constance's new family consisted of her biological father, his wife and their children; "all these children ... shitty pampers, babies in a little apartment. I didn't know how to cuss. I didn't know anything about cigarettes, drugs or anything. My parents taught me. My sister and brothers taught me the evil side of life. Nothing stable, always fussing, arguing, fighting, ... it was terrible. I got hit. My money was stolen ... My clothes were gone. I learned foul language. I learned how to fight. I had to be very defensive."

Constance lived with her father's family on and off throughout her childhood and adolescence. She continues to have nightmares about his treatment of her. Her father saw Constance as defiant and "stubborn and bullheaded." His usual form of punishment was to tell Constance to go to her room and wait for him to come and punish her, "The thing is, you know you are going to get an ass whopping, but you don't know what he is going to hit you with. You stand there butt bald, naked, pacing the floor ... (thinking) please finish your tricking and get this shit over with. And sometimes he would leave me standing there. He couldn't make it up the steps. He'd be that drunk. And sometimes he'd make it up the steps and beat the living shit out of me ... You never knew." After the beatings, Constance's sister would take care of her, "Put peroxide on it, wipe the blood, put pamper pads on my back, make a cushion pad for my butt."

Constance ran away twice. When she was located, she told the police that she was being beaten by her father at home. They were unconvinced. All she had to show for these beatings were bruises; only "lumps" counted. Two months later, after another beating by her father, Constance ran away again. "This time I had something to

197

show. I took off my clothes and I said, 'see, he beat me.' I had cuts and bruises all over me."

The authorities believed Constance this time. They cleaned her up, treated her wounds and sent her to a children's home. She knew how to cuss and fight and take care of herself. "So I got it in my mind, if I act tough they won't bother me. But I was very afraid. And I kept that image to protect myself." One day, "I had taken a shower and these girls came in the bath when I was in there and wouldn't let me out. They said since you think you're so tough, we're going to show you how tough you are ... Someone shoved me and I slipped and fell back on the floor. The girls held me down, kissing me all over and playing with the private parts of my body. I was crying; (they) stuffed my mouth with towels. They raped me, stuck a broom-stick up my vagina." Once again, Constance had trouble getting anyone to believe her story. One nurse was willing to look at her and discovered her injuries. Constance was transferred to another unit to await a more appropriate permanent placement. Constance thinks that she was ten years old when this happened.

This event was not Constance's introduction to sexual abuse. She recalls a rape by a stranger when she was five or six. Constance cannot recall with whom she was living at the time, but does remember the incident: "... I was going to the store and a guy approached me to help him clean up the front. He would give me some change ... and some candy." He told Constance to meet him in the alley. When they met there, he told her they had to go to his house to get the money. Constance, at first, refused, but the man convinced her. When they got to the house, "He shut the door. He gave me a dollar and said, 'I'll give you another dollar if you take your pants down.' I took my pants down and lay on the bed. He penetrated me and I bled. I had to get stitches. He hurt me. I was just a baby."

In seventh grade, Constance was placed in a new group home for girls. It was small, five or six residents. It was a new neighborhood for her and she could not go out by herself, her activities were restricted but she liked the small size of the place and the fact that, "so many things went on there. Girls would have sex with each other – drink and smoke."

The relative freedom and excitement of the house were appealing to Constance. However, she once again found that her tough pose could not compete with other girls' roughness. Constance was the youngest in the house and often got set up to take the blame for others. If someone had been smoking in the bathroom, Constance would always be made to look like the guilty party by the others. Constance realized what was going on and did not like it; she decided, "I'm going to have to stand up to these girls because they're using the hell out of me. So I got into my first fight. I won. I wasn't satisfied. I wanted her dead. I didn't want to have to deal with her again or apologize … I stayed mad for a couple of months or so. I was taking no shit; when I'd pass her, I'd say: 'Little shit, I'm going to kill you bitch.' And all that kind of shit. I was on a wild horse." Constance was out of control. She was sent to the state mental hospital for one month, one of many trips. Constance did not find these hospitalizations pleasant or helpful and they did not seriously affect her behavior. She returned to the same environment and the same friends, "so naturally … if you go back to your old friends, you do the old things again."

The group home did offer Constance something she had seldom had before. She connected strongly with one of the counselors. This woman took the time to educate Constance about sex and birth control and menstruation, information Constance had not been exposed to before.

Constance also had her first experience with getting high. "Then the scary part came in. I went out and got high for the first time. I took a hit off a joint and freaked out. They had to take me home. They said, 'Whatever you do don't tell them where you were and don't tell them what you had.' Later on, about a couple of hours passed by, I began to get my vision back. My thoughts came back. I had never felt like that before in my life. So I went into it more."

Constance started using regularly and found that her status with the other residents in the house improved. 'I would take my allowance and buy a bag of reefer. Get up on the bed. We'd all drink and smoke cigarettes. Laugh and tell jokes, eat munchies all the time. So they got to like me. I could do all of those things."

Not only did using drugs establish Constance's position among the girls, it also established it on the streets. Constance was befriended by a woman named Sparky, a woman with a pink Cadillac, fancy clothes and gold jewelry, "and she'd always give me money when she'd see me." Constance realizes now that Sparky was a "pimp" and a "hustler," but to Constance, living in a group home in her early teens, she was great, she became Constance's best friend. Constance became a trusted reefer seller for Sparky. Constance was not using much herself, so she always turned all of the money in to Sparky. Sparky would then give Constance thirty or forty dollars. Constance thought that she was rich.

Constance got so caught up in her new life. She got careless about house rules. She came in late one night. The counselor noticed that she was high and made her empty her pockets. Constance refused to tell the counselor where she had gotten all of the money in her pockets. Constance was restricted to the house. She kept her relationship with Sparky going through the other girls in the house who would bring her money and things from Sparky. When the restriction ended, "I ran up the hill to see her, the first person I wanted to see. We went for a ride, went to McDonald's. She gave me some money and a gold chain she put around my neck. I was really happy and I told her, "I need a watch to tell time so I won't be late for curfew.' She said, 'I'll get you a watch," so I said 'Sparky, I like you.' She said, 'You do? I like you too.' Sparky kissed me and I didn't know what to do. I felt good. Little sparkles. But I didn't know if it was real. You know it shocked the hell out of me. I said 'Sparky, what did you do that for?' She said 'shhhhhh.' So, I said, 'shhhhhh.' We won't talk about it anymore." Constance returned home. Her money was well hidden in her shoe. She was not high, but she had been smoking cigarettes which violated the rules. "Damn, every time I turned around I was on restriction."

Restrictions and short stays at the local mental hospital came and went. Constance always returned to the same setting. One day she tried her first snort of cocaine "because everybody else was doing it." This is how she describes the experience: "I was on a trip. I had a heartbeat that was going real fast. I was breathing real fast, sweating, my eyes were big, my nose was running ... I felt like I was going to explode. When I started walking it started really taking effect on me because I was walking very fast and was wondering why I was speeding. All of a sudden I was perspiring and it was in the spring ... I said, 'Oh shit, I'm tripping. I'm tripping. You all are going to have to take me to the hospital.' (The people with me) said: 'You'll be all right, you'll be all right! Just keep on walking.' We stopped in the store and got a beer and prayed the beer would cool me off and bring me down, which it did. I was calm for a while."

The company that ran Constance's group home for girls also ran one for boys. The girls were taken to visit the boys sometimes and eventually the two programs were combined in a duplex, boys in one house, girls in the next.

On Constance's first visit to the boy's home, she made three new friends, Billy, Dave and Jack, "And we were all wild, we were really wild. We rode bicycles up and down the streets, stole batteries from people's cars. We sucked gas out of people's cars and put it in our little go-cart and we'd be able to take the go-kart on a long haul. We were real devilish. We were smoking marijuana. We drank a lot of beer too. The other kids called us the "beer drinkers." We were real tight. If you found one of us, you'd find all of us. We started skipping school and staying out late and getting into all sorts of trouble." Constance thinks that she was 14 or 15 years old at this time.

One day, Constance and her friends stole the keys to the group home's van. "We were all playing in the back of the van when Billy discovered the keys. He started the van; he pulled it forward, then backward. I wanted to drive everyone else had a try but me. I thought 'R' was for run, so I put it on 'R' stepped on the gas and boom! 'R' was for reverse. The van hit the telephone pole, knocked it down, damaged the van. We jumped out of the van so fast, we left the keys in there. We ran across the street, climbed over the fence and across the field. I got stuck on the fence." A counselor caught them and demanded to know where they had gotten the keys. Constance said she did not know. She was just riding with her friends. The boys, some of whom were brothers, all turned and pointed at her. In the end, they all got restricted to their rooms.

Constance found in the "beer drinkers" a kind of family. "We'd go to school together. We'd eat together. We crashed together. We got sick together. We did a lot. They were like brothers to me. I was the only girl in the group. I was special to each and every one of them. Bill became my boyfriend. We never had sex, but we'd smooch and kiss in the laundry room."

During the years Constance was in group home and treatment programs, she was often sent home for periods of time and on weekend passes. This home was with her father and his family ... the home that she had run away from as a child because of beatings and abuse.

Sometimes, her father would tell her to do the dishes, "I would go in there and start running water, getting the dishes ready and while I was standing up there ... a rat would run across the top of the sink. I'd run out of the kitchen. He said, 'Where you see a rat at? Go on in there, get your ass in there and wash them goddamn dishes.' " Constance returned to washing dishes. This time the rat ran across her feet; she jumped and bumped her head on a kitchen cabinet. She still bears a scar from the cut. Her father refused to believe her; he said he did not see any rats. Constance told him to stay in the kitchen with her and be quiet and he would see the rat. This time he did see the rat running across the counter. Constance tried to run out of the kitchen but instead ran into her father who was blocking the door. He asked her if she was afraid of the rat. She told him she was. Her father responded: " 'Well they're afraid of you. And you're afraid of them so you'll just run the opposite way from each other. There isn't anything to be afraid of, they aren't going to hurt you. They are more scared of you than you are of them.' He used to say that kind of stuff to me. He'd push me back in the kitchen or raise his hand to smack me or something."

When Constance turned eighteen, her involvement with the group home program ended. She had been in and out of school over the years and finally dropped out in eleventh grade. Constance worked at an adult education center doing housekeeping chores and studying for her G.E.D. Constance is uncertain about whether she ever actually passed the G.E.D. test. She took it twice but never got any notification of results in the mail. Constance thinks it may never have gotten to her because she had so many addresses.

Constance tried the Job Corps twice. She wanted to learn a trade. Both times she was expelled not too long after entering the program because she was found to have another girl in her room. The Job Corps restricts participants to their dorms and forbids sex of any kind for the life of the program.

Constance's life has been full of confusion about her sexuality and her sexual identity. Constance had dealt with a number of rough situations with women in institutions, but she has felt for a long time that she would rather deal with women than men. "I was afraid of men ... seeing a penis would just tear me apart. Because I had been raped several times, abused a lot by men. And a woman is so sensitive, so lovable and caring and very feminine." Constance is clear that when she is with women she takes the masculine role, "I like being aggressive. I started out saying I'm going to show a man what it means to be a man ... how to be a man to a woman, showing her all the affection that is supposed to be in a relationship between a man and a woman." Sometimes Constance's strategy of being tough and aggressive and being like the men tripped her up. She would find herself, "putting myself in bad spots trying to play the role of a man, going gambling and drinking. The men didn't like that. They'd put me down and sometimes I got myself into situations I couldn't get out of. It was either have sex or get your ass whipped. I couldn't fight, so I had sex. Then they say, "that's what I mean, you're not a man, you're still a bitch. You can get fucked like anybody else.'"

Constance had sex with men for money. She had a number of pregnancies and abortions. She always regretted the abortions deeply, but she felt that she could not raise a child alone and did not want her child to go through what she had in her life. She feels abortion is murder and does not like the idea that she was "killing somebody just to have sex and get money." Sometimes the money was for drugs and alcohol; often it was to go to gay bars and find a woman. When Constance had a relationship with a woman, "I'd go to work and be faithful for a while, then she'd leave and I'd be back dealing with men."

Constance remembers that she did have times in her twenties when she lived with a female lover and worked. They would share an apartment and Constance would work construction jobs, sometimes doing "man's" work, sometimes having it relatively easy, directing traffic. Constance remembers her early twenties as a good time in her life, having independence, a succession of steady lovers and money to spend. She also recalls that things did not go well when her relationships ended. She was often expelled from her lover's apartment. Sometimes she went to shelters or lived on the streets. She would start living the fast life again, putting herself in dangerous situations. She would use drugs and alcohol. She would spend periods of time on a psychiatric ward. Constance's life continued to cycle. There would be good relationships and work and there would be mental hospitals, drugs and shelters.

During a period of homelessness, Constance was referred by a shelter to an outreach program within a local mental health agency. The agency provided clinical case management services to individuals with persistent and severe mental illness. Constance was referred for ongoing psychiatric and substance abuse treatment and housing. Her clinician was a young, caring woman. Constance thought that she was "very attractive and had a beautiful personality." Constance had never known anyone like her, "Anything I wanted or needed to talk about, she was there … and she would tell me things like, 'You can do it, you can do it, if you put your heart into it … You're capable. You're lovable and you have talent. Just slow down and things will come to you.' I started to believe her. So I stopped smoking, drinking, hanging out at nights partying."

Constance did so well she was able to move to an agency-run apartment. At this time Constance was working and making good money. She felt that she could use and get away with it. She smoked more than $100 worth of crack. She realized that somehow her case manager, Kim could tell that she had been using. Kim did not directly accuse Constance but she encouraged her to tell her what was going on. When Kim did catch her using, Constance told her the truth about her drinking and drug use. Kim was not angry and punitive. Instead she calmly told Constance that she would move her from the apartment she was sharing with two other clients to a more structured living situation. Constance, who had lost her job, was willing to go.

Constance moved to a supervised group home and liked it. "I had my own room and it was kind of quiet. We had curfew. It was fine because I was there with people my own age. I could relate to them." With the help of the structure and the support of her case manager, Constance had only one brief relapse with alcohol while in the group home. She remembers being clean for eighteen months. This was a good time for Constance. Her case manager gave her a lot of special attention.

This good time ended abruptly when Kim told Constance that she was leaving her job because she was going to have a baby. Constance had trouble understanding the news. She told her case manager that she loved her and wanted her for a girlfriend. Kim left the agency, leaving Constance "crying like a baby." Constance was angry and upset. "I couldn't trust anybody. I didn't want to be around anybody or anything."

Constance remains ambivalent about what she wants from life and about what she may be able to attain. Even with her frustration and anger at her treatment program, she feels that a number of people there do care about her. She credits the program with keeping her alive this long. She is grateful for that as it allows her to continue to struggle with her addictions and gives her hope that someday she may get the life she wants. She and her treatment team have tried many things over the last six years. She has been in 34 different housing settings; she has lived on the streets at four different times; she has had 33 hospitalizations. Nothing has been quite enough.

It seems that the only constant in Constance's life is change, from program to program and from worker to worker. Constance wants to once again be the person she feels she was while working with Kim, but it is hard. "I've been trying to go every way to get there, to be like it was but it can't be. She's gone. These people are here. I have to do what they want me to do and start putting my trust in them. But I'm scared that if I do, they'll leave me just like Kim did. Every time I get close to somebody, real close … they leave. Then I'm sitting there, fucked all over again. Just like when my mother and father dumped me off. And I hurt. I really hurt."

Barbara's story

As told to Christine L. Landis, M.S.W.

Let me tell you about my story. My name is Barbara Brown. I'm a 46 year old Black woman, 5′ 1″, with hazel eyes. I have a seventh grade education. I was the youngest of twelve children. My mother really should have known how to raise kids, since she had so many, but she didn't. I don't know why she didn't care about us. I'm still trying to understand that. I do know that she was a functional alcoholic. She would go to work and not drink until the weekend, but then she would drink a lot.

My godmother, Nettie Catherine Young, tells me stories about when I was a baby. You see, my godmother had a rooming house and would usually let construction workers rent from her. Well one day my mother showed up and my godmother let her stay because she had a baby. When my godmother asked to see the baby my mom opened up her coat and there I was, with my head hanging this way and my feet hanging that way. My godmother felt sorry for her and let us stay on the second floor. My mother put an army blanket on the floor for me and put a rag around my hips for a diaper. Even though it was winter time she would leave the window open. She slept on the bed and I slept on the floor.

A couple of weeks after we arrived, my godmother came upstairs to use the bathroom. She said that she had been hearing this cat meowing so she decided to walk around in the house to see if she could find it. So my godmother came in our room and looked around and found me by the bed. My godmother said she had a hard time believing her eyes, I looked that pathetic. I was bald-headed, had little eyes and she said that she could count every rib on my body. I was three pounds, 14 ounces when I was born and when she found me I didn't weigh any more than five pounds.

After that my godmother took me, bathed me, greased me and then I started getting well. So from then on I lived between my mother, godmother and my older sister's house. It wasn't an easy childhood. My godmother used to beat me with her cane, hard enough to leave welts. My mother used to make me work a lot around the house. All three were controlling. They wouldn't let me go outside and play with the other kids. I had to sit at home with the adults. I never could understand that, but I do remember feeling lonely and very hurt. I was stuck in the house while the other kids could play whenever they wanted. The other kids would call me crazy. That hurt my feelings and I used to cry about it until they made fun of my crying, so I had to teach myself not to cry.

One of the ways I coped during those years was to act like a clown. It was a way to help me deal with the pain of not being wanted or accepted. I would try to make people laugh by teasing them. Usually they would just look at me and say, "Wow, she is really crazy." I didn't know the meaning of that word until I went to school. When I found out what it meant, I didn't like it and told the kids not to call me that, but they did anyway.

When I was five years old, I had a nervous breakdown. I saw snakes and felt as if they were coming after me. I was hollering and screaming and telling people to come and get the snakes off me because they were eating me up. I ran out of the house and down the street. This man said to me, "Come here little girl, what are you doing out here this time of morning in your pajamas?" I told him, "Snake, snake!" So he picked me up and went to call the police. These two big cops came and as we were walking down the street, my godmother saw us and came to get me. The cops told me that I was safe now. I said, "No! Snake, snake!" One of the officers picked me up and threw me on the bed. By the time I hit the bed I bounced back on the floor and was screaming about snakes. The officers told my godmother to take me to the hospital to see what was wrong with me.

I don't know how long I stayed in St. Elizabeth's, the state mental hospital. There were no other children around there at that time. I had to stay with the grownup females. I was kind of scared and shocked when I went in. I didn't have anybody to play with so I played the piano. They took that and closed it up because I didn't know anything about playing pianos. They had a radio in there which they took away because I had it on loud and was dancing around and it was disturbing the other patients. My godparents brought me storybooks, but they kept them at the nurse's station and I couldn't see them.

There was this one little old church lady who would sit down and draw and talk with me and read me stories at night. I saw the psychiatrist and everything was going along all right until one day when this one nurse gave me a tube of lipstick and told me to give it to another nurse. All of them looked alike to me in their white dresses. I couldn't tell one from the other. So the first nurse came up to me later and asked me if I had given the lipstick to the other lady. I said "I don't know who I gave it to. It was somebody in here." She was angry and she took me and put me in the hallway. She told me to stand in the corner and not move. So I'm standing there in the corner for a long time when a third nurse came along and asked what I was doing there. I told her one of the staff had put me there because I gave a lipstick to the wrong woman. So she took me out front again. When that nurse went back into her room, the nurse that gave me the lipstick picked up a folding chair and hit me in the back of my head. BAM! I fell and hit the floor. The other nurses came running out there saying, "Oh no! I know she didn't do that!" They had the doctors check me out to see if I had any brain or head damage. That nurse had come straight down on my head with that chair. I think that's the reason that they don't have folding chairs in the hospital anymore. They have chairs connected to each other, so you can't pick them up. Anyway, I stayed there for a little while and then they took me back home.

On my eighth birthday my mother told me how many times she went to wrap me in newspaper and put me in the trash. She said the only thing that saved me was my big mouth. I asked her why she said that. She said because there were so many times she went to put me in the garbage, but she was afraid that I was going to cry and she thought that would draw attention to her.

When I was about ten years old, my mother, my oldest sister, my sister's boyfriend and I were driving in the car. They were trying to see where they could find the bootlegger to get some alcohol. So we were passing this large building that was St. Elizabeth's Hospital. I was looking at the light green fence and at the big buildings. I said, "Dag mommy, I been over there." My mother said "No baby, you haven't been over there." Then my oldest sister said "Yeah mommy, she was over there! Don't you remember that time she went crazy?" My mother hit my oldest sister upside the head and told her to shut up. But that's when it came to me. That's when I realized that was the hospital I had been in.

My nieces and nephews felt that they could beat me up and take advantage of me when I first moved in with them. I let them go ahead and pull my hair and tear my clothes off and scratch my face. I didn't do anything because they were my sister's kids and she told me to tell her when they messed with me. Well, I went up there and told her about it one day and all she did was laugh. She didn't control her kids. So I told my mother and she said, "You got a mouth full of teeth, two hands and two feet, now you deal with it the best way you can. If you don't beat their butts, I'm gonna beat yours when I come home because I'm tired of hearing your stories every day."

The next day they got home before I did and were waiting in their favorite places to jump on me and pull my hair. Well, I surprised them because I grabbed them first, rammed those heads together and then turned around, threw one against one wall and the other against another wall. My sister came in and started yelling, "What are you doing to my children?! You're crazy! Leave my children alone!" So I knocked my sister down and sat on her. My mother came through the back door and walked in on us. She called me upstairs and I thought she was going to beat me up, but she said, "See how easy that is? All you got to do is beat up the leader and all the rest of them will leave you alone." I said, "I see."

When I was twelve years old I was raped two times, once by my mother's boyfriend and once by my godmother's son. At that time my mother was living with my oldest sister. My sister's kids were in one room, my mother, her boyfriend and I were in another room and my sister and her boyfriend had the third room. I didn't want to sleep in there because my mother and her boyfriend might be doing something that I didn't want to see. I went in though and lay on the floor. Just as I was about to dose off to sleep, I went to turn over and there my mother's boyfriend was with a knife at my throat, telling me to be quiet and don't say a word. He told me to just lie there. Then he raped me. While this was going on I asked God, "If you love me why do you take me through these changes?"

About a month after that I started getting very sick and had to go to the hospital. My godmother took me over there and they examined me and realized that somebody had had sex with me. They kept asking me who the guy was and I wouldn't tell them. Then they had the priest come and I did tell him who had done it. He told my godmother and my godmother told my mother. My mother told them that I was lying because her boyfriend wouldn't do anything like that. How would she know? She was drunk and passed out on the bed, when all of this was going on. Anyway, I stayed in the hospital about three weeks. They found out who the man was, I don't know if they put him in jail or not. I didn't hear anything else about it, but it was my word against his.

I then moved back into my godmother's house where I was the only child. I had one bed in the basement and my godmother's fifty-five year old son had a bed there too. My godmother was the kind of woman who didn't keep secrets. So she told her son about the rape that I had been through. One night he came over to me and told me that I could have anything and everything I wanted as long as I took care of the men in my life. He then raped me. Afterwards he asked me if I wanted anything from the store. I said yes, that I wanted a pack of false fingernails. He got them for me and I glued them on and sharpened each nail to a sharp point. That night he came over to me and I had my hands behind my back and was leaning on my elbow. He put those big droopy lips over my mouth and it felt as if he was going to smother me. I took both of my hands and scratched him from his forehead all the way down his cheeks. I dug those artificial blades into him with the sharp points. He jumped up and looked at me as if he was in total shock. I guess he expected me to go along with him as I had the night before. I told him that if he touched me again I was going to tell his mother. After that he moved out of his mother's house and got his own apartment. He said it was my fault for carrying on so, but I was just a kid and didn't understand what was going on. I knew those men were doing something bad toward me though, because they kept telling me to keep it a secret. I grew up with much pain and agony because of that.

It wasn't easy living with either my godmother, or my mother, but living with my mother was worse. She would drink so much. A couple of nights I woke up with her standing over me with a butcher knife in her hand, saying, "You want me to kill you?" I was so scared. I would get out of the bed and watch her for the rest of the night. We didn't have a telephone, so I couldn't call anyone. I never told anyone about it because I didn't think that they would believe me, or they would laugh at me.

My godfather was a strong working man, but after he retired, he didn't have anything to do. He started drinking a lot. I could get away with a lot in those days. He would go in the bedroom and get his wife's pocketbook, where all the money was and have me go to the liquor store for him. I would go to the store and get half a gallon of liquor. He would say, "Come here and pour yourself a drink. Go downstairs in the basement to drink it and don't act crazy." Well, I took more than one drink and then I tried to bring the stereo, radio and the television, downstairs to the basement where I was. He caught me and said, "How come every time you get drunk you do something stupid?" I didn't know why.

I got pregnant when I was sixteen after having sex with a neighbor boy. My godparents had never told me about birth control. I was scared when I found out, mostly because I was afraid of their reaction. At the same time I was excited because I thought that now I would have someone to love me. After having my son, I got pregnant again and at age eighteen had a daughter. I thought that I would be the perfect mother, instead I saw my children go through things that even I hadn't gone through. I was getting a welfare check and working also, but I still didn't have enough money for food or heat. My poor kids didn't even have those basic things.

I turned to alcohol and drugs heavily when I was twenty-one. I was very depressed, feeling like a failure and paranoid too. One night I came in and threw up in my room. My mother cleaned up after me, but told me I ought to quit drinking because I was getting sick. I went out the following week and I got drunk again, came back and messed up the room as I did before and the only thing my mother did was give me the broom and dustpan and told me to help myself. She cleaned up after me the first time because she didn't think I was going to go back out there and do the same thing again, but I did.

Around that time I also got involved in peep shows. I would get high and go downtown. I would go in and ask them if I could get on stage and they would say yes. I did that for a while. I did it to earn money. I would sometimes turn tricks there too. I wasn't standing on the corners, or anything, but I did make some money at the peep shows. That went on for a couple of years. I ran around with many different men until I started hearing about AIDS and that it can kill you. That was when my sex life slowed down.

My life was pretty miserable. If I wasn't the one making it miserable, I went and found somebody to make it worse than it already was. When I was twenty-three years old I started living with my boyfriend who was verbally and physically abusive towards me. He used to call me whore, tramp, slut and dog. Those were things I was used to hearing because my mother, godmother and sisters would call me those nasty names too. My boyfriend would blacken my eye almost every other week. One time he hit me on my head and I fell down. He threw his foot back to kick me in my face, but one of his buddies grabbed him in time and pulled him back.

I got so depressed during that time that he was battering me that I tried to commit suicide by drinking Clorox. My boyfriend actually ended up saving my life because when he saw me staggering around

211

he slapped me on my back until I threw up. He wondered where that Clorox smell was coming from and then realized that I had drunk some. I told him I made a mistake, that I had thought it was beer. He didn't buy it and said "No one would make a mistake like that." He wanted to drive me to the hospital, but I didn't want to go. So I drank a lot of milk that night which flushed it out of my system. That was my first suicide attempt. Years later I tried taking an overdose of my medications, but I just got sleepy. I think that was my way of crying out for help.

When my boyfriend and I were drinking and drugging, everything seemed OK to me, but when we were sober that's when we got into big fights. During those years he would say "I'm gonna beat you up so that nobody else will want you. I'm gonna kill you and your kids." He didn't want me, but he didn't want anybody else to want me either. So I had a hard time getting rid of him.

One time he grabbed one of my kids in the chest and raised him off his feet and rammed him into the wall. Something snapped in me when he did that. I went to the kitchen and got the butcher knife and was sticking it in his back and when he turned around I put the blade at his throat. I told him if I was dumb enough to let him hit me that was my problem, but he wasn't going to hit any of my kids.

I finally got away from him, but it was a slow process. My fear turned to anger and I just got fed up with his foolishness, especially with him saying he was going to kill me and my kids. I had to break it off before it got any worse, so I did. We wound up going to court. I told the judge to get him out of our lives or one of us was going to end up dead. The judge asked my boyfriend if he understood that he was to stay away from me and he said yes. That night he called me at my mother's house and told me to meet him, that he still loved me and forgave me. I told him no. Later on that night he went back and destroyed our apartment. First he slashed the mattresses, pillows and sofa. He stuffed most of it in the tub, toilet and sink. He scattered food all over the kitchen. He then lit the place on fire. Because I didn't go back to him, he destroyed all of our things. I couldn't get a witness to say that they saw him in the area, because if they did, he would have served time in jail and people were afraid of him.

I was hearing voices during that time because of my mental illness. It was during treatment for my alcohol abuse at St. Elizabeth's

Hospital that they started me on the medication, Haldol, which helped me not to have hallucinations. Those voices were very disturbing, telling me to hit other people. Over the years I've had about seven psychiatric hospitalizations at different hospitals.

My children ended up going to a foster home because they considered me to be an unfit mother. I would drink and drug and run after other women's husbands. I would go off and leave my kids for two or three days and then come back. One time I was partying hard, drinking liquor and smoking pot. I heard a voice telling me to get a knife and stab my daughter. So I went and got a butcher knife and was standing over her bed staring at her. Just as I drew the knife back something told me, "No. Don't do it. That's your baby." So I didn't do it. I took the knife back to the kitchen. I was so shaken by what I had almost done that I immediately gathered a few clothes and money and caught a bus to Baltimore. I stayed in Baltimore for a couple of months, until the urge to kill my child left me. I didn't know anyone there. It was just a place to escape to. At that time I didn't have anyone to talk to about what I was going through, so the only thing I knew to do was to run.

I did go back to D.C., but continued with my old behavior of leaving my kids while I went out to party. One winter day my children went over to a neighbor's house when I didn't return home and nobody could find me. They decided to call the police. The police came and got my children and took them to the social service building. That's when they were placed in a foster home.

I never could get my kids back because of my addictions. I became homeless after I lost my kids. I stayed in shelters and sometimes with family. Staying with family was not always a good idea. When I would stay with my mother we would drink together every day. Her alcoholism was getting worse and whenever she would get drunk, she would call my older sisters and brothers and tell them to come beat my butt because I wasn't acting right. Then they would come over and give me a piece of their mind.

I remember the time when my mother slipped on the ice and fractured her hip. She went to the hospital and had her leg all wrapped up in a cast. I was the one who took care of her. This one morning I had fixed breakfast for her and was sitting by her bed while she ate. The expression on her face was sad. I asked her what was wrong. She said,

213

"If I knew that you were gonna turn out to be like this, I never would have said or done them things like trying to get rid of you when you was a baby." I told her not to worry, that everything turned out all right. She asked why I was so good to her, knowing all the things that she said and did. I said, "Well, because Jesus told me to love everybody and that's what I do. God can forgive people like you."

My mother died at the age of 63. She had cirrhosis of the liver due to her heavy drinking. Yet till the end she wouldn't stop drinking or smoking. She died on November 25 and her birthday was on Christmas day, so that has always been a hard time of the year for me. For many years I would relapse on that date. This past year I didn't relapse though because I thought of the good and happy times we had and not about the negative and bad times.

I'm more alert now. I've been off drugs and alcohol for seven months now. I know how to deal with situations in a more positive way. For one thing I don't go back to where the bad things happened to me. I used to go to my sister's house, but that would bring back memories about the way they treated me and about getting raped by my mother's boyfriend. I stayed away from that man too because the memories would come back when I saw him. For a long time I couldn't express my thoughts and feelings to anyone. I kept it inside because I was afraid that my family would call me names or would tell me that I wanted it to happen. They would put the blame on me, as if it was my fault.

I used to think that the rapes were my fault because of the way I was shaped. I thought that was why men would come after me. I only found out recently that it wasn't my fault. I went into the hospital and while I was there I had a good psychiatrist. I told my story about the way I've been treated in her group. I let it all hang out there and they told me I wasn't to blame. They also gave me a wonderful book called "The Courage to Heal," that has meant a lot to me.

Now I'm in a trauma group that helps me to express myself, how I feel today and what I've been through when I was growing up. I feel my self esteem is not so low anymore. I feel good about myself. I'm not as paranoid as I used to be. I also keep myself as busy as possible by going to groups. I want to become a good grandmother for my grandson. I want to be able to enjoy my family. The past has tormented me a lot and now I just want to stay calm.

I've learned from my mistakes and I've tried to pass that along to my children. I especially didn't want my daughter to go through what I went through. I taught her to stand up for herself and not let others bully her. There was one case when I thought that she might have been sexually assaulted. I asked her about it and she said no. She told me that she would tell me if anything like that happened. I would believe her too. It's so important to be believed. She's now learning to take responsibility for herself and her son.

Now when I wake up in the morning I feel good and even if I don't feel good, I try to make myself feel better. I look in the mirror and I say, "I'm somebody special." Then I put on my radio so that I can dance around until its time for me to go.

I don't want to be bothered with a man right now. Sometimes that's just as if you have another child you have to care for. I don't have the patience for it anymore. If you're not mature enough to deal respectfully with me, then I'm not going to deal with you. I might kid and play around sometimes, but there is a time to be serious also and I'm serious when I say I don't want to get back into being battered as I was before. Love can be hazardous to your health, if you're in love with someone who hurts you. No woman should have to put up with abuse.

Chapter Ten

The House on Phillips Avenue

Rae E. Unzicker

THIS story should really be told by others, by Anne, Clare, Patti, Marie, Susan,* and the others who have come to teach us, and who, in the process, honored us with their deep sense of truth and wisdom, with their sensitivity and courage and humor.

These are the "psychotics" who have lived with us, shared our food and hearts and lives, and who have assuredly challenged and enriched us.

We did not know we were moving to a sacred place when Jim and I got married in 1974 and had to find a house to accommodate not only us, but Jim's four children, three teenagers and a five-year-old. Jim, a local native, remembers the house from his childhood. He'd ride his bike down the short hill, and take the curve in front of the house slowly. He remembers the ladies sitting on the front porch watching him. He discovered as an adult that ours had been the most revered house of ill repute in town.

The basement is still cut up into tiny bedrooms, and our neighbor tells stories of learning what he knows about sex by watching through the windows when he was a little boy. Jim thinks the house

---

*all names changed.

has female karma. I think it's paying its dues to women for having abused them in the past.

It hasn't always been women who've come to stay. It started with the minister who officiated at our wedding. Six months later, shortly after we were settled in the house, he needed a place to stay for a night. We didn't know that he was doing what alcoholics call "hitting bottom," that he would burst into our bedroom in the middle of the night, demanding the keys to Jim's car. He spent the next night, drunk, in a hotel room, and started a fire. He was charged with arson, and his church sent him off to a rehabilitation center for alcoholic clergy.

There were many about-to-be-divorced people then, and we provided a way station for them. One was a jazz piano player who was an inveterate early-morning talker. He still plays "Here's That Rainy Day" whenever we visit the French restaurant where he holds forth on the piano. Another was my best friend, who concocted luscious meals in the crock pot almost every day.

We didn't view what we were doing as "therapeutic" or even palliative. For me, it was a way of carrying on a tradition and repaying a debt to a family who had provided loving foster care in the midst of my own career as a mental patient.

One afternoon, I came home to find a person in our living room, crying and frightened, talking to Jim. That wasn't so unusual, except that he was my former shrink, a rigid behavioral psychologist who had, quite literally, thrown me out of his office following a suicide attempt several years earlier.

He stayed with us for nearly two years. He didn't live with us, actually; he had an apartment somewhere, and he usually went there to sleep. He eventually bought the duplex that adjoins our back yard. But he was at our house every day, sharing meals, vacations, holidays, and parties. At varying times, he treated me like a patient, friend, bad mother, good mother, housekeeper, child and shrink. I suppose I did the same with him.

The awakening

We went together – the shrink, my husband, and I – to the Esalen Institute in Big Sur, California. It was at Esalen that I experienced an awakening. Esalen was started in the 1960's by two counterculture

218

Stanford grad students, Dick Price and Michael Murphy. Price had been incarcerated and electroshocked in the worst kind of mental hospital. All he really wanted was to create a safe place for himself, believing, as I do, that the worst thing about being crazy is never feeling you're safe. On Murphy's grandparents property, they put together a place that I call a "summer camp for grown ups." Esalen offers a rich palette of experiences from the human potential movement – massage, gestalt practice, intuitive awareness, bioenergetics, movement, yoga, dance, quantum physics, and all kinds of self-expression.

For me, it was the asylum I'd always been looking for. I'd not found it in five mental hospitals, with nineteen professional "helpers," nor in the plethora of psychotropic drugs I'd wanted but didn't know how to get: safety, isolation, nonjudgmental support, environmental beauty, healthy food, and techniques and practices for personal growth. I was ready. I don't think I would have been so inclined five years earlier, but I'd given up on psychiatry and settled into the belief that life is painful. Resigned to living with discontent, I settled. I settled for the best psychiatry had to offer: a life without psychiatry. The psychologist had done his job. I "behaved" perfectly well. I was no longer "schizophrenic."

Esalen is not a mental hospital, nor a place for people in "psychotic states." For me, it was a starting place from the gray pointlessness of my inner life into a rich well of feelings. I'd felt them before but, whenever I tried to express them, usually through suicide or catatonia, I was drugged, locked up, or, worst of all, told it – I – didn't matter.

During this trip to California, at the City Lights Bookstore in San Francisco, I discovered "Madness Network News," a now-defunct newspaper published by, and for, ex-psychiatric patients. They called themselves psychiatric inmates. It was the summer of 1978; between Esalen and the Madness Network News, I experienced an epiphany.

I *knew* that I would never again submit to the dehumanizing process of traditional psychiatry. Through "*Madness Network News*," I knew that I wasn't alone. I began to get angry about what had been done to me in the name of help, and this was the door to my personal healing. Confronting my own anger, I encountered the people and the literature of the mental patients' liberation movement, and this also validated my anger and sense of betrayal.

219

The next step was to get involved, and I soon found myself entrenched with the local Mental Health Association, which had its own very different agenda. I remember distinctly an expensive booklet they were distributing at the time, which promoted drugs as the "cure" for depression. My involvement in the "radical" cause of the mental patients' rights movement garnered some media attention and launched my second career, that of an advocate for psychiatrically labeled people.

With a small grant from the National Institute of Mental Health's (now the Center for Mental Health Services) Community Support Program, I started one of the first federally-funded advocacy programs, and quickly learned the rules of co-optation. Working adjacent to the bureaucratic structure, and ultimately answering to them, I found my emerging values and principles challenged on a daily basis. While we were helping people stay out of the hospital – I'd naively thought that was our goal – we were forced underground. We took people across the state line to avoid commitment, and out of their "catchment areas" to other mental health centers; we told people they didn't *have* to take drugs, even if their shrinks prescribed them. To this day, I am frequently publicly vilified for "telling people to go off their drugs."

The disillusionment

I began to feel philosophically crushed under the powerful political weight of the mental health system. When we tried to be innovative, we were told that we only represented a small (though unhappy) segment of the recipients of mental health services. What about the people who *liked* partial care, they asked. Finally, they told me straight out that I couldn't criticize their oppressive policy in public, even if it was the truth. I could compromise, or be compromised. In the end, it didn't matter. They, the bureaucrats, pulled the funding for the project.

That grant, however, paved the pathway to our house that had already been cleared by our friends.

First, there was Anna, a woman diagnosed as paranoid schizophrenic and, later, as manic depressive. One Sunday afternoon, Jim and I responded to a call from one of her friends, and we discovered

Anna in her apartment. She'd tied bows on, around, and in every-thing – curtains, towels, food, shoestrings, belts – and she was curled up on her bed rocking and talking gibberish. I did what was instinc-tive: I crawled into her bed and began rocking her, talking softly and gently, reassuring her she was safe. Jim picked up the hundreds of pieces of clothing and other paraphernalia that covered every surface. We tried to reach her case manager, who didn't make herself available on weekends. We brought Anna home.

She stayed several days, until we figured out that she was toxic on an overdosage of lithium her psychiatrist had prescribed, but not properly monitored. She slept occasionally, but more often wan-dered, talked loudly, tried on our clothes, and interrupted our lives. Jim remembers standing in the bathroom shaving, and Anna coming in to sit on the toilet. I remember her coming into our bedroom at 6:00 a.m., crawling in between us in our bed. Anna was (and is) a large woman – 5′ 9″, 250 pounds. In one of her night wanderings, she knocked over the massage table and television in her room, causing the most property damage we have ever sustained through having a crazy person stay with us.

Through these days, Anna would have moments of absolute clarity, times in which she knew exactly where she was and why she was there. This recognition would make her feel desolate and she would cry inconsolably, comforted only when I held and rocked her.

It's important to say here that Jim and I both reject the label "mental illness" and all of the expected behaviors and outcomes attendant to it. We use the word "crazy" because it is much less stig-matizing than "mentally ill"; "crazy" has a generic meaning easily understood by most people. We do not embrace the current dogma of biological psychiatry, that people are simply organs or combina-tions of chemicals to be manipulated. We clearly reject the model of "brain disease."

Instead, we view people as complicated human organisms who are profoundly affected by what happens to them, both historically and in the present. Every single person who has come for respite has had a history of physical, sexual, or psychological abuse, or personal or environmental neglect. We believe that what is commonly called "mental illness" is not an illness at all, but an example of emo-tional suffering brought on by a disturbance in a whole field of

221

relationships, primarily the family of origin. The symptoms of mental illness are the unique ways people develop to cope. As Joe Berke writes in *Two Accounts of a Journey Through Madness*, "Mental illness reflects what is happening in a disturbed and disturbing group of people, especially when internalized in and by a single person … a person diagnosed as mentally ill is the emotional scapegoat for the turmoil in his or her family or associates and may, in fact, be the 'sanest' member of this group."

We found this to be true. It is clear that trauma, particularly childhood trauma, is imprinted. It becomes deeply rooted and affects every aspect of the person – the physical, psychological, spiritual, and social. Trauma manifests itself at every level, and ricochets off its own energy, like a horrible house of mirrors. Sexual abuse is evil, and its survivors are wondrous, complex human beings who develop a seemingly instinctive array of skills to cope that should be honored, not "diagnosed."

To call people who have experienced childhood trauma, especially sexual abuse, "mentally ill" is not only a tragic mistake, it is an insult to the fiery truth of personal experience. This is not a mere "misdiagnosis"; it is, instead, systematic venal denial of a human being's most important self-definition: her truth, her experience, her history, her reality, her humanity.

Simplicity and common sense

Perhaps because we are naive, or more likely because of my own devastating experiences as a long-term "professional schizophrenic," we do not attempt to impose our view of sanity, nor do we view others' behavior as "sick." With Anna, and everyone else, we started with the simplest acts of kindness. Sleep. Food, often fed by hand, sometimes in a baby's bottle. Human contact – we'd read stories, or Jim would give non-sexual and non-threatening mini-massages … lots of warm baths, in candlelight with soothing music.

We did not know that, at almost precisely the same time we were attempting to calm the chaos of people's inner lives, non-traditional researchers were developing the theories and building the philosophical underpinnings that might someday validate what we, two uneducated but well-meaning nonprofessionals, were doing. In *The*

Dancing Healers, Carl Hammerschlag writes, "When it comes to understanding the mind, we are like children. Even if we someday know the brain and its chemistry, the mind will always have a mind of its own. The mind is a multifaceted jewel that snatches at whatever light comes in from many angles and creates a myriad of hues and colors. There are many ways to see the light as there are ways to create it."

I was lecturing at a local college when I first encountered Clare. She was not, to say the least, my kind of person. She affected a punk style and a look that were threatening. I forgot her, so I didn't know who she was when she called and asked to meet with me. We missed each other in the restaurant, but finally connected later, and she was blunt and to the point. She wanted me to "help" her.

By this time, I was very busy with my work in the mental patients' liberation movement, and I'd started a tiny "private practice" in my house, teaching people some of the techniques that had been useful in my own healing – gestalt, transactional analysis, bodywork, and meditation. I made it clear that I wasn't a professional. Perhaps the most important choice, however, was my decision that I wasn't intending to "help" anyone. "Help" is something people receive, not something given, especially intentionally or in a formalized structure. I am cynical about systematized "help" of any kind. In truth, my primary focus was in keeping people from being drugged or involuntarily treated in a hospital setting, rather than in providing psychological help.

Clare was a serious abuser of drugs. Her drug of preference was amphetamines, but she used anything she could get. She was going to school (more or less), working, and taking care of a huge dog – and she was struggling with a very real internal demon named Monad.

She'd created him while she was being brutally raped as a child. Monad had turned from a protective guide to terrorizing demon when she was again raped in a mental hospital, where she spent her senior year of high school. There, she was labeled as "schizophrenic."

She moved in with us, terrified that we'd repeat the abuse she'd experienced in the hospital. The bed frame in her room had some small-chain apparatus that had once been used to hold two frames together. Much later, Clare told me she was convinced the chains

223

were a device to restrain her. She was also subject to seizures, which were exacerbated by her drug use. When she had a grand mal seizure in the middle of the night, I awakened, gave her a warm bath, changed the soaked sheets, and tucked her back into bed. Clare says this was an important reference point in our relationship, when she began to believe I'd be there for her, in spite of any messes she might make.

She'd moved in with the agreement that she'd stop using drugs, and within two weeks, overdosed in our house. We were able to negotiate with our family physician to admit her to a medical floor, where a clinical pharmacologist experienced in street drug use and abuse supervised her physical withdrawal from speed. Back at home, she began a series of self-mutilations. Clare still bears the scars of slicing her arms and shoulders with serrated knives, trying to exorcize her demon. I responded in a human way, by getting angry with her. Clare has told me that she experienced this in a wholly different way than the pseudo-caring therapeutic or punitive-behavioristic responses she'd received from mental health professionals. I was willing, instead, to engage with her human-to-human. I had to. We were living together. It was a process of "being with," as opposed to "doing to," which is at the core of most psychiatric treatment.

She raged. Twice a week or more, for more than a year, Clare arranged for people to keep her safe while she screamed, hit, bit, kicked, swore, and released a lifetime of anger. Jim helped occasionally, and was amazed when I suggested he put his hand over her abdomen, the place in her body Clare identified as holding her anger. It was white-hot.

Like most experienced mental patients, Clare looked to me for authority and sometimes punishment. When I didn't comply, she was often confused and angry. She also expected me to abandon her, to tell her she was "too difficult" and send her off to a shrink. One woman therapist had done exactly this.

With constant reassurance, her self-destruction decreased. She was able to grieve and, finally, to forge a relationship with me on equal footing.

Because I believe that nurturing physical contact is essential to healing, I've always touched or hugged people. Clare wouldn't tolerate it at first, flinching or even screaming at the slightest touch. This

224

changed quickly, however, and she began to crave contact. We talked at times, about her childhood, where her parents demanded only that she accede to their religion, while ignoring her obvious drug use and "hallucinations." We also talked about the politics of psychiatry, and how she'd been victimized by the system she wanted desperately to believe in. Clare became active in the local mental patients' liberation group, finished college, and went on to work with developmentally disabled adults.

When she left to live on her own, she maintained very close contact, calling our house "home," going fishing with Jim and shopping with me, learning to cook and play bridge.

She was finished when she believed she'd gotten enough. While Clare no longer participates in the day-to-day activities of our home, we see her frequently. She's active with her friends, her job, and her life.

Authenticity and autonomy

In my work as an advocate, we were often able to "divert" people from the mental health system. In my experience, people in emotional crisis are most often asking for safety and support – two commodities least likely to be found in a mental hospital. Members of our ex-patient group, called the Mental Health Advocacy Coalition, would frequently offer both short-term living space and emotional support to each other.

It is that quality of consistent personal presence which we call emotional support that is most difficult to define or quantify. To participate fully in another person's "psychosis" is a potentially enriching and always enlightening experience – if it is not interrupted by mechanistic "medical" treatment. It is, after all, an invitation to participate in the joy of human re-emergence.

There were others. There was Patti, who came from a religious cult, and was attempting to starve herself to death. We dealt with this by feeding her by hand. She was also educationally disadvantaged, and college and beauty school provided a valuable exposure to life for her. She has been working successfully with disabled adults for more than seven years now, owns her own home, and has deep and intimate relationships with others.

Revictimization by professionals

Marie was someone to whom I felt instantly spiritually connected, as though I'd known her before. Repeatedly abused in childhood by her father, she was "catatonic." When she stopped being withdrawn, she tried to kill herself. I discovered her, unconscious, and arranged for medical services without psychiatric intervention. In the emergency room and in intensive care, I sat by her head for hours while she was comatose, whispering over and over again, "I love you. I want you to live." Marie says that, some weeks later, she "knew" she was loved and that life was worth living. Later, she set up a re-birthing process for herself, inviting her friends to participate in a ritual of re-emergence.

Deplorably, Marie was later subjected to sexual exploitation by a mental health professional, a licensed psychologist. After a period of denial and "acting out," she eventually filed charges against him and, as a result, his license to practice was suspended. I was aware that there were more than a dozen women who had been similarly victimized by this well-regarded professional, and eventually discovered there were five other licensed professionals in the area who were routinely sexually abusing or exploiting female clients. Marie still bears the scars of this re-victimization, and is understandably unable to bring herself to trust yet another professional to assist her through the natural process of anger and grief that is the result of the abuse. Nonetheless, she is living on her own in a distant location, and works in a profession for which she earned her degree while she was part of our family.

Susan helped us design a marathon, an extended period of time in which the focus was on her. It was based on an experience I had created for myself some years earlier, which I called my "madness marathon." She arranged for several people, including three therapists/healers of her choice, to be present, and used 48 continuous hours to explore the boundaries of her madness. She regressed spontaneously, becoming a hungry infant, an angry two-year-old, then an appealing four-year-old. By agreement, we acted as "ideal parents," providing protection for her vulnerable child. Susan says the marathon helped contain her madness. Since then, we've frequently utilized the marathon structure for people wanting an intensive experiential process. I have spoken with others who have set up similar "interventions," either purposefully or without intent, and believe that people can and will respect boundaries, as long as they are an integral part of the decision-making process. For example, I often tell people who are suicidal that I will stay with them for up to three days, which is my personal level of tolerance. Not surprisingly, the crisis usually passes within this period of time. If not, we jointly devise back up strategies I have used for myself during times of feeling self-destructive, such as asking friends to simply be present, without needing to "do" anything.

Limited and liberated

Over a period of ten years, we opened our home to more than five hundred people. We did not promise healing, or hold out false hope. It didn't always work out. There were times we felt exploited, and certainly times we felt we were in way over our heads. We often felt both limited and liberated by our lack of formal education and training. I'm sure some of the people who came thought we were peculiar or weird or that we had some ulterior motives.

We see ourselves as ordinary people doing ordinary things. I believe we simply did what people in many cultures do. Native Americans, particularly, view "mental illness" as a spiritual sickness and provide holistic remedies along with support from the community and counsel with shamans. In many "underdeveloped" countries, what would be labeled as "mental illness" is seen through a spectrum; in some, "crazy people" are revered as mystics.

Many churches provide emotional, personal, and financial support to their members and others. So do more loosely structured social groups, especially those of oppressed minorities, such as gay and lesbian people.

Since the vast majority of people who would be labeled as mentally ill – if only they were "caught" by the psychiatric system – don't seek "treatment," we can surely speculate that they are receiving help, support, and caring from their families and friends. Since "mental illness" existed long before psychiatry came into being, it seems to me that most people have an innate sense not only of what they want as "help," but also of how to "help" others. Psychiatry, in this way, has caused many people to abandon their own wisdom, and to turn over their sense of community responsibility to so-called experts. In doing so, we have all undermined the human family and each person in it.

We emphasize that our way is not the "right" way. It is only our way, and it's in a constant state of change and flux as we learn from the people who have come to us. With this perspective, it is easily apparent that we are not only teachers but, perhaps more importantly students who are learning from women who dare to paint with all the hues on their rich spiritual palettes.

Further, we recognize that being part of an extended family is not for everyone; it requires a degree of commitment and responsibility from all the participants, no matter how functional or "dysfunctional" they may be. (We recognize that these are subjective terms.) Living in community is often difficult for people who have been conditioned by the mental health system to be passive recipients of services and who can't envision wholeness for themselves. By and large, these are the people whom we have failed. It's not our failure, really, but the system's, which has promoted passivity, compliance, and spiritual death, and which offers "good" incentives to "good" patients – disability income, housing, drugs, approval by authority figures, and absolution from responsibility.

Rejecting psychiatric presumptions

What do we offer that's different? First, we do not make psychiatric presumptions, nor do we accept labeling, either by the system or the person. If a person comes with a long psychiatric history – and most do – we reassure her that we're not interested in knowing her "diagnosis," which often becomes self-fulfilling prophecy. We don't use MMPI's or other psychiatric schemes to measure outcomes, but encourage each person to trust her own knowing about what "sanity" is for her. We attempt to honor each person's madness and her unique way of expressing that madness, and we try to adapt the environment to fit the person. Most often, this is a simple matter of providing physical and emotional sanctuary – as the person defines it – whether that means designating a space she can occupy as a mad person, making creative arts tools or children's toys available, providing corrugated boxes to tear up or towels to twist, or supporting her as she screams. In this process, we often find ourselves teaching basic pretexts of gestalt practice and developmental theory, which can provide a framework for illumination. This usually comes later, though. In the meantime, the ongoing promise of presence is perhaps the most important gift we give. Perhaps there is no single effort more radical in its potential for healing broken hearts and souls than a transformation of the way in which we function as metaphorical gardeners, growing people.

We have attempted, at times, to bring more structure to our process. We've had regular dinners and "community meetings." At one time, we embraced the reparenting model and "adopted" several people. It eventually became apparent that this set up artificial boundaries and that what we were doing began to look more like therapy, albeit "good therapy," and less like the extended family we intended. We have now returned to a less formal structure, though we've built in some time for privacy and have expanded our social circle to include more people without direct experience as recipients of mental health services.

We strive to keep in touch with the inherent imbalance of power between givers of care and receivers of care, and to cope with this by continuously acknowledging the dangers of exploitation, and sharing the day-to-day substance of our own lives.

Personal transitions and transformations

In 1988, Jim had a serious heart attack. While it was terrifying, it was also extremely gratifying to watch as every member of our extended family came to the coronary care unit to give and receive support. I remember Joan, our newest person, bringing her teddy bear and – for the first time – allowing herself to be touched and comforted without recoiling.

Jim's illness, however, caused us to reevaluate the level of energy we were able to invest in people with formidable needs. We decided that we would no longer open our home to people on a long-term basis. We would still make long-term personal commitments to people, and retain our open-door policy for people needing a place to be during crisis or transition. It has been illuminating to see how

229

well people do "on their own" as long as they know a back up resource is available.

In 1990, I was diagnosed with breast cancer. In 1991, another, rare cancer was detected, for which I am still receiving ongoing treatment. While not life-threatening, it has deeply affected my level of energy. These events were cataclysmic, both personally and within our extended family. They brought a clear opportunity to evaluate the more recondite meaning of my life, work, and passion, as well as another refocusing of my energies. While I am still deeply committed to serving as a teacher/healer and learning more about the process of personal growth – both my own and others – it seemed time to shift more of my individual resources into the work of impacting public policy.

Reflections

Almost every person who finds us has two primary concerns. First, they're afraid they'll "lose control." Usually, this turns out to mean they're afraid of going crazy. Those who've been in psychiatric hospitals have a valid fear, and we promise them that it's safe to "lose control," even to "go crazy," that we'll do whatever is humanly possible to keep them from being locked up.

Secondly, people often demand "a way out," and they believe we'll take them out of their pain, fear, despair, anger, and loneliness. Through my own experience, I know that there is no "way out," that the way out is through, that by dipping into their personal reservoirs of primitive feelings, their "madness," they will no longer be at the mercy of their emotional disarray.

As St. Exupery wrote in *The Little Prince*, "What's essential is invisible to the eye." For us, the essential truth lies in what Laing describes as the etymological definition of "schizophrenia." "Schiz" means "broken." "Phrenos" means "soul" or "heart." For survivors of sexual abuse and trauma – those who are truly brokenhearted – we believe the elemental factors in healing and growth are also the most basic: love and compassion. Though this is a heretical notion in traditional psychiatry, we hope that it is not only revolutionary, but also evolutionary. This is where it all begins, and this is where it never ends.

References

Barnes, M. and Berke, J. (1971) *Two Accounts of Journey Through Madness.* London: MacGibbon and Kee.

Hammerschlag, Carl A. (1988) *The Dancing Healers: A Doctor's Journey of Healing with Native Americans.* San Francisco: Harper and Row.

Laing, R.D. (1967) *The Politics of Experience.* New York: Ballentine Books.

St. Exupery, Antoine De (1943) *The Little Prince.* New York: Harcourt, Brace, World.

Part IV

Policy and Research

Chapter Eleven

A Question of Illness, Injustice, or Both?

Mary Anne Reilly

How We Choose to Perceive the Impact of Abuse on People's Lives Will Help Determine the Future Direction of Health Care Policy

Mary Anne Reilly, M.A.

"It is elementary psychology that those who wish to change the world for the better should not begin by vilifying the public they seek to persuade, or by confronting it with a task that seems impossible."

Theodore Roszak (1995)

"We have a body of knowledge (about human behavior) that for the most part, we ignore. The policies (being pursued) have no logical or rational connection to the best scientific research that is available to us."

Former Democratic Congressman Ted Strickland,
an Ohio psychologist who lost his 1994 re-election bid.
(*Mental Health Weekly*, 1995)

Background

Throughout the better part of 1994, a small, stalwart band of survivors of childhood sexual abuse and their supporters took turns

235

advancing on Capitol Hill. Some of those involved were setting foot in congressional offices for the first time. Others were old hands on the topic and seasoned players in the policy game.

What brought the group together was the prospect of health care reform, or more accurately, the unwelcome prospect of health care reform legislation that failed to directly address most abuse-related issues-that, in fact, declined to identify child abuse as a public health issue. Stunned by the lack of discussion about such issues and frustrated by the press and policy focus on individual disorders and cost-rather than context-driven benefit packages, participants in the Moving Forward Health Care Reform Project★ presented congressional staff and organizations with the latest research on abuse-related medical and psychological aftereffects, previewed original work on the health care and societal costs of abuse and wrote legislative language that sought to designate abuse survivors of all ages as a "medically underserved" population requiring focused public health services. Above all, the group brought survivors who were willing to tell legislators and their staffs about the havoc that abuse had wrought in their lives and to explain how system after system had failed (sometimes spectacularly) to meet their needs.

Such testimony did not go unheeded. Some legislators' staffs had already begun to draw similar conclusions about the need to address abuse issues in health care reform and suggested specific ways to enhance the legislation. Senator Paul Wellstone's (D-MN) office tried to offer an amendment using the "medically underserved" language.

Eventually, however, it became harder and harder to be heard above the cacophony of voices demanding "special" consideration. Ultimately, like so many others', survivors' voices were drowned out by opponents of reform. By October, federal health care reform efforts were headed for hibernation – at least, many thought, until January brought a new congressional class to Washington.

Few envisioned just how new that class might be.

★NOTE: The Moving Forward Health Care Reform Project began in 1993 under the auspices of Moving Forward, Inc., a non-profit organization that publishes *Moving Forward: A Newsjournal for Survivors of Sexual Child Abuse and Those Who Care For Them*. Moving Forward, Inc. now belongs to several coalitions, including the Working Group on Violence, a Washington, D.C. area-based coalition committed to ending abuse and its impact across the lifespan. Health care issues are a primary focus of the Group.

A new congress and a hand-off to the States

New congressional realities

That all seems so long ago now. Since that time, organizations used to hectic, yet relatively routine, reauthorizations of federal laws regarding Medicaid, Medicare and other programs have found themselves scrambling to adjust and in many cases, defend their constituencies against budget-axes being wielded by federal and state-level policymakers.

In view of this *fin de siecle* focus on deficit reduction and shift of programatic responsibility to the states, it seems imperative that those interested in the policy implications of these developments take another look at the ways the public and private sectors have conceptualized and administered services to survivors of abuse – and indeed to all of those who have been diagnosed as having a serious mental illness. It also seems time to incorporate what the research is saying about the physiological, psychological and fiscal consequences of a history of abuse, because if even a portion of what is now being posited is true, such data have tremendous implications for the way individual and social problems are viewed in this society. And that, it almost goes without saying, can have a transformative impact on public policy.

Fifty States, fifty administrations and more: potential disasters and opportunities

In the wake of the demise of federal health care reform efforts, rising health care costs and a presumed mandate to limit social program spending, state officials are pushing for belt-tightening "reforms" of their own. In the State of New York, for example, new Republican Governor George E. Pataki introduced a Medicaid waiver proposal designed to install health maintenance organizations (HMOs) as mental health services "gatekeepers" for Medicaid recipients.

This proposal produced an outcry from mental health advocates, not only because HMOs and other managed care entities have yet to establish a consistent, positive reputation with providers and recipients of mental health services, but also because such entities have had little, if any, experience in administering services to those diagnosed with serious, or chronic, mental illness. In New York, as elsewhere, many of the services directed to this population have been provided by voluntary agencies – agencies that have yet to establish relationships with managed care organizations. In addition, fully cap-itated plans (plans that allow for a pre-approved "cap" on the amount of money that can be expended on services for each person enrolled in the plan) like the one proposed by Pataki, have been known to lack the flexibility necessary to provide more than marginal services to this population (*Mental Health Weekly*).

High-stakes political environments like this can and often do, produce intense and destructive competition among those attempt-ing to wrest what funding remains available for their specific projects and populations. Cooperation might better serve clients' needs. Congressional efforts to relegate responsibility for other social pro-grams to the states may further exacerbate such dynamics at the local level.

Thankfully, the challenge that these developments represent is becoming more clear to health care and other human services advo-cates. In Washington, D.C., as well as in states like Illinois, coalitions containing women's health and other groups have begun taking steps to avert the duplication and sabotaging of efforts that have some-times compromised the effectiveness of organizations under similar political conditions. Assessments of current political realities have also uncovered the need to find a common theme that unites the interests of constituencies of all ages and backgrounds and offers the public a different and effective way to analyze and solve social problems.

Developing a theme that makes common and political sense

A theme beginning to resonate with advocates, researchers and service providers stresses the interconnectedness of issues such as homelessness, unwanted pregnancy, substance abuse and inadequate and mistargeted health care. It incorporates a vision of a healthier, less-divided nation that empowers rather than stigmatizes those who

238

find themselves on the banks of mainstream American culture. Proposed independently by several sources in Washington, D.C. and elsewhere, this theme involves the relationship between violence and its impact on the health of those who have been abused at any point during their lifetimes and, indeed, the consequences of such violence for everyone in this society. Lastly and most pointedly, given the current political climate, it focuses on the need to assess the dollar-for-dollar cost of violence and communicate it to a public focused on waste and hungry for solutions.

This is not exactly a new idea. More than a century ago, neurologist Jean-Martin Charcot and his students Pierre Janet and (however temporarily) Sigmund Freud, became aware that trauma and specifically childhood sexual abuse, played a pivotal role in women's physical and mental health. Much closer to the present time, the concurrent political pressure provided by the modern women's movement and Vietnam veterans' groups, as well as research conducted with Holocaust survivors, resulted in an unprecedented interest in women's health and research on the aftereffects of trauma (Alpert, Brown and Courtois, 1995).

Also during the 1970s, the federal government began to respond to similar pressures. Congress enacted legislation that created a National Institute of Mental Health research program that focused on rape and other acts of violence (Salasin, 1995) and The United States Commission on Civil Rights sponsored a consultation entitled *Battered Women: Issues of Public Policy*. Finally, The President's Commission on Mental Health published a report that listed issues involving physical and sexual abuse in the family and sexual abuse and harassment outside of the family among the priorities that needed to be addressed in services being provided to women diagnosed with serious mental illness (Salasin, 1995).

During the early 1980s, as now, the political tides effectively turned against further examination of such issues. In the 1990s, however, a broader constituency has begun forming to address these issues in a more comprehensive way. This constituency is motivated by its exposure to a growing body of research on abuse and trauma *and* by the active participation of abuse survivors, members of the federal bureaucracy, long-time advocates and other groups and individuals formerly uninvolved in violence issues, including health

239

professionals. Such a development has the potential to transform the way abuse survivors, other advocates, researchers, health, mental health and legal professionals see themselves, the work that they do and the strategies they employ to improve the lives of those who have been abused *and* the community at large.

Will such efforts be successful in ways that previous ones were not? Or will attempts to discredit research and testimony on the subject distract policymakers and the press and ultimately defuse the energy needed to present such a case to the public?

A lot depends on the way we view the problem.

The personal is political – or is it?

But what do they want?

As the previous statement implies, there are many ways to analyze violence-related issues. But how, one might ask, does that process affect policy? The short answer to this question is that it *can* in many ways. When crafting a piece of legislation, or formulating policy that reflects a legislative mandate, for example, policymakers at all levels of government rely on a variety of sources to aid and focus that analysis. In addition, policymakers rely on the testimony of "experts" which, to a varying extent, reflect the populations affected by proposed changes in laws or agency priorities – and, often to a significant degree, the political agendas of those in charge of arranging such testimony.

While those concerned about influencing health care policy on abuse-related issues can have an impact on this process at points along the way, public hearings and other types of meetings offer the most common opportunites for larger audiences to hear such concerns. At gatherings like these, policymakers may accept such testimony without much comment – or interest, for that matter. At other times, however, they may be quite receptive.

In such cases, a key question policymakers are likely to ask is "Okay, but what do you want?" Many involved in abuse-related issues have not been used to answering that question in specific terms. Nonetheless, it is one that abuse survivors and their allies in the public and private sectors must address as they seek to transform the way policy is conceptualized and conducted.

Regrettably, determining what is needed and which strategy will be the most effective in providing it can prove to be a protracted process. In fact, no matter how grueling and frustrating it may be to respond to the changing demands of policy efforts that one has no initial role in crafting (such as health care reform), that quick-response process is generally more contained, (e.g., how can we draft legislative language that addresses our concerns about the need to train medical students to recognize the signs of abuse), than the more global re-thinking that seems necessary now.

Given the diminishing resources available to taxpayer-financed social programs, however, it's hard to argue that we have a choice in the matter. There probably will, for example, continue to be cuts of some sort in Medicaid and possibly in SSI and other disability programs. Further, managed care companies will continue to make substantial inroads into the public health delivery system ("Congress Moving to Slash SSI," 1995). There will be, as members of the Substance Abuse and Mental Health Services Administration's (SAMHSA) National Advisory Committee on Women stated during a June 1995 meeting, a smaller safety net than the one that currently exists for vulnerable populations, including those diagnosed with a serious mental illness. And community organizations undoubtedly will be faced with having to further pool their collective resources to maintain that net.

In that case, the question becomes: What do survivors, advocates, clinicians and researchers need to think — and hopefully reach some agreement about — to determine what is needed, so that all can effectively respond to questions such as "What do you want?" As individuals and groups begin, or in some instances, continue to embark on this process, there are a number of issues that warrant discussion. The remainder of this chapter will explore some of them.

Ways of viewing the problem of abuse in society: the victim-blaming, illness, recovery, social justice and emerging models

To determine what is needed, or more specifically, what would be most effective at the policy level, it seems necessary to return to an "umbrella issue" that has been the focus of debate — and rancor — for more than a century: how to conceptualize the problem of abuse. The models described below attempt to provide a framework for that process.*

The victim-blaming model. A variation on what may be termed the *Victim-Blaming* model has flourished for quite some time. Until recently, it virtually dominated the fields of psychiatry and psychology and figured prominently in public discourse on the subject of violence. "It has led," as psychiatrist Judith Lewis Herman (1992) has noted, "researchers and clinicians to seek an explanation for the perpetrator's crimes in the character of the victim."

Such attempts to blame acts of violence perpetrated on a victim on that victim's character are rarer today than they once were (with the notable exception of the courtroom). At some point during the evolution of the public's familiarity with psychological terms, however, the notion of character and psychopathology have become – to use a clinical term – enmeshed. Thus it is with sad conviction that Herman (1992), like those providing services to people diagnosed with a serious mental illness and those who have themselves been diagnosed as such, can state that "Social judgment of chronically traumatized people therefore tends to be extremely harsh."

This overall perception accounts for the particularly brutal fate that befalls those survivors of abuse who are also traumatized by poverty, community violence, racism, or other factors; in other words, it transcends sexism, as central as gender-related politics may be to this discussion. Not only are many of those diagnosed with serious mental illness plagued by the consequences of the misdiagnoses that psychiatrist Elaine Carmen has so aptly described, but they are often also subject to harsher stigmatization and treatment conditions than trauma victims with economic means. As psychiatric survivor and psychologist Pat Deegan (1995) recounts:

> During a therapy session my friend's therapist essentially apologized for having my friend wait in the same waiting room as the

---

*NOTE: For a fuller discussion, see Armstrong, L. (1994). *Rocking the Cradle of Sexual Abuse: What Happened When Women Said Incest.* Reading, MA: Addison-Wesley; Dobash, R. Emerson and Dobash, Russell P. (1992). *Women, Violence & Social Change.* London: Routledge; and Herman, J.L. (1992). *Trauma and Recovery: The Aftermath of Violence – From Domestic Abuse to Political Terror.* New York: Basic Books.

'severely and persistently mentally ill.' Although this did not bother my friend in the least, her therapist assured her that a separate waiting area in the hallway of the trauma clinic was soon to be established. Trauma survivors were to be segregated from exposure to "really crazy" people.

This poignant example of the tenacity of the victim-blaming model is even more tragic and ironic, given what is now becoming known about the prevalence of a trauma history in those who have been diagnosed with a serious mental illness. In truth, prevailing preconceptions about the demographic profiles and symptomatology of abuse survivors have been very – if unwittingly – effective. Until very recently, survivors with the radically different diagnoses and prospects described above, have barely known about, much less spoken to, one another.

The illness model. One model that arose to challenge this victim-blaming model – but one which has rarely focused on abuse as a factor in the etiology of mental disorders – may simply be termed the *Illness Model.* For several decades, a number of psychiatrists and other mental health professionals, families of psychiatric patients and advocates have sought to destigmatize those with psychiatric problems by emphasizing what they see as the *biological* origins of such difficulties. Chief among the goals of this effort has been to convince the public that the vast array of psychiatric difficulties enumerated in the *Diagnostic and Statistical Manual of Mental Disorders* (DSM) are *illnesses* rather than character flaws and that proper intervention, ranging from short-term psychotherapy to long-term institutionalization, can mitigate the effects of such maladies. This conceptualization is often accompanied by a belief in the ameliorative effects of psychotropic drugs that are used to treat these "mental illnesses," some of which are posited as having solely genetic, as opposed to environmental, components.

To be sure, psychotropic drugs are known to relieve symptoms and to assist functioning, especially in cases where the context of an individual's suffering is acknowledged and understood. In addition, being labeled "ill" as opposed to "evil" can provide some protection from at least one form of stigmatization, particularly in instances where organic brain disease or other conditions precludes full

243

integration into the community. But it is unclear whether such conceptualizations can endure in the future. Diminishing tolerance of vulnerable populations and the programs aimed at servicing their needs – and this conceptualization's dependency on compartmentalized diagnoses and apparent lack of focus on the role of abuse in the lives of many of those diagnosed with a mental illness – make it particularly vulnerable to reassessment.

The recovery model. Much of the work described in this volume seeks to apply the best aspects of the recovery model to the needs of those diagnosed with a serious mental illness, so there is little need to explore this model here in depth. However, a few points seem particularly germane to this discussion. First, there are many variations of the recovery model; one may find adaptations of it in psychoanalytic approaches to therapy, in therapeutic formulations firmly grounded in traumatic stress studies and in the modified precepts of twelve-step and other forms of self-help programs. Recovery models also have come to be associated with experiential as well as cognitive therapies, such as art and movement therapies of various types and outdoor programs.

Second, the most important contribution such models have made is to shift the theoretical responsibility, if not always the actual burden for the actions that precipitated victims' coping difficulties on those who have perpetrated such crimes, rather than to assign blame to some moral failing or biological abnormality in the victims themselves. In a significant number of cases, particularly when victims either have or develop financial or social resources, this shift from repentance to recovery has enabled former victims to redefine themselves and their world and to begin to create a better future for themselves and those close to them.

Third, with the exception of some self-help and other therapy models, much of the vocabulary and analytic interpretations of individual experiences characteristic of the recovery model remain relatively clinical in nature. In some instances, therapists and other service providers are compelled to devise a clinical diagnosis simply to ensure insurance reimbursement for their work with clients. Fee-for-service and managed care companies alike expect diagnoses based on the conceptualizations outlined in the *DSM*, a volume published periodically by the American Psychiatric Association. In any case, relatively little interest or attention was paid to the potential political ramifications of the recovery model, until the well-publicized, but meagerly understood, abuse memory controversy gained notoriety in the 1990s.

The social justice model. While the recovery model has gained ascendancy over the past decade and a half or so, it does not lack critics: women and men, feminists and human rights advocates, have indicated their dissatisfaction with what they see as the apolitical nature of such a model. Some, such as R. Emerson and Russell Dobash (1992), contend that therapeutic professionals have "co-opted" the violence against women movement begun by American feminists during the 1970s, robbing it of the analytical potency that, in their view, characterized the movement's early days. "An important contribution of feminism," they write, "has been to show how the 'personal is political' and to have revealed the importance of intimate personal domination. But this should not mean the collapse of one into the other or lead to equating the political with an exclusive focus on the person – yet this trajectory has at times led to the minimization and neglect of economic and social factors."

They conclude that this lack of emphasis on relevant socioeconomic factors may compromise efforts to end abuse. "The more women are seen as clients in need of therapy rather than people in need of alternatives and choices, the less the movement challenges prevailing conceptions of the problem."

Others are less charitable in their assessment of the evolution of conceptual approaches to abuse-related issues. In *Rocking the Cradle of Sexual Politics: What Happened When Women Said Incest (1994)*, author Louise Armstrong, a consistent proponent of developing a political response to the issue, quotes British authors Kelly, Regan and Burton, as follows:

> The notion of a "journey" to survival, where one is "healed" is both naive and idealistic.... The medical metaphors of "healing" and "recovery" offer a false hope that experiences of abuse can be understood or responded to in a similar way to illness: where both symptoms and cause can be "got rid of" if one can simply find the right "treatment." Thus interactional and social events which are fundamentally about inequality and

245

use of power-over are transformed into individual encounters equivalent to the contracting of germs or viruses.

Exclusively political or therapeutic approaches to the problem of abuse, while interesting, are certainly vulnerable to being viewed as reductionist and unsatisfying. In fact, few would credibly argue that human experience can be reduced to a display of symptoms needing individual treatment *or* to the sum of one's interactions with vast social, political and economic forces that require mass political participation to change.

In that case, how can the best of these perspectives be brought together to form a more integrated view of how to address the problem?

An emerging model. One more and final perspective offers a way to answer this question. It acknowledges that some clinical approaches can positively benefit abuse survivors but underscores the need to see the problem is its broader social context – and it appears to be gaining ground among advocates and clinicians alike. Law professor and advocate Susan Stefan (1995), who is developing litigation strategies designed to improve the mental health system's treatment of sexually abused women, has expressed one such view this way:

> I think there are a lot of very good people out there who are trying their best in a very tough system. Individual women have been helped by individual therapists, just like individual women have been hurt by individual therapists. I'm not saying people don't work hard and with good faith within the system, but I *am* saying it's not helpful to stress adjustment to a society that condones and in some ways encourages rape.

Some clinician/researchers in the trauma field also concede that their work must be examined in the full political, social and economic context of the times in which it is conducted. In fact, this point was quite deliberately brought home by psychologist and International Society for Traumatic Stress Studies (ISTSS) past president John Wilson (1995) during a speech he delivered on "Integrated (Trauma) Models for the Future" at a conference held in Washington, D.C.:

When we think about an integrative model and we think about directions for the future, we must always think about the context in which we think, we write, we work – because it's always affected by historical circumstances. It's affected by the culture in which we live, the events that are transpiring and our own philosophy and the experiences we bring to them. This is true whether you're a clinician or a researcher.

Drawing on his observations of the history of trauma research, its evolution through several editions of the *DSM* and a recent trip to Bosnia, Wilson asked his audience to consider whether it was time to depathologize responses to abuse and other forms of trauma. He reiterated what he and author Robert Jay Lifton have previously suggested, namely that post traumatic stress disorder (PTSD) may be a "normal response to an abnormal situation." "What's abnormal or sick," he asked, "about having memories of watching people die as they were interned in Nazi death camps? What's sick about that? Anything? I don't think so – I think it's human. And that raises another very interesting philosophical question," he added, "Do we really want to codify all of this stuff as pathological in nature?"

His comments struck a nerve in many of those present. Amid enthusiastic applause, he concluded his presentation by saying:

> There's a higher message I believe in all this and it's that the true nature of the human spirit is not to walk around banged up and beat up by horrific circumstances that are either historical, familial, or accidental but to transcend them – and our task as helpers, as researchers, as educators, is to recognize that, to acknowledge it and do everything we can to put ourselves out of business.

While still in the early stages of formulation, a vision that acknowledges the role of power in abusive behavior and destigmatizes the impact of trauma and abuse – indeed of all types of psychological difficulties – but that also allows individuals to address their own situations with support from peers and/or therapeutic professionals, seems to stand the best chance of bridging the gap between clinical and political views of the problem.

247

Some questions to consider

The previous section discusses some of the ways the impact of abuse has been conceptualized until now. Hopefully, it begins to raise some of the questions that those involved in this issue need to address in order to influence policy as effectively as possible. These questions may include:

- Should the victimization of women and children and the consequences of that victimization, be viewed as a political/human rights/feminist issue, requiring political solutions?
- Should such victimization be viewed, instead, as a health problem, requiring appropriate intervention and treatment?
- Finally, can an effective approach include a combination of both and if so, to what extent and purpose?

Other factors that affect answers to such questions. Of course, these questions can be answered in a variety of ways, depending – to a larger degree than some might admit – on one's cultural and economic background, current economic status, gender and profession, as well as one's experience with the legislative or judicial process, political movements in general and the medical and mental health care delivery systems.

While the sheer number of such factors may prompt one to want to postpone the discussion to an indefinite "later", it's important to remember that the effectiveness of policy often depends on the fullness of its response to these considerations. The way chosen to address them can literally mean the difference between life and death for some and affect the quality of life of others.

Some examples. Depending on whom you talk to, access to care can mean a host of different things. For example, imagine for a moment how the following individuals might define access to care. Susan is an employed abuse survivor with generous insurance benefits who, after a relatively few unsuccessful experiences in private sector therapy settings, finally finds a therapist willing and able to assist her. She is likely to respond that abuse is a health care issue and that policymakers need to make sure that if she leaves her job, she won't be forced to forego therapy for six months to a year before becoming eligible for similar benefits.

248

But her concerns may seem like relatively luxurious ones to Laura, an abuse survivor on Medicaid whose only therapy is provided occasionally and free by a clinician who began working with her when she was employed. She undoubtedly wants to know how she can qualify for mental health benefits, period.

To someone like Evelyn, an abuse survivor who is diagnosed with a serious mental illness and is being mistreated in an inpatient unit, access to care is less important than her personal safety. She is desperate to learn how she can be protected from hospital staff who "slam me down when they put me in seclusion" (Wisconsin Coalition on Advocacy, 1994).

Finally, access to care in the traditional sense may appear irrelevant to Denise, a woman with an abuse history who has been revictimized by clinical professionals in the past and vows to avoid formal "treatment" in a state mental health system at all costs in the future. She would like to see policymakers formally support alternative services that she feels stand a better chance of meeting survivors' needs.

To varying degrees, each of these situations can be addressed at the policy level. To date, however, they have not been presented in a comprehensive fashion for a variety of reasons. Some may cite societal denial of and resistance to dealing with abuse issues as one reason – and that has considerable merit. Others may hold the legacies of social science methodology and the medical model responsible for the compartmentalization of data that obscures the pervasiveness of the problem – and they have a point. Still others may justifiably argue that while there has been a considerable amount of separate activity on the part of child abuse- and partner-abuse issue activists, that grassroots support for abuse-related policy changes across the lifespan has yet to make itself substantially felt. Finally, the paucity of evidence about the cost of such violence to the health and mental health delivery system indicates that policymakers have not yet been given a compelling enough fiscal reason to introduce changes to a system that's as uncomfortable about the issue as the public is.

Nonetheless; all that is changing – slowly but surely. What is driving that change, to a significant extent, is the research now emerging on the medical, mental health and systemic consequences of abuse.

The medical and psychological consequences of abuse: a brief overview

Research findings on the medical consequences of abuse

Research on the medical consequences of abuse has grown considerably in recent years. Study results suggest that a history of abuse may have a variety of complex effects on a number of bodily systems, some of which will be summarized below. As these effects are described, it is important to keep in mind that some – but far from all – of these medical problems may have a psychological component and that some of them represent physical damage that has directly been caused by the abuse itself. In all cases, they can have a significant impact on the day-to-day lives of people of all ages and backgrounds.

A history of abuse may affect the central nervous system in a variety of ways. These include the neurochemical problems that research indicates may be the result of trauma (van der Kolk, 1988), as well as the physical trauma and injury that has been caused by physical abuse itself. One study, for example, found that among those participants who could be diagnosed with epilepsy – that is, where the presence of the epilepsy was documented – 52 percent had been hit in the head or face during repeated physical abuse. A connection has also been postulated between a history of abuse and what are known as non-epileptic seizures, which account for half of inpatient and 20 percent of outpatient epilepsy visits. That same study, conducted just a few years ago, determined that 77 percent of those experiencing non-epilieptic seizures – those are seizures that do not seem to have any organic cause – had been sexually abused during childhood or adulthood, while 70 percent of those experiencing such seizures had been at least physically abused during their lifetimes (Bowman, 1993).

A variety of sleep disorders, including sleep apnea, which has been found to relate to obesity, may also bear a relationship to past or present abuse (van der Kolk and Fisler, 1993). Finally, migraines and other kinds of headaches can be indicative of an abuse history (Wahlen, 1992).

Respiratory system-related ailments that can afflict those with a history of abuse include: asthma and other signs of respiratory distress, such as gagging, choking and shallow breathing. This problem often comes to light in the dentist's office and is one reason survivors of abuse avoid dentists and wind up with more serious dental, as well as medical, problems than the general population (Reilly, 1992).

Cardiovascular system problems include stress-related ailments such as hypertension, coronary artery disease and cardiac arrythmia. One survivor of childhood abuse, for example, recently learned from a psychologist at a veterans's administration hospital that the type of cardiac arrythmia she suffers from is also commonly found in combat veterans and prisoners of war.

Endocrine system-related problems include hormone dysregulation. Research by Dr. Frank Putnam of National Institute for Mental Health (NIMH), for example, suggests that sexually abused girls reach puberty a year or two before their non-abused peers and that they seem to have much higher levels of several hormones – these include cortisol, which bears a relationship to stress, testosterone and an adrenal hormone that is associated with sexual maturity (Jancin, 1991). Another problem relates to diabetes, probably the best-known endocrine system disorder. When diabetics have been abused, a variety of problems arise that stem from an inability to control one's diet and the influence of chronic stress on such conditions.

The gastrointestinal and genito-urinary systems are vulnerable to a host of conditions that either defy traditional diagnosis or emerge as a direct result of abuse. Chronic pelvic pain has been the subject of several studies that indicate that those with a history of abuse are more likely to experience such pain than those who claim not to have such a history (Walker et al., 1988). Physical damage due to injuries inflicted during the abuse may also be reflected in problems affecting this system. A survivor of childhood sexual abuse once visited a urologist to detemine whether or not her current physical problems, such as a permanently damaged urethra, could have been caused by the abuse. In fact, they were (Reilly, 1992). Other system-related problems include bladder problems, sexually transmitted diseases and pelvic inflammatory disease (Wahlen, 1992). Rounding out the list of problems that may have a connection to a history of abuse are reproductive problems, including complications stemming from earlier pregnancies, longer amounts of time in labor and post partum difficulties (Jacobs, 1992). Lastly and not surprisingly, survivors of abuse may experience a range of sexual difficulties and dysfunctions (Westerlund, 1992).

A word on the psychological consequences of abuse

The potential psychological consequences of abuse have been enumerated elsewhere in this volume, so it is unnecessary to reexamine them in depth here. Nonetheless, it seems pertinent to touch on the impact that some of these consequences may have on medical and mental health care delivery systems, since this area will be of greatest interest to policymakers. For example, it is not uncommon for survivors of childhood abuse to deem themselves undeserving of timely and consistent medical care, which is why they may experience a medical or psychiatric emergency, such as a suicide attempt, before they seek help. This behavior, as well as the misdiagnosis still all too common in emergency settings, has potentially massive, as yet uncalculated, cost implications for hospitals and clinics of various types.

Medical and mental health system costs

Research studies are beginning to show that a significant number of other abuse survivors respond very differently to medical concerns. Some frequent, rather than avoid, medical facilities, in the often unrealized hope that the symptoms they present will be accurately diagnosed and treated. A study (Felitti, 1991) published in the *Southern Medical Journal*, for example, revealed that 17 percent of those who indicated they had been sexually abused as children saw a physician more than ten times per year, roughly five times the national average. One preliminary estimate of the costs involved in cases like this, which was based on statistics involving the prevalence of childhood sexual abuse and the average cost of an office visit, calculated the cost of such visits in the billions of dollars annually (Pedigo and Reilly, 1994).

Misdiagnosis-related costs are regularly incurred by the mental health system as well. A Canadian study suggests the magnitude of costs involved. The study (Ross and Dua, 1989), which focused on the psychiatric health care costs of 15 female abuse survivors diagnosed with multiple personality disorder (MPD) (now referred to as dissociative identity disorder (DID)), found that the subjects of the study spent an average of 99 months in the Canadian mental health care system before being properly diagnosed – at a cost of $3.8 million (in U.S. dollars). The author estimates that savings of more than $347,000 (in U.S. dollars) per person could be achieved if earlier and accurate diagnosis were to occur in the mental health system.

The importance of a life-span perspective

As has been noted earlier in this chapter and throughout this volume, researchers, clinicians and abuse survivors themselves are becoming increasingly aware of the need to address the consequences of abuse as they affect people across the lifespan. From that perspective, young abuse victims being seen in publicly-funded school-based clinics and elderly nursing home residents with undocumented or ignored histories of abuse who have been misdiagnosed and overmedicated in such facilities, or treated for substance abuse at community mental health centers (Moseley, 1995), must also be seen as the focus of policy concerns. Viewed in this context, costs related to substance abuse, HIV/AIDS and other sexually transmitted diseases, homelessness, other forms of domestic violence and teenage pregnancy, may also legitimately be considered part of the fiscal legacy of this society's relative tolerance of abuse.

Influencing future health care policy

But the problem's so big – what do we do?

When presented with abuse-related information during last year's health care reform debate, one Capitol Hill staffer replied: "But the problem's so big – what can we focus on?" It's a fair question – and a far different one than many of us are used to hearing. But how does one answer it?

There are several ways to do so. Not surprisingly, one's response depends in part on some of the issues discussed earlier in this chapter. Responses may vary, in other words, in relation to how one interprets the current political situation, whether one decides to focus exclusively on health and/or on broader issues that affect it and how one translates the information on abuse-related consequences.

One way to respond, as smaller or still-organizing groups and lobbyists have done, is to focus on specific aspects of federal, state and local legislation and regulation that address particular issues. An example of this approach would be legislation requiring health insurance companies to issue policies to those with a history of abuse, instead of disqualifying them on the basis of a victim-blaming "pre-existing condition."

Those involved in such efforts could also demand that the "outcome research" being touted by managed care companies and supported by employer dollars not only contain medical and mental health services data related to the assessment and treatment of abuse (currently, they may or may not), but also include evaluations of such services from those who use them. Apparently this rarely happens. Activities like these could help stem the tide of misdiagnosis that is so costly in human and economic terms, without necessarily venturing outside the "abuse is a health care issue only" paradigm.

If, however, one views such current practices as discriminatory towards those with such a history then one has entered different, though still related, territory. In that case, it may become necessary to concede that the problem is so big that it needs to be analyzed and thought through piece by piece so that collective action can be pursued in an effective, coherent way.

Undoubtedly, talk of more massive efforts to influence public policy will make some feel squeamish, either because they have never been involved in such efforts and do not know what to expect. Conversely, they have been involved in similar efforts and do not feel they have the energy or motivation to "do it again."

While that is an understandable response, it is hard to imagine that neither individuals diagnosed with a serious mental illness nor their advocates will get the policy hearing they deserve without the coordinated efforts of providers, survivors and others of both genders to link up their concerns with the need to address abuse issues in a more comprehensive way. Elected officials and many hired to advise them, have long been convinced that Medicaid recipients and their advocates just are not organized enough ("Republicans Eye Medicaid Cut," 1995). It will take work to change their minds.

But this has not been done before — or has it?

Other compelling objections can inevitably be raised about the wisdom of proposing a more coordinated response to abuse issues. There is too much stigma attached to issues involving abuse, some might say, let alone to those diagnosed with mental illness. Nothing that comprehensive could ever happen, others might conclude.

Recent history seems to prove those contentions wrong. Legislative efforts to end violence against women, such as the Violence Against Women Act, as well as the successess brought about by AIDS and breast cancer activists, indicate that such initiatives can not only survive, but can become highly successful. AIDS activists, many of whom have been stigmatized by their sexual preference, have nonetheless had major impacts on health care policy.

According to Margo Michaels, M.P.H., (1994) who has written about the accomplishments of the AIDS Coalition to Unleash Power (ACT-UP) and the National Breast Cancer Coalition (NBCC), AIDS activists have been credited with playing a significant role in procuring unprecedented amounts of funding for AIDS research under difficult political conditions and credited with contributing to policy changes at the Food and Drug Administration. In 1993, Michaels also notes, the National Breast Cancer Coalition delivered a petition — signed by 2.6 million people — to President Clinton. The petition "demanded that the breast cancer epidemic be declared a National Health Emergency and that a national strategy be developed to end the epidemic." In response, Health and Human Services Secretary Donna Shalala gathered researchers, activists and policy makers together to devise a "National Action Plan on Breast Cancer."

Each of these efforts, or movements, as they are sometimes called, have involved what Michaels refers to as "boundary spanners." She describes such individuals as people who "share divergent identities, such as scientist/activist, policymaker/activist, or clinician/activist."

From their respective points-of-reference, such individuals have historically helped to ease communication between activists and the individuals and institutions challenged by their demands. Together they have made a difference.

Political conditions and the policies affected by them, change – sometimes predictably and, other times, without apparent warning. It is impossible to discern ahead of time what will happen in November of 1996, much less what the political landscape will look like in the year 2000. What can be predicted, however, is that the legacy of abuse will remain largely unchecked, unless a concerted effort is made to engage policymakers in its eradication.

References

Alpert, J.L., Brown, L.S. and Courtois, C.A. (1995) "Symptomatic clients and memories of childhood abuse: What the trauma and child sexual abuse literature tells us," In *Working Group on Investigation of Memories of Childhood Abuse, Final Report (Draft)*. Washington, D.C.: American Psychological Association, pp. 4–7.

Bowman, E.S. (1993) "Etiology and clinical course of pseudoseizures: Relationship to trauma, depression and dissociation", in *Psychosomatics*, 34(4), pp. 333–341.

Deegan, P. (1995) "Before we dare to vision, we must be willing to see." *Dare to Vision: Shaping the National Agenda for Women, Abuse and Mental Health Services: Proceedings of a Conference Held July 14–16, 1994 in Arlington, VA*, pp. 6–16.

Dobash, R. Emerson and Dobash, Russell P. (1992) *Women, violence and social change*. London: Routledge, p. 234.

Felitti, V.J. (1991, March) "Long-term medical consequences of incest, rape and molestation", in *Southern Medical Journal*, 84(3), pp. 328–331. See also: Springs, F.E. and Friedrich, W.N. (1992). "Health risk behaviors and medical sequelae of childhood sexual abuse", in *Mayo Clinic Proceedings*, 67, pp. 527–532.

Herman, J.L. (1992) *Trauma and recovery: The aftermath of violence – From domestic abuse to political terror*. New York: Basic Books, pp. 115–116.

Jacobs, J.L. (1992) "Child sexual abuse victimization and later sequelae during pregnancy and childbirth", in *Journal of Child Sexual Abuse*, 1(1), pp. 103–112.

Jancin, B. (1991, December) "Sexually abused children found to have lasting hormone effects", in *Clinical Psychiatry News*, pp. 3, 22.

Kelly, L., Regan, L. and Burton, S. (1992) "Beyond victim to survivor: The implications of knowledge about children's resistance and avoidance strategies" (London: Child Studies Unit, University of North London, June 1992). In L. Armstrong (1994). *Rocking the Cradle of Sexual Abuse: What Happened When Women Said Incest*. Reading, MA: Addison-Wesley, p. 235.

Michaels, M.I. (1995) *Health activism in breast cancer and AIDS: A conceptual framework*. Unpublished manuscript. University of North Carolina, Chapel Hill, Department of Health Behavior and Health Education.

Moseley, S.M. (1995, Spring) "Elderly Incest Survivors: A Hidden Problem in a Hidden Population", in *Dimensions: A Quarterly Newsletter of the Mental Health and Aging Network of the American Society on Aging*, p. 1.

Pedigo, M.K. and Reilly, M.A. (1994) "The health and societal costs of childhood sexual abuse." Presentations conducted for congresssional staff and national organizations, p. 4.

Reilly, M.A. (1992, January–February) "Medical community takes notice of survivors' health concerns", in *Moving Forward*, 1(2), pp. 1–11.

Ross, C.A. and Dua, V. (1993) "Psychiatric health care costs of multiple personality disorder", in *American Journal of Psychotherapy*, 47(1), pp. 103–112.

Rozak, T. (1995) "Where Psyche meets Gaia." In T. Rozak, M.E. Gomes and A.D. Kanner (Eds.), *Ecopsychology: Restoring the Earth/Healing the Mind*, ed. (pp. 1–17). San Francisco: Sierra Club Books.

Salasin, S. (1995) "Looking back, looking ahead: Shining a light on the abuse of women." In *Dare to Vision: Shaping the National Agenda for Women, Abuse and Mental Health Services: Proceedings of a Conference Held July 14–16, 1994 in Arlington, VA*. Holyoke, MA: Human Resource Association of the Northeast, pp. 1–5.

Staff. (1995, March 3) "Congress moving to slash SSI for mentally ill", in *American Psychiatric News*, p. 1.

Staff. (1995, March 20) "In case you haven't heard", in *Mental Health Weekly*, p. 8.

Staff. (1995, March 20) "Proposed N.Y. Medicaid Waiver Threatens Agency Structure", in *Mental Health Weekly*, pp. 2–3.

Stephan, S. (1995) "The protection racket – Violence against women: Psychiatric labeling and the law", in *Dare to Vision: Shaping the National Agenda for Women, Abuse and Mental Health Services: Proceedings of a Conference Held July 14–16, 1994 in Arlington, VA*, pp. 25–30.

van der Kolk, B.A. (1988) "The trauma spectrum: The interaction of biological and social events in the genesis of the trauma response", in *Journal of Traumatic Stress*, 1, pp. 273–290.

van der Kolk, B.A. and Fisler, R.E. (1993) "The biologic basis of posttraumatic stress." In B.A. Elliott, K.C. Halverson and M. Hendricks-Matthews, (Eds.). *Primary Care Clinics of North America. Special Issue on Family Violence and Abusive Relationships* (June, 1993), 20(2), pp. 417–432.

Wahlen, S.D. (1992) "Adult survivors of child sexual abuse." In M. Hendricks-Matthews, (Ed.). *Violence Education: Toward a Solution.* Kansas City, MO: The Society of Teachers of Family Medicine, pp. 89–102.

Walker, E.A., Katon, W.J., Harrop-Griffiths, J., Holm, L., Russo, J. and Hickok, L.R. (1988) "Relationship of chronic pelvic pain to psychiatric diagnoses and childhood sexual abuse", in *American Journal of Psychiatry*, 147, pp. 75–80.

Westerlund, E. (1992) *Women's sexuality after childhood incest.* New York: W.W. Norton.

Wilson, J.P. (Speaker) (1995) "Toward integrative models for the future." *Proceedings of the Conference on Trauma, Loss and Dissociation: The Foundations of 21st Century Traumatology, February 16–20, 1995.*

Wisconsin Coalition for Advocacy (1994) *Report on patient treatment concerns and use of restraint and seclusion in violation of Sec. 51.61, Wis. Stats. at the STEP unit, Winnebago Mental Health Institute, June 22, 1994*, p. 14.

Chapter Twelve

Treatment Research on Sequelae of Sexual Abuse

Stanley D. Rosenberg, Robert E. Drake and Kim T. Mueser

C OMMUNITY mental health clinicians and researchers are in the midst of a profound sea change in understanding the role of trauma in the development and exacerbation of various disorders. In a sense, this change is analogous to the shift which occurred when the first conceptualizations of dual diagnosis emerged and we began to recognize that the course of psychiatric illness, treatment response and recovery were markedly affected by comorbid substance use disorders. We have now become aware of the degree to which substance abuse had been overlooked by mental health professionals and the degree to which clients had not even been asked the relevant questions about their substance use behavior. In the current situation, we are finding that another set of questions we have neglected to ask-relating to trauma history-may have also distorted our view of our clients' problems and what is needed to aid their recovery (Rose, Peabody and Stratigeas, 1991). This change in awareness goes beyond the confines of community mental health and is emerging in all aspects of the psychiatric and medical care delivery system. Where the physical and sexual victimization of patients had been almost totally invisible, there is now a growing belief among many professionals that abuse and its sequelae may be one of our most profound public health problems. The purpose of this paper is to review the emergent literature on abuse, its sequelae and treatment, especially as it relates to people with severe mental illness. We will focus on the research implications of this data in relation to new treatment models for trauma recovery in this population.

Prevalence of childhood sexual abuse

The occurrence of sexual abuse in childhood is increasingly recognized as an important etiologic component in a number of psychiatric disorders (Briere, 1992; Browne and Finkelhor, 1986; Bryer, Nelson, Miller and Krol, 1987; Green, 1993; Greenwald, Lettenberg, Cado and Tarran, 1990; Kendall-Tackett, Williams and Finkelhor, 1993; Surrey, Swett, Michaels and Levin, 1990; Wyatt, Guthrie and Notgrass, 1992). Childhood sexual abuse is most commonly defined as any sexual contact (including caressing, fondling or stimulating the genitalia of a child; having the child stimulate the perpetrator's genitalia; and/or oral, anal or vaginal rape) occurring with anyone five or more years older when the subject was under age 16 (Briere, 1984). Epidemiological studies report prevalence rates of childhood sexual abuse ranging from 6.8% to 62% (Russell, 1984; Walch and Broadhead, 1992; Wyatt, 1985). Most researchers in the field estimate that one-quarter to one-third of all female children in our culture suffer sexual abuse before their eighteenth birthday (Browne and Finkelhor, 1986).

The prevalence of childhood abuse in help-seeking populations appears to be even higher than in the population as a whole. Recent studies find relatively high rates of childhood molestation in such clinical populations as chronic pain patients, women seeking routine gynecologic services (Walch and Broadhead, 1992) and those seeking treatment from primary care physicians (Bachmann, Moeller and Bennett, 1988; Greenwood, Tangalos and Maruta, 1990; Lechner, Vogel, Garcia-Shelton, Leichter and Steibel, 1993). Briere and Zaidi (1989) found that 70% of non-psychotic women seeking psychiatric emergency room services acknowledged, on direct questioning, a history of sexual abuse in childhood. Studies of sexual abuse among female psychiatric inpatients suggest a prevalence rate of 59–63% percent (Bryer et al., 1987); while the comparable figure for female outpatients appears to be at least 40% (Surrey et al., 1990).

Childhood sexual abuse in severely mentally ill women

The few available studies assessing abuse history in women with severe mental illness (both inpatient and outpatient) have found rates of childhood sexual victimization varying from 34% to 54% (Beck and van der Kolk, 1987; Craine, Henson, Colliver and McLean, 1988; Jacobson and Herald, 1990, Muenzenmaier, Meyer, Struening and Ferber, 1993; Rose et al., 1991). The lower figure was obtained using a non-standard, brief measure and produced a rate substantially lower than that in the four other cited studies. The remaining studies report disclosure of abuse in approximately half of the patients interviewed. Goodman, Dutton and Harris (in press) have documented that a very high percentage of dually diagnosed homeless women have a premorbid history of childhood victimization. However, the implications of childhood sexual abuse for understanding the symptomatology and life course of dually diagnosed women are not well understood. This field of inquiry is quite new and the literature is rife with ambiguities and controversy. One of the few points of agreement between researchers and clinicians working in this area is that much investigation into the impact of early abuse, its relation to other types of vulnerability and the treatment of its long-term effects, is required.

At the same time, clinical researchers working in the area of severe mental illness have been understandably wary of focusing on the problem of early abuse in this population. There has been reluctance, for example, to disinter the theoretical trend of blaming families for causing major psychiatric disorders. Current treatment models emphasize enhancing current adjustment rather than understanding past events; and many researchers mistrust historical information provided by psychotic, substance-abusing respondents. On the other hand, trauma is a ubiquitous issue for clinicians who treat homeless, dually diagnosed people. Even though we currently lack proven treatment strategies for the amelioration of post-abuse effects, it is difficult to argue for continued ignorance. It should also be noted that many homeless people have histories of being raised by non-relatives, such as foster homes (Susser, Moore and Link, 1993) and

261

have early trauma histories that may not be related to direct familial experiences. The comparative rates and clinical correlates of incestuous and non-incestuous abuse in this population are another of the many issues requiring further elucidation.

The sequelae of sexual abuse

To date, the reported sequelae of physical and sexual abuse in childhood appear to be diffuse, overlapping and confounded by other variables such as family pathology and substance abuse. Childhood victimization appears to be a risk factor for a wide variety of symptoms including depression, character disorders and alcohol abuse (Nash, Hulsey, Sexton, Harralson and Lambert, 1993). The most commonly discussed long-term effect of childhood sexual abuse is Post Traumatic Stress Disorder (PTSD) (Courtois, 1986; Eth and Pynoos, 1985; Goodwin, 1985). However, a number of researchers have raised questions about the applicability of the PTSD model, based largely on the study of adult victims of discrete, time-limited traumas, to patients who have been victims of incest and other forms of chronic childhood victimization (Wasserman and Rosenfeld, 1992). These writers posit a more complex and unique set of chronic, symptomatic effects resulting from early and chronic sexual abuse (Finkelhor and Browne, 1985; Briere, 1984; Goodwin, 1990; Herman, 1992) including feelings of powerlessness, self-blame, tendency towards dissociative symptoms and a variety of pathologies of self. However, there is not a standard definition of a post-abuse syndrome and even less established is measurement technology for its assessment.

It is unclear how the vulnerable population described in this volume (women with major mental illness and substance use disorders) may also meet criteria for either the more narrowly defined syndrome of PTSD or the varieties of post-abuse disorders described by Herman (1992) and others. It is certainly not known what the treatment implications might be of a patient's status on some continuum of focal pathology associated with early victimization, whether those suffering only adult trauma require modified interventions, or how the phase of trauma response affects treatment response. While Stowe and Harris (this volume) report that psychosis and substance abuse do not disqualify patients from participation in treatment for abuse recovery, the field currently lacks data on outcomes for patients with early vs. later trauma, those with and without PTSD, those with and without active substance use disorders and those with and without psychosis.

Problems in assessing abuse prevalence and sequelae

Further complicating the issue of specific sequelae is the fact that sexual abuse may be confounded with other pathogenic factors. Families where abuse occurs are more likely to evidence numerous pathogenic features (Harter, Alexander and Neimeyer, 1988; Hulsey, Sexton and Nash, 1992; Wyatt and Newcomb, 1990) such as enmeshment, isolation, increased role confusion and a rigid, authoritarian parenting style. (Alexander, 1985; Alexander and Lupfer, 1987; Blick and Porter, 1982; Pelletier and Handy, 1986; Tierney and Corwin, 1983). Indeed, a constellation of variables frequently associated with the development of psychopathology are almost always present in the families of abuse victims (Beitchman, Zucker, Hood, DaCosta, Adman and Cassavia, 1992).

Although the long-term sequelae of sexual abuse are variable, complex and frequently elusive in their clinical presentation, they have also been alleged to be etiologic factors in a number of psychiatric disorders (Gelinas, 1983), including Somatization Disorder, Borderline Personality Disorder and Multiple Personality Disorder (O'Donohue and Greer, 1992). Some authors (e.g., Nigg, Silk, Western, Lohr, Gold, Goodrich and Ogata, 1991) see the effects of abuse on the development of object representations as predisposing survivors to develop borderline and similar personality disorders. Others argue that applying personality disorder diagnoses to abuse victims indicates a misunderstanding or denial of the etiology of their symptoms and places blame for abuse sequelae on the survivor (Herman, 1992).

The problems of parsing the differential etiologic contributions of early trauma, major mental illness and substance use disorders to current symptomatology represents an even more difficult conundrum. These clients are often reluctant, as are many abuse victims, to report early abuse; especially intra-familial abuse (Williams, 1993; Della Femina, Yaeger and Lewis, 1990). They may also become confused as to the chronology of events and, when psychotic, may be prone to persecutory delusions and delusions with bodily and/ or explicitly sexual content. The general issue of the validity of "repressed memory" (Loftus, 1993) and the potential for false accusation of abuse have not yet been focused on this population. For example, when abuse rates are reported for the severely mentally ill in the few available studies, there is no data on whether these events were "repressed" or forgotten for periods of time and remembered in the context of treatment and/or later retraumatization. However, the general issue of suggestion and the problems of interpreting confused, poorly articulated early memories may be further compounded by the general problems of memory, language and cognition imposed by both major mental illness and substance abuse. This population is also particularly vulnerable to the commingled effects of childhood physical abuse and neglect and of adult physical and sexual abuse.

It would also appear that, as in the population as a whole, the nature and intensity of post-abuse sequelae are quite varied. While many dually diagnosed homeless women have been traumatized, we do not know how many meet criteria for PTSD, or for the other types of chronic post-abuse syndromes described by Herman (1992), Briere (1984) and others. The delineation of various psychiatric syndromes that are the sequelae of trauma remains relatively uncharted territory. Identifying specific, discrete syndromes resulting from trauma could have implications for predicting which patients will mostly likely respond to which psychotherapeutic interventions. At the present, the majority of research on the sequelae of trauma has focused on PTSD, with some attention directed to the controversial category of multiple personality disorder (Piper, 1994). Despite some agreement about the core defining characteristics of PTSD (unpleasant memories of the traumatic event, avoidance, heightened physiological arousal), it is unclear which other symptoms should be included in the complex.

Depression is widely recognized as a common secondary symptom of PTSD (Rundell et al., 1989) and has been assessed in most controlled treatment studies of PTSD (e.g., Cooper and Clum, 1989; Resnick and Schnicke, 1992). There is less agreement as to whether psychotic symptoms (other than flashbacks or reexperiencing the trauma) can also be a part of the PTSD syndrome. Some

264

evidence suggests a link between PTSD and psychotic symptoms. Several studies of comorbid psychiatric disorders in patients with PTSD have reported higher than expected rates of schizophrenia (Escobar, Randolph, Puente, Spiwak, Asamen, Hill and Hough, 1983; Davidson, Swartz and Storck, 1985; Faustman and White, 1989). For example, Faustman and White (1989) reported that 29 out of 536 (5.4%) veterans with PTSD were also diagnosed as having schizophrenia, a rate approximately five times that in the general population (Robins and Regier, 1991).

Psychotic symptoms are common in patients with chronic PTSD. Mueser and Butler (1987) in a study of inpatient veterans with PTSD, reported that hallucinations were associated with more severe symptoms and higher levels of combat exposure. In a subsequent study of outpatient veterans (Butler, Mueser, Sprock and Braff, 1994), those with PTSD had significant elevation on the Scale for the Assessment of Positive Symptoms (SAPS; Andreasen, 1984) compared to veterans without PTSD. Specially, the PTSD group had higher scores on the hallucinatory experiences, delusional thought and bizarre behavior subscales of the SAPS, but not the formal thought disorder subscale.

Along with this evidence that chronic PTSD may present with psychotic symptomatology, at least one case study (Waldfogel and Mueser, 1988) reported that a chronically ill patient's schizophrenic-like symptoms remitted when an earlier sexual trauma was revealed and he was treated with an imaginal exposure approach (Keane and Kaloupek, 1982). While further study is needed, especially with traumatized women, these limited findings suggest that the PTSD syndrome may extend beyond the widely accepted cluster of symptoms specified by DSM-IV. If psychotic symptoms do co-occur in even a relatively small proportion of traumatized persons, such symptoms could result in misdiagnosis and unnecessary chronicity due to the failure to treat the underlying post-traumatic disorder.

Significance of trauma and its effects

The research reviewed suggests the possibility that, for a subset of dually diagnosed women, their chronic symptoms in fact derive from PTSD: that we have misdiagnosed them as having affective or schizophrenic disorders. We currently lack information on how their post-abuse sequelae interact with other vulnerabilities in this population and on how the relief of PTSD or post-abuse symptoms may affect other symptoms and these clients' general level of functioning.

In this context of increasing clinical awareness but continued scientific ambiguity, it is important that programs serving severely mentally ill clients begin to develop effective strategies for dealing with the primary symptoms and problems in living which characterize a highly vulnerable group of abuse victims: dually diagnosed homeless women. Harris' chapter (this volume) represents one model for accomplishing this task and is quite congruent with many of the principles which underlie a treatment model for a parallel, but somewhat less ill chronic population recently proposed by Herder and Redner (1991). Both models emphasize the need for intensive case management, crisis intervention and other ongoing support services for women with chronic mental illness being treated for post-traumatic symptomatology. Both recognize that the trauma intervention should involve group support, the opportunity for cognitive reframing, social-skills enhancement and psychoeducation. Harris, working with clients with more Axis I disorders and higher rates of co-morbid substance use disorder, argues for fewer exclusionary criteria for trauma treatment as long as adequate supports are available.

We would argue that both the available research data, as well as clinical experience, support many of Harris' key contentions. First, there are costs to attempting to ignore the problem of early abuse experiences when providing services to women with severe mental illness. Both directly and indirectly, public sector clients are expressing needs related to past sexual victimization and can become alienated from service providers if they refuse to confront these concerns. Secondly, many of their most significant functional problems and difficulties in accepting services may be related directly to their post-abuse reactions (e.g., distrust of authority). Moreover, treatment need not raise the specter of decompensation for these clients if adequate attention is paid to their needs for structure and safety. Many women with severe mental illness express a need for processing this "secret" and shameful aspect of their history. While less structured forms of psychotherapy may be difficult for these clients to manage, concrete and psychoeducationally structured approaches appear to be strategic in allowing them to engage in the process of reframing their experiences. Such reworking of the meaning of the trauma in relation to current behavior can be effective in reducing self-blame, revictimization and other self-harming behaviors. It is also clear that the multi-faceted treatment approaches advocated by both Harris and Herder and Redner are congruent with current knowledge of effective services for clients who are severely mentally ill (Torrey and Drake, 1994). These include: the importance of engaging the client in a working alliance; direct efforts at improving adaptive functioning in adult social roles; enhancing environmental supports; use of well integrated, multi modal interventions; dealing with the heterogeneity of the schizophrenic disorder in treatment planning; adopting a long-term perspective towards rehabilitation rather than pursuing a rapid cure; and addressing basic issues such as physical well being and homelessness as a precondition to treatment.

Treatment implications

In recent years a multitude of different treatment strategies have been proposed for PTSD or other syndromes that result from trauma. Unfortunately, the amount of research on these interventions is quite limited. In fact, if one examines controlled research on treatment, only three studies have been conducted, two on combat veterans (Cooper and Clum, 1989; Keane, Fairbank, Caddell and Zimering, 1989) and one on rape victims (Foa, Rothbaum, Riggs and Murdock, 1991). A fourth quasi-experimental study has also been conducted on rape victims which did not randomly assign patients to treatment groups (Resnick and Schnicke, 1992). All four studies were time-limited, employed cognitive-behavior interventions that included imaginal exposure to feared memories and produced positive results that were maintained at follow-up.

This research is promising, but the effects of the interventions on early sexual assault and incest have not yet been the focus of controlled study. However, several case studies employing these cognitive-behavior approaches to women with histories of childhood sexual abuse and PTSD have reported positive results (Rychtarik, Silverman, Van Landingham and Prue, 1984; Vaughan and Tarrier, 1992). More work is needed in this area and the systematic study of

267

cognitive-behavioral treatments to traumatized individuals with severe mental illness appears to be warranted.

Implications for services research

Research is clearly needed to examine whether particular patient characteristics, or characteristics of the traumatic events suffered, are related to differential response to post-traumatic interventions for clients with severe mental illness. We would raise the questions, for example, of whether the particular treatment interventions are more appropriate and effective for women victimized in childhood, more recent trauma victims, or both. Histories of childhood victimization are clearly common among dually diagnosed homeless women, but further investigation is needed to determine if symptoms, course of illness, adaptation and treatment responses are differentially affected in this population by the developmental stage at which abuse first occurred and by the type of those trauma experiences. Previous investigations, for example, have cited differential long-term effects mediated by such factors as whether the abuse was incestuous or non-incestuous; the presence or absence of direct physical violence associated with the abusive episode; single vs. multiple perpetrators, the presence of opportunity to disclose the incident; and more chronic versus acute instances of victimization (Briere and Runtz, 1988, Briere and Zaidi, 1989; Wyatt and Newcomb, 1990). Further complicating this question is the fact that women victimized in childhood, especially victims of incestuous abuse, are also much more likely than the population as a whole to suffer adult victimization. Many dually diagnosed homeless women probably have suffered both childhood and adult victimization.

Another point requiring further elucidation is whether treatment models are equally relevant for males in the dually diagnosed, homeless population. Recent findings suggest that men are half as likely as women to be physically and/or sexually abused in childhood (Findelhor and Dziuba-Leatherman, 1994). This would imply that substantial numbers of men suffering chronic mental illness and substance use disorder have post-abuse reactions which may be as those observed in homeless, dually diagnosed women. Both the phenomenology and treatment of these problems should be investigated.

Given the paucity of data from controlled studies treating child-hood abuse sequelae generally and its total unavailability for patients with severe mental illness, our emergent awareness of the scope and significance of childhood traumatization in this population raises many questions and challenges for services researchers. First, the extent and nature of the problem of post-abuse reactions in women with severe mental illness require further investigations. In order for this goal to be achieved, we will have to learn more about assessing the problem with reliable and valid techniques, a task which has proven technically complex in less ill populations (Rosenberg, Hulsy and Rosenberg, submitted for publication; Resnick, Falsetti, Kilpatrick and Freedy, in press; Foa, Riggs, Dancu and Rothbaum, 1993). Longitudinal data will also be useful in documenting the complications related to abuse sequelae in women with severe mental illness. Clinical researchers must work to identify innovative or "best clinical practice" models to treat identified problems related to abuse and its aftermath. Treatment models will need to be care-fully defined and operationalized, preferably in the form of manuals which can guide service delivery across a range of clinical settings where this population seeks services. Ideally, open clinical trials could be conducted to demonstrate the utility of one or more treatment approaches as well as providing evidence that highly vulnerable clients are not harmed by attempts to ameliorate abuse sequelae.

Once empirical evidence on these issues has been gathered, inves-tigators should initiate controlled experiments with identified sub-groups of patients most likely to benefit from specific interventions. Almost all of the proposed models for treating trauma sequelae in those with chronic disorders are complex and multifaceted (Herman, 1992, Seidel, Gusman and Abueg, 1994), as well as being aimed at many different levels of functioning and pathology (mood, self-concept, addictive behaviors, risk taking, psychotic decompensa-tion). Although this complexity may well be demanded by the clini-cal and practical realities of working with patients with both severe mental illness and post-abuse effects, it creates challenges in deter-mining which are the most potent ingredients in a given interven-tion, or for whom (e.g., patients with or without PTSD *per se*). Additional controlled experimentation should ultimately be con-ducted by decomposing efficacious models to isolate their active

269

ingredients, establish their domain of validity and assist costs and benefits.

It would also seem important to emphasize how early we are in the process of developing effective, practical treatment models for post-abuse symptoms in patients with severe mental illness. Clear evidence on treatment efficacy for approaches to chronic PTSD in women and especially on its variants in the "post-abuse" spectrum, is not yet available. When we try to export existing, minimally researched technologies – derived primarily from outpatient studies of acutely traumatized – to the population with chronic and severe mental illness, we are forced to make broad extrapolations. To some unspecified degree, we will need to adapt treatment approaches introduced in other contexts for less ill clients, or invent quite new treatment technologies for treating people with both major mental illness and trauma histories. Still another degree of complexity is added in providing treatment to women who are both abusing substances and homeless, making them more vulnerable to re-victimization.

References

Alexander, P. (1985) "A systems theory conceptualization of incest", in *Family Process*, 24, 79–88.

Alexander, P. and Lupfer, S. (1987) "Family characteristics and long-term consequences associated with sexual abuse", in *Archives of Sexual Behavior*, 16, 235–245.

Andreasen, N.C. (1984) *Scale for the Assessment of Positive Symptoms (SAPS)*. Iowa City: University of Iowa.

Bachmann, G., Moeller, T. and Bennett, J. (1988) "Childhood sexual abuse and the consequences in adult women", in *Obstetrics and Gynecology*, 71, 631–642.

Beck, J.C. and van der Kolk, B. (1987) "Reports of childhood incest and current behavior of chronically hospitalized psychotic women", in *American Journal of Psychiatry*, 144, 1474–1476.

Beitchman, J., Zucker, K., Hood, J., DaCosta, G., Adman, D. and Cassavia, E. (1992) "A review of the long-term effects of child sexual abuse", in *Child Abuse and Neglect*, 16, 101–118.

Blick, L. and Porter, F. (1982) "Group therapy with female adolescent incest victims." In S. Groi (Ed.), *Handbook of clinical intervention in child sexual abuse* (pp. 145–175). Lexington, MA: Lexington Books.

Briere, J. (1984) *The effects of childhood sexual abuse on later psychological functioning: Defining a "post-sexual abuse syndrome."* Presented to the Third National Conference on Sexual Victimization of Children, Washington, D.C.

Briere, J. (1992) *Child abuse trauma: Theory and treatment of the lasting effects.* Newbury Park: Sage Publications.

Briere, J. and Runtz, M. (1988) "Symptomatology associated with childhood sexual victimization in a nonclinical adult sample", in *Child Abuse and Neglect*, 12, 51–59.

Briere, J. and Zaidi, L. (1989) "Sexual abuse histories and sequelae in female psychiatric emergency room patients", in *American Journal of Psychiatry*, 146, 1602–1606.

Browne, A. and Finkelhor, D. (1986) "Impact of child sexual abuse: A review of the research", in *Psychological Bulletin*, 99(1), 66–77.

Bryer, J., Nelson, B., Miller, J. and Krol, P. (1987) "Childhood physical and sexual abuse as factors in adult psychiatric illness", in *American Journal of Psychiatry*, 144, 1426–1430.

Butler, R.W., Mueser, K.T., Sprock, J. and Braff, D.L. (1994) "Positive symptom comorbidity in posttraumatic stress disorder." Manuscript under review.

Cooper, N.A. and Clum, G.A. (1989) "Imaginal flooding as a supplementary treatment for PTSD in combat veterans: A controlled study", in *Behavior Therapy*, 20, 381–391.

Courtois, C. (1986) "Treatment for serious mental health sequelae of child sexual abuse: Post-traumatic stress disorder in children and adults." Paper presented at the Fourth National Conference on Sexual Victimization of Children, New Orleans, LA.

Craine, L.S., Henson, C.E., Colliver, J.A. and MacLean, D.G. (1988) "Prevalence of a history of sexual abuse among female psychiatric patients in a state hospital system", in *Hospital and Community Psychiatry*, 39, 300–304.

Davidson, J., Swartz, M., Storck, M., *et al.* (1985) "A diagnostic and family study of posttraumatic stress disorder", in *American Journal of Psychiatry*, 142, 90–93.

Della Femina, D., Yaeger, C. and Lewis, D. (1990) "Child abuse: adolescent records vs. Adult recall", in *Child Abuse and Neglect*, 14(2), 227–231.

Escobar, J.I., Randolph, E.T., Puente, M.A., Spiwak, F., Asamen, M.A., Hill, M. and Hough, R.L. (1983) "Post-traumatic stress disorder in Hispanic Vietnam veterans: Clinical phenomenology and sociocultural characteristics", in *The Journal of Nervous and Mental Disease*, 171, 585–596.

Eth, S. and Pynoos, R.S., (Eds.) (1985) *Post-traumatic Stress Disorder in Children*, Washington, DC: American Psychiatric Press.

271

Faustman, W.O. and White, P.A. (1989) "Diagnostic and psychopharmacological treatment characteristics of 536 inpatients with posttraumatic stress disorder", in *The Journal of Nervous and Mental Disease*, 177, 154–159.

Finkelhor, D. and associates (1986) *A Sourcebook on Child Sexual Abuse*, Beverly Hills, CA. Sage.

Finkelhor, D. and Browne, A. (1985) "The traumatic impact of child sexual abuse: A conceptualization", in *American Journal of Orthopsychiatry*, 55(4), 530–541.

Finkelhor, D. and Dziuba-Leatherman, J. (1994) "Victimization of children", in *American Psychologist*, 49(3), 173–183.

Foa, E.B., Riggs, D.S., Dancu, C.V. and Rothbaum, B.O. (1993) "Reliability and validity of a brief instrument for assessing post-traumatic stress disorder", in *Journal of Traumatic Stress*, 6, 459–473.

Foa, E.B., Rothbaum, B.O., Riggs, D.S. and Murdock, T.B. (1991) "Treatment of posttraumatic stress disorder in rape victims: A comparison between cognitive-behavioral procedures and counseling", in *Journal of Consulting and Clinical Psychology*, 59, 715–723.

Gelinas, D. (1983) "The persisting negative effects of incest", in *Psychiatry*, 46, 312–332.

Goodwin, J. (1985) "Post-traumatic symptoms in incest victims." In S. Eth and R. Pynoos, (Eds.), *Post-traumatic stress disorder in children* (pp. 157–168). Los Angeles, CA: American Psychiatric Association.

Goodwin, J. (1990) "Applying to adult incest victims what we have learned from victimized children." In R. Kluft (Ed.), *Incest-related syndromes of adult psychopathology*. Washington, DC: American Psychiatric Press, pp. 55–74.

Green, A. (1993) "Child sexual abuse: Immediate and long-term effects and intervention", in *Journal of the American Academy of Child and Adolescent Psychiatry*, 32(5), 890–902.

Greenwald, E., Lettenberg, H., Cado, S. and Tarran, M. (1990) "Childhood sexual abuse: Long-term effects on psychological and sexual functioning in a nonclinical and nonstudent sample of adult women", in *Child Abuse and Neglect*, 14, 503–513.

Greenwald, C., Tangalos, E. and Maruta, T. (1990) "Prevalence of sexual abuse, physical abuse and concurrent traumatic life events in a general medical population", in *Mayo Clinic Proceedings* 65, 1067–1071.

Harris, M. (in press) "Treating sexual abuse trauma with dually diagnosed homeless women", in *Community Mental Health Journal*.

Harter, S., Alexander, P.C. and Neimeyer, R.A. (1988) "Long-term effects of incestuous child abuse in college women: social adjustment, social cognition and family characteristics", in *Journal of Consulting and Clinical Psychology*, 56, 5–8.

Herder, D. and Redner, L. (1991) "The treatment of childhood sexual trauma in chronically mentally ill adults", in *Health and Social Work*, 16(1), 50–57.

Herman, J.L. (1992) *Trauma and Recovery*. New York: Basic Books.

Hulsey, T., Sexton, L. and Nash, M. (1992) "Family characteristics associated with the occurrence of childhood sexual abuse", in *Bulletin of the Menninger Clinic*, 56, 438–450.

Jacobson, A. and Herald, C. (1990) "The relevance of childhood sexual abuse to adult psychiatric inpatient care", in *Hospital and Community Psychiatry*, 39, 300–304.

Keane, T.M., Fairbank, J.A., Caddell, J.M. and Zimering, R.T. (1989) "Implosive (flooding) therapy reduces symptoms of PTSD in Vietnam combat veterans", in *Behavior Therapy*, 20, 245–260.

Keane, T.M. and Kaloupek, D.G. (1982) "Imaginal flooding in the treatment of a posttraumatic stress disorder", in *Journal of Consulting and Clinical Psychology*, 50, 138–140.

Kendall-Tackett, K., Williams, L. and Finkelhor, D. (1993) "Impact of sexual abuse on children: A review and synthesis of recent empirical studies", in *Psychological Bulletin*, 113(1), 164–180.

Lechner, M., Vogel, M., Garcia-Shelton, L., Leichter, J. and Steibel, K. (1993) "Self-reported medical problems of adult female survivors of childhood sexual abuse", in *The Journal of Family Practice*, 36(6), 633–638.

Loftus, E. (1993) "The reality of repressed memories", in *American Psychologist*, 48(5), 518–537.

Muenzenmaier, L., Meyer, I., Struening, E. and Ferber, J. (1993) "Childhood abuse and neglect among women outpatients with chronic mental illness", in *Hospital and Community Psychiatry*, 44(7), 666–670.

Mueser, K.T. and Butler, R.W. (1987) "Auditory hallucinations in chronic combat-related posttraumatic stress disorder", in *American Journal of Psychiatry*, 144, 299–302.

Nash, M., Hulsey, T., Sexton, M., Harralson, T. and Lambert, W. (1993) "Long-term sequelae of childhood sexual abuse: Perceived family environment, psychopathology and dissociation", in *Journal of Consulting and Clinical Psychology*, 61(2), 276–283.

Nigg, J., Silk, K., Westen, D., Lohr, N., Gold, L., Goodrich, S. and Ogata, S. (1991) "Object representations in the early memories of sexually abused borderline patients", in *American Journal of Psychiatry*, 148(7), 864–869.

O'Donohue, W. and Geer, J. (Eds.) (1992) *The sexual abuse of children: Theory and research* (Vol. 1). Hillsdale, NJ: Lawrence Erlbaum Associates.

Pelletier, T. and Handy, L. (1986) "Family dysfunction and the psychological impact of child sexual abuse", in *Canadian Journal of Psychiatry*, 31, 407–412.

Piper, A. (1994) "Multiple Personality Disorder", *British Journal of Psychiatry*, 14, 600–612.

Resnick, P.A. and Schnicke, M.K. (1992) "Cognitive processing therapy for sexual assault victims", *Journal of Consulting and Clinical Psychology*, 60, 748–756.

Robins, L.N. and Regier, D.A. (Eds.) (1991) *Psychiatric disorders in America*, New York: Free Press.

Rose, S.M., Peabody, C.G. and Stratigeas, B. (1991) "Undetected abuse among intensive case management clients", in *Hospital and Community Psychiatry*, 42, 499–503.

Rosenberg, S., Hulsey, T. and Rosenberg, H. "Detecting childhood sexual abuse through adult speech content." (Submitted for publication).

Rundell, J.R., Ursano, R.J., Holloway, H.C. and Silberman, E.K. (1989) "Psychiatric responses to trauma", *Hospital and Community Psychiatry*, 40, 68–74.

Russell, D. (1984) *Sexual exploitation: Rape, child sexual abuse and sexual harassment*, Beverly Hills, CA: Sage Publications.

Rychtarik, R.G., Silverman, W.K., Van Landingham, W.P. and Prue, D.M. (1984) "Treatment of an incest victim with implosive therapy: A case study", in *Behavior Therapy*, 15, 410–420.

Seidel, R.W., Gusman, F.D. and Abueg, F.R. (1994) "Theoretical and practical foundations of an inpatient post-traumatic stress disorder and alcoholism treatment program", in *Psychotherapy*, 31, 67–78.

Surrey, J., Swett, C., Michaels, A. and Levin, S. (1990) "Reported history of physical and sexual abuse and severity of symptomatology in women psychiatric outpatients", in *American Journal of Orthopsychiatry*, 60(3), 412–417.

Susser, E., Moore, R. and Link, B. (1993) "Risk factors for homelessness", in *American Journal of Epidemiology*, 15, 546–556.

Tierney, L. and Corwin, D. (1983) "Exploring intrafamilial child sexual abuse: A systems approach." In D. Finkelhor, R. Giles, G. Hotaling and M. Strauss (Eds.), *The dark side of families: Current family violence research* (pp. 102–116). Beverly Hills, CA: Sage Publications.

Torrey, W. and Drake, R. (1994) "Current concepts in the treatment of schizophrenia", in *Psychiatry*, 57, 278–285.

Vaughan, K. and Tarrier, N. (1992) "The use of image habituation training with post-traumatic stress disorders", in *British Journal of Psychiatry*, 161, 658–664.

Walch, A. and Broadhead, W. (1992) "Prevalence of lifetime sexual victimization among female patients", in *Journal of Family Practice*, 161, 658–664.

Waldfogel, S. and Mueser, K.T. (1988) "Another case of chronic PTSD with auditory hallucinations", in *American Journal of Psychiatry*, 145, 1314.

Wasserman, S. and Rosenfeld, A. (1992) "An overview of the history of child sexual abuse and Sigmund Freud's contributions." In W. O'Donohue and J. Gear (Eds.) *The sexual abuse of children: Theory and research* (Vol. 1). Hillsdale, NJ: Lawrence Erlbaum Associates.

Williams, L. (1993) "Adult memories of childhood abuse: Preliminary findings from a longitudinal study", in *The Advisor*, 5(3), 19–21.

Wyatt, G. (1985) "The sexual abuse of Afro-American and White-American women in childhood", in *Child Abuse and Neglect*, 9, 507–519.

Wyatt, G., Guthrie, D. and Notgrass, C. (1992) "Differential effects of women's child sexual abuse and subsequent sexual revictimization", *Journal of Consulting and Clinical Psychology*, 60(2), 167–173.

Wyatt, G. and Newcomb, M. (1990) "Internal and external mediators of women's sexual abuse in childhood", *Journal of Consulting and Clinical Psychology*, 58, 758–767.

---

*This chapter has been previously published in Community Mental Health Journal, 1995.

Chapter Thirteen

Prevalence and Impact of Sexual and Physical Abuse

Lisa A. Goodman, Melanie Johnson, Mary Ann Dutton and Maxine Harris

Introduction

Born and raised in the rural south, Diane, a 53-year old African American woman, describes a history of abuse which began in childhood and continued through four marriages. At the age of six, Diane went to live with her father after her parents' divorce. He was alcoholic and soon sent Diane to live with an aunt, who threw things at her, threatened her with a knife and repeatedly beat her. At about the same time, Diane was first raped by an older cousin with whom she lived. He repeatedly abused her physically and sexually throughout her childhood. Diane recounts that she took charge of protecting her younger female cousin, who was the only other female child in the household. Despite Diane's efforts, however, this girl was sexually abused by the same man, beginning at the age of 3 or 4. Diane escaped this frightening household only to enter into a succession of abusive marriages. Each of Diane's four husbands had a "drinking problem" and each frequently slapped, hit and beat her. Fifteen years ago, Diane left her fourth husband when she could no longer tolerate his abuse and subsequently became homeless. Diane attributes not only her homelessness, but also a major depressive disorder, to her long history of physical and sexual abuse. When she finally received help from a community mental health center, she had been homeless and clinically depressed for 15 years.

Melissa is a Caucasian woman who appears much younger than her 31 years. Her father repeatedly beat her as a child, kicking and hitting her and throwing a knife at her on one occasion. The beatings continued into adulthood when Melissa moved back home after suffering a "breakdown" in her first year at college. Sadly, both her parents and several doctors convinced Melissa that she had provoked the violent outbursts from her father. At times, her mother went as far as denying that the abuse had occurred. As horrifying as these experiences alone might be, three teenaged neighbors also raped Melissa at the age of seven. To this day, Melissa believes that she was responsible for the rapes. Melissa became homeless when she left home in her twenties, unable to endure further abuse from her father. Melissa is deeply depressed, expresses a low opinion of her self-worth and holds little hope of changing her life.

These women and many other episodically homeless, seriously mentally ill women who were interviewed during 1994[1], tell harrowing stories of sexual and physical abuse, often at the hands of family members, husbands, or romantic partners. Their stories are particularly compelling and important in light of our findings on the prevalence of violence in these women's lives. Of the 99 women we interviewed, nearly all had experienced some form of physical or sexual abuse. In fact, it was difficult to find a woman in our sample who had *not* been attacked or violated in some way. This chapter will describe our study and its findings with regard to

---

[1] Substantial portions of this chapter are based on or excerpted from two previously published articles describing this research. These articles include Goodman, L., Dutton, M. and Harris, M. (1995), Episodically homeless women with serious mental illness: prevalence of physical and sexual assault. *American Journal of Orthopsychiatry*; and Goodman, L., Dutton, M., and Harris, M., (in press). The relationship between violence dimensions and symptom severity among homeless, mentally ill women. *Journal of Traumatic Stress*. For information on cognitive schemata held, and risky behaviors demonstrated by our sample, see, respectively, Goodman, L. and Dutton, M. (in press). The relationship between victimization and cognitive schemata in episodically homeless, seriously mentally ill women. *Violence and Victims*; and Goodman, L. and Fallot, R. (under review). The association of physical and sexual abuse with HIV risk behaviors and revictimization in urban women with serious mental illness.

the extent, nature and impact of violence in the lives of these women. Following a brief review of the literature and description of our sample and methods, we will describe the results obtained in each of two parts of our study. In the first part, we examine the extent of physical and sexual assault in childhood and adulthood among a group of predominantly African American, formerly homeless women diagnosed with a serious mental illness and receiving services from a large, urban community mental health center. In the second part, we explore the degree to which specific dimensions of violence – frequency, recency and the number of types of violence experienced – were related to symptom severity.

Background

Prevalence of physical and sexual violence

Sexual and physical violence against women in the United States is widespread. Rigorous, community-based representative studies have demonstrated that between 19 and 28 percent of all women were victims of sexual abuse as children (Finkelhor, Hotaling, Lewis and Smith, 1990; Kilpatrick, Edmunds and Seymour, 1992; Russell, 1986). Between 14 and 25 percent of adult women have been raped (Koss, 1993; Searles and Berger, 1987). And, intimate partners will physically assault between 21 and 34 percent of women in the United States (Browne, 1993a). Unfortunately, these statistics may underestimate the actual incidence of sexual and physical abuse in this country. These studies, based on national surveys, excluded women who were non-English speaking, hospitalized, homeless, institutionalized, incarcerated or without telephones (Browne, 1993a; Goodman, Koss, Fitzgerald, Russo and Keita, 1993).

A particularly vulnerable, yet understudied subgroup may be homeless women with serious mental illness. Indeed, homeless mentally ill women may represent the most vulnerable segment of our society (Harris, 1991). Homeless individuals frequently must choose between the dangers of life on the street and the hazards of overcrowded, unsafe and poorly supervised shelters (Hope and Young, 1986; Stefl, 1987). Their relative lack of emotional, material and social resources make *mentally ill* homeless women especially vulnerable to these dangers. For many, these difficulties did not begin in adulthood. For example, compared to housed women, homeless women report a significantly greater likelihood of having spent time in a foster or group home (D'Ercole and Struening, 1990; Goodman, 1991b; Wood, Hayashi and Shen, 1990), having run away from home (Shinn, Kenickman and Weiteman, 1991) and having come from homes where their parents abused drugs or alcohol (Wood *et al.*, 1990).

Victimization in homeless women. Studies investigating the prevalence of victimization among *homeless* women (Bassuk and Rosenberg, 1988; Bassuk, Rubin and Lauriat, 1986; D'Ercole and Struening, 1990; Goodman, 1991a; North and Smith, 1992; Ryback and Bassuk, 1986; Shinn, Knickman and Weitzman, 1991; Simons, Whitbeck and Bales, 1989; Wood *et al.*, 1990; Whitbeck and Simons, 1993) indicate relatively high levels of physical and sexual abuse. An integrative analysis of these studies reveals that 12% to 60% of the female homeless respondents reported being physically abused in childhood; between 10% and 42% reported being sexually abused in childhood; between 27% and 74% reported being physically abused; and between 7% and 43% reported being sexually attacked as adults.

Victimization in seriously mentally ill women. Studies have shown that seriously mentally ill women are also at high risk for physical and sexual violence. Combining studies of inpatient (Beck and Van der Kolk, 1987; Bryer, Nelson, Miller, *et al.*, 1987; Carmen, Rieker and Mills, 1984; Cole, 1988; Crane, Henson, Colliver, *et al.*, 1988; Jacobson and Herald, 1990; Jacobson and Richardson, 1987) and outpatient (Herman, 1986; Jacobson, 1989; Muenzenmaier, Meyer, Struening, *et al.*, 1993; Rose, Peabody and Stratigeas, 1991; Rosenfeld, 1979) mentally ill women, between 35% and 51% of respondents report histories of child physical abuse; between 20% and 54% report histories of child sexual abuse; between 42% and 64% report being physically abused as an adult; and between 21% and 38% report being sexually assaulted as an adult. Thus, it appears that a disproportionate number of homeless and seriously mentally ill women have been victimized.

Despite the importance of the studies described above, none set out to gain information from women with histories of prior homelessness *and* mental illness. Further, none examined in great detail various dimensions of the violence experienced, including the type, frequency, severity, or recency of the abuse and the identities of the perpetrators. Finally, none investigated the relationship between specific demographic and diagnostic factors and prevalence rates.

Impact of physical and sexual violence

Although researchers have made great headway in assessing the psychological impact of violence against women, they have largely overlooked those women who may be most vulnerable to its effects, including homeless, seriously mentally ill women (Goodman, Koss, Fitzgerald, et al., 1993). In fact, only four studies have investigated the relationship between victimization and symptoms among homeless women, without regard to their psychiatric diagnosis. D'Ercole and Struening (1990), for example, found significant correlations between histories of victimization and depressive symptoms in homeless women. North and Smith (1992) found that 34% of a sample of homeless women in shelters met criteria for a lifetime diagnosis of PTSD. Among those women reporting at least one trauma, more than half had developed PTSD, with rape being the most frequently cited stressful event. Using the same sample, North, Smith and Spitznagel (1994) found Axis I disorders to be associated with a history of violent trauma. Finally, a fourth study by Simons, Whitbeck and Bales (1989) identified a relationship between criminal victimization and increased levels of general psychological distress in a sample of adult homeless individuals (both male and female).

Other studies have examined the relationships among types of abuse and psychiatric symptoms in samples of inpatient or outpatient recipients of mental health services, without regard to their history of homelessness. For example, in a sample of inpatients, Beck and Van der Kolk (1987) found that those with a history of childhood incest were significantly more likely than those without such a history to have sexual delusions, preoccupations, depressive symptoms, substance abuse and major medical problems. Among outpatient women with chronic mental illness, Muenzenmaier and her colleagues (1993) found that those with a history of childhood abuse had higher levels of both depressive and psychotic symptoms.

Two studies provide evidence that experiencing multiple types of abuse may be associated with especially serious psychiatric symptoms. Carmen, Riker and Mills (1984) found that inpatients who were both physically and sexually abused were more likely to turn their anger inward in uncontrolled ways than those who were victims of physical or sexual abuse alone. Similarly, Bryer *et al.* (1987) found that in a sample of female inpatients, sexual or physical abuse in childhood was significantly associated with somatization, interpersonal sensitivity, depression, anxiety, paranoid ideology and psychoticism. Moreover, patients who had experienced both physical and sexual abuse in childhood reported more severe symptoms than those with a single type of abuse.

Our study: sample and procedures

During 1993 and 1994, we interviewed 99 episodically homeless women with diagnoses of serious mental illness. All of our participants had been referred from a local shelter or psychiatric hospital to a major urban community mental health center. For the purposes of this study, we defined homelessness as having lived in a shelter or on the street, or having no fixed address at the time of discharge from the hospital. By the time of the interview, most (93%) of our respondents had regained some form of housing with the help of the mental health center, thus differentiating our respondents from those in other studies of currently homeless individuals.

We recruited participants from among the 199 women active on the caseload at the mental health center. For a variety of reasons, we were able to interview only 99 women. Forty-four women were unreachable (hospitalized, living on the street, highly irregular in their attendance at the center). Thirty declined to be interviewed or failed to show up for at least two scheduled interviews. In 25 cases, the case managers determined that the client was too fragile psychologically to be interviewed. Finally, one woman became psychotic during the interview, making the protocol invalid.

Four female graduate students in clinical psychology, one experienced female counselor and four case managers working at the community mental health center conducted the interviews. Clients could decline to be interviewed and 7% of the women chose this option. Most interviews took place in a private therapy room at the mental health center. Respondents received $10 for the one to one-and-a-half hour interview. Although a few respondents showed obvious emotional strain during the interviews, most of the women expressed appreciation for the opportunity to talk about highly significant events in their lives.

Instruments and definitions

The interview protocol, described below, covered a wide range of information, including background information (residential status, family constellations, educational levels, employment histories and current substance abuse), physical and sexual assault histories and symptoms. In addition, we solicited information from case managers about primary and secondary diagnoses made at the time of intake.

Child and adult physical and sexual abuse. To measure the *prevalence and severity of physical abuse during childhood and adulthood*[2], we modified the Violence Subscale of Straus' (1979, 1989a) Conflict Tactics Scale (CTS). The CTS consists of an ordered series of violent behaviors. Participants were asked to report the number of times each behavior had been perpetrated against them by anyone during their childhood or adulthood. *Physical assault or abuse* was defined as acts of intentional physical aggression ranging from repeated slapping to kicking, beating, burning, choking or threatening with or using a knife or gun. We categorized reported incidents of physical violence into two levels of severity, based on their presumed risk of injury (Straus, 1989b). *Minor violence* included throwing an object, pushing, shoving or slapping. *Severe violence* for childhood included kicking, biting, hitting with a fist or object, beating, burning and threatening with or using a knife or gun. The criteria for *severe violence* in adulthood were identical, except that burning (more commonly associated with child abuse) was replaced with choking (more frequently associated with spouse abuse).

We used Russell's (1986) semi-structured interview to investigate the respondents' experiences of *child and adult sexual abuse*. The questionnaire avoids the use of "loaded" terminology, such as rape, incest and molestation, relying instead on open-ended questions

---

[2] 18 years was used as the cutoff between childhood and adulthood.

about specific sexual behaviors, perpetrated by a range of people. We defined *sexual assault or abuse* as unwanted sexual experiences with relatives or acquaintances, intimate partners, or strangers, ranging from forcible heavy petting to rape. As with physical abuse, we classified sexual violence items into two levels of severity. *Severe sexual abuse* included attempted or completed rape (penile-vaginal penetration), fellatio, cunnilingus, anilingus or anal intercourse. *Minor sexual abuse* included forced genital or breast contact.

Symptoms. We used several instruments to assess the *range and severity of symptoms* among our participants. The Symptom Checklist-90-R (SCL-90-R; Derogotis, 1977) is a 90-item self-report symptom inventory designed to assess extent of symptomatology across nine primary symptom dimensions. In this study, we focused on four clinical scales commonly associated with violent victimization – anxiety, depression, hostility and somatization – and one global measure of distress, the Global Symptom Index (SCL-GSI). In addition, we used the Crime-Related PTSD Scale (CR-PTSD), developed by Saunders, Arata and Kilpatrick (1990), which was derived from the larger SCL-90. The authors of the scale have established a cut off score (.89) which has correctly classified 89.3% of women as PTSD-positive or PTSD-negative after exposure to violent crime, including sexual assault, aggravated assault, robbery and burglary. Although the original scale was developed using a community sample of largely white, middle-class, well-educated women, the internal consistency reliability of the scale for our study was extremely high, with a coefficient alpha = .94.

The Dissociation Scale (Briere and Runtz, 1988) is composed of five items that use the same format as the SCL-90. This scale has successfully discriminated between college students with and without childhood sexual abuse histories. As with the CR-PTSD Scale, the Dissociation Scale was developed using primarily white, middle-class women as respondents. Nevertheless, internal consistency reliability for our respondents was .73.

Sample characteristics

The women we interviewed ranged in age from 21 to 71, with a mean age of 42. As indicated in Table 1, a majority of the sample

TABLE 1
Demographic Characteristics of Sample

CHARACTERISTICS	% OF SAMPLE
Ethnicity	
African-American	80
Anglo-American	16
Asian-American	2
Other	2
Marital Status	
Single	50
Divorced	24
Separated	11
Married	10
Windowed	5
Sexual Orientation	
Heterosexual	83
Bisexual	12
Lesbian	5
Education	
HS-drop-out	40
HS graduate	33
Some college	26
Employment History	
Worked less than 2 years	16
Worked for 2–5 years	26
Worked for over 5 years	58
Sources of Income★	
SSI/SSDI	73
Partner/friend/relative	26
Job	12
Panhandling	8
Prostitution★★	8
Residential Status	
Own apartment	35
Group home	24
Transitional housing	12
SRO/boarding house	9
Shelter	8
Residential treatment	4
With friend/relative	3
Other	4

★Income categories are not mutually exclusive.

★★Only 51 respondents were asked this question.

(80%) was African American. Half of the sample had never been married, another quarter were divorced and the remaining women were either married, separated or widowed. Although none of the women were currently caring for children, 71% were mothers. Other background characteristics are described in Table 1.

Our interviewees represented a wide range of severe psychiatric disorders. According to case managers, 59% of the women interviewed were diagnosed with schizophrenia or schizoaffective disorder as their primary disorder. Another 14% were diagnosed with bipolar disorder and 14% with major depressive disorder. The remaining 11% had been given a number of primary diagnoses including alcohol or other drug dependence, psychotic disorder (not otherwise specified) and borderline personality disorder. Finally, substance abuse played an important role in many of our respondent's lives. Thirty-six percent of the women reported that alcohol was a current "problem." Thirty-eight percent and 20% respectively reported that cocaine or another substance was a current problem. Combining substance types, 44% reported a "problem" with some substance.

Results from our study

Prevalence of victimization. As discussed below, most of our participants had experienced severe, ongoing abuse at the hands of multiple perpetrators, usually beginning in childhood and extending into adulthood. The nature and extent of the abuse and the identities of perpetrators varied widely, as illustrated by the story of one woman who had been beaten as a child by her grandmother, raped by three strangers one evening as a teenager and then beaten by her husband as an adult.

Abuse in Childhood. As Table 2 shows, 87% of the women reported physical abuse in childhood and 65% reported sexual abuse. Furthermore, 82% of the physical abuse and 88% of the sexual abuse was categorized as severe.

Sexual abuse assailants included strangers (40%), caretakers or acquaintances at least five years older (51%) or both (29%).

Abuse in adulthood. The pervasive and severe child abuse described by respondents also extended into adulthood. As Table 2 indicates, 87% of the women had suffered some form of adult physical assault

TABLE 2
Prevalence and Severity of Abuse

| | VIOLENCE LEVEL | | |
FORM	NONE	MINOR	SEVERE
Child Physical	13%	13%	74%
Child Sexual	35%	07%	58%
Adult physical	13%	03%	84%
Adult Sexual	24%	11%	65%

and all but 3% of these had been assaulted severely. Strangers had physically assaulted 53% of the women and intimate partners had assaulted 80% of them. As shown in Table 2, 76% of the interviewees had been sexually assaulted, most of them severely. Fifty-seven percent had been sexually assaulted by a stranger, 40% by a relative or acquaintance and 40% by an intimate partner.

Co-occurrence. When different aspects of abuse are examined together, a more comprehensive and even more alarming picture of the pervasiveness of victimization in these women's lives emerges. Combining child and adult abuse, 87% of the sample had been abused both as children and as adults. When physical and sexual assault are combined, 92% of the total sample had experienced either physical or sexual abuse or both.

In addition, as shown in Table 3, most respondents had experienced multiple types of abuse. Only 4% had experienced one type of abuse and a half of the sample had experienced all four types of abuse. Combining types of abuse, 97% of the women interviewed had been abused at some point during their lives. The picture does not change appreciably when one looks only at severe violence. Only 6% of the respondents had *not* experienced some form of severe violence during their lives. Finally, the conditional probability of revictimization as an adult was .64 for women with no history of child abuse and .97 for those who experienced either sexual or physical abuse in childhood. Thus, adult assault appears to be almost inevitable for urban, homeless, mentally ill women with histories of being abused as children.

Recency. During the month prior to the interview, 20% of the women interviewed reported being physically assaulted and 15%

TABLE 3
Number of Categories of Abuse Experienced

	NO. OF CATEGORIES				
SEVERITY LEVEL	0	1	2	3	4
Minor & Severe	3%	4%	18%	25%	50%
Severe Only	6%	6%	26%	25%	36%

reported sexual victimization. Combining both types of abuse, 28% of the total sample had been victimized within the last month.

Finally, we investigated the possibility that four background factors – ethnicity, educational level, psychiatric diagnosis and age – might be related to the prevalence and recency of each form of abuse. No significant differences were found across categories of ethnicity, education or diagnosis. Investigating the interaction between age and form of abuse, we found that the youngest and middle groups (ages 21–40 and 41–50, respectively) reported more physical abuse than the oldest group (75%, 83% and 43% respectively; $X^2 = 8.3$, d.f. = 2, $p < .05$). None of the other forms of abuse, nor recency of abuse, however, differentiated these age groups. This latter finding contrasts with findings from other studies, in which younger women are usually at greater current risk for abuse (Koss, Goodman, Browne, et al., 1994). In our sample, however, the oldest group was just as likely as the middle and younger group to have experienced recent physical or sexual abuse, perhaps because our participants live in environments that make them particularly vulnerable to victimization, regardless of age.

Victimization and symptom severity

Given the startlingly high proportion of women experiencing abuse in our sample, we could not compare symptom severity for those with and without abuse histories. Instead, we examined how various dimensions of violence (frequency, recency and the addition of physical to sexual abuse) related to levels of psychological distress, expecting to find positive correlations between the various dimensions and the severity of distress.

We used one-way multivariate analyses of variance (MANOVAs) followed by one-way analyses of variance (ANOVAs) to explore the relationships between symptom levels and dimensions of violence. In addition, we used a multiple regression analysis to assess the relative degree to which dimensions of violence predicted levels of psychological distress, controlling for relevant background variables.

Frequency. Women with frequent abuse (six episodes or more) reported higher symptoms levels than did women with less frequent abuse (1–6 episodes), Wilks lambda = .83, F (6,89) = 2.99, p < .05. As Table 4 shows, we found significant differences among the groups on four of the seven symptom measures (depression, hostility, total symptom score and PTSD), using a relatively stringent criterion[3]. The groups also differed significantly on anxiety at the less stringent, generalized alpha criterion of .05.

Physical vs. Physical and Sexual Abuse. Our analysis also revealed differences in overall symptom severity between respondents who had experienced child physical abuse alone and those who had experienced both child physical and child sexual abuse, Wilks lambda = .83,

TABLE 4
Symptom Scores by Abuse Frequency

SYMPTOM SUBSCALE	INFREQUENT (N = 29)		FREQUENT (N = 67)		
	MEAN	SD	MEAN	SD	F(DF = 2)
Anxiety	.68	.67	1.12	.94	5.50[a]
Depression	.79	.66	1.46	.93	12.36★
Dissociation	.71	.82	.93	.87	1.36
Hostility	.40	.70	.88	.85	7.24★
PTSD	.72	.56	1.19	.86	7.24★
Somatization	.63	.79	.93	.84	2.83
Global Severity Index	.73	.58	1.19	.78	7.95★

★p < .10, Sidak criterion; p < .001 − .01 for individual analyses.
[a]p < .05, generalized alpha level.

---

[3] To reduce inflation of the experimentwise Type 1 error rate, we used a sequentially-rejecting Sidak procedure to evaluate tests for statistical significance (Holland and Copenhaver, 1987; Maxwell and Delaney, 1990; Sidak, 1967). This procedure is more powerful than Bonferroni-based procedures (Maxwell and Delaney, 1990).

TABLE 5
Symptom Scores by Single vs Multiple Abuse Types

SYMPTOM SUBSCALE	CHILD PHYSICAL ABUSE ONLY (N = 27)		CHILD PHYSICAL AND SEXUAL ABUSE (N = 59)		
	MEAN	SD	MEAN	SD	F(DF = 1)
Anxiety	.76	.72	1.16	.96	3.76
Depression	.92	.77	1.51	.94	8.08★
Dissociation	.68	.75	1.02	.92	2.77
Hostility	.52	.72	.88	.90	3.28
PTSD	.78	.61	1.25	.87	6.35[a]
Somatization	.90	.95	.89	.81	.01
Global Severity Index	.81	.60	1.22	.81	5.57[a]

★$p < .10$, Sidak criterion; $p < .01$ for individual analysis.
[a]$p < .05$, generalized alpha level.

$F (6, 79) = 2.74$, $p < .05$. As shown in Table 5, respondents with both types of abuse reported significantly higher levels of depression when we used our more stringent alpha criterion. Using a generalized alpha criterion of .05, the groups differed significantly on total symptoms scores and PTSD as well. With regard to adult abuse, however, we found no significant differences between the 16 respondents with only physical abuse and the 70 women with both physical and sexual abuse.

Recency. Finally, we found significant differences between women who had experienced abuse in the last month and those with prior adult abuse but none during the last month, Wilks lambda = .81, F (6.84) = 3.21, $p < .01$. As Table 6 shows, respondents who had been sexually or physically abused in the last month reported significantly higher scores on all seven symptom clusters (anxiety, depression, hostility, somatization, total symptoms, PTSD and dissociation) than those who had not been victimized in the previous month.

Multiple Regression. We used a multiple regression analysis to examine the proportion of variance in total symptom severity (GSI score) accounted for by dimensions of abuse, controlling for relevant background variables. First, we looked at the relationships between relevant background variables (ethnicity, education, age, substance abuse) and GSI. We found only one significant relationship – that

TABLE 6

Symptom Scores by Recency of Adult Abuse

SYMPTOM SUBSCALE	NON-RECENT ADULT ABUSE (N = 63)		RECENT ADULT ABUSE (N = 28)		
	MEAN	SD	MEAN	SD	F(DF = 1)
Anxiety	.79	.68	1.56	1.08	16.96★
Depression	1.07	.78	1.87	.93	18.03★
Dissociation	.70	.76	1.36	.92	12.68★
Hostility	.55	.68	1.21	1.01	13.23★
PTSD	.87	.60	1.59	.99	18.24★
Somatization	.71	.75	1.23	.94	7.93★
Global Severity Index	.87	.60	1.56	.87	18.72★

★$p < .10$, Sidak criterion; $p < .001–.006$ for individual analysis.

between substance abuse and GSI, $F (1,97) = 9.25$, $p < .01$. Women who were identified as having a "problem" with substance abuse were also more likely to score higher on the GSI. Thus, we included substance abuse in our model as a predictor variable. We also examined potential interactions between the dimensions – recency, frequency and abuse type – and substance abuse. The final model explained 29% of the variation in symptom severity (based on an adjusted R^2). Substance abuse and recency contributed significantly unique predictive power and abuse type contributed marginally to predictive power (see Table 7). Although frequency took on the expected sign, it did not contribute significantly to the variation in symptom severity, possibly due to multicollinearity with recency and abuse type (phi correlations between both these variables and frequency were .29 and .40, respectively and were significant at $p <.01$). None of the interactions, however, were significant.

Discussion

Our study underlines the need to focus attention on the important role that victimization plays in the lives of homeless women with serious mental illness. Key findings of our study include:

• Victimization is nearly normative in the lives of homeless, seriously mentally ill women;

TABLE 7

Linear Regression Model for the Prediction of Symptom Severity
(SCLGSI) from Substance Abuse and Trauma Dimensions

INDEPENDENT VARIABLES	BETA
Substance Abuse	.25*
Recency	.40*
Abuse Type	.17**
Frequency	.07

$*p < .01$
$**pp < .10$

- Various dimensions of violence – specifically, frequency, recency and the addition of child sexual abuse to child physical abuse – are associated with a broad range of psychiatric symptoms. The more frequently or recently that abuse had occurred, the more severe was the woman's psychological distress. And similarly, women who had experienced multiple types of abuse, such as childhood sexual and child physical abuse, were also more likely to suffer more severe symptoms.

While our study had several limitations, as discussed below, our results point to the need for more research into the difficulties and needs of this particularly vulnerable population; for mental health care providers to pay closer attention to the role that victimization has played in the etiology and course of these women's illnesses; and for interventions to be designed that address not only women's emotional needs, but issues of safety and security as well.

Prevalence and impact of victimization

Our results suggest strongly that for episodically homeless women with serious mental illness, the lifetime risk for violent victimization is so high that rape and physical battery are normative experiences. Only 3% of the 99 respondents had *not* experienced either physical or sexual abuse as either a child or an adult. Not only was the violence pervasive, most of it was also quite severe. Further, the risk for recurrent abuse was extraordinarily high. A full half of the sample had experienced all four forms of abuse at some point in their lives; 36% had experienced all four forms at the most severe levels. In fact, for those who had experienced child physical or sexual abuse, the probability of being victimized as an adult was .97 – difficult odds to beat. Perhaps most relevant for service providers, much of the abuse was ongoing, extending into respondents' current lives. More than one in four had experienced at least one episode of abuse during the month preceding the interview.

The study also demonstrates that for this population, dimensions of violence, including frequency of violence across the lifespan, recency and the addition of child sexual abuse to child physical abuse, are associated with a broad range of psychiatric symptoms and in combination with substance abuse, account for 29% of the variance in overall distress. These findings suggest that environmental stressors, such as exposure to violence, may contribute to the presence and severity of psychiatric symptoms among this population. Additionally, these results suggest that multiply traumatized women *do not* become numbed to the impact of new violence, even when they have been exposed to extensive prior violence. In fact, for a woman with a serious mental illness and, perhaps, symptoms associated with prior victimization, a new assault can deepen her psychological distress.

Of course, the strong association between dimensions of violence and severity of symptoms does not necessarily mean that violence causes symptoms. Certain symptoms, for example, may heighten a woman's vulnerability to victimization. Alternatively, a third factor may contribute to both victimization and symptom severity. Nor does the association found between dimensions of victimization and symptoms illuminate the mechanisms by which the former may influence the latter. For example, victimization may shape symptoms by increasing the risk of symptom relapse, maintaining symptoms that would otherwise diminish, increasing the severity of already existing symptoms, or some combination thereof.

Limitations of the current study

Several limitations constrain the generalizability of this study. First, we faced the issue of accurate reporting. Because our participants were seriously mentally ill, their descriptions of prior abuse may have arisen from fixed delusions or hallucinations of a sexual nature rather than from actual violent encounters. This possibility, especially salient for the 59% of women with diagnoses of schizophrenia or schizo-affective disorder, may have artificially increased the prevalence rates obtained in the study.

On the other hand, however, participants may have underreported some abuse experiences because our measures were not developed for this population and may not have been sensitive to differences in terminology. For example, many respondents looked at their inter-viewers blankly when asked about unwanted touching of their genitals. Thus, we may have superimposed categories or used termi-nology that made little sense to these women. And a substantial minority did not understand the meaning of terms such as "oral sex", "intercourse" or "penetration." In addition, our measures did not allow for full diagnoses of trauma-related disorders such as PTSD or Dissociative Identity Disorder. A more complete set of outcome measures should be used in future research. Further, new measures for violent experiences should be developed that better reflect the language and cultural constructions of violence held by homeless and seriously mentally ill women.

A second limit to generalizability is that the episodically homeless, mentally ill women we interviewed may be lower functioning than other homeless, mentally ill women. In our study, all respondents had been identified by a social service provider as needing an intensive case management intervention to regain housing and reestablish sta-bility and security in their lives. Further, as noted earlier, none of our participants were caring for their children, in large part because they had given them up to other caregivers. Finally, our sample was largely African American and nearly half identified alcohol or cocaine as a problem. Their status as minorities may have increased their sense of marginalization and stigma, thereby decreasing their chances of seeking help from available social institutions. Substance abuse may also have placed them at added risk by forcing them into dangerous places and situations. Future research on the prevalence of abuse in this population could address some of these limitations by recruiting larger samples from several towns and cities, allowing comparisons between urban and rural populations, different ethnic minorities, women in resource-rich and resource-poor cities, or even women in different geographic regions of the country.

Implications for policy and service delivery

Three policy imperatives emerge from the findings reported in this study. First and most obviously, regular and ongoing inquiry into women's present and past experiences of abuse must be made a routine part of service delivery to this population. Bryer and his colleagues (1987) point out that failure to address abuse histories may, in effect, confirm clients' belief that they need to deny the reality of abuse experiences. Cole (1988) concludes that ignoring histories of assault will result in an inadequate basis for formulating treatment strategies as the link between a client's history and her presenting problem.

Second, shelter and mental health center staff who work with this population must be educated about the prevalence of past and present abuse in this population, the potential links between prior abuse and current symptoms and life situations and methods to address the current consequences of past abuse as well as the present danger of recurrent abuse. Knowledge about the social context of constant threat and danger that homeless mentally ill women face may help service providers understand otherwise inexplicable behaviors and responses to new events as well as how their clients perceive themselves, the world and other people.

Finally, broad-based interventions must be developed that address victimization histories among homeless, seriously mentally ill women. Most important, whether in a shelter or a community mental health center, a physically safe environment must be ensured so that women can begin to develop a sense of personal control (Browne, 1993b; Goodman, Saxe and Harvey, 1991). Women cannot begin the healing process if they are in imminent danger within the walls of their residence (no matter how temporary) or place of treatment. Additionally, every attempt should be made to increase a sense of community among clients and between clients and staff within these settings. Without social support and consequent development of trust, women may be unable either to disclose abusive experiences or to accept any help offered.

References

Bassuk, E.L. and Rosenberg, L. (1988) "Why does family homelessness occur? A case-control study", in *American Journal of Public Health*, 76, 783–788.

Bassuk, E.L., Rubin, L. and Lauriat, A. (1986) "Characteristics of sheltered homeless families", in *American Journal of Public Health*, 76, 1097–1101.

Beck, J.C. and Van der Kolk, B.A. (1987) "Reports of childhood incest and current behavior of chronically hospitalized psychotic women", in *American Journal of Psychiatry*, 144, 1474–1476.

Briere, J. and Runtz, M. (1988) "Symptomatology associated with child-hood sexual victimization in a nonclinical sample", in *Child Abuse and Neglect*, 12, 51–59.

Browne, A. (1993a) "Violence against women by male partners: Prevalence, outcomes and policy implications", in *American Psychologist*, 48, 10, 1077–1087.

Browne, A. (1993b) "Family violence and homelessness: The relevance of trauma histories in the lives of homeless women", in *American Journal of Orthopsychiatry*, 63, 3, 370–384.

Bryer, J.B., Nelson, B.A., Miller, J.B. and Krol, P.A. (1987) "Childhood sexual and physical abuse as factors in adult psychiatric illness", in *American Journal of Psychiatry*, 144, 11, 1426–1430.

Carmen, E., Rieker, P.P. and Mills, T. (1984) "Victims of violence and psychiatric illness", in *American Journal of Psychiatry*, 141, 3, 378–383.

Cole, C. (1988) "Routine comprehensive inquiry for abuse: A justifiable clinical assessment procedure", in *Clinical Social Work Journal*, 16, 33–42.

Craine, L.S., Henson, C.E., Colliver, J.A. and MacLean, D.G. (1988) "Prevalence of a history of sexual abuse among female psychiatric patients in a state hospital system", in *Hospital and Community Psychiatry*, 39, 3, 300–304.

D'Ercole, A. and Struening, E. (1990) "Victimization among homeless women: Implications for service delivery", in *Journal of Community Psychology*, 18, 141–152.

Derogatis, L., Rickels, K. and Rock, A. (1976) "The SCL-90 and the MMPI: A step in the validation of a new self-report scale", in *British Journal of Psychiatry*, 128, 280–289.

Finkelhor, D., Hotaling, G.T., Lewis, I.A. and Smith, C. (1990) "Sexual abuse in a national survey of adult men and women: Prevalence characteristics and risk factors", in *Child Abuse and Neglect*, 14, 19–20.

Goodman, L.A. (1991a) "The prevalence of abuse in the lives of homeless and housed poor mothers: A comparison study", in *American Journal of Orthopsychiatry*, 61, 489–500.

Goodman, L.A. (1991b) "The relationship between social support and family homelessness: A comparison study of homeless and housed mothers", in *Journal of Community Psychology*, 19, 321–331.

Goodman, L.A. and Dutton, M.A. (in press). "The relationship between victimization and cognitive schemata in homeless, seriously mentally ill women", in *Violence and Victims*.

Goodman, L.A., Dutton, M.A. and Harris, M. (1995). "Episodically homeless women with serious mental illness: prevalence of physical and sexual assault", in *American Journal of Orthopsychiatry* 65(4), 468–478.

Goodman, L.A., Dutton, M.A. and Harris, M. (in press). "The relationship between violence dimensions and symptom severity among homeless, mentally ill women", in *Journal of Traumatic Stress*.

Goodman, L.A. and Fallot, R. (under review). "The association of physical and sexual abuse with HIV risk behaviors and revictimization in urban women with serious mental illness."

Goodman, L.A., Koss, M.P., Fitzgerald, L.F., Russo, N.F. and Keita, G.P. (1993) "Male violence against women: Current research and future directions", in *American Psychologist*, 48, 10, 1054–1058.

Goodman, L.A., Saxe, L. and Harvey, M. (1991) "Homelessness as psychological trauma: Broadening perspectives", in *American Psychologist*, 46, 11, 1219–1225.

Harris, M. (1991) *Sisters of the Shadow*. Oklahoma: University of Oklahoma Press.

Harris, M. and Bachrach, L.L. (1990) "Perspectives on homeless, mentally ill women", in *Hospital and Community Psychiatry*, 41, 23, 253–254.

Herman, J.L. (1986) "Histories of violence in an outpatient population", in *American Journal of Orthopsychiatry*, 65, 137–141.

Holland, B.S. and Copenhaver, M.D. (1988) "Improved Bonferroni-type multiple testing procedures", in *Psychological Bulletin*, 104, 145–149.

Hope, M. and Young, J. (1986) *The faces of homelessness*. Lexington, MA: Lexington Books.

Jacobson, A. (1989). "Physical and sexual assault histories among psychiatric outpatients", in *American Journal of Psychiatry*, 146, 755–758.

Jacobson, A. and Herald, C. (1990) "The relevance of childhood sexual abuse to adult psychiatric inpatient care", in *Hospital and Community Psychiatry*, 41, 154–158.

Jacobson, A. and Richardson, B. (1987) "Assault experiences of 100 psychiatric inpatients: Evidence of the need for routine inquiry", in *American Journal of Psychiatry*, 144, 908–913.

Kilpatrick, D.G., Edmunds, C.M. and Seymour, A.K. (1992) *Rape in America: A Report to the Nation*. Arlington, VA: National Victim Center.

Koss, M.P. (1993) "Rape: Scope, impact, interventions and public policy response", in *American Psychologist*, 48, 10, 1062–1069.

Koss, M.P., Goodman, L.A., Browne, A., Fitzgerald, L.F., Keita, G.P. and Russo, N.F. (1994) *No safe haven: Male violence against women at home, at work and in the community*. Washington DC: American Psychological Association Press.

Maxwell, S.E. and Delaney, H.D. (1990) *Designing experiments and analyzing data*. Pacific Grove, CA: Brooks/Cole Publishing Company.

Muenzenmaier, K., Meyer, I., Struening, E. and Ferber, J. (1993) "Childhood abuse and neglect among women outpatients with chronic mental illness", in *Hospital and Community Psychiatry*, 44, 7, 666–670.

North, C.S. and Smith, E.M. (1992) "Posttraumatic stress disorder among homeless men and women", in *Hospital and Community Psychiatry*, 43, 10, 1010–1016.

North, C.S., Smith, E.M. and Spitznagel, (1994) "Violence and homelessness: An epidemiological study of victimization and aggression", in *Journal of Traumatic Stress*, 7, 1, 95–110.

Rose, S.M., Peabody, C.G. and Stratigeas, B. (1991) "Undetected abuse among intensive case management clients", in *Hospital and Community Psychiatry*, 42, 5, 499–503.

Rosenfeld, A. (1979) "Incidence of a history of incest among 18 female psychiatric patients", in *American Journal of Psychiatry*, 136, 791–795.

Russell, D. E. H. (1986) *The secret trauma: Incest in the lives of girls and women*. New York: Basic Books.

Ryback, R.F. and Bassuk, E.L. (1986) "Homeless battered women and their shelter network", in *New Directions in Mental Health Services*, 30, 55–61.

Saunders, B., Arata, C.M. and Kilpatrick, D.G. (1990) "Development of a crime-related post-traumatic stress disorder scale for women within the symptom checklist-90-revise", in *Journal of Traumatic Stress*, 3, 439–448.

Searles, P. and Berger, R. J. (1987) "Factors associated with a history of childhood sexual experience in a nonclinical female population", in *Journal of the American Academy of Child Psychiatry*, 23, 215–18.

Shinn, M., Knickman, J. and Weitzman, B.C. (1991) "Social relationships and vulnerability to becoming homeless among poor families", in *American Psychologist*, 46, 11, 1180–1187.

Sidak, Z. (1967) "Rectangular confidence regions for the means of multi-variate normal distributions", in *Journal of the American Statistical Association*, 62, 626–633.

Simons, R.L., Whitbeck, L.B. and Bales, A. (1989) "Life on the streets: Victimization and psychological distress among the adult homeless", in *Journal of Interpersonal Violence*, 4, 482–501.

Stefl, M. (1987) "The homeless in contemporary society", in R. Bingham, R. Green and S. White (Eds.), *The homeless in contemporary society* (pp. 46–63). Newbury Park, CA: Sage.

Straus, M. (1979) "Measuring intra-family conflict and violence: The Conflict Tactics (CT) scales", in *Journal of Marriage and the Family*, 4, 1, 75–88.

Straus, M. (1989a) "Measuring intra-family conflict and violence: The Conflict Tactics Scales", in M. Straus and R. Gelles (Eds.) *Physical violence in American families: Risk factors and adaptations to violence in 8145 families* (pp. 29–47). New Brunswick, NJ: Transaction Books.

Straus, M. (1989b) "New scoring methods for violence and new norms for the Conflict Tactics Scales", in M. Straus and R. Gelles (Eds.), *Physical violence in American families: Risk factors and adaptions to violence in 8145 families* (pp. 535–559). New Brunswick, NJ: Transaction Books.

Whitbeck, L.B. and Simons, R.L. (1993) "A comparison of adaptive strategies and patterns of victimization among homeless adolescents and adults", in *Violence and Victims*, 8, 2, 135–152.

Wood, D., Valdez, R.B., Hayashi, T. and Shen, A. (1990) "Homeless and housed families in Los Angeles: A study comparing demographic, economic and family function characteristics", in *Journal of Public Health*, 80, 1049–1052.

Part V

Special Issues

Chapter Fourteen

Care of Clinicians Doing Trauma Work

Ellen Arledge Blanchard and Mirta Jones

P SYCHOTHERAPISTS who treat trauma survivors face a unique set of issues and demands stemming, in part, from the powerful emotional needs of these clients. Survivors often exhibit intense fear, anger, neediness, shame and denial (Courtois, 1988). Re-enactments of past abuse can be enormously painful to the client and unbearable for the therapist to witness (Saakvitne, 1991). In addition, their deep mistrust and inability to be soothed make traumatized clients difficult to engage and place them at increased risk for premature termination from treatment (Schauben and Frazier, 1995). Systemic issues such as limits on mental health coverage and an unjust legal system can make working with survivors even more difficult (Schauben and Frazier, 1995). The therapist can be further demoralized by having to face the ugly reality of child abuse and public apathy towards violence against women and children in a misogynist society. The societal taboo against acknowledging incest can leave therapists who engage in this work isolated and without adequate professional support (Pearlman and Saakvitne, in press).

Working with survivors of trauma, however, can have a transformative effect on the therapist. These effects include profound changes in core aspects of the therapist's self (Pearlman and Saakvitne, in press). Clinicians may notice changes in their identity, world view, ability to manage feelings and spirituality. Indicators of changes in identity can include questioning one's gender roles, self-esteem and one's own history. A change in world view may result in abandoning "beliefs that people behave according to a set of values, that the world is fundamentally just, that people can influence outcomes in their lives and that the future is bright" (Pearlman and Saakvitne, in press). Therapists may alternate between feelings of numbness and hypersensitivity that can lead to feeling out of control. A sense of isolation in the world and disconnection from loving others, one's self and one's god reflect alterations in the therapist's spirituality.

The therapist's own history plays a role in her response to trauma work. High ideals, rescue fantasies, or overinvestment in meeting all her clients' needs may result in inadequate self-care. She may be prone to ignoring her own emotional, spiritual, psychological and physical needs (Pearlman and Saakvitne, in press). Another risk for the therapist unaware of the impact of her own history is that she will seek to have her needs met at the expense of the client. Awareness of one's own issues facilitates self-care of the clinician.

Trauma recovery work with women diagnosed with severe mental illness poses further hazards for the therapist. The high prevalence of abuse within this population ensures the therapist a caseload which includes a number of survivors (Harris, 1995). These clients often present with histories of multiple abuse, revictimization and ongoing abuse (Harris, 1995). Among these women, the incidence of violent victimization was so high that experiences of rape and physical battery became almost normative (Harris, 1995). The effects of homelessness, mental illness and substance abuse only exacerbate difficulties in working with this population of survivors. Racism, sexism and the scarcity of resources highlight societal unwillingness to recognize and develop specialized treatment for women survivors diagnosed with mental illness.

Trauma occurs in an interpersonal and relational context and it is within this context that healing also takes place. The therapeutic relationship is the setting which provides the client with the opportunity to experience relating to another in safe intimacy. Since what the clinician brings to this relationship is crucial, attention to how the work affects the clinician is a critical part of the process.

304

Recognizing signs of distress is an important first step in addressing the impact of this difficult work on psychotherapists, case managers, residential specialists and other treatment providers. Throughout this chapter the word *therapist* will be used generically and can be understood to mean any treatment provider. Therapists who treat trauma survivors are vulnerable to vicarious traumatization, powerful countertransference issues and burnout due to a lack of resources and support from the system.

Vicarious traumatization

Vicarious traumatization refers to the transformation in the therapist's inner experience resulting from empathetic exposure to clients' trauma material (McCann and Pearlman, 1990). Vicarious traumatization can lead to disrupted beliefs about the goodness of others and safety in the world (Pearlman and Saakvitne, in press). The therapist may experience a sense of heightened vulnerability to trauma and fear for her own well-being. Symptoms of secondary PTSD often manifest themselves in the form of intrusive imagery from the client's traumatic material as well as in nightmares, anger and anxiety and a tendency towards dissociation. McCann and Pearlman (1990) suggest that these disturbances can affect all aspects of a therapist's life and that they may be permanent. Personal accounts by therapists currently engaged in work with trauma survivors will illustrate some of these issues and their effects on clinicians.

Linda, a counselor at a residential program for disadvantaged mothers, was stunned to hear the horrendous stories of abuse these young women confided to her.

> I had heard about sexual abuse on television, but it was always something that happened to others. Now it has really hit home for me because these are people I know, care about and see every day. I remember my first client; she was very open about her abuse. She went into the graphic details and I almost lost it. I wanted to cry and scream, but instead I sat there stone faced and disbelieving. I had this strong sense that the things she had described were impossible and unreal. Yet, there she was, crying, her pain so raw, so real, I just couldn't deny it. To be honest, I was kind of relieved when the session was over. It was so painful

for me to watch her relive her experience as she spoke. I knew I had to remain strong, be professional. She needed that from me.

I don't think I am the same person I was before I began to do this work. I have been doing this four years now so I've learned to adjust. The first six months I had nightmares frequently. I couldn't stop thinking about the horrible traumatic lives these women had survived. I grew up in a loving, supportive family. I felt so guilty about my happy childhood. For a while I was unable to enjoy life anymore. I wouldn't go out or socialize, I just wanted to talk about my clients' lives. I became mistrustful of others, even my friends. I started looking under my car before I got in and running from my car into my house as fast as I could. I still do that. I do weird things now, for example, when people walk by me on the street, I memorize their faces just in case I need to identify them later. I can't stop myself, whenever I see men with little girls I wonder if they are molesting them. Luckily, I have support from the other staff here at work and we talk about our feelings. I am also in therapy and that helps a lot.

The impact of this work has clearly affected Linda's life in many ways. She has become more fearful for her own safety and suspicious of the motives of others. She also experienced secondary symptoms such as nightmares, hypervigilence, anxiety and intrusive thoughts. In spite of support from her therapist and colleagues, Linda states, "Once I began to do this work, I realized that part of me will never be the same."

Countertransference

Vicarious traumatization represents the cumulative effect on the therapist of exposure to traumatic material across clients (Pearlman and Saakvitne, in press). In contrast, countertransference describes the therapists' unresolved and unconscious issues raised by a particular client's material, race, gender and transference response. The therapist's attitudes and beliefs inevitably influence her interaction with the client. When the therapist's comfort level is challenged by the client, she may respond defensively. Work with trauma survivors in particular can evoke ambivalent or judgmental feelings in the therapist. Countertransference can be a useful tool if acknowledged, or conversely, can result in reactions and behaviors on the part of the therapist that can be harmful to both the client and the therapist herself. Acting out countertransference issues can lead to feelings of incompetence and loss of control in the therapist. Courtois (1988) describes horror, denial, avoidance, guilt and rage as some common responses to stories of abuse. Martha works at an outpatient mental health agency and co-leads trauma groups for mentally ill women in the inner city. She noted that "you can't do the group without it having a major effect on you." Martha also discussed the disparity between her life and the lives of the women in her group:

> To say that it made me feel guilty is probably too strong a word. Call it privileged, not so much because I'm white or middle-class, but because I grew up in a fairly sane and sensible environment. I wasn't expected to take care of my siblings. I didn't have parents who were throwing knives at each other. It seems that the only way these women could handle their situations was to run away and to end up living in shelters. The women talked about how hard it was to escape homelessness and drugs and how people are always trying to lure them back into it. It just seemed like once things started going wrong for people they would either go crazy and end up in a hospital or lead a marginal existence on the streets. I'm not sure I would have been able to come through all the things these women survived.

By distancing her own experience from that of her clients', Martha was able to titrate the feelings of dread and horror elicited by the group members' accounts. In discussing incest horror, Meiselman (1978) says, "A horrified attitude prevents us from recognizing the true scope of the problem by relegating incest to the realm of events that are so bizarre that they occur only among the scum of society or in the context of extreme psychopathology." At times, Martha experienced the group as so overwhelming that she responded physically to what she heard. In her words: "When I heard really bad stories I would sometimes get a feeling in my legs that they wanted to get up and walk out on their own. I almost felt like I should put my head between my knees to avoid passing out. I'm willing to sit there and listen to these horror stories, but my body is screaming, 'get me out of here!' " Therapists also protect themselves from the impact of intolerable affect by minimizing 'the severity of the abuse, questioning the passivity of the victim and implying that the victim played a role in the abuse. Some therapists gain a sense of control and efficacy by maintaining a rigid and distant professional role (Courtois, 1988). This detachment from the survivor and her story enables the therapist to contain her own anxiety within the relationship. Therapists may adopt a rescuing or caretaking role in an effort to assuage their own feelings of guilt and powerlessness when faced with the survivor's profound pain. The boundaries of the therapeutic relationship may become blurred as the therapist attempts to remedy the deficiencies of the client's past. The therapist allows for extended sessions, late or nonpayment, phone contact at any time of the day or night, irrespective of the therapist's personal needs. These allowances cast the survivor as fragile, overly special and in need of, extraordinary arrangements (Courtois, 1988).

Emily is a therapist in private practice in a large city. When Emily reflected on her work with trauma survivors, she acknowledged overextending herself.

> I had a particular client who presented with a very intense and severe trauma history. I was appalled at the cruelty and deprivation she had suffered as a small child. I found myself wanting to hold her and comfort her and erase her pain. I desperately wanted to fill the voids of her young life. When I went away on vacation, I decided to give her my phone number in case she needed me. I wasn't sure this was a good idea, but I felt she needed it. We had 90 minute sessions to accommodate her difficulty with trust. I often called her at home to check up on her. Eventually, I began to resent what I saw as her over dependency on me. This made me feel incredibly guilty, like I was another abusive parent she couldn't count on.

This overextension on the part of the therapist can then lead to feelings of rage toward the client for being overly dependent and demanding (Courtois, 1988). It is important for the therapist to realize that she cannot change the past or eliminate the pain, but rather must assist the client in integrating these feelings to achieve healing. Rage may also manifest itself against the perpetrator and society at large, as well as towards the client herself. While co-leading a trauma group for young women at a residential facility, Karen was aware of strong feelings of anger in herself. Her frustration with the women in the group stemmed from their denial that the abuse had any impact on their lives.

> It seems really contradictory to me for these women to be in a group to receive treatment and then deny that they need help. I felt enraged at them and wondered if they were simply avoiding being seen as 'victims' in society. I then felt intensely pissed off at the world for denigrating women in this fashion. I became consumed with the plight of women in our patriarchal society. I feel that perhaps I was less effective in dealing with these young women's individual issues because my angry feelings got out of control.

Countertransference dynamics can differ according to gender. Herman (1981) suggests that female therapists are at risk for over identification with the victim and rage at the perpetrator, while male therapists may experience over identification with the aggressor. The female therapist's attunement to the victim position, both from personal experiences and the fact of being a woman, often fosters feelings of hopelessness and powerlessness. These, in turn, may result in overprotection, over gratification and a loosening of boundaries with the survivor client. Conversely, male therapists tend to struggle with power issues in relation to their female clients and thus are more likely to rationalize the behavior of the perpetrator and emphasize the victim's possible complicity. They may conversely feel guilty and try to compensate for what "bad men" have done in the past.

Excessive voyeuristic interest in the details of the abuse can be harmful to survivors already burdened by shame issues. Male therapists must be aware of their reactions to a sexualized transference. Unfortunately, sexual exploitations of survivor clients by their male therapists have been found to occur quite regularly (Courtois, 1988). On the other hand, a relationship with a male therapist that models caring and clear sexual boundaries can be ultimately healing for the survivor. Nicholas, a therapist in private practice in the suburbs, describes his experience in working with a female trauma survivor:

> This woman presented with a terrible history of severe physical, emotional and sexual abuse. She can be very rageful and often

309

comes in roaring, "I hate men!" I think that male therapists who work with female clients tend to hear that a lot. I try to get the issue on the table for discussion, but, if the hatred is directed at me, I have a really hard time with it. Sometimes I feel like shouting back. It makes me so angry. Naturally, I don't. In some ways I can identify with being a victim. I've felt cornered and attacked and felt homicidal rage about it. Actually, I was sexually assaulted as a teen by an older guy in the locker room. It only happened twice and there was no penetration, so I didn't identify this as a major piece of my life. Nevertheless, I can identify with that intense fear and sense of vulnerability.

Sometimes I think I overidentify with her around issues of dissociation. She really dissociates when she talks about the sexual abuse. She goes into a trance and won't listen to me, won't stop talking until she is done with her story. I try and stay with her, but I find myself going into a trance as well. It feels scary and slippery and I find myself getting really sleepy. I think one way I defend myself is by becoming a little more distant and less spontaneous. The other extreme is that I go into these trances where I might as well be dead. There have also been times when I feel she is having a sexualized transference towards me. This happens when she is talking about her adult relationships with men. I feel myself becoming sexually aroused and I don't quite know what to do with it. I'm not interested in her. I just feel a physical reaction. When I was a lot younger, my pull to have sex with a client was much stronger. One time I remember thinking, "to hell with my career" because the pull to act on it was so intense. I have had female patients try and seduce me, but I've felt comfortable not acting on it. What stops me is a moral code and the threat of losing my career. I am also active in getting my needs met in outside relationships which I think is important in keeping good boundaries with clients.

The clinician survivor

Given the high incidence of sexual abuse among the general population, it seems unavoidable that the population of therapists in general and female therapists in particular, will include survivors of childhood trauma. Psychotherapists often choose their profession based on a need to understand their family history and resolve their own conflicts (Saakvitne, 1991). It is often no accident that an individual who has been traumatized as a child would be drawn to a field that promotes introspection and personal exploration (Saakvitne, 1991). Certainly the personal characteristics of trauma survivors are apt to predispose them to become attentive to the needs of others and to be gifted caretakers. This personal history can make survivors compatible with the role of therapist due to their acute sensitivity to the affects, needs and unspoken defenses of another as well as their highly developed capacity for empathy (Saakvitne, 1991). Survivor therapists bring their own unique issues of countertransference to the therapeutic process.

It is crucial that the therapist who is a trauma survivor engage in her own personal therapy. Issues of trust, control, boundaries, safety and self-esteem are paramount in work with survivors and the therapist survivor must acknowledge and explore her own limitations in order to be available to the client. It is inevitable that at some point there will be an overlap between the therapist's and the client's experiences. The affect generated by the client's story can be particularly intense for the therapist survivor. She must be acutely aware of her own countertransference response and what she brings into the relationship with the client in order to fully utilize her self as a therapeutic tool. Defensive reactions to the often evoked affective responses of fear, anger, shame, anxiety and grief will be mobilized to protect the therapist's self in the face of overwhelming, intolerable affect in much the same way they were when she was a child (Saakvitne, 1991). This may result in the therapist's inability to hear or believe the client, especially if the therapist is unaware of her own abuse history. Alternately, the therapist may assume that she knows exactly what the client is saying or experiencing because she mistakenly identifies the client's conflicts and coping strategies as being similar to her own. Therapist survivors must also guard against the tendency to dissociate during moments of high stress.

Disclosure of the therapist's trauma is a complicated issue that should be carefully evaluated to ensure that the therapist is not unconsciously seeking to have her own needs met by the client. Disclosure poses the risk of inviting the client to care for the therapist (Saakvitne, 1991). Fantasies about the therapists' pain, fragility, or strength can inhibit a client's sense of safety and openness (Saakvitne, 1991). Saakvitne (1991) strongly suggests that it is rarely, if ever, appropriate or useful for the therapist to disclose past abuse within the therapeutic relationship. The issue of disclosure and its relevancy with a particular client should always be discussed in supervision.

Leslie is a psychotherapist who works with mentally ill women who are survivors of trauma. As she began to do this work, she was simultaneously learning about the effects of trauma in her own life:

> I was driven to do the professional work with clients and strongly committed to it. In fact, it was the most important aspect of my work, so it was really important to get it right. I had to get it right and get it better than others because I was a trauma survivor. It was very scary, but also exciting to realize that who I was and what I had experienced, came from my traumatic background. There was a reason for things, now they made sense. This gave me hope, both for myself and for my clients. In the beginning, I became pretty cluttered and over-whelmed in listening to their stories. It was difficult for me to separate out my own stuff. One of my biggest clinical errors was assuming I knew what was going on with my client because it was the same as my stuff. I remember actually telling the client what she was feeling and going through. I would hear a client's story and pick out the parts that resonated for me and tell her what was going on inside her head. I've learned to let clients tell their own stories and to check things out with them.
>
> I was always great at sitting through a client's horrible story and taking care of her. However, as soon as she left, I would unravel. My emotions were so intense, I would get flooded and just sit there, staring into space for hours, feeling like my heart was about to explode. I think it is something about being a trauma survivor, that you can be strong for someone else because they need you. You don't have to focus on yourself. Later though, it can be hell. I realize now that I also used to focus on the trauma itself and how awful it was and not at all on the women's strengths, their ability to heal or other aspects

of my clients' selves. I was able to do that once I became more integrated in my own therapy. I think that people who are not survivors have much less of a sense of what these people have survived and less of a sense of the process of healing and how difficult it is. My expectation is to help someone have a better and more alive life and be less affected by the trauma. I know from personal experience that it is not something that will ever go away. It will always be there. Hopefully though, it won't haunt you as much.

For me as a therapist, I have to be careful and keep up limits and boundaries so as not to overextend myself. Otherwise, I tend to try and do everything, I give too much and have nothing left. It was definitely something I had to learn how to do. Trauma survivors are not known for their ability to comfort or take care of themselves. I strongly believe that my own personal therapy was crucial in healing me and enabling me to be an effective therapist. Everyone doing this work needs to have done their own therapy. I also absolutely depended on supervision to help me process my feelings and reactions. Lately, I've been getting massages and have been taking care of my body through good nutrition. I also get a lot of support from my husband. Last, but certainly not least, I have stayed sane through this all by being able to talk to other survivor therapists. I encourage others to do the same. Nobody can or should do this work alone.

Self-care

As discussed previously, there are many factors that place the trauma therapist at risk for vicarious traumatization. In order to continue to do this work compassionately and well, one must be prepared to give serious consideration to one's own welfare. Unfortunately, little has been written about care of the clinician doing trauma work. Interventions to allay the impact of trauma work may fall into three categories: personal, professional and organizational (Pearlman and Saakvitne, in press). Psychotherapy is of primary importance in a clinician's personal care. Being in a therapy provides a number of safeguards for both the client and the therapist. The therapist who is

313

aware of her own issues and countertransference is in a much better position to respond empathically and consciously to what her clients present. She is better able to maintain appropriate boundaries and to make conscious choices about relaxing or tightening those boundaries. Therapy also provides a supportive arena in which the trauma therapist can ventilate her frustrations and explore her reactions to vicarious traumatization. It is essential that clinicians seek for themselves the same respectful attention and caretaking they give to their clients (Saakvitne, 1991).

Other valuable ways to cope with work-related stress include: active coping (concentrating one's efforts on doing something about the problem); seeking emotional support from friends or relatives; making a plan of action; seeking instrumental social support (advice from someone about what to do); and humor (Schauben and Frazier, 1995). Schauben and Frazier (1995) found that all of these coping strategies were associated with a lower prevalence of symptoms of vicarious trauma in therapists. Respondents in Schauben and Frazier's study were also asked to include additional strategies they had found helpful in coping with work related stress. Many answered that they participated in activities that focused on physical health such as exercising, eating healthy foods and getting adequate sleep. Spiritually-oriented activities such as keeping a journal, meditating, or being outdoors were the second most reported coping strategies. Also reported were leisure activities such as reading, listening to music and gardening. For example, Martha describes other ways in which she cares for herself:

> When things get really bad I go to a movie. I do have a support system outside of work that I keep in contact with. Sometimes after a group I would literally go home and go to bed. I have always been pretty good at comforting myself and distracting myself. Some of the greatest impact of the group process was fairly subtle and I didn't necessarily know what was percolating inside of me until it began to make sense. It was not an immediate thing. One of the co-leaders and I kept in contact and talked about it. I managed to deal with some of the impact by looking for activities and exercises for the group trauma manual which was something that I felt more comfortable with because it was

314

something concrete. I could go out and buy a book of poetry or something like that and try to hold on to some of the less threatening parts of the group.

Also important is the support of co-leaders, colleagues and supervisors. Without this kind of support, this work can be isolating and overwhelming. "In order to understand the victim's internal situation the therapist must be a willing participant in the drama, a situation that of necessity causes a loss of objectivity. The only compensation for this necessary loss is an embeddedness in a social situation in which the therapist can rely on colleagues to provide the same zone of safety that the therapist is providing for the patient" (Bloom, 1993). Co-leaders of groups and other colleagues doing trauma work must build trusting relationships in which they feel safe enough to share thoughts and feelings that are evoked during sessions with survivors. Karen used her relationship with her co-therapist to process her frustrations around how their group was going. "We would stay behind and talk to each other after the group. For me that's the most important kind of self-soothing or processing. I mean, I need to verbalize it and get it out. If I have someone that I can talk to about it who understands and then complain about it, I'm more likely to be able to let it go." When discussing the experience of working with co-leaders and participating in a supervision group, Martha says:

> Being honest I realize that when I felt very exhausted and very burnt out and very depressed that a lot of it did come from spending time with the group. It was hard sometimes to get out from under it. It was very difficult to have a lot of friends in the outside world and know it isn't something you can talk to them about, nor is it something they want to hear about even if you could. I also felt that they couldn't really appreciate the impact of this work. That's why it has been so important to share this with colleagues and my supervisor, they understand and sympathize.

Some clinicians have found a team approach to be of help in protecting therapists from secondary trauma. Munroe and Shay (1993) find that prevention of vicarious trauma "lies in alliance among therapists who see their own responses as clinically relevant, identify engagement patterns and offer alternatives." They also recommend discussion among team members about feelings aroused by the clients' traumatic material and of feelings toward the clients. Team members from different professional backgrounds are further encouraged to work together to make this discussion safe. Additionally, whenever possible therapists should try to vary their professional responsibilities. Therapists should consider limiting the number of trauma survivors they treat. Other suggestions include working on a committee in the community, taking on a writing or research project, attending conferences, or teaching.

While personal and professional support are important, the need for a broader range of support offered by the organization, system, or society cannot be underestimated. "While individual self care is important, it is not solely the individual's responsibility to provide the tools or the environment conducive to self care. In fact, individual self care has only limited effect or value unless social and environmental factors are also implemented (Yassen, 1993)."

Jane, a journalist, shared her experiences about the impact an organization can have on fostering a healthy environment in which to do this work:

> It was not at all by chance that I got into the line of work I did. I started working in a battered women's shelter in Boston. I really identified with these women and felt a certain familiarity with them and that this was very important work to do. At the same time I felt disconnected from their stories. Over time it seemed I had heard a million stories of abuse but I didn't relate those stories to similar occurrences in my own life. Not really a repression, but more of a dissociation. I developed intense bonds with these women.
>
> One time I was working with a young girl who had been misdiagnosed as mentally retarded and learning disordered, but I could see that she was really bright. She was being abused at the time and after she told about the abuse, she was placed in special classes and her story dismissed. I didn't know what to do. As I

listened to her, I became intensely fascinated and attached. When I decided to go to graduate school, I realized that the girl felt very betrayed by my leaving. Looking back, I know I should have set better boundaries and not have seen myself as her savior.

I used to try and help everyone. I had lots of friends who were abused and I had great sympathy and compassion for them. At that time I didn't consciously know about my own abuse history. In part, I believe I was able to avoid my history because when I worked in these women's organizations, staff were not encouraged to explore their own issues and in fact were discouraged from it.

I eventually wound up in treatment myself, but it was 18 months before I had my first memory of abuse. I realized I couldn't ignore it. I was overwhelmed, but also relieved. A lot of things fell into place for me and I spent time re-evaluating my whole life. I wanted to be involved in helping people with trauma histories, but I also knew my limits, so I decided to make my contribution through my journalism.

I have found that everyone brings their own issues to bear in how they deal with trauma. Tremendous energy is required to address these issues and if you can't or don't deal with your own past you can develop defenses that are destructive to someone's treatment. People are at different places regarding their awareness of their own issues. It is so important to be open to looking at yourself. Otherwise, you are at risk for acting stuff out unconsciously. Having a supportive community in which to explore these areas and talk about your countertransference can honestly help eliminate a lot of problems in the treatment itself and among colleagues.

I am very concerned about how organizations handle the support of their staff doing trauma work. In universities, agencies, inpatient facilities, etc. care givers are not encouraged to look at themselves and consider how to take care of themselves. This is a very dangerous situation. A lot of healers are overwhelmed. People need more than "professional" help. They also need community support.

Conclusion

Clinicians need to focus on their own care when working with survivors of trauma. Therapy with survivors in all populations is an extremely difficult and taxing process. The therapist must not only contend with the challenges of treating clients that present with a myriad of painful symptoms, but also with a society that alternately denies the existence of such abuse and attributes blame for it on the victim. In order to be effective as a healer and maintain personal well-being, therapists must have support in the personal, professional and organizational realms.

References

Bloom, S.L. (Summer 1993) "Vicarious traumatization and therapist self-care", in *Traumatic StressPoints: News for the international society for traumatic stress studies.* 7(3) New York: W.W. Norton.

Courtois, C.A. (1988) *Healing the Incest Wound.* New York: Norton.

Harris, M. (1995) "Trauma Recovery Skills: Development and Enhancement" (Unpublished).

Herman, J.L. (1992) *Trauma and Recovery.* New York: Basic Books.

Herman, J.L. (1981) *Father-Daughter Incest.* Cambridge, MA: Harvard University Press.

McCann, I.L. and Pearlman, L.A. (1990) "Vicarious traumatization: A framework for understanding the psychological effects of working with victims", in *Journal of Traumatic Stress*, 3(1), 131–149.

Meiselman, K.C. (1978) *Incest: A psychological study of cause and effects with treatment recommendations.* San Francisco: Jossey-Bass.

Munroe, J.F. and Shay, J. (Summer 1993) "Prevention of secondary trauma in therapists", in *Traumatic StressPoints: News for the international society for traumatic stress studies,* 7(3), 3.

Pearlman, L.A. and Saakvitne, K.W. (in press). "Constructivist self development theory approach to treating therapists with secondary traumatic stress disorders." In C. Figley (Ed.), *Compassion fatigue: Secondary traumatic stress disorders from treating the traumatized.* New York: Brunner/Mazel.

Saakvitne, K.W. (1991) "Countertransference in psychotherapy with incest survivors: When the therapist is a survivor of child abuse." Paper presented at the 99th Annual Convention of the American Psychological Association, San Francisco, CA.

Schauben, L. and Frazier, P. (1995) "Vicarious trauma: The effects on female counselors of working with sexual violence survivors", in *Psychology of Women Quarterly*, 19, 49–64.

Shengold, L. (1989) *Soul murder: The effects of childhood abuse and deprivation.* New Haven, CT: Yale University Press.

Yassen, J. (Summer 1993) "Taking care while giving care: Guidelines for treaters of trauma", *Traumatic StressPoints: News for the international society for traumatic stress studies*, 7(3), 4.

Chapter Fifteen

Sexual Trauma and African American Women

Bronwen L. Millet

THE experience of sexual trauma in the African American community is a complex issue to both assess and treat. The difficulty
stems from the culture of African American people. The legacy of
African American women, in particular, has been one shaped by
stories of sexual trauma passed from generation to generation. Rape
and sexual abuse have occurred over a period of several hundred
years. Traditionally African American women were sold, with their
price being determined by their child bearing capacity. The children
were routinely conceived as a result of forced sexual relations with
both African male slaves and white slave masters (Greene, 1994).
African American women have heard stories of their great-grand-
mothers, great-aunts and other relatives being victims of random
rape and sexual abuse. Thus, when the daughters, granddaughters and
great granddaughters of these women experience sexual trauma, it
often becomes difficult for them to determine if these acts are
merely a "rite of passage" or if they have in fact been victimized. An
awareness of such issues is paramount in treating African American
women. Because it is often a difficult and confusing experience for
African American women to state they are survivors of sexual
trauma, providers of mental health services must be aware of the
specific cultural issues that make treatment difficult.

The focus of this chapter is twofold. First, a presentation of the difficulties clinicians may encounter in attempting to assess sexual trauma in African American women will be presented. This overview will outline several "trouble" areas, along with examples that suggest ways to enhance the cultural sensitivity during the assessment process. A similar approach will be applied to the second area that will be discussed, treatment issues addressing potential "trouble" areas in treating African American women who are victims of sexual trauma and then offering recommendations for culturally sensitive intervention.

The material in this chapter is based on informal interviews which were conducted with both African American and Caucasian female case managers at Community Connections. All of the interviews were conducted in small groups in a space within the work setting. All participants were assured of anonymity and were informed of how the information they provided would be used. All interviews lasted approximately 40 minutes and clinicians were informed that they did not have to continue to participate in the process if it made them uncomfortable in any way. The data obtained will be referred to and used to illustrate specific points throughout this chapter.

Assessment issues

Identifying oneself as a victim of sexual trauma is a complex issue for many African American women. African American women have traditionally taken care of themselves and provided for their families. This care and support have at times been given in the midst of sexual abuse by the African American male. These women continue to support their families at their own expense and to remain silent. To do otherwise would be to risk ridicule by family members and to struggle with feelings of guilt. This difficulty is further complicated when these women attempt to identify themselves as victims within mainstream society. African American women have historically been victims of oppression, discrimination and racism. Such consistent and intense victimization often results in their feeling too uncomfortable to give voice to any sexual abuse that might have occurred.

Because African American women have such difficulty identifying themselves as victims, it becomes critical that any assessment procedures used are clear and specific. Such techniques will leave little room for doubt by the women and will lessen the likelihood for their feelings of guilt. Objective and specific assessment procedures allow women to identify themselves as victims without worrying about the appropriateness of their response to the perpetrator.

It is also important that assessment procedures avoid blaming the women. While this issue is important across cultures, it is critical for African American women, especially when the abuser is an African American male. Because African American women have traditionally been the caretakers within the community, they are expected to take care of and provide for the African American male (Greene, 1994). Implicit in this is the injunction that African American women are not to engage in activities that might make the life of African American men more difficult than it already is, even at the expense of their own well being (Greene, 1994). African American women may thus choose to remain silent in the midst of much abuse (Greene, 1994). Because African American women have concerns and issues of guilt about identifying themselves as victims of abuse by African American males, it is important for clinicians to be aware of this conflict. It is critical that clinicians help identify these women when they are victims and take special care not to blame them for the abuse or consequences to the perpetrator.

Language

Language (both verbal and nonverbal) is a critical component of the assessment process. The actual words used to convey the thoughts and feelings of African Americans are important in understanding and appreciating this unique culture. Sensitivity to language is also necessary to lessen the chance of misinterpretation and misunderstandings during exchanges.

The actual language used to address African Americans can either promote or hinder their willingness to participate in the assessment process. More specifically, within the African American community older persons are addressed with the use of a title, or "Handle" as it is called within the African American culture. Thus, when greeting an older person, younger persons initiate conversations with the use of Miss, Mrs. or Mr.. To do this demonstrates respect and gives older persons recognition and appreciation. If, however, young people do not address their elders using a title, it is often interpreted as a sign of disrespect and is met with distance and hostility on the part of older African Americans.

During the informal interview with African American case managers, one case manager spoke of her experience of referring to a client by her first name as opposed to greeting her using a title. The case manager told of how upset and defensive the women became, stating that the case manager was young enough to be her daughter. The older woman also reported that just because one has a degree and a professional job is no reason for one to be disrespectful. Although attempts were made to rectify this situation, the woman remained distant for the duration of the assessment. Thus, even when one has the best of intentions, it is paramount to have a framework for understanding particular differences from mainstream culture so that persons are not inadvertently offended.

There are also particular words and phrases used specifically within the African American community (Randall-David, 1989). Again a familiarity with such words and phrases is necessary to increase the likelihood that persons will be appropriately understood.

African American clinicians reported that their African American clients often referred to each other as "bitches." The use of this word is not always an intentional put down, but may be an attempt to "reclaim the language." Frequent use of this word helps to desensitize women from the hurt and pain that has often been associated with its use during abuse.

The term "my friend" is another word whose usage deviates from mainstream society. Whereas "friend" usually has a platonic connotation within the mainstream, the use of the term within the African American community often implies an intimate, romantic involvement. Such a distinction is critical in helping clinicians understand the dynamics of a reported relationship. Again, when clinicians understand these particular linguistic nuances, it not only helps them understand their clients better, but it also conveys that the particular culture is respected and appreciated.

During the interview with the African American clinicians, another example was given in which an understanding of the

324

language was critical. An African American client referred to a Caucasian clinician as being "phat." The Caucasian clinician was offended and reported this insult, wanting an apology. An African American clinician overheard the exchange and assured the Caucasian clinician that the use of the word she heard was not "fat," but "phat" which in the African American community can be translated to mean "pretty hips and thighs."

African American case managers reported that many African American women also used the term "girl" or "girlfriend" when speaking to each other. This term demonstrates feelings of affection and connectedness among these women. Group members occasionally referred to each other as "nigger" or to their male partners as "my niggah." Although at first glance, mainstream culture may wonder how to interpret such an exchange, it can be easily understood when the dynamics of the African American culture are known. Traditionally the term "nigger" has been used by mainstream society to oppress and ridicule African Americans. The use of the term by African Americans in relation to each other, however, is again an attempt to "reclaim the language," thus taking the negative connotation out and replacing it with a positive one. African Americans frequently use the term "nigger" as a term of endearment and affection.

Additionally, the African American case managers reported that many of their African American clients speak in a loud tone, while using the words "bitch" and "nigger." Such interactions are often misinterpreted by mainstream society as the beginnings of a disruption. One African American case manager gave an example of actually having to explain this difference to a Caucasian clinician who had called for security backup because she misinterpreted the use of the language and thought that a fight might occur.

The importance of such an understanding was further demonstrated when Caucasian clinicians were interviewed. When asked about language differences Caucasian clinicians immediately spoke of the use of the word "nigger" during therapy. The Caucasian clinicians were uncomfortable with the use of the term and did not have an appropriate context for understanding its use. Caucasian clinicians also reported not feeling comfortable enough to question African American clients about their use of the term. Again, there is a need

325

for mainstream society to be sensitive to language differences and realize that while they may not actually use the language themselves, they must understand its use within the African American culture.

It is also important to be sensitive to the tone of voice in which African Americans speak. It is often thought that African Americans speak in an angry way. When African Americans talk, Caucasian clinicians can misunderstand the exchange and assume that a violent episode is about to occur. Opal Palmer Adisa (1990) discusses the pent up anger often felt by African Americans. This anger has been reportedly built up over a life time of discrimination and oppression. African Americans thus often feel full of rage and have very few appropriate outlets for these feelings. Consequently it becomes understandable that African Americans may look and act in an angry way that is often misinterpreted as an impending violent act by clinicians unfamiliar with the culture. Angry words and loud voices are sometimes only the packaging of oppression and racism. Opal Palmer Adisa (1990) attempts to explain anger in African American women in a passage from the Black Women's Health book. She states:

> Did you ever wonder why so many sisters look so angry? Why we walk like we've got bricks in our bags and will slash and curse you at the drop of a hat? It's because stress is hemmed into our dresses, pressed into our hair, mixed into our perfume and painted on our fingers. Stress from the deferred dreams, the dreams not voiced; stress from the broken promises, the blatant lies; stress from always being at the bottom, from never being thought beautiful, from always being taken for granted, taken advantage of; stress from being a black woman in white America. How long do you think you can hold our breath without asphyxiating? Yes, black women do commit suicide. We kill ourselves when we cease to smile; when we take drugs to deaden the pain of being black; when we allow a partner to physically and mentally abuse us because we are desperate to have 'somebody'; when we allow ourselves to be divided by class privilege, income, preoccupation with skin color, look or sexual preference; when night after week after month we sit alone in our apartments and cry, or eat packaged death, or watch televi-

sion because there is no one to call and say, 'Hey girl, what's happin?' we are stressed out.

Nonverbal communication styles also vary between cultures and again differences should be acknowledged and explored so that unintentional offenses do not occur. For instance, within the African American community prolonged eye contact is often considered starring or an act of defiance, although within mainstream culture it is often interpreted as a display of interest and understanding (Randall-David, 1994). Since African Americans do not maintain direct and continual eye contact to demonstrate their attentiveness, clinicians must not assume that the lack of it implies a lack of interest or involvement. Members of the African American community demonstrate their attentiveness by other forms of nonverbal communication such as head nodding or "umm, umm ..." responses (Randall-David, 1989).

The negotiation of space is another form of nonverbal communication that is culturally specific. Within mainstream culture, physical distance is maintained during verbal exchanges. African Americans, in contrast, tend to speak with relatively little physical space between them (Randall-David, 1989). Such little physical space is often used to convey feelings of warmth and a sense of community between people. Thus, during exchanges, it becomes important for clinicians to understand the implications behind physical distance. Distances with too much physical space may unintentionally offend people and cause them not to participate fully in the assessment process. The negotiation of space for African American trauma survivors is complex. Close consistent physical contact with others is often difficult for trauma survivors in general. As stated earlier, African Americans often interact within a close physical space. Thus while African Americans traditionally prefer close interactions, African American trauma survivors may find this uncomfortable. It is thus critical for clinicians to be aware of these dynamics so that their behaviors can be modified as necessary.

A Caucasian clinician gave an example of an assessment she conducted with an African American woman. Upon their initial meeting, both women shook hands and continued to stand while discussing the assessment process. As the African American women spoke, she continued to approach the Caucasian clinician. The

Caucasian clinician began to back up until there was literally no place else to go. The Caucasian clinician reported feeling invaded and was uncomfortable and awkward. Although the Caucasian clinician did not ask the interviewee how she felt, we can speculate that she too felt ill at ease with the clinician's movement away from her. Even with knowledge of the culture, the Caucasian clinician may have still felt uncomfortable with such a close physical proximity. Knowledge, however, may have provided her with a more appropriate framework for interpreting the woman's behavior.

Treatment issues

Engagement issues

From the onset, treating African Americans within a traditional mental health agency can prove to be a difficult task regardless of whether the issue is trauma or some other mental health concern. Much of this is related to the reluctance of African Americans to seek help from public agencies. African Americans have traditionally been subjected to oppression and institutionalized racism by the mainstream culture and are thus reluctant to seek help outside their culture. Thus, initial attempts to treat African Americans are often met with suspiciousness and distance.

Treating African American survivors of sexual trauma can prove to be an even more complicated task especially when the abuser is a family member. African Americans are instructed from a young age to be distrustful of mainstream society and not to discuss "family matters" with outsiders. Historically, it has been beneficial for African American families to keep family business private. Progress was traditionally made more quickly when mainstream society was not aware of the advancements of African American people. African American women often find it difficult to report abuses by African American men especially when they believe that these men are already victims of mainstream society. African American clients often blame their victimization not on the male but on the society that consistently discriminates against him. Such a belief not only takes away the responsibility of the perpetrator but also allows the women to rationalize remaining silent.

The healing that needs to occur for women who have been victims of sexual trauma, however, can only occur when there is a degree of openness and honesty. True healing can only take place when the woman feels comfortable enough to experience vulnerability and helplessness and to know that she will be protected and cared for. It is thus critical for clinicians to understand the special concerns and inhibitions that African American women may have in discussing their trauma.

Greene (1994) reports of a client who lamented that although her live-in boyfriend was intermittently abusive to her, she often felt that he got abused by white people all day and did not deserve "trouble" from her too. Additionally, many women in these situations observe that if they report an abusive partner, he will be treated more harshly by law enforcement officials because he is an African American (Greene, 1994). Thus, there is a conflict for African American women between their personal needs and those of their African American male partners. Although women may be correct in their assessment of the harsher treatment received by African American males, Greene (1994) states that it remains important for these women to avoid feeling responsible for taking care of the perpetrator. She further states that while it is imperative for clinicians to understand the struggle these women face, they must also consistently encourage them to seek help and to take care of themselves.

Another example of the difficulty that African American women have in reporting family members was demonstrated by an African American member of a trauma group at Community Connections. Although the member reportedly spoke freely of the abuse committed by her father, it was still difficult for her to find fault with him. It is important to note that while difficulty reporting abuse is true for most victims of sexual trauma, the role African American women have played in protecting their males makes this type of disclosure particularly problematic.

During the informal interview, African American case managers recommended ways to engage women in treatment. One way was through the use of culturally relevant readings such as the *Black Women's Health Book* (White, 1990) or Sisters of the Yam: Black Women in Self-Recovery (Hooks, 1993). Suggestions also included using culturally relevant examples as role models. This allows the participants to identify with women of the same culture who have gone through similar experiences, helping them to feel more connected to the material, thus making for a better emotional transition from victimization to recovery. An example of this was given by an African American woman who is a sexual trauma survivor. The trauma group leader consistently drew similarities between Maya Angelou's work and the struggles of group participants. When the leader referred to Maya Angelou's journey to self-recovery, she continued to discuss the similarities between Maya Angelou and the group members. The leader reports that the group members felt a connection with the example and found it much easier to relate to each other's struggles. Such experiences make an internal transition much more likely.

During the informal interview, African American case managers also agreed that another way to facilitate the treatment process was to have the African American women listen to each other. Although it is common knowledge that trust is built within a group as its members self-disclose and are responded to by other members in a caring, appropriate manner, this dynamic has special implications for African American women. As stated earlier, African American women are taught to be mistrustful of the mainstream culture because of years of racism and oppression. African American women have also learned to protect, nurture and keep the family together (Greene, 1994). Thus necessary support and understanding can occur when African American women encourage and reassure each other that they are not alone in their struggle.

Therapy issues

Group therapy and other similar treatment interventions are effective ways of treating survivors of sexual trauma. Within the African American community, however, counseling is often viewed with suspicion and thought to be threatening (Randall-David, 1989). Many African Americans do not refer themselves to mental health agencies because to do so is viewed as an admission that there is a problem with them. While some members of mainstream society associate visits to psychiatrists or psychologists as a status symbol, African Americans often translate such contacts to mean that society is again telling them that something is wrong with them. It is possible that African Americans may believe that information discovered about them during a therapy group might be used against them in an attempt to continue their oppression. Again, issues of trauma and abuse are difficult for most people to discuss across cultures, but the racism and discrimination against people of color makes this population less likely to share information that may make them appear vulnerable or helpless. Given that such issues exist within the African American community, it is paramount for providers of mental health to understand the difficulty African American women may have in agreeing to receive help from a mental health agency. It is crucial for providers to stress the importance of seeking professional help for sexual trauma victims while being sensitive to the stigma associated with counseling within the community (Randall-David, 1989).

Members of the African American community often rely on their own resources in taking care of their problems. There is often a downplay in the severity of their problems and a tendency to convince others that they have the situation under control when they do not. African American women who are survivors of sexual trauma may not want to appear weak or in need of help and thus may opt to present a more controlled and indifferent facade. It is important for providers of mental health to be sensitive to this and to give women permission to have problems, thus letting them know that they have been violated and that it is not their fault (Randall-David, 1989). As stated earlier, having African American women discuss with or listen to other African American women's stories of sexual abuse may be a first step in letting them know that they are not alone. It is critical that providers do not misinterpret a calm exterior or a lack of verbalization of stress to mean that there is not any genuine distress.

An African American case manager told of a group encounter where one of the African American members consistently reported that the abuse she experienced in her past did not affect her at all. The group member further stated that she was not angry about being abused nor did she feel a need to discuss it. Over the course of many months the woman remained quiet and seemingly uninterested in the group although she attended every session. Approximately six months into the therapy sessions, the group leader had an emergency and the group was canceled. At the following

331

session this woman was found crying in the therapy room 45 minutes before the scheduled start time. When this was discussed in group, she told of the difficulty she had in telling her story. She further told of how invested she was in the group and how disappointed and abandoned she felt when it did not meet. This situation may have been magnified for this woman if she historically had been rejected or abandoned in the past. Although this woman had been judged as uninterested or uninvolved, her calm exterior and lack of eye contact were not indicative of her level of connection.

There are many reasons African American women may appear to be uninterested when they are, in fact, very interested and invested. The apparent lack of interest may be used as protection from feelings of helplessness or vulnerability. Additionally, many African American women have been consistently and routinely discriminated against, resulting in a dulling of senses and a lack of any real display of emotions.

Another way to make the therapy more inviting is to be sensitive to the spiritual dimension of recovery. Religion is an appropriate source of comfort and support for African American persons and should be included during treatment. Religion has traditionally been an important aspect in the daily lives of most African Americans. Religion often provides an oasis from the daily struggles with life, poverty and conflict within the community (Randall-David, 1989). During the informal interview, case managers reported that their African American clients often used prayer as a source of coping. Group members suggested that they lean on God for their support.

An African American case manager reported that she included prayer in the beginning of each session at the suggestion of the participants. This practice appeared to both sooth and comfort members, placing them in a space where they were able to receive help and guidance. The inclusion of culturally specific supports also demonstrates to group members that their culture is important and respected. Other case managers reported that they supported members' suggestions of inviting a minister and attending church services together.

Another African American case manager told of an experience that demonstrated a clear lack of understanding of the religious component of the African American culture. A 42 year old African American woman with a long history of mental illness was in the

332

process of becoming stabilized via therapy and medication. Because of her progress, independent housing options were being explored for her. As a part of this process, the woman was to be interviewed by the housing staff to assess her ability to live independently. As a part of the assessment process, the woman was asked about her support networks. More specifically, she was asked to whom she talked when she was having problems and needed help or guidance. The woman quickly responded that she often spoke to God. She reported that she told God all of her problems and that God often talked back to her. While such a response may be viewed as psychotic within mainstream society, frequent two-way conversations with God are a way in which many African Americans have been instructed to seek help and support. Without such knowledge and sensitivity to the culture, this response and ones similar to it would be misinterpreted and an inappropriate intervention might be made.

Besides providing a consistent level of support, religion also influences African Americans' conceptions about illness, health and what happens in their lives. African Americans often speak of the problems they have in life as being a direct consequence for disobeying God (Randall-David, 1989). Thus African American women who have been victims of sexual trauma may blame their victimization on their disobedience towards God. It thus becomes critical for clinicians who do incorporate religion into their treatment to assess the ideology of the religion so that women are not incorrectly blamed for their abuse. It is critical that the clinicians not disrespect or disapprove of the religion in general, but be sensitive and creative in reframing beliefs that may inappropriately blame women.

It is also important that the styles of the intervention be culturally sensitive. Randall-David (1989) reports that African American women respond better when the intervention includes some type of physical action. Such an intervention in the work with trauma survivors may prove useful in providing immediate and specific solutions for women. It is often difficult to talk about a subject as powerful as trauma. African Americans are a people for whom movement is a large part of their daily interaction. Trauma interventions should thus also include action and movement. Such an intervention allows women an alternative way to process very intense emotional material and gives them a familiar way to express themselves.

Additionally, exercise and the use of music was suggested by African American case managers as a way of relaxing members and providing comfortable and familiar surroundings for interventions to take place.

One African American case manager reported that she always began each session with culturally sensitive music. She reported that the music provided the women with a sense of community as well as connection through the lyrics that were used which were culturally relevant. In songs that speak to the issue of abuse in African American women, the actual words can be used as a source of bonding between women and can be used for inspiration and guidance. For example, songs such as Tina Turner's "What's Love Got to Do With It," in which she sings about an abusive relationship where love was not enough to make her stay, may be used to begin a more personal discussion about trauma.

Discussion

It is virtually impossible to separate one's self from one's culture. Culture is all inclusive. It consists of one's orientation to music, food, clothing and art, but also includes how people construct their relationship with the planet, how they view aging, define male-female relationships and define illness and health (Mason, Benjamin and Lewis, in print).

In the psychological treatment of people of color, Lum (1983) suggests that open discussions concerning racial awareness, family and social history and personal or cultural beliefs about the presenting problem's etiology are important. Pinderhughes (1989) suggests that such discussions can provide an indication of the client's ethnic awareness and esteem.

Treatment of a different culture often tends to be culturally blind. In the informal interviews which were conducted as part of this study, it is interesting to note that African American case managers consistently addressed the importance of culture in treating African American women. These case managers readily cited examples of its importance and made recommendations for culturally sensitive interventions. Caucasian clinicians, on the other hand, consistently either found culture not to be an issue or found themselves to be exempt from issues of cultural sensitivity. Although these interviews were by no means exhaustive, nor should the results be interpreted as an actual study, it is important to note the consistency with which persons outside of a culture ignored its impact. Mason *et al.*, (in print) suggests that treating everyone the same (if that is possible) can lead to ignoring the impact culture can have on the delivery of services. Jones (1988) comments:

> ... that the culturally blind approach assumes that the problem is somehow biological. It asserts that there are no meaningful differences and that race doesn't matter, we are all the same. Although race does not matter, culture does. We are all not the same, as we evolved from and continue to evolve different cultural legacies.

In an attempt to become more culturally sensitive, providers must pay attention to simple things such as dress, holidays celebrated and musical or food interests. Family networks and authority figures can give key insights as to the client's level of acculturation or assimilation (Mason, *et al.*, in print). It is also important to keep in mind that when providers do not know they should ask questions.

Mason, *et al.*, (in print) suggests that a natural beginning point is with one's own cultural orientation or that of one's agency in terms of its similarities and differences from other cultures. How people feel about their own cultural identity is often indicative of how they feel about themselves. As Pinderhughes (1989) suggests, "Practitioners who value their ethnicity are in a better position to value that of their clients, more ready to help clients learn to value themselves and to use ethnic identity as yet another avenue for building self-esteem."

The benefits of becoming culturally competent are manifold. It allows practitioners to better understand the issue of cultural diversity and to consider areas such as the historical underutilization and the premature termination of services among African Americans (Sue and Sue, 1990).

Summary

It is critical that clinicians have a basic understanding of the cultural background of the people they are treating. More specifically, it is important that clinicians understand the language of the people.

Such knowledge helps to ensure that misinterpretations and misunderstandings are minimal. It is also important to incorporate culturally sensitive interventions. Such an inclusion demonstrates an appreciation and acknowledgment of a culture.

References

Adisa, O.P. (1990) "Rocking in the sun light: Stress and black women." In E.C. White (Ed.), *The black women's health book: Speaking for ourselves.* Seal Press, Washington.

Greene, B. (1994) "African American Women." In L.Comas-Diaz and B. Greene (Eds.), *Women of color: Integrating ethnic and gender identities in psychotherapy.* Guilford Press, New York.

Hooks, B. (1993) *Sisters of the Yam: Black women and self-recovery.* South End Press, Boston.

Jones, J.M. (1988) "Racism in black and white: A bicultural model of reaction and evolution." In: P.A. Katz and D.A. Taylor (Eds.). *Eliminating racism: Problems in controversy.* Plenum Press, New York.

Lum, D. (1992) *Social work practice and people of color: A process-stage approach.* 2nd edition. Brooks/Cole Publishing Company, Belmont, CA.

Mason, J.L., Benjamin, M.P. and Lewis, B.S. (in press) "The Cultural Competent Model: Implications for child and family services." In L.A. Heflinger and C.T. Nixon (Eds.), *Families in the Mental Health System for Children and Adolescents: Policy, Service and Research.* Sage Newberry Park, California.

Pinderhughes, E.B. (1989) "Significance of culture and power in human behavior curriculum, ethnicity and race." In Bowles and Hardy, *Critical concepts in social work.* National Association of Social Workers, Inc. Silver Spring, MD.

Randall, E.D. (1989) *Strategies for working with culturally diverse communities and clients.* 1st edition. Association for the Care of Children's Health, Washington, D.C.

Sue, D.W. and Sue, D. (1990) *Counseling the culturally different.* John Wiley and Sons, New York.

White, E.C. (Ed.). (1990) *The black women's health book: Speaking for ourselves.* Seal Press, Washington.

Chapter Sixteen

Spirituality in Trauma Recovery

Roger D. Fallot

Introduction

At Community Connections, a recent survey asked 100 consumers about their religious commitment, activities and satisfaction (Fallot and Azrin, 1995). In this predominantly African American group of people with histories of multiple problems (severe mental disorders, frequent substance abuse difficulties, homelessness and poverty as well as sexual and/or physical abuse), the findings were instructive. Fifty-eight per cent of the survey participants reported that religion was "very" or "extremely" important to them while only 18% said it was "not very" or "not at all" important in their current lives. Further, 74% of the respondents said they were "mostly satisfied," "pleased," or "delighted" with the amount of satisfaction they got from religion while only 8% felt "mostly dissatisfied," "unhappy," or "terrible" about this aspect of their experience. Not only do these individuals find religion a highly significant part of their daily lives but they derive a great deal of fulfillment from their religious faith and practice. It is striking, then, that this very salient and potentially powerful aspect of experience is so often neglected in mental health services.

Understanding the spiritual and religious dimensions of human experience has become an increasingly important challenge for those working in the mental health field. While studies suggest that many therapists may not differ markedly from the general population in their openness to *spirituality*, they are in fact less *religiously* committed (Lukoff, Lu and Turner, 1992).* Achieving an understanding of these dimensions may be especially difficult for providers who do not share consumers' convictions about the value of religious experience or activities. In order to empathize adequately with consumers, though and in order to offer culturally competent and responsive services, it is important for mental health professionals to become aware of the ways in which religious and spiritual perspectives may be related to the entirety of consumers' lives. While many people frame their spiritual concerns in explicitly religious language, many others do not. The abilities to recognize, understand and respond to the implicit as well as explicit dimensions of spirituality are thus key skills in this arena.

Trauma and spirituality

People experienced in working with trauma survivors are not univocal about the place of spirituality in understanding and responding to traumatic experiences. On one hand, there is increasing emphasis on the potential power of spirituality in recovery and growth. Recognizing the complex interconnections among biological, psychosocial and spiritual dimensions of experience, many holistic programs attempt to bring together these perspectives as mutually reinforcing avenues to personal and social empowerment. This is true not only in religious settings involving pastoral care and counseling (e.g., Cheston, 1993) but in recent secular work as well. Without labeling it spirituality, Herman (1992) has described the loss of

---

*I am adopting a convention here which distinguishes between "religion" as that which involves the beliefs and practices of a church or other organized religious group and "spirituality" as involving a person's ultimate values, or their relationship with God, the sacred, or a higher power. The overlap between these categories is of course considerable. I will often refer to spirituality alone as the more inclusive term; a person's spirituality may or may not find expression in organized religion while virtually all religions offer some view of the ultimate.

meaning and faith which may accompany trauma and the importance of empowerment and reconnection as meaning-giving themes
in recovery. In assessing the capacity of armed services veterans to
cope with the effects of trauma exposure, Foy (1994) and his colleagues have included a "spiritual/philosophical" domain in their
coping resources inventory. Drescher and Foy (1995) have recommended the possible use of several spiritually-based activities, including the exploration of spiritual autobiographies, in trauma recovery.

On the other hand, there is often skepticism between trauma survivors and mental health professionals about the role of spiritual or
religious factors in abusive relationships. Religious beliefs and communities have frequently implicitly sanctioned or provided justification for the abuse of power in certain relationships (Capps, 1992;
Fortune, 1983; Poling, 1991). Further, religious institutions have
many times ignored or minimized reports of abuse and protected
perpetrators at the expense of their victims (Fortune, 1983; Poling,
1991). From this point of view, there are certainly grounds for wari-
ness of religious involvements: they may reinforce victimization and
revictimization and inhibit survivors' capacities for self-protection
and recovery.

Dual diagnosis and spirituality

In the literature describing services for people with severe mental
disorders and substance abuse/dependence problems (individuals
with "dual diagnoses"), there is a similar divergence of opinion about
spirituality. Some view spirituality as a key, often underutilized,
resource in personal and social integration for people with serious
mental illnesses (Aist, 1987; Sullivan, 1993; Lindgren and Coursey,
1995). And spirituality has of course been at the heart of many self-
help programs, especially twelve-step models such as Alcoholics
Anonymous and Narcotics Anonymous (Alcoholics Anonymous,
1976).

At the same time, some mental health professionals express concern
about the potentially destructive role of spirituality and religion. For
people with severe mental disorders, religious ideas and experiences may tap into (perhaps at best) confusing abstractions and (at
worst) actively disorganizing religious delusions and preoccupations

339

(Noordsy, Schwab, Fox and Drake, 1994). At the institutional level, certain religious groups may support exclusively "spiritual" means of healing (including prayer, healing rituals and participation in other activities of religious life). The opposition of these groups to their members' involvement in mental health treatment is likely to bring their views into direct conflict with those of providers and present consumers with an extremely difficult forced choice between the two groups and their modes of healing.

These apparently divergent valuations of spirituality are not inconsistent with the research literature on religion and mental health more generally. The bulk of this evidence points to a modest positive relationship between religion and mental health (Chamberlain and Zika, 1992); greater religiosity is associated with many indices of emotional well-being. But this literature also indicates that a more useful way of framing this issue is in terms of the *function* of religiousness: what *role* does spirituality or religion play in a particular person's life at a particular time? Religion or spirituality *per se* cannot be assumed, then, as a consistently positive (or negative) factor in the recovery and growth process because these dimensions of experience can function in such a multiplicity of ways. The suggestion Masters and Bergin (1992) offer researchers is equally useful for clinicians: "to go beyond asking, 'Is the person religious?' and move to the question, 'How is the person religious?' " (p. 221).

One woman at Community Connections described this difference vividly in discussing her drug use pattern and her love of gospel music. Music had always played a large part in her religious life. When she was using drugs, she "would get high and listen" to certain songs, "like a ritual." On the other hand, gospel music became an equally important resource for her in attempts to remain clean, contributing to her daily sense of courage for recovery. The same religious resource thus took on starkly contrasting functions at different points in her life.

This chapter will describe some of the *positive* roles spirituality may play in the lives of people with trauma histories and severe mental disorders. This is not meant to imply that spirituality always functions in a way which facilitates recovery and growth but that for many people spirituality and religion can and do offer unique resources central to the healing process. For people with many overlapping and thoroughly interconnected problems, recovery in one sphere may well foster the possibility of recovery in another. Abstinence from drugs, for example, may set the stage for greater involvement in and more effective use of other therapeutic relationships. Or conversely, addressing a trauma survivor's need for self-soothing and exploring ways to comfort oneself may enhance the likelihood of abstinence. While I will focus mostly on the place of spirituality in recovery from trauma, it is important to recall that, because of the tightly interwoven nature of this set of problems, spirituality's contributions to recovery in any one domain are likely to be reflected in another.

In work describing the potentially positive roles religion may play in relation to mental health (e.g., Schumaker, 1992), little attention has been given to the specific concerns of people with mental disorders and trauma/abuse histories. The following discussion and its major themes are drawn from individual interviews, focus groups and clinical discussions at Community Connections. Virtually all of the participants have reported histories of sexual and/or physical abuse in childhood, adulthood, or both. Most have also experienced substance abuse or dependence problems and significant periods of homelessness. All have been diagnosed with a major mental disorder. This complex set of highly correlated and recurring experiences forms the backdrop against which their spiritual lives have taken shape.

Spirituality and religion as self-strengthening

Among the sequelae of trauma are difficulties in the consolidation (or, for adults, reconsolidation) of a firm sense of self. From the vantage point of self psychology, trauma survivors are often vulnerable to experiences of fragmentation and discontinuity, to persistent low self-esteem and to disrupted feelings of agency and subjectivity (Peoples, 1991). Sexual and physical abuse are massive intrusions; they interfere with the development of a cohesive sense of oneself as a valuable individual capable of pursuing goals with energy and vitality. Sensitive, then, to the possibility of further damage, survivors develop a range of responses to salvage, protect, regain and/or stimulate important feelings of worth, strength and competence. Other people play a key role in the potential restoration of this firmer sense of self by adequately responding to the survivor's needs for mirroring, idealizing and belonging. Thus, they may provide appropriate affirmation when the individual needs to feel valued and important; offer consistently idealizable soothing and comfort when the person needs to rely on a strong and caring other; and acknowledge the survivor's needs to be a part of relationships with others who are similar in significant ways. Both relationships with God and with other people may be essential elements in the experience of self-strengthening which is central to trauma recovery.

Relationships with god as self-strengthening

Self psychologists have pointed to the ways in which a person's image of and relationship to God may serve "selfobject" functions, that is, may serve to maintain and bolster a healthy and mature sense of self (Randall, 1988; Jones, 1991). Drawing on object relations theory, other psychologists of religion have emphasized the image of God as a "transitional phenomenon" in the world of relationships, powerfully situated between the realms of internal and external reality (Winnicott, 1971; Rizzuto, 1979). Precisely because God exists, psychologically speaking, in this realm between the subjectively and objectively experienced world, one's relationship with God can carry with it significant capacities for adaptation as well as defense (Meissner, 1984). Indeed, this relationship may reflect a "psychological space" of creative and transforming possibilities, a relational arena in which the self may be sustained and strengthened (Jones, 1991). Survey research has supported the notion that relationships with "divine others" may be connected to psychological well-being (Pollner, 1989). Trauma survivors who use such religious language often describe in their relationship with God key moments and phases related to their recovery.

A sense of safety. Trauma survivors feel an acute need for a sense of safety. They need reassurance that the world and other people are not uniformly dangerous or abusive. One woman, raped by her father when she was nine years old, had a long history of homelessness, drug abuse and prostitution. She captured implicitly the sharp contrast between God and unnamed others in saying, "[God] is *good* and He's not here to hurt me; He's here to help me." Another woman talked about the many ways in which God had served as her protector, even warning her to leave the boyfriend who later became physically abusive. Repeatedly, God emerges in the stories of these survivors as a trustworthy and constant refuge, a relationship haven reliably available to those who believe. The trust implicit in this view was captured by one woman who said, "The will of God will not lead you where His grace will not protect you."

A sense of being comforted and soothed. The intense, recurring distress associated with physical and sexual abuse often makes it difficult for survivors to experience calming relief. In the midst of such pain, God may be experienced as a source of comfort and soothing. One interviewee described the contrast between her mother's neglect and rejection of her with God's constant "presence and understanding." Another woman talked about dealing with the hurt of insults and the threat of abandonment by recalling her experience of the stead-fastness of God: "Nobody can take [God's] love for you away." Especially striking in the context of these stories of chaos and destructiveness was the possibility of "peacefulness" in the relation-ship with God. Whether they found it in worship or in prayer, those who felt God's reassuring presence described a sense of tranquility and relief from excessive worry.

Self-acceptance and self-affirmation. Given their histories of trauma, of substance abuse, of homelessness and of mental illness, it is not sur-prising that themes of self-denigration and social stigmatizing pervade the accounts of many of these individuals. For many, spirituality has offered an avenue to realistic self-acceptance. Several people described how important it was to experience God's love for them "in spite of" their social marginalization, their weaknesses, their guilt or shame, their apparently "unacceptable" behavior. One survivor of childhood rape had abused "crack, alcohol, PCP, LSD, cough syrup ... the whole nine yards" and felt tremendously ashamed of her sexual activities. For her, a renewed closeness to God meant the reversal of a long-held belief in her own pervasive "badness." Recognizing that she was, in God's eyes, "more good than bad" marked a turning point in her engagement in the recovery process. Baptism occasioned another interviewee's experience of "security about myself. I could accept myself as I am *really*, [with] flaws and foibles."

Just as the experience of God's acceptance was tied to self-acceptance for some survivors, self-affirmation often was related to a belief in God's valuing and affirming them. A woman who was

343

sexually abused by her father spent years living on the streets, using drugs heavily and prostituting to get drugs. In returning to church after many years, she was surprised to discover that she could actually "feel good about myself ... [that God] wants the best for me ... gives me a feeling I can't explain." Survivors able to draw on such spiritual resources may well find in the process a firmer and more stably valued sense of self.

A *"real relationship" with God*. Certainly there are idealizing processes involved in many of these images of God as a powerful source of nurturance and protection. It is especially noteworthy, then, that for many interviewees God was not depicted in distant or inaccessible ways. Nor was the effect of God's activity in their lives seen as overriding the unavoidable limits of human reality. Instead, there was a level of comfort and ease in discussing God. One interviewee talked about the necessity of having a "working relationship" with God. In contrast to some other relationships, she noted that she had always felt capable of standing up to God. "God had to prove to *me* He was real. I wasn't going to confess without proof." Another woman described her prayer conversations with God in this way: "I make a joke with God. I fuss with Him if it doesn't work out – like Job."

In this particular religious and cultural context, God as a friend and partner may live comfortably alongside God as the powerful governor of the world. So it is perhaps not surprising that God's role in enhancing the lives of these women has "realistic" limits. Some were acutely aware of the possibility of expecting too much and then being disappointed. "When you do make that commitment [to God], life is not always going to be glorious," as one woman put it. Others talked about the importance of recognizing that there will be "ups and downs" in their lives, that there will always be "some upset," and that these experiences do not mean that God has become indifferent. Rather than pulling these trauma survivors into an unrealistic realm of inflated hopes, their relationship with God seemed to ground them in life's day-to-day realities.

Relationships with others as self-strengthening

For some individuals, it is a small step from a relationship with God to relationships with other people. One interviewee captured the

344

way in which she saw this often serendipitous connection: "God works through other people, so you have to be alert." Whether others are seen as extensions of God's activity or not, however, religious involvement often provides significant social support (Taylor and Chatters, 1988). For people with severe mental disorders, religious activities may contribute to an enlarged and strengthened social network as well as to an enhanced sense of community (Sullivan, 1993). Those with abuse histories may be especially responsive to such support because their self-protective needs have often led to considerable interpersonal isolation and distance. Their experiences of trauma, stigmatization and marginalization and their ways of adapting to dangerous situations (e.g., in homeless shelters or on the streets) often result in stances of hypervigilance, hostility and mistrust. So the contrast between these feelings and those of inter-personal acceptance and comfort is often a very striking one. One woman who had been homeless for over a decade thought she would never be able to "be around a bunch of people." She was more than surprised to discover, in attending church with her sister, that she could indeed feel like part of the group and "realize I could sit around people *anywhere*." And, very importantly for her, the new group could supplant her former network of "get-high partners." Having these new friends and acquaintances (in both church and recovery groups) "keeps me sane and keeps me going."

An important bolstering of one's sense of self is possible by way of this acceptance and belonging. One pastor was particularly adept at creating a welcoming atmosphere.

> "He knows I'm recovering and some of my girlfriends have joined, too ... [we] have a little flock. The minister says, 'Bring 'em on in.' Some of the choir members had trouble [with this] at first. [But he says], "There's always one more space ...""

Participation in such a church group was indeed a key part of this woman's feeling strengthened and renewed each week.

Religion and spirituality as coping resources

In addition to this general role in confirming and strengthening the survivor's sense of self, there are several more specific ways in which

345

spirituality may assist in coping with trauma and its sequelae. Shifting emphasis from the relational processes outlined above to more cognitive and behavioral ones, these resources focus on the survivor's capacity to understand and solve the wide range of problems which may follow from traumatic experience.

Finding meaning

For many people, religious beliefs provide a vital context of meaning for life's events. Not only does faith structure individual experience but it orders the world at large. Religion and spirituality can play a very important role, then, in the *interpretation* of destructive acts and circumstances. For trauma survivors the experience of abuse often calls into question the very foundation of their religious faith: "If God truly cares about me, how can such painful and dehumanizing things happen? If God is just, what did I do to deserve this suffering?" Theologians have addressed these questions under the rubric of *theodicy*, the justification of evil in a world created and governed by a good and all-powerful God. For people with recurrent and complex histories of trauma, this often becomes an issue of ongoing, practical significance. Whether people talk about it in terms of maintaining faith, or keeping a good relationship with God, or finding some meaning in and through their suffering, a substantial understanding of their pain and its place in the larger scheme of things are fundamental to self-sustenance.

One woman expressed it this way: "God created me, not to suffer, but with what He feels we need to be what He wants us to be ... to develop strengths and accept weaknesses ... I can say I know who I am." Another woman, a victim of childhood physical abuse and sexual abuse in adulthood, recalled thinking, "Why is this happening?" and coming to the conclusion that "the Lord will put us through trials ... kind of a learning experience, a strengthening. [This] has helped me to help [others]. There is a reason why [God doesn't take away our problems]." Different spiritual perspectives may value such explanations quite differently. But for these individuals, developing a clear idea of God's greater purpose in permitting their suffering, a purpose often difficult to fathom, has enabled them to place their experiences in a meaningful perspective and has enhanced the possibility of recovery.

346

Experiencing purpose

In addition to this understanding of some larger meaning, many people describe the experience of renewed *personal* purpose, that they more readily focus on important goals and have more motivation for following through. Some couch this is terms of vocation, of doing what God has called them to do. In describing her active role in the ministries of a local church, a woman with a history of depression and homelessness said that she had experienced a new sense of hope: "My joy is being able to do what I'm inspired to do." Whether in an organized religious context or not, people recount the importance of (re)discovering goals consistent with deeply-held values and of feeling committed to reaching these goals.

Solving problems

Sources of guidance. Recent research in the psychology of religion has demonstrated several ways in which people's spirituality and, specifically, their relationship with God may become part of their general approach to problem-solving (Pargament *et al.*, 1988). Trauma survivors, perhaps especially those with substance abuse problems or mental disorders, may distrust their own perceptions and question the validity of their social judgment. Several interviewees talked about their prayerful conversations with God and their sense of God's guidance as sources of clarity in the midst of uncertainty. "[Prayer gives me] a clearer understanding of what's going on," said one woman in describing how God's counsel helped her to be more patient and discerning about her daily life decisions. Another woman's experience of God's support helped her to stick with difficult situations longer than she thought she would otherwise have been able. "[I became] capable of going through a problem and seeing it all the way to the end ... [could] find solutions within [myself] ... gained an understanding of myself."

Sources of self-control. As many twelve-step programs have posited, spirituality can be a potent ally in attempts to control addictive behavior. For trauma survivors who are homeless and addicted, gaining a sense of self-control is a core part of recovery, essential not only to controlling substance use but to avoiding the often drug-related situations which lead to revictimization. One woman described a very specific way in which her religious experience assisted her both in maintaining abstinence from drugs and in avoiding the dangerous consequences to which she had been exposed in living on the streets.

> "Going to church helps me a lot. It keeps me on the right path. Sometimes my mind has little slip-ups and I want to drink and drug. I just tell the devil, 'Get behind me.' And then I don't drink and drug. I go home or go to the movies with a girlfriend. I just have fun. It reminds me I can do these things if I put my mind to it."

As did some others strongly engaged in the recovery process, this interviewee actively integrated her involvement with the church, Alcoholics Anonymous and mental health services. They had become mutually reinforcing aspects of her daily efforts to stay clean and to stay safe.

Spirituality and religion and recovery virtues

While it is important to understand the potentially valuable psychological functions of religion and spirituality, using only social scientific concepts neglects the more indigenous and experientially immediate, language of the trauma and substance abuse (and, to an increasing extent, mental health services consumer) recovery movement as well as that of many religious groups. Throughout the discussions of spiritual issues, these other ways of talking about healing, recovery and growth were prominent. Several recurring themes emerged which may be thought of as "virtues," in the classical sense of personal and characterological strengths.

Developing hope and enthusiasm

Trauma and abuse have a numbing, deadening and demoralizing impact. Rekindling a sense of hope and enthusiasm for the future often seems futile. So when interviewees talked about feeling "uplifted" spiritually, they often did so with a profound sense of its importance. While it is difficult to describe succinctly the various aspects of this experience, the uplifting quality of religious life carries with it connotations of inspiration, of hope, of energy. People described the way in which spiritual uplifting empowers them and equips them for facing daily struggles with a realistic optimism.

Developing courage and strength

Not unrelated to hope is the attribute of courage. Once the future is seen to hold out alternative possibilities, the difficult work of moving toward those possibilities can begin. People with complex and recurring trauma experiences need sustenance for facing the inevitable pain and disappointments of the recovery process. Many view this internal fortitude as simply courage, the courage to face things as they are and the courage to make changes. The way to genuine recovery seems to require this in one woman's view: "Going *through* [problems] is what makes you what you are; going *around* causes you to think you are what you are."

Developing patience and tolerance

Powerful needs and feelings and strong reactions to social situations are often difficult for trauma survivors to modulate and even more difficult for those who have used drugs or alcohol to assuage distress. The development of patience and the capacity to tolerate uncomfortable emotions and situations without dissociating and without substance abuse is experienced as a signal achievement. One woman described how she began to "tune out the world" after she saw "that it wasn't a pretty picture." Drugs used to distract her and minimize her hurt and disappointment. But "now, when I get worried or upset, I have no desire to use. I still have some upset [but I am] learning some patience, some tolerance, some acceptance." For her, as for some others, the so-called "Serenity Prayer" was particularly important in daily meditation.

Other women noted how their experiences as part of a religious group had expanded their capacity to empathize with others and tolerate interpersonal differences. In describing her own sense of being loved by God, one interviewee discussed her commitment to

349

"accepting people as people," in spite of their obvious differences and potential antagonisms. Another described the way in which "being there for someone else … is the most help to me … I know what it is like to be rejected … outcast … homeless."

Developing gratitude

There may appear to be few occasions for gratitude among people whose life experiences have been so harsh. Yet perhaps precisely because of this harshness, gratitude emerges as a core response in the recovery process. One woman described going away from worship services with the sense that "I've made it through another week and that [worship] tops it off. I get to start another week and I give [God] some praise." Survival, safety, or abstinence may become reasons for gratefulness. "I thank God every morning for waking me up. I have a prayer that came to me and I always say this. 'Thank God … Alleluia … Praise the Lord … Amen.' "

Developing forgiveness

There are clear dangers in any emphasis on forgiveness in work with survivors of abuse. Some religious approaches call for premature forgiveness of perpetrators of violence; some expect victims to deny or minimize their hurt, anger and pain. It is not at all clear that forgiveness is an appropriate value at all times or in all relationships. But for those committed to the importance of forgiveness, spirituality and religion offer some important avenues for its expression. Sexually abused as a child by a family member, one woman talked about how this abuse:

> It made me think that God had let me down. [Later] I learned how to forgive people … I was angry at [the perpetrator] for a long time. He did this to me and made me feel like I could never have a normal life. The Lord taught me it's better to forgive and forget. [Now] I don't consider [the abuser] an enemy.

This woman saw forgiveness as a personally freeing experience, coming after a long period of anger and hatred.

350

Spirituality and the process of change

Trauma survivors for whom spirituality is explicitly important present several different patterns of connection between their spiritual lives and their engagement in the recovery process. Two of them are especially noteworthy.

Spirituality motivates change

Some people describe spiritual or religious experience as the primary motivating force in their engagement in recovery. Metaphors of conversion, redemption and being offered "new life" are central ones. At age 35, one woman was baptized and reports feeling that:

> The old me had died and the new had come forth. The old me constantly doubted – fought to do the right, battling the wrong. [The new] had a sense of security about myself ... could think in a way that was godly-righteous ... could pertain to problems I was facing.

Facing reality; dealing with problems "as they are" rather than denying, minimizing, or dissociating; seeing clearly the consequences of substance abuse – all of these might emerge from a powerful, spiritually-based recognition of the most fundamental life dilemmas and choices. And these recognitions become in turn the basis for beginning the process of recovery.

For some, only God or a higher power could make possible the changes necessary in their lives. They experience themselves as having reached the limits of their own efforts and motivation, as having become so entrenched in their ineffective or destructive ways of handling their problems that only a transcendent force could turn their lives in a different direction. One abuse survivor had been using drugs heavily for years and summarized her experience this way:

> [God] is about the only one [who] could bring me back about as stable as I am now. I had been in treatment eight or nine times [in the last twelve years]. I knew the book-knowledge ... but I wasn't willing to do any of that ... didn't want to. It was definitely God.

Survivors may thus offer spiritual answers to clinical questions; no other explanation seems as cogent to them and no other force appears as powerful as that of the spiritual realm.

Spirituality consolidates change

Other survivors describe spirituality becoming important only *after* they had become actively involved in recovery. One woman described feeling able to return to church only after she had begun making other changes in her life. Religious activities then became an important source of reinforcement for recovery, especially by integrating her now revitalized beliefs with family and social support and mental health services:

> [Before] I thought the Lord didn't love me. Once I was in church, I figured it out that He loves me and wants the best for me … I've gotten over [childhood sexual abuse] through the help of [case management and therapy], my sister and the Lord.

For many people who have experiences like this, spiritual change and development strengthen other avenues to recovery by providing an overarching framework in which the totality of change can be understood and valued. Self-help groups, mental health services, social network changes, family support, residential and vocational assistance come to interact in a synergistic fashion with the person's spirituality. Spirituality can make more coherent the various aspects of recovery by emphasizing the all-encompassing nature of personal change and providing key images for its enactment ("coming back to myself," "becoming whole," and "being the person God intends me to be" are examples of this language). Whether by reconnecting with former spiritual resources or by developing new ones, individuals may find in their religious lives significant avenues for integrating and thus enhancing the power of the recovery process.

Conclusion

It is often difficult to identify factors which make possible recovery from trauma for people with so many closely connected and complicating problems. One of the resources commonly noted by survivors themselves, however, is spirituality. This chapter has provided brief descriptions of some of the functions and processes by which spirituality may motivate and enhance trauma recovery (and, in this population, coping with other difficulties as well). Filling powerful experiential and explanatory roles, religion or spirituality is often reported as both a central foundation and a key sustainer of recovery.

Such accounts have direct implications for assessment and services for trauma survivors with mental and/or substance use disorders. Because this dimension of experience is often so important, a careful assessment of spirituality's place in the trauma survivor's life is increasingly valuable. A number of current models are available for describing the functions and/or core themes of an individual's spiritual life (Fitchett, 1993). Making the religious dimension part of an overall assessment allows the mental health professional to see reinforcing (or conflicting) relationships between spirituality and other aspects of the survivor's recovery.

Mental health services may also incorporate context-appropriate and individually sensitive spiritual resources for trauma recovery. Exploring with survivors the spiritual meanings attached to their experiences; attending to stories and metaphors related to religious and spiritual frameworks; recognizing the power of ritual to structure and renew people's lives; eliciting and discussing spiritual autobiographies; examining the ways in which religious communities may shape self-understanding; developing spiritually-focused discussion and support groups – these are just some of the ways in which greater attention to spirituality may be made part of ongoing recovery work. For many individuals, not to do so risks neglecting a potentially powerful source for healing and integration.

References

Aist, C.S. (1987) "Pastoral care of the mentally ill: A congregational perspective", In *The Journal of Pastoral Care, XLI*(4), 299–310.

Alcoholics Anonymous (3rd ed.). (1976) New York: Alcoholics Anonymous World Services, Inc.

Capps, D. (1992) "Religion and child abuse: Perfect together", in *Journal for the Scientific Study of Religion*, 31(1), 1–14.

Chamberlain, K. and Zika, S. (1992) "Religiosity, meaning in life and psychological well-being." In Schumaker, J.F. (Ed.), *Religion and mental health* (pp. 138–148). New York: Oxford University Press.

Cheston, S.E. (1993) "Counseling adult survivors of childhood sexual abuse." In Wicks, R.J. and Parsons, R.D. (Eds.) *Clinical handbook of pastoral counseling* (Vol. 2). New York: Paulist Press.

Drescher, K.D. and Foy, D.W. (1995) "Spirituality and trauma treatment: Suggestions for including spirituality as a coping resource", in *The Clinical Quarterly*, National Center for PTSD, 5, 4–6.

Fallot, R.D. and Azrin S.T. (June, 1995) Consumer satisfaction: Findings from a case management program evaluation survey. Paper presented at the Annual Conference of the International Association of Psychosocial Rehabilitation Services, Boston, MA.

Fitchett, G. (1993) *Assessing spiritual needs: A guide for caregivers.* Minneapolis: Augsburg Press.

Fortune, M. (1983) *Sexual violence: The unmentionable sin.* New York: Pilgrim Press.

Foy, D.W. (November, 1994) PTSD assessment and treatment. Paper presented at the New Hampshire-Dartmouth Psychiatric Research Center, Lebanon, NH.

Herman, J.L. (1992) *Trauma and Recovery.* New York: Basic Books.

Jones, J.W. (1991) *Contemporary psychoanalysis and religion.* New Haven: Yale University Press.

Lindgren, K.N. and Coursey, R.D. (1995) "Spirituality and mental illness: A two-part study", in *Psychosocial Rehabilitation Journal*, 18(3), 93–111.

Lukoff, D., Lu, F. and Turner, R. (1992) "Toward a more culturally sensitive DSM-IV: Psychoreligious and psychospiritual problems", in *The Journal of Nervous and Mental Disease*, 180(11), 673–682.

Masters, K.S. and Bergin, A.E. (1992) "Religious orientation and mental health". In Schumaker, J.F. (Ed.), *Religion and mental health* (pp. 221–232). New York: Oxford University Press.

Meissner, W.W. (1984) *Psychoanalysis and religious experience.* New Haven: Yale University Press.

Noordsy, D.L., Schwab, B., Fox, L. and Drake, R.E. (1994) In Powell, T. (Ed.) *Understanding the self-help organization: Frameworks and findings* (pp. 314–330). Thousand Oaks, CA: Sage Publications.

Pargament, K.I., Kennell, J., Hathaway, W., Grevengoed, N., Newman, J. and Jones, W. (1988) "Religion and the problem-solving process: Three styles of coping", in *Journal for the Scientific Study of Religion*, 27(1), 90–104.

Peoples, K.M. (1991) "The trauma of incest: Threats to the consolidation of the self." In Goldberg, A. (Ed.), *The evolution of self psychology: Progress in self psychology* (Vol. 7). Hillsdale, NJ: The Analytic Press.

Poling, J.N. (1991) *The abuse of power: A theological problem.* Nashville: Abingdon Press.

Pollner, M. (1989) "Divine relations, social relations and well-being", in *Journal of Health and Social Behavior*, 30, 92–104.

Randall, R.L. (1988) *Pastor and parish: The psychological core of ecclesiastical conflicts.* New York: Human Sciences Press.

Rizzuto, A.M. (1979) *The birth of the living god: A psychoanalytic study.* Chicago: University of Chicago Press.

Schumaker, J.F. (Ed.). (1992) *Religion and mental health.* New York: Oxford University Press.

Sullivan, W.P. (1993) "It helps me to be a whole person: The role of spirituality among the mentally challenged", in *Psychosocial Rehabilitation Journal*, 16(3), 125–134.

Taylor, R.J. and Chatters, L.M. (1988) "Church members as a source of informal social support", in *Review of Religious Research*, 30(2), 193–203.

Winnicott, D.W. (1971) *Playing and reality.* London: Tavistock Publications.

Chapter Seventeen

Trauma and Trauma Recovery for Dually Diagnosed Male Survivors

David W. Freeman and Roger D. Fallot

Introduction

Men with "dual diagnoses" (i.e., who have both a severe mental disorder and significant substance abuse problems) frequently have histories of trauma exposure. Because this group of men has usually been excluded from trauma studies, however, the existing literatures on men (e.g., Silverberg, 1986), male trauma (Hunter, 1990; Briere, Evans, Runtz, and Wall, 1987; Elliot and Briere, 1992; Thomas, 1989), and trauma in general (Briere, 1989; Herman, 1992; McCann and Pearlman, 1990) can make only a partial contribution to our understanding of their experience. The cumulative impact of recurrent, multiple, complex trauma has caused significant difficulty for this population, especially for those individuals who are also impoverished and periodically homeless. Many such men, for example, indicate that they were physically and sexually abused many times in childhood and adulthood and/or have been involved in multiple episodes of street violence. Community and institutional violence as well as combat trauma may thus be added to other experiences of physical and sexual abuse.

The vulnerabilities associated with mental and substance use disorders, trauma, and life's more common difficulties coexist and amplify each other in the lives of these men. A psychotic episode, an involuntary hospitalization, a severe substance abuse relapse, or an eviction, for example, can increase one's chances of exposure to trauma, especially in an inner city context. Trauma, in turn, can exacerbate symptoms of mental illness or lead to an increase in substance abuse. Each kind of difficulty can serve as a precipitant for another in a circular or spiraling fashion.

John, for example, was suspended from his group home for repeated violations of the substance abuse rules. He found the shelters too dangerous so he slept on the street in a local park. He was chased in the middle of the night from his bench by another homeless man wielding a broken bottle. The incident served as a trigger for a severe worsening of his relapse. John then had much greater difficulty renewing his recovery so that he could return home. In another example, Alvin, who had been severely physically abused as a child, was devastated by the death of his parents in a car accident when he was fourteen. His post-traumatic stress disorder was complicated and exacerbated by the later onset of a disabling psychotic spectrum disorder. Self-medicating alcoholism led to his exclusion from most mental health services for many years and to subsequent periods of homelessness. Homelessness then left him vulnerable to witnessing and suffering community violence.

The temporal chain of events in these stories illustrates just a few of the ways in which multiple problems interact; a single causal line rarely provides an adequate explanation. Acute exacerbation of a mental illness can serve as a trigger for or as a consequence of relapse. Community violence can restimulate an underlying chronic post-traumatic stress disorder and precipitate an episode of homelessness. Homelessness can make a man more vulnerable to community violence. We will focus, therefore, on the contribution of these interconnected difficulties to the disruption of men's overall development.

Sources of information

Our investigation of the impact of trauma on men diagnosed with serious mental illness has been informed primarily by discussions with clients, the clinical experience of other male clinicians who have provided services for this population, and our own clinical experience. The authors conducted a series of three different focus groups which addressed issues of male identity, a wide range of positive and negative life experiences, and the recovery skills men perceived as necessary for an adaptive lifestyle. Additional discussion groups included male clinicians who had an interest in trauma and who had experience with a traumatized male population.

Life goals of dually diagnosed male trauma survivors

One of the striking themes of our focus groups was the value these men placed on achieving more settled and well-modulated lives. Having lived on society's margins and having seen the impact of their own and other's behavioral extremes, they wanted to be known and accepted for their strengths. Some expressed the desire to be able to fit in, to have behavioral choices, and to have some influence over how they were perceived by others. Stability, consistency, and predictability emerged as primary goals. Some men were in search of reasonable pleasure: "I want to rest, walk on the boardwalk, watch the sunrise, have sex, be on an even keel, and not get sick." Other men sought outlets for productive creativity including music lessons, artwork, and song writing. Others wanted to assume more responsibility by working. Many were interested in helping family members who had life difficulties less severe than mental illness, substance addiction, or homelessness.

Developmental dimensions in the lives of male survivors

Our focus groups helped us identify five developmental dimensions in the core identity of these men: 1) Self-esteem; 2) Self-protection; 3) Self-direction; 4) Mutuality; and 5) Responsibility. From an experiential perspective, these dimensions describe fundamental ways individuals think and feel about themselves and the world around them. From a more distant perspective, they provide a framework by which clinicians may organize behavioral observations. Each dimension is associated with fundamental capacities and skills that characterize the psychosocial adaptation of the individual. Personal growth along these dimensions leads to a life of greater consistency, coherence, and flexibility.

Self-esteem grows out of a man's capacity to develop and preserve a sense of positive self-worth and is widely regarded as a key correlate of mental health.

Self-protection has to do with a man's capacity to protect himself from emotional and physical danger. The development of a sense of security sufficient to support emotional and physical boundaries is often difficult for this population.

Self-direction is the capacity to develop, maintain, and enhance effective, flexible action plans. Purposeful action is most effective when it is well informed by all of one's internal resources, including both thought and feeling; and also when behavioral skills are in place to carry out the plan. An inability or unwillingness to use one's inner resources diminishes the capacity to be self-directed.

Mutuality is characterized by good communication; an easy and fair give and take between people; a well-negotiated exchange of tangible and emotional support, information, and advice; a reasonable trust in the consequences of honest disclosure of thoughts and feelings; a care and concern for the impact of one's statements and actions on another, and a reasonable faith in another's commitment to an equivalent care and concern; and interdependence in the pursuit of shared goals.

Responsibility is the basic capacity to hold oneself and others accountable in a manner that is appropriate to the context.

The impact of trauma

Trauma can cause depression, anxiety, numbing, hyperarousal, PTSD, substance abuse, interpersonal difficulties, and a host of other symptoms and syndromes (Briere, 1989; Herman, 1992; Hunter, 1990). Consequently, trauma can damage the capacities needed for successful progress along each of the developmental dimensions. The abilities to develop a positive sense of self-worth, to protect oneself, to sustain a purpose, to express interests and concerns, to manage mutual relationships, and to assume appropriate levels of responsibility can be undermined by traumatic experience.

The achievement of personal stability and flexibility is also undermined by trauma. Traumatic disruptions in these men's lives express themselves in fragile, brittle, and unstable solutions to the specific issues raised by each of the developmental arenas. Trauma thus predisposes men to less mature, less adaptive, and less well-integrated coping responses.

Traumatic disruptions tend to produce pairs of opposite responses along each of the five developmental dimensions. One member of each pair is organized around the experience of deficit and weakness while the other is characterized by a sense of considerable power. For example, trauma disrupts self-esteem by channeling men into positions of shame or grandiosity. Both positions are extreme and neither are stable. There can be rapid oscillations of experience between these two extremes with grandiosity yielding to shame, and vice versa. While shame is associated with the experience of weakness, grandiosity is tied to that of power. In parallel ways, the dimension of self-protection may be expressed with poles of vulnerability and invulnerability; self-direction with rigid over control and impulsiveness; mutuality with dependence and independence; and responsibility with over-responsibility and under-responsibility (See Table I).

TABLE I
EXPERIENCE OF:

Developmental Dimension:	**Weakness**	**Power**
Self-esteem	Shame	Grandiosity
Self-Protection	Vulnerability	Invulnerability
Self-direction	Rigid self-control	Impulsiveness
Mutuality	Dependence	Independence
Responsibility	Under-responsibility	Over-responsibility

361

Disruptions of self-esteem

Trauma usually threatens the development and stability of positive self-esteem by leaving dually diagnosed men susceptible to experiences of grandiosity and/or shame.

Grandiosity is characterized by the experience of success inflated far beyond one's actual achievement and capacity. In its most extreme and disabling form grandiosity can be intertwined with a delusional disorder, although grandiosity need not assume psychotic proportions to cause severe difficulties. Eric, for example, who was physically abused by his mother and father and who was treated violently by the police during his many episodes of involuntary hospitalization, believed he was a superhero and an agent of God, battling a cult of evil on earth. He used his size, intensity and rage to assert his power over other people. When he observed the fear that he instilled in others, his inner convictions about his absolute superiority were confirmed. His grandiosity was nearly all-encompassing; even when he was reasonably stable, he said: "It's still hard for me to realize that I was sick during my superstar odyssey."

The grandiose position is not always delusional or psychotic; it can also be a feature of one's character style. Randy almost always felt that he was correct. "I feel very confident that I'm right. I can see the cycles and manifestations of perfection in words, mind, and spirit." His grandiose sense of self-perfection disarmed efforts by others to help him live more effectively. He was very reluctant to accept help he did not "need." Perhaps as a result, he was more prone to substance abuse relapse, medication refusal, and disabling social conflict.

Shame, at the opposite extreme from grandiosity, is the feeling of inadequacy and worthlessness exaggerated beyond any actual failure. Shame is accompanied by a dreadful fear of the exposure of one's bad but true nature, especially one's shortcomings and weaknesses. Shame is widely associated with abuse survivors, but is also common among scapegoats, victims of public humiliation, people saddled with the stigma of a chronic mental illness, substance abusers, children of substance abusers, people unable to live independently without supervision, and those unable to assume their preferred social roles. The men in this study struggled with all of these difficulties.

Darrell, for example, was the neighborhood scapegoat on local street corners as a teenager and told of the feeling of great shame he experienced when he was the object of this physical and emotional abuse. His shame was intensified by his father's alcoholic behavior, and, later, his own mental illness and alcoholism. The cumulative effects of the different kinds of trauma he experienced contributed to an inner experience of crippling shame which interrupted his ability to assemble and sustain a positive sense of self esteem.

In another example, Jimmy, who was a combat veteran and survivor of multiple kinds of abuse, experienced a shame that was intensified by group home restrictions on his efforts to see his family. These restrictions limited his capacity to exercise and practice normal adult responsibilities. "I want to hold out an image for my sons that I'm not retarded or mentally sick."

John, who has suffered from severe and persistent psychotic symptoms since early adulthood, was badly whipped by his father as a teenager. When his whipmarks and welts were exposed in the shower during gym class, other boys teased him mercilessly. As an adult, John has refused to shower. He can describe the humiliation he experienced as an adolescent, but attributes his refusal to shower to fears of being maimed by an army of persecutors.

Disruptions of self-protection

Invulnerability and vulnerability are the two most common results of traumatic disruptions in the area of self-protection. Invulnerability is characterized by rigid, impermeable emotional boundaries. Men who adopt an invulnerable position believe themselves to be untouched by the actions and communications of others. They quickly minimize or deny the traumatic impact of others on them, as if their very experience of others is irrelevant.

An overly fluid and easily dissolved emotional boundary characterizes the vulnerable position. Men who are extremely vulnerable have little or no ability to preserve an emotional boundary with others, to protect themselves from traumatic incursions across that boundary, or to care for their own needs in the presence of someone who is threatening. Men who have been diagnosed with a psychotic spectrum disorder often have particular difficulty managing their boundaries with others. We have found that trauma intensifies that difficulty.

Eric, who was physically abused by his parents as a child, and exposed to extensive community violence throughout his life, oscillates between vulnerability and invulnerability. He believes there is a master of the universe, Spindle, who creates and destroys at will. When she speaks to him, he has no capacity to withstand her instruction or demand, or to create a safe haven for himself where he is free of her influence. Eric has another delusion, however, in which he experiences himself as absolutely invulnerable. In this delusion he is Superman. When he feels the silk boots on his feet he can fly into the Oval Office at the White House and present his arguments to the President. When under the influence of this delusion nobody can redirect Eric or intrude on his psychic state of complete well-being. He is invulnerable to the intrusions of the outside world. Eric can cycle between vulnerability and invulnerability within the few moments of a brief interaction.

Some of these men have delusions which help them feel somewhat less vulnerable. Although these delusional "solutions" are not adequately self-protective, they do mollify some pain. John, for example, ran away from home when he was 14 to escape his father's violence. When he was on the street, he hid from every passing car in fear that his father had come to retrieve him. When he was finally returned to his father by the police, he was severely beaten again. He worked harder than ever to keep peace in the family, but all his efforts could not protect him from his father's eventual frustration and wrath. Several years later, after the first episode of his psychotic illness, John developed the delusion that his "real" parents had died in a transatlantic plane crash and that he had been adopted by a cruel and neglectful couple (his abusive parents). The delusion of adoption helped explain the behavior of his father. No "real" father would hurt his children as his father had hurt him. The delusion also put a psychological distance between John and his father.

Bill is a huge man who was raped in jail as an adult, and threatened with guns and other weapons by his father during childhood. Bill intimidates others with his size, his verbal bluster, and his well-known history of nearly killing a man in a drunken fight. Bill expe-

364

riences himself as invulnerable when he is threatening others. Like Eric, Bill oscillates between vulnerable and invulnerable positions. Although Bill's capacity to overwhelm others usually supports his experience of invulnerability, he feels extremely vulnerable during nonviolent social negotiations. At these times, he is aware that his social skill deficits and his problems with impulse control render him incapable of effectively protecting himself.

Disruptions of self-direction

Rigid over control and impulsiveness are the two common experiences associated with disruptions of self-direction. Rigid over control delays behavior, but also inhibits thought and feeling from informing the behavior that eventually emerges. Impulsive action is characterized by a seeming absence of thought and feeling and an outburst of behavior. Eric frequently moved between these two positions. He described a long period of tightly controlled arguments with his wife that suddenly erupted into impulsive violence that ended only after he beat her brutally with a boot. Doug, a physical and sexual abuse survivor, was able to stay clean for brief periods of time by rigidly avoiding women and fellow "crack heads." He could not preserve this posture of over control for long, however, despite his best intentions. After a few hours of rigid resistance to drug cravings, he impulsively pursued offers of drugs and sex from both men and women.

Jimmy first explained that he would do anything in his power to avoid replicating his father's violence and then told a series of fragmented stories about his own experiences as a father. When Jimmy's youngest son played with the television remote in an irritating fashion, Jimmy – who would use his black belt karate skills to intimidate others – became extremely angry. Although he could recognize that he was about to act like his father, he was unable to formulate an intervention that would de-escalate the situation. He struggled with his feelings of rage for what seemed to him like a long time before suddenly and impulsively hitting his son. Jimmy responded to his own impulsiveness with intense feelings, primarily guilt.

Jimmy was unable to form and implement effective plans for managing his children's behavior. He was alternately empathic with

365

the pain suffered at the hands of an abusive father, and then extremely impatient with his sons' suffering. He abhorred violence in one moment, but behaved violently the next. Jimmy could not channel or process his anger effectively, nor could he use his considerable verbal skills to manage provocative situations.

Disruptions of mutuality

Men who have been traumatized can be rendered so unsure of themselves and uncertain of their own capacities that they constantly seek and create dependent relationships. Alternatively, they can be so distrustful and wary that they become isolated and overly independent. Men who are too independent have a heightened fear of being misused or betrayed, and easily become unrealistically self-sufficient. Men who are too dependent fail to contribute in a positive way to the success of any relationship.

Justus, a victim of severe physical abuse at the hands of his father, vacillates between the independent and dependent responses. Justus often rejects all emotional assistance, advice, and information. At significant risk for exposure to HIV, for instance, he steadfastly and angrily refused all information about testing. His angry, paranoid postures (even about the negotiation of much simpler social exchanges) intimidates others who, in turn, keep their distance. Justus is, however, extremely dependent on his mother for help with even minor decisions and is unwilling to negotiate with other adults without her assistance. When deciding whether or not to get a telephone, for example, Justus sought his mother's opinion in a way that seemed more like he was asking her permission than merely her advice.

The development of mutuality is uniquely challenged when there is a history of sexual abuse. Tad was raised in a family with multiple overlapping sexual relationships among most of the family members. His guilt, shame, and confusion about the sexual abuse complicate his emotional and sexual relationships with adult peers. His adult sexual behavior recreates his childhood experience and is aggressive and highly intrusive. He does not take the rights of others into account, claiming that his independence exempts him from social concerns. Almost simultaneously, however, he is extremely dependent on professional staff to help him identify his own desires.

366

Disruptions of responsibility

Trauma can disrupt a man's progress along this developmental dimension by eliciting the extremes of under- or over-responsibility. Over-responsibility is associated with the belief that "Nothing will go wrong if I do it all." George, for example, made several appropriate efforts to get a cocaine addicted roommate into treatment, but also tried to provide for his other roommate's medical, emotional, financial, psychiatric, and interpersonal needs. The extreme extension of over-responsibility is evident when a man is concerned that his actions will result in cataclysmic consequences for others. Sean's delusion that his smallest movement might destroy the universe is characteristic of an extremely over-responsible position. Many men, however, first experienced the over-responsible position before the onset of their mental illness. John, for example, took responsibility for his sibling's homework to minimize his father's violence. As a teenager John often fought with older men who physically abused his mother.

When men despair of assuming responsibility successfully, they often retreat to a position of under-responsibility. Severe depression can lead to an episode of lower functioning, where it is nearly impossible to adequately discharge one's responsibilities. Trauma can also precipitate under-responsibility by contributing to a sense of helplessness and futility.

Internal experience is crucial to an understanding of under-responsible behavior. The burdens of over-responsibility often lead men to assume a position of apparent under-responsibility. Rick was a sexual and physical abuse survivor who was institutionalized and homeless from his early teenage years. He experienced himself as terribly burdened with responsibility – "I carry the weight of the world on my shoulders" – but gave every appearance of having no responsibility whatsoever.

Recovery

Recovery work for dually diagnosed male trauma survivors requires a (re-)development and integration of a cohesive response to the demands of each of these developmental dimensions. The

367

development and enhancement of fundamental skills and capacities support this integrative process. A mature, integrated response improves a person's capacity to preserve a positive self concept, protect oneself, take reasonable risks, be effective and appropriately spontaneous, assume an appropriate level of responsibility, modulate affect, develop and sustain focused and effective activity, soothe and be soothed, empathize with others, establish realistic dependencies and trust, and be emotionally available to others. As men grapple successfully with each of these developmental dimensions, there is a relatively greater freedom in the choice of adaptive style and greater stability in the sense of self. Correspondingly, there is less fluctuation of experience between one extreme and another.

Recovery of self-esteem. The maturation of self-esteem requires a movement away from the positions of grandiosity and shame and toward the development of positive self-regard and worth. Acceptance of the self, acknowledgment of difficulties imposed by the outside world, and the capacity to make plans that address difficulties and shortcomings are the signs of positive self-esteem.

Real world accomplishments contribute to the process of recovery. Examples of such achievements in this population of men include extended periods of abstinence from illegal drugs and alcohol, residential stability, successful work experience, artistic productivity, and the experience of sharing successfully in a community. The development of positive relations with family members is another indication of successful recovery of self-esteem. Several men had the rewarding experience of being reaccepted by their extended family after stabilizing their mental illness, developing a period of recovery from substance abuse, and maintaining residential stability.

Eric, for example, whose life on the streets had once become precarious after a series of violent muggings, was the success story of a family reunion many years later because he was clean and sober, and psychiatrically and residentially stable. In previous years, his family could not locate him on the street, or they avoided him because he was too disruptive. John made a very preliminary move toward developing a greater degree of self-esteem. After several years of relative stability in his life, he was able to begin showering on a weekly basis, although at first he did so furtively and in fear of reprisal. After five years of recovery with the support of AA and intensive case management services, Darrell began a rap group that was well attended by other members of the treatment community. The success of his group significantly buttressed his sense of self-esteem.

Recovery of self-protection. Recovery in this area requires a man to increase his capacity to protect himself from emotional and physical dangers, and also to develop the capacity to take risks and be open to the influence of others. The development of a greater sense of personal security is at least partially contingent on the development of one's own power and a clear sense of one's own limitations. Personal security also depends on an appreciation of the power of others, the ability to contend with another's powerful presence, and a willingness to be influenced by that power when appropriate.

Eric's preoccupation with Spindle and Superman distracted him from successful negotiation of a safe emotional and sexual relationship with his girlfriend. With emotional support, practical advice, and education, Eric was eventually able to recognize the dangers of unprotected sex. He became increasingly receptive to the need to protect himself and to discuss safe sexual practices with his girlfriend. Over time, he learned to negotiate a relationship with her that was relatively free of dangerous activity and abuse.

After five years of case management interventions, psychotherapy, residential stability, and sobriety, Alvin, who wore makeup to school as a child to hide signs of physical abuse, was able to have a respectful conversation with a brother he had avoided for 30 years. Previous attempts at conversation had ended in violent arguments where both Alvin and his brother felt alternately desperate and imperious. This conversation was more successful because Alvin felt more secure, protected himself more successfully, and did not act on impulses to hurt his brother's feelings.

Recovery of self-direction. The mature integrated response to the challenges of self-direction enable a person to engage in purposeful behavior mediated by a full range of thought and feeling. Eric's impulsive drug use, for example, and his efforts to guarantee the conspiratorial silence of housemates through threat and intimidation led to a major verbal confrontation with his group leader. After several months of moderate social withdrawal, an increase in psychotic symptoms, but a decrease in drug use, Eric followed up on the confrontation by discussing his concerns about being treated fairly and

369

with respect. He acknowledged the problem of his intimidating style, but spoke about his need to feel free to behave as he thought right so long as others were not hurt. Eric's self-directed pursuit of this resolution was largely free of impulsive threats and efforts to control what others said.

Recovery of mutuality. Maturity along this developmental dimension is achieved when a man is able to move appropriately among handling life's difficulties independently, seeking needed help, and offering assistance to others. Mutual relationships provide a social resource that serves as a buffer against disrespect, rejection, and betrayal elsewhere in the social network. The development of confidence and skill in dealing with life's ups and downs, and also the ability to read social situations well enough to avoid danger are improved as men retreat from the extremely independent and/or dependent positions.

Progress along this developmental dimension requires both intrapersonal and interpersonal growth. The intrapersonal process involves the development of an image of oneself as competent and effective in dealing with life's problems and opportunities, and is clearly related to the development of positive self-esteem that we have already discussed. The interpersonal process involves the development of adequate social skills and effective problem solving abilities.

George was physically and sexually abused as a child and was dually diagnosed as an adult. Estranged from his wife and then involuntarily hospitalized, George professed an extreme independence and withdrew from the social world. After several years of residential stability, psychiatric stability, and sobriety, George made cautious forays into the world of relationships, and eventually developed a romantic relationship. A fragile person herself, his girlfriend was at first afraid of George and acted to keep him at a distance. Rather than reverting to an isolationist independence, however, George minimized his contact with her for two months while she adjusted to the relationship. His success in developing a reasonably mutual relationship served as a buffer against the painful negotiation of his divorce.

Recovery of responsibility. Trauma experiences, mental illness, and substance abuse all make it extremely hard to develop and maintain a mature, consistent level of responsibility. George was rejected by his family after several years of institutionalization and homelessness. After regaining psychiatric and residential stability, and achieving three years of sobriety, he enrolled in a job program and began working in the meat department of a discount grocery store. As his paychecks started to come in on a regular basis, George's ex-wife resumed contact with him and began to ask for money. Increased contact with his ex-wife and children rekindled delusional ideas about his responsibility for his son's future. As George accumulated financial resources, he became increasingly afraid of being asked to manage responsibility he thought was beyond his ability. After several weeks of growing tensions which were fueled by cycles of delusional preoccupation and moments of psychological clarity, George quit his job abruptly and returned to his former position of under-responsibility. Just as quickly, the demands from his social network fell away. After several weeks of unemployment, however, George returned to a volunteer job that gave him some responsibility without the threat of too much independence.

Conclusion

We are recognizing the enormous impact that recurrent, multiple, and complex trauma have on the lives of urban, dually diagnosed men. The five developmental dimensions and the trauma-associated disruptions we have identified help us organize our conceptualization of trauma and recovery. The specific skills that support success along these developmental dimensions can help men in the integrative work that is central to their trauma recovery.

References

Briere, J. (1989) *Therapy for Adults Molested As Children: Beyond Survival.* New York: Springer Publishing Company.

Briere, J., Evans, D., Runtz, M. and Wall, T. (1987) "Symptomatology in men who were sexually molested as children: A comparison study", in *American Journal of Orthopsychiatry*, 58, 457–462.

Clatterbaugh, K. (1994) "Men and masculinity", in *Serials Review*, 20(1), 94–106.

Elliott, D.M. and Briere, J. (1992) "The sexually abused boy: Problems in manhood", in *Medical Aspects of Human Sexuality*, 26(2) 68–71.

Finkelhor, D., Hotaling, G., Lewis, I.A. and Smith C. (1990) "Sexual abuse in a national survey of adult men and women: Prevalence, characteristics, and risk factor", in *Child Abuse and Neglect*, 14, 19–29.

Fogel, G., Lane, F. and Liebert, R. (Eds.) (1986) *The Psychology of Violence*. New York: Basic Books.

Foy, D.W., Siprelle, R.C., Rueger, D.R. and Carroll, E.M. (1984) "Etiology of posttraumatic stress disorder in Vietnam veterans: Analysis of premilitary, military, and combat exposure influences", in *Journal of Consulting and Clinical Psychology*, 52, 79–87.

Goldner, V., Penn, P., Sheinberg, M. and Walker, G. (1990) "Love and violence: Gender paradoxes in volatile attachments", in *Family Process*, 29(4) 343–364.

Herman, J.L. (1992) *Trauma and Recovery*. New York: Basic Books.

Hunter, M. (1990) *The Sexually Abused Male, Volume I: Prevalence, Impact and Treatment*. New York: Lexington Books.

Hunter, M. (1990) *The Sexually Abused Male, Volume II: Application of Treatment Strategies*. New York: Lexington Books.

Lisak, D. (1994) "The psychological impact of sexual abuse: Content of interviews with male survivors", in *Journal of Traumatic Stress*, 7(4) 525–530.

McCann, L. and Pearlman, L.A. (1990) *Psychological Trauma and the Adult Survivor: Theory, Therapy and Transformation*. New York: Brunner/Mazel.

Rausch, K. and Knutson, J.F. (1991) "Assessing Environments III", in *Child Abuse and Neglect*, 15, 29–36.

Silverberg, R.A. (1986) *Psychotherapy for Men*. Springfield, IL.: Charles C. Thomas.

Straus, M.A. (1979) "Measuring intrafamily conflict and violence: The Conflict Tactics Scales", in *Journal of Marriage and the Family*, 41, 74–85, 1979.

Thomas, T. (1989) *Men Surviving Incest*. Walnut Creek, California: Launch Press.

Index